AIEL Series in Labour Economics

AIEL Series in Labour Economics

Published Volumes:

F. E. Caroleo, S. Destefanis (Eds.)
The European Labour Market
2006. ISBN 978-3-7980-1679-2

Nicola Acocella · Riccardo Leoni
(Editors)

Social Pacts, Employment and Growth

A Reappraisal of Ezio Tarantelli's Thought

With 41 Figures and 33 Tables

Physica-Verlag
A Springer Company

Professor Nicola Acocella
University of Rome 'La Sapienza'
Department of Public Economics
Via Castro Laurenziano 9
00161 Roma
Italy
nicola.acocella@uniroma1.it

Professor Riccardo Leoni
University of Bergamo
Department of Economics
Via dei Caniana 2
24128 Bergamo
Italy
leoni@unibg.it

Library of Congress Control Number: 2006938911

ISSN 1863-916X
ISBN 978-3-7908-1915-1 Physica-Verlag Heidelberg New York

Physica-Verlag is part of Springer Science+Business Media

springer.com

Production: LE-TEX Jelonek, Schmidt & Vöckler GbR, Leipzig
Cover-design: Erich Kirchner, Heidelberg

SPIN 11916178 88/3100YL - 5 4 3 2 1 0 Printed on acid-free paper

Preface

I still feel deeply moved, many years after Ezio Tarantelli's tragic death, as I dedicate these words to the works of a man who was a valued and sadly-missed aide of mine during my years with the Bank of Italy.

From 1966, when he passed the Bank of Italy examination, to 1973 when he left the Bank's Research Department to devote himself to research and university teaching, and still later when he became an external consultant with the Bank of Italy, Ezio Tarantelli was appreciated by all for his gifts of analysis, reflection and initiative. His interest mainly focused on the real economy – as shown in the texts collected here. His contribution to the issues involved, from production to prices and income distribution, was fundamental to the debate – within and even more outside the Bank – on finding a balance between growth, price stability and social equity.

In the Eighties Tarantelli devised a model of 'concertation', or close consultations between employers and unions aimed at breaking out of the perverse wage–prices inflationary spiral. He was a strong advocate of that model and he made it known at large. That, perhaps, was the real reason for his murder.

The force of his ideas brought about a gradual change which, in 1992–93, led to the signature of an agreement between the Government, employers and unions which had a decisive role in halting inflation.

As I had occasion to recall at the inauguration of the University of Calabria's Library, which is named after him, that agreement never had a name. But were it to have one, it should by rights be Ezio Tarantelli's.

Carlo Azeglio Ciampi
President of the Italian Republic

January, 2006

Contents

PART III: SOCIAL PACTS IN EUROPE

PART IV: INDUSTRIAL RELATIONS AND MACROECONOMIC PERFORMANCE

Introduction

Nicola Acocella[1] and Riccardo Leoni[2]

[1] University of Rome 'La Sapienza', Italy
[2] University of Bergamo, Italy

1 The role of labour economics and social pacts in Tarantelli's thought

The expression 'Tarantelli proposal' occurs repeatedly in this book. Therefore, it must be explained, mainly for the benefit of those readers who, being too young and/or not familiar with the Italian setting, don't know either Ezio Tarantelli or the evolution of Italian labour market institutions.

In Italy, until 1992-1993, there was no experience of incomes policy and there existed an automatic mechanism for indexing nominal wages to past inflation ('scala mobile' or sliding-scale mechanism). In 1992-1993 this mechanism was replaced with one where wage increases would be consistent with the government's target rate of inflation, with some allowance for recouping the difference between actual and target inflation, to safeguard the purchasing power of wages. This was largely what Tarantelli had advocated at the beginning of the previous decade.

Tarantelli thought that, if it is true that (i) in an open economy operating under fixed exchange rates, the rate of inflation should be strictly controlled, (ii) monetary policy tends to supply the quantity of money necessary to satisfy such external constraint, (iii) price inflation depends on the dynamics of wages and productivity, then a coordinated policy of wage moderation (where nominal wages are determined on the basis of the target future – rather than the real – rate of inflation) would guarantee the same disposable income to wage earners as that which would be available in the absence of such a policy, but with the added benefit of higher employment and lower inflation (Acocella and Ciccarone, 1995).

According to Tarantelli (1986), in setting low nominal wages rise the trade union(s) would play a coordination role and influence future price expectations and, thus, the effective rate of inflation. As a result, they would have a positive influence on the external balance, thereby reducing the deficit to be financed by foreign capital. Real wages would be substantially preserved. However, were this not the case, the government could compensate the trade union(s) through reduced interest expenditure, reduced tax evasion or increased public expenditure ('politico-economic exchange'). Even a non inflation-averse union would find it beneficial to engage in a policy of wage moderation.

Pierluigi Ciocca reconstructs Tarantelli's policy proposal as an alternative to monetarism. Both Pierluigi Ciocca and Mario Sarcinelli reconstruct the economic, social and political environment in which Tarantelli's thought emerged and which it was intended to address.

2 The implementation of Tarantelli's proposals

Tarantelli's proposal was partially implemented in Italy in February 1984, with an agreement applying the principle of wage pre-determination and its enforcement by law. It was not until 1993 that a comprehensive incomes policy along the lines he had suggested was adopted, 'the July 1993 Protocol'. In his preface to this book, Carlo Azeglio Ciampi, the Italian Prime Minister in 1993 and President of the Italian Republic at the time it was prepared, rightly states that the Protocol should bear Tarantelli's name. Even though it was being shaped as a social pact, with reciprocal concessions by the parties, the 1993 agreement was implemented mainly in so far as the aspects of incomes policy were concerned, partly because of the circumstances in which it was signed.

The Protocol introduced two separate, non-overlapping bargaining levels, recalled in both Tronti's and Brandolini et al.'s papers: a national level bargaining lasting two years, where wage increases should be consistent with the planned rate of inflation, but with the possibility to recoup differences with the real rate of inflation at the end of the period (thus fully accepting Tarantelli's proposal), and a firm level, where a system of efficiency wages was conceived.

The overall impact of this bargaining system is investigated by Leonello Tronti, who recognises the extraordinary merits of the Protocol in curbing inflation while underlining the incompleteness (with respect to Tarantelli's proposal) in the way the incomes policy was implemented in Italy. Similarly, Andrea Brandolini et al. analyse the broad picture emerging from the Protocol as well as other policy actions (and omissions).

Annalisa Cristini and Riccardo Leoni take into consideration the effects of the wage determination mechanism based on bargaining and efficiency wages introduced in Italy in 1993. The analysis looks at the productivity-enhancing effects of the efficiency wage approach and tests the role of specific profit-sharing schemes based on formal performance evaluations agreed upon with the trade unions' representatives. Compared to decentralized wage bargaining, which in itself gives rise to a positive rent sharing, the wage premium increases further if a performance evaluation procedure is also implemented, or alternatively, if the incentive mechanism is negotiated between management and the trade union's representatives. Moreover the extent of rent sharing is highest when the evaluation performance scheme is agreed upon between management and the trade union's representatives. It is worth mentioning that this is a typical situation where traditional indicators, related to output-based variable pay (such as turnover, productivity, defects and cost targets), are abandoned for new, input-based indicators, which stimulate employees to improve their skills by learning, job rotation, team working, suggestion system and involvement. While the former refers to a traditional design setting, the latter is consistent with Business Process Reengineering (BPR), which is a prerequisite for the so-called high road to innovation and development.

The results constitute a sort of confirmation that, on the one hand, both good incentive schemes negotiated with trade union's representatives and good industrial relations lead to more efficient workplaces[1] and, on the other hand, efficient bargaining/Coase theorem (see Freeman and Acocella et al., *infra*) really offer a good starting point for analysing EU social dialogue economies.

3 The history of social pacts and social pacts in Europe

Tarantelli advocated more than purely centralised collective bargaining and incomes policy. He was aware of the many aspects involved in wage policy and claimed that a sort of social pact should be pursued by social partners, as an outcome of successful social dialogue.

A precise definition of social pacts is hard to find as they are variously rooted in the political, economic, social, and industrial relations culture of countries and differ rather significantly in form, content and outcomes. Tarantelli defined them loosely as cooperative agreements between unions, employers' organisations and, possibly, the government to determine wage policy and other aspects of economic and social life. They represent a consensus on the main directions of economic and social policy. The domain of bipartite agreements (those between firms and workers) may simply include terms and conditions of employment. Tripartite agreements usually cover macroeconomic and social policy issues.

Social pacts have been adopted extensively mainly in European countries and, to some extent, in Asian, Central and Latin American and African countries since the 1960s. Their diffusion in Europe is one of the dominant differences with the United States, as Richard Freeman documents. Their domain is usually macroeconomic and social policy and related issues rather than strictly terms and conditions of employment, which are instead the focus of purely collective bargaining.

The social pacts stipulated in some European countries have evolved towards what Tarantelli called 'decentralised corporatism', showing the institutional flexibility of collective agreements, emphasised by Jelle Visser, largely documents. Tarantelli's assassins robbed him of the time needed to develop the concept of decentralised corporatism, but he did not consider this to be flimsy. As Dell'Aringa reports, there have been developments in this direction in a number of economies in the 1980s and 1990s in English-speaking countries and elsewhere. In some cases, as in Sweden, there has been a kind of 'organised decentralisation', which may be of interest at the European level, too. As Dell'Aringa puts it, this might offer the 'best opportunity for combining the benefits of coordination in terms of internalisation of various effects caused by wage pressures… with the benefits of increased flexibility of relative wages' (p. 169).

---

[1] The positive role of trade unions for firm productivity is shown in Black and Lynch (2001, 2004) and Cristini, Gaj, Labory and Leoni (2003).

4 The significance of industrial relations for macroeconomic performance

Dell'Aringa reminds us that, according to Flanagan (1999: 1157) 'the notion of corporatism suffers from uncertain theoretical foundations' and a lack of attention to the micro-economic and social foundations that produce superior results. Centralisation of wage bargaining has not always proved very important in explaining macroeconomic performance *vis-à-vis* other features of the labour market and industrial relations or the orientation of monetary policy and other institutional aspects of an economy. According to Dell'Aringa, also welfare expenditure, which was one of the terms of the political exchange advocated by the first neo-corporatists, has not proved beneficial to macroeconomic performance and welfare reform has become central in the political agenda. He adheres to a school of interpretation which is sceptic with respect to the virtues of neo-corporatism. He asserts that several other institutional aspects, referred both to the labour market and the overall economic system, affect macroeconomic performance. His scepticism is manifested also with regard to the idea of decentralised corporatism (which Tarantelli instead considered positive: see Tarantelli, 1986), claiming that unemployment in Europe is a regional problem (located mainly in Italy, Germany, Spain and France), and – as such – possible solutions should be tracked down at this level through greater flexibility in the geographical wage structure. This, in turn, requires a reduced level of coordination, both formal and informal, at the national level. The question, however, arises whether heterogeneous territorial groups, with dissimilar endowments and abilities, are likely to bargain efficiently, instead of using their resources for rent-seeking.

Piero Ferri is more open to the possible positive effects of centralisation. His contribution is based on a model somehow inspired to Tarantelli. He first shows how important the value of the parameters reflecting nominal rigidities and industrial relations can be for the dynamics of the system. The indexation system has a certain influence on the former, in line with Tarantelli's intuition and suggestion of a reduction in the sensitivity of nominal wages to past inflation as a disinflationary measure. In addition, industrial relations can influence the dynamics of the system in his model through their influence on expectations and learning. In particular, centralisation of bargaining, together with other conditions, can make the business cycle less pronounced or even disappear (Ferri, p. 186).

Croci Angelini and Farina, too, refer to the nature of industrial relations as a determinant of macroeconomic performance, through their influence on the degree of wage dispersion. One could be led to think that social pacts have a negative influence on the employment level as they reduce wage dispersion. However, first there is mixed empirical evidence – as Croci Angelini and Farina remind us – of the relation between employment and wage inequality. The latter is usually thought to be lower with labour market institutions such as those stemming from social pacts and, more generally, protective regulation. However, in the case of Scandinavian countries, social pacts have been compatible with an increase in wage dispersion. Croci Angelini and Farina track the rising trend in wage inequality in Europe and trace it back to a number of factors. Overall, labour market deregulation and decentralised wage setting increase wage inequality, but the effect can to some extent be offset by income redistribution policy. In any case, the increase in wage inequality in Europe is inconsistent with those theories (like Krugman's) holding a negative causal relationship between wage compression and low-skilled employment (pp. 199–200).

5 For a theory of social pacts

Richard Freeman laments the lack of a theory of social dialogue (p. 222). He refers to general methodologies able to explain or reject cooperation, such as, respectively, the Coase theorem, which predicts that bargaining always produces efficient outcomes, and the prisoners' dilemma, which predicts flawed behaviour. On these grounds, empirical evidence sometimes appears contradictory. But he argues that – in spite of the fact that market-driven economies (like the US) show that the market often falls short of efficiency – the competitive model still provides a valuable framework for analysing market performance. In a similar vein, and by analogy, he thinks that efficient bargaining/Coase theorem can still be a valuable framework for illuminating social dialogue systems (like EU), even thought the real world does not offer any evidence of efficient bargaining as a general rule. To this end, he draws on behavioural economics and efficient bargaining as well as game theory and institutional design to infer that it is neither logical nor rational to throw away the baby with the bathwater and to claim at the same time that, were he with us today, Ezio Tarantelli would look favourably upon these areas (efficient bargaining/Coase theorem) and contribute to them.

Nicola Acocella et al. give us a theory of social pacts. In their model, where the union is interested in the levels of wages, employment and public expenditure, social pacts not only lead to superior macroeconomic performance, but are also acceptable by trade unions. The key to their acceptability lies in the benefit the trade unions derive from higher public expenditure, in line with Tarantelli's thought. By reflecting on the fact that public expenditure is financed through distortionary taxation, however, their model offers also the possibility to explain the evolution of social pacts in Europe in the last decades. The rules adopted for gaining access to the European Monetary Union in the early 1990s might have put pressure on both the governments and the trade unions to adopt social pacts, as the social partners were prompted to put greater emphasis on the pursuit of inflation and public expenditure targets.

6 Alternative solutions to conflicts and sources of a better macro performance in Europe

Social pacts are by no means the only possible way to improve macroeconomic performance. The economic literature, from Barro and Gordon (1983) to Lawler (2000a, b; 2001) and Coricelli et al. (2000, 2004), has discussed three main often interrelated solutions to improve macroeconomic performance: the conservative central banker, union coordination (centralisation), and corporatism (the cooperative solution between the government and the trade unions).

In his paper Fabrizio Coricelli adds to the literature and his own previous findings in claiming that monetary authorities' conservatism is needed to improve macroeconomic performance, the more so the higher the degree of product market competition. Contrary to a widespread belief (see, e.g., Guzzo and Velasco, 1999), central bank conservatism and market competition are complements, rather than substitutes. This could justify the presence of a conservative European Central Bank in the process of strengthened European integration.

Fabrizio Coricelli is aware that his conclusion holds only to the extent that bargaining is not centralised. Thus, he implicitly points to an alternative way to orient European institutions, more in line with the Lisbon strategy. This could be based on social pacts at the European level (as suggested by Crouch, 2000), on the one hand, and accompanying labour market policies, on the other.

Robert Lindley in fact strongly advocates Lisbon-oriented policies, such as an increasing educational attainment and participation in education and training, higher investment in human capital and mobility. But at the same time, he recalls the mistake of the supply-side orientation of policy in paying too much attention to the behaviour of individuals in the 'markets for learning and labour', and too little to issues relating to organisational effectiveness, which strongly influence the dynamism of the economy and the quality of working life. This is a source of major concern, since the knowledge-based economy is fundamentally about the behaviour of organisations rather than individuals. Without disentangling this point, the problem of low productivity in Europe remains unsolved: in fact even if employment were to increase, new labour forces would be attracted into labour markets (thereby raising the employment ratio, one of the Lisbon targets), but the problem of how to improve organisational efficacy remains. The rational and efficient solution is to make work-based learning feasible, which requires an organisational design and setting of workplaces consistent with the creation and diffusion of tacit and informal knowledge.

7 New contents for a social pact in the age of the knowledge economy

In recent decades three interrelated features have characterised economic systems: an increasing stress on public expenditure, a growing globalisation process and the pervasive role of knowledge. According to some authors these features call for increased flexibility and a reduced role of social pacts and centralised wage bargaining, as these impose rigid wage differentials and policy attitudes. Specifically, this would be a recipe suitable for those European countries whose labour markets are still different from the Anglo-American one.

Contrary to this position, however, it can be argued that it is not social pacts *per se* that should be questioned, but their contents. Actually, limits to the growth of public expenditure, globalisation and the knowledge economy require social pacts with contents and orientation different from those that have characterised the last three decades or so. The first generation of social pacts exchanged wage moderation for an increase in social spending. Social pacts of the second generation traded wage moderation for a reduction in public expenditure, mainly in order to facilitate entry in the EMU. Social pacts in the age of globalisation and the knowledge society should trade wage moderation for commitment by both governments and firms to undertake high investment in ICT, organisational capital and skills development. The background of this proposal can be summarised as follows.

David Metcalf (2003: 133) points out that 'labour economists are going "inside the firm" more frequently now than in the past', in search of detailed knowledge of the operations of the firm with modern technologies. There is a reason for that, as in these new contexts it is impossible to determine a priori whether industrial relations *per se* raise or lower labour productivity.[2] But the empirical literature points out the general conditions for a positive causation between unionism and productivity: cooperative – or at least non-adversarial relations – and centralisation of bargaining and organised decentralisation. In addition, the most interesting and promising approach appears to focus on high-performance work practices (adopted in bundles, and including good industrial relations). The main findings in this sphere are that skill-biased technological change (which affects all sectors and jobs) and the complementarity between capital investment (mainly ICT), intangible assets (organisational capital) and skilled workers are responsible for the high increase in labour productivity and firm performance. Only rarely can better performance be ascribed to natural monopoly or competition-constraining regulation (i.e. to the market structure for goods); the main explanation refers instead to a set of 'new' intangible elements of the economic activity.

High-performance work organisations (HPWO) (recalled both in Cristini and Leoni's paper, in Tronti's contribution and Lindley's analysis), incorporating characteristics of learning organisations and knowledge production and sharing, constitute the cornerstone of a programme aiming at enhancing competitiveness, on the one side, and a new organisation of the firm and job design, on the other. Empirical evidence in this area is growing day by day. For instance, Black e Lynch (2004) show that the average annual growth of output in US manufacturing in the second half of the Nineties (4.7 per cent) has been sustained by a sharp increase in productivity, equal to 1.6 per cent, of which 1.4 per cent (89 per cent of the productivity itself) is due to the reengineering of the job place and the implementation of new practices in the human capital management, resulting in an empowerment of human resources. In particular, new practices include: reduction in hierarchical levels, increased autonomy of teamwork, workforce training in cognitive and relational aspects, a system of incentives which promotes learning and better performance of the workers instead of the mere quantitative effort, and finally a large involvement of employees and trade unions[3].

---

[2] For a survey of these effects see Metcalf (2003).

[3] On this stream, see, for example, the results of Ichniowski, Shaw and Prennushi (1997) based on data for the US steel industry, according to which productivity is 6.7 per cent higher under the innovative human resource management system, 3.2 per cent higher un-

Other economists have pointed out not only that investment in intangible assets matters, but also that investment in tangible assets, namely ICT, influences productivity growth.[4] The main result of this literature regards not so much the 'additive' contribution of specific investment to the whole firm performance as the strong complementarities among different investments. The original idea of the organisation of the firm as a complementarity of heterogeneous parts, as opposed to the neoclassical paradigm of the firm as a 'black box', dates back to the work of Milgrom and Roberts (1990 e 1995). The authors introduce a rigorous representation of the organisation complementarities based upon the characteristics of supermodularity of the profit function, and model the clustering of practices resulting from complementarity between technological innovation and organisational changes directed towards greater 'internal' (*versus* external) firm flexibility.

Confronted with this bulk of empirical evidence, we believe – paraphrasing Richard Freeman (*infra*) – that, were Ezio Tarantelli with us today, he would look favourably upon these outcomes for a new 'social pact' aimed at establishing (at a central level) the general tracts of HPWO, *to be specified and implemented* through decentralised agreements between workers representatives and the firm. This would activate the huge repository of intelligence and tacit knowledge not only of employees engaged in organisational units devoted to the development of codified knowledge (R&D departments), but also (and perhaps, mainly) of those in the operative nucleus, where tacit knowledge streams out in the daily problem setting and problem solving activities. At the firm level, in fact, trade unions and managers have a lot to do in designing, selecting and monitoring those mechanisms suitable for such targets.

Within the 'political exchange' policymakers have to coherently channel resources to introduce and diffuse business process reengineering (which is costly), and to provide economic incentives to compensate workers for their cognitive and learning efforts, since today's costs to develop competencies represent tomorrow's welfare improvements, as skill obsolescence will be reduced. Higher productivity and propensity to innovate[5] are the reward of the firm, which benefits from inter-

der the 'high-teamwork' system and 1.4 per cent higher under the 'communications' systems. For the UK, Patterson, West, Lawthom and Nickell (1997), on the basis of a longitudinal study of 67 British firms (mostly with one location and one product), show that 17 per cent of the changes in firms' profitability is due to HRM practices and organisational innovations, while only 8 per cent is due to R&D expenditure, 2 per cent to strategies and 1 per cent to technology and quality. For Germany, Bauer (2002) and Zwick (2003) find a significant positive impact of HPWO on the productivity of the average establishment. Greenan (1996) on French data, Caroli and Van Reenen (2001) on both French and UK data, and Askenazy (2000) on US data, find that workplace reorganisation and the adoption of new practices foster, and are fostered by, high-skill levels in the workforce. For Italy, only Cristini, Gaj, Labory and Leoni (2003) are able to document – even if, unfortunately, in a very small sample of industrial firms – the positive relationship between bundles of new work practices (a combination of workplace re-engineering, new human resource management and good industrial relations) and firm performance.

4 See Brynjolfsson et al., 2000; Breshnahan et al., 2002; Brynjolfsson et al., 2002.

5 See Michies and Sheehan, 2003; Laursen and Foss, 2003; Pini and Santangelo, 2005.

organisational capabilities[6], since all the complementarities are affected in sequence. Virtuous circles, due to their path-dependent nature and their reciprocal interactions, tend to take the form of a spiral inscribed (or locked) into trajectories that may well be superior or inferior, according to the 'selection' and the 'intensity' of organisational specificities (Cristini, Gaj and Leoni, 2005).

The need for a new social contract is even more profound in Southern European countries (Italy included) as the HPWO only timidly emerges in the debate on employment as an antidote to simplistic ideas of what to expect from labour market de-regulations and the preoccupation with 'unburdening management' by removing constraints on their prerogative to manage. A social pact like that sketched above could constitute a big push in the right direction.

A warning should, however, be issued against the possibility that also this new type of social contract (as happened in some cases in the past) is not honoured by either the governments or the firms.

Acknowledgments

The editors are grateful to AIEL (Italian Association of Labour Economists), Bank of Italy, CISL (Italian Confederation of Worker's Trade Unions), Tarantelli Foundation, SIE (Italian Society of Economics), the University of Rome 'La Sapienza' and the Third University of Rome for their financial support to the international seminar on Ezio Tarantelli's thought, which took place in Rome (31st March – 2nd April 2005). The seminar would have not been successful without the contribution of ideas of the President of the Scientific Committee, Luigi Frey, and its members, including Marcello De Cecco, Angelo Gennari, Guido M. Rey, Antonio Pedone, Salvatore Rossi, Leonello Tronti, in addition to the editors.

We acknowledge also the contribution of several other colleagues, whose papers – for several reasons – are not included in this volume: Alberto Bagnai, Francesco Carlucci, Giuseppe Croce, Emanuela Ghignoni, Frederic Gravel, Pedro Lages Dos Santos, Isabelle Lebon, Roberto Schiattarella, Massimiliano Tancioni, Giuseppe Tattara, Marco Valentini and Andrew Watt.

The seminar benefited from a political discussion on Ezio Tarantelli's economic policy proposals. We thank the participants to the round table, chaired and coordinated by Pierre Carniti: Luigi Angeletti, Mario Baldassarri, Guglielmo Epifani, Paolo Garonna, Savino Pezzotta and Tiziano Treu.

We wish also to thank Gabriella Pappadà for her invaluable technical assistance in preparing the conference, and Angelo Gennari, Luigi Frey and Leonello Tronti for their very helpful comments on a earlier draft of this introduction.

---

[6] Inter-organisational capabilities refer to the results of a co-evolving system of 'cumulative changes', due to a set of complementarities like those between basic schooling and work-based learning (in a HPWO environment), ICT and skills, ICT and new organisational settings, new work practices when they are implemented in bundles, and finally new work practices and propensity to innovate processes and products.

Our final and most respectful thanks are for Carlo Azeglio Ciampi, former President of the Italian Republic and the Italian Prime Minister in 1993, who honoured us with his speech at the seminar and prepared the preface to this volume.

References

Acocella, N. and G. Ciccarone (1995), 'Moderazione salariale e "scambio politico": un'analisi microfondata', *Rivista Italiana di Economia*, **0**:111–38.

Barro, R.J. and D.B. Gordon (1983), 'Rules, discretion and reputation in a model of monetary policy', *Journal of Monetary Economics*, **12**:101–121.

Black, S. and Lynch L. (2001), 'How to compete: the impact of workplace practices and information technology on productivity', *Review of Economics and Statistics*, **83**(3): 434–45.

Black, S. and Lynch L. (2004), 'What's driving the new economy? The benefits of workplace innovation', *Economic Journal*, **114**:97–116.

Bresnahan, T., E. Brynjolfsson and L.M. Hitt (2002), 'Information technology, workplace organization and the demand for skilled labor: firm-level evidence', *Quarterly Journal of Economics*, **117**(1):339–76.

Brynjolfsson, E. and L.M. Hitt (2000), 'Beyond computation: information technology, organizational transformation and business performance', *Journal of Economic Perspective*, **14**(4):23–48.

Brynjolfsson, E. and L.M. Hitt (2003), 'Computing productivity: firm-level evidence', *Review of Economics and Statistics*, **85**(4):793–808.

Brynjolfsson, E., L.M. Hitt and S. Yang (2002), 'Intangible assets: computers and organizational capital', *Brooking Papers on Economic Activity*, **1**:137–81.

Caroli, E. and J. Van Reenen (2001), 'Skill-biased organizational change? Evidence from a panel of British and French establishments', *The Quarterly Journal of Economics*, **4**:1449–92.

Coricelli, F., A. Cukierman and A. Dalmazzo (2000), 'Monetary institutions, monopolistic competition, unionized labor markets and economic performance', *CEPR DP 2407*.

Coricelli, F., A. Cukierman, and A. Dalmazzo (2004), 'Economic performance and stabilization in a monetary union with imperfect labor and goods markets', *CEPR DP 2745*, in H.W. Sinn and M. Widgren (eds), *Issues of Monetary Integration in Europe*, Cambridge, MA: MIT Press.

Cristini, A., A. Gaj, S. Labory and R. Leoni (2003), 'Flat hierarchical structure, bundles of new work practices and firm performance', *Rivista Italiana degli Economisti*, **2**: 313–41.

Cristini, A., A. Gaj, S. Labory and R. Leoni (2005), 'Dynamic organisational capabilities: a unifying framework for new work practices, product innovation and competences formation', in R. Leoni and G. Usai (eds), *Organisations Today*, London: Palgrave/Macmillan, pp. 241–84.

Crouch, C.J. (2000), 'The euro and labour market and wage policies', in K. Dyson (ed.), *European Strategies and the Euro*, Oxford: Oxford University Press, pp. 278–304.

Flanagan, R.J. (1999), 'Macroeconomic performance and collective bargaining: an international perspective', *Journal of Economic Literature*, **37**(3): 1150–76.

Guzzo, V. and A. Velasco (1999), 'The case for a populist central bank', *European Economic Review*, **43**:1317–44.

Ichniowski, C., K. Shaw and G. Prennushi (1997), 'The effects of HRM systems on productivity: a study of steel finishing lines', *American Economic Review*, **87**:291–313.

Laursen, K. and N.J. Foss (2003), 'New human resource management practices, complementarities and the impact on innovation performance', *Cambridge Journal of Economics*, **27**(2):243–63.

Lawler, P. (2000a), 'Centralised wage setting, inflation contracts, and the optimal choice of central bunker', *Economic Journal*, **110**:559–75.

Lawler, P. (2000b), 'Union wage setting and exchange rate policy', *Economica*, **67**:91–100.

Lawler, P. (2001), 'Monetary policy, central bank objectives, and social welfare with strategic wage setting', *Oxford Economic Papers*, **53**(1):94–113.

Metcalf, D., (2003), 'Unions and productivity, financial performance and investment: international evidence', in J.T. Addison and C. Schnabel (eds), *International Handbook of Trade Unions*, Cheltenham (UK) and Northampton, MA (USA): Edward Elgar, pp. 118–71.

Michie, J. and M. Sheehan (2003), 'Labour market deregulation, "flexibility" and innovation', *Cambridge Journal of Economics*, **27**(1):123–43.

Milgrom, P. and J. Roberts (1990), 'The economics of modern manufacturing: technology, strategy, and organization', *American Economic Review*, **80**:511–28.

Milgrom, P. and J. Roberts (1995), 'Complementarities and fit: strategy, structure and organizational change in manufacturing', *Journal of Accounting and Economics*, **19**:179–208.

Pini, P. and G. Santangelo (2005), 'The underlying internal processes of incremental and radical innovations: an empirical analysis of the Reggio Emilia industrial districts', *working paper CREIC*, n.3, Università di Ferrara.

Rhodes, M. (1998), 'Globalization, labor markets and welfare states: a future of "competitive corporatism"?', in M. Rhodes and Y. Mény (eds), *The Future of European Welfare: A New Social Contract?*, London: Macmillan.

Tarantelli, E. (1986), *Economia politica del lavoro*, Turin: UTET.

Zwick, T. (2003), 'The productivity impact of lean management', *Discussion paper*, Centre for European Economic Research (ZEW), Mannheim.

PART I

SOCIAL PACTS IN TARANTELLI'S THOUGHT

1 'Doing good'. Ezio Tarantelli's Approach to Political Economy

Pierluigi Ciocca

Bank of Italy, Italy

1.1 Beyond monetarism: the role of institutions in shaping economic policies

In the early 1980s the Italian indexation mechanism compensated about 80 per cent of past inflation each quarter. It was broadly recognized that that mechanism had to be revised to prevent an inflationary spiral. A ready-made recipe was to discipline nominal wage claims through monetary policy. This remedy seemed to have worked in other countries. Ezio Tarantelli was among the few who understood why what worked in Germany and elsewhere could not work in Italy. He forcefully explained that monetary policy could be either unsuccessful or very successful depending on the institutional setting. It took another ten years for this idea to gain consensus and for econometricians to start regressing the inflation rate on the degree of centralisation of wage bargaining.

Tarantelli's thesis, shared by others, was that the inflation of the '70s was the result of the income distribution struggle that had started in the late '60s and sharpened when the bill for the first oil shock came due. In this new context, the traditional policy trade-off between inflation and unemployment was no longer tenable. The econometricians termed this new phenomenon the 'instability of the Phillips curve': Tarantelli called it 'the indeterminacy of the solution of the post-Keynesian model'.

The conflict over income distribution could still be settled through monetary policy only where a small change in unemployment could effectively discipline wage claims. In other contexts such an option was no longer available. In institutional settings where strong centralized unions could resist real wage cuts, additional tools were required. The choice of leaving it to the market and to monetary policy to sort out winners and losers in the income battle could be extremely costly in terms of the Okun index. In the '70s it was already clear – as Tarantelli demonstrated in various works – that an uncooperative game between a central bank, committed to fighting inflation with monetary policy, and a strongly centralized union with bargaining power over wages could be disruptive for the economy. On the contrary the successful anti-inflationary policies in Scandinavia, Germany and Austria provided a case in which central bank and unions played cooperatively to bring inflation down. However, resolving the income distribution issues was a precondition for involving unions in the definition and the implementation of consensual policies. Tarantelli's idea was that this conflict should be shifted from the market sphere into the political agenda.

Tarantelli's tool kit for governing a modern capitalist economy with centralized representation of interests consisted in a non-market arena to deal with income distribution and an incomes policy to guide the economy toward consensual targets. The non-market arena, where employers' associations, unions and government were supposed to be represented, was more appropriate than the market for solving the income distribution problem. Fiscal policy could reconcile the twofold nature of wages as income for workers and costs for firms. Wage moderation would not imply a reduction in the share of income going to workers if at the same time the state used fiscal resources to provide direct services in education, health and housing. This 'political deal' – or 'scambio politico' – was the tool devised by Tarantelli to solve the indeterminacy of the post-Keynesian model in the absence of an agreed income distribution.

The second tool – incomes policy – was the instrument of coordination to achieve the policy goals. The simultaneous announcement of consistent, coordinated action by the central bank, unions and government was a potent device for credibility. It could shape agents' expectations, making the achievement of the announced targets more likely.

This mode of economic governance – which took the name of 'neo-corporatism' from political science – was postulated on trust between the actors involved (employers, government and unions). Tarantelli's thinking drew on the most advanced game theory, which was looking for ways out of the 'prisoner dilemma'. It was suggested that cooperative solutions, as we now know, can emerge when games are repeated, as it is rational to trust other players in the early stages of the game. At the same time the principles underlying Olson's 'logic of collective action' and the theory of public goods were at the base of Tarantelli's search for the conditions that fostered cooperative solutions.

These essential characteristics of any industrial relations system were captured in three aspects of neo-corporatism. First, the degree to which unions are willing to use real wages as a policy instrument and to leave the distribution issues to the political arena – that is, the willingness of the unions to enter the *scambio politico* – was a pre-condition needed for building mutual trust. Second, the degree of bargaining centralisation measures the system's ability to prevent free riding. Finally, the extent to which *pacta sunt servanda* – the commitment to the honour the pact – is related to the probability that actors will engage in cooperative solutions in the early stage of the game. Tarantelli devoted an entire book to the theory behind these three elements and the institutional features underlying them. In a number of empirical papers he showed that a synthesis of these elements was a good predictor of macroeconomic performance in a set of OECD countries from 1968 to 1983, as measured by the Okun index.

The idea of testing the implications of an institutional theory by cross-country regressions gained currency in the 1980s and 1990s. In the process, however, the richness of description was somewhat diminished, and in later work only one yardstick was used: the degree of centralisation of the wage bargaining.

For Ezio Tarantelli this conceptual framework was not of merely academic interest. He used it to take an active part in the policy debate and to advance practical proposals on crucial issues. Together with his contribution on the *scala mobile* – the Italian wage indexation system – we cannot forget his tireless battle against unemployment. Ezio considered unemployment a really intolerable disgrace for a modern capitalist market economy. Most provocative was the idea – perhaps too advanced in 1985 when he first suggested it – of coordinating incomes policy with an expansionary fiscal policy within the European Community. The budgetary deficit would be financed by ECUs printed by the Community. More plausibly he also suggested exchanges between flexible employment rules and jobs, decent unemployment benefits and less stringent employment protection legislation, part-time jobs and a shorter work week.

1.2 The theory at work. The reform of wage indexation

At the end of 1980 the Italian inflation rate soared beyond 20 per cent, after two years of rapid increase. Both domestic and external factors were at work: rising administered prices for utilities and public services, depreciation of the lira, and the second oil shock. But those inflationary factors were amplified by the wage indexation system.

The inflation differential with respect to Italy's trading partners put constant pressure on the exchange rate and the current account balance. Closing the inflation gap became the top priority. The most commonly advocated policy was to reduce the degree to which wages were indexed to past prices.

Technically, it was suggested that wage indexation should be sterilized vis-à-vis oil prices and/or the appreciation of the dollar against the basket of currencies included in the ECU. The major drawback was that even in the absence of new external shocks high inflation would persist simply because indexation to past price rises. In 1980 the elasticity of earnings to the previous quarter's prices was about 75 per cent: the indexable average inflation rate was 18.2 per cent. In the face of this momentum effect, sterilization alone would not be enough to ensure consistency with the stance of monetary policy. What is more, convergence towards the inflation rates of other countries could be halted if wage increases from collective bargaining were out of line with productivity gains. All in all, then, this proposed solution was unsatisfactory: wage trends were more a mirror of the past than a guide to the future.

In an article in *La Repubblica* in April 1981, Tarantelli proposed to predetermine wage increases in order to guide prices along a path agreed upon by unions, employers and government. As an incentive-compatible device, the proposal included an 'insurance clause' under which workers would be compensated for any unexpected cut in real wages.

The novelty of the suggestion consisted in using wages as a policy instrument. In the months that followed there was a lively discussion over the proposal, and a few technical adjustments were added.

It took two years, a deep recession, and Confindustria's repudiation of the 1975 wage indexation deal to create the conditions for an agreement that, at least partially, reflected Tarantelli's ideas. On 22 January 1983, the government, the unions and the employers' associations signed the 'Scotti Agreement' named after the Labour Minister Enzo Scotti. The agreement was the first attempt in Italy to broker a *scambio politico* – a political deal – in which the unions accepted a 15-point cut in the degree of indexation, the sterilization of price increases due to indirect taxes, oil price rises and devaluation. In exchange workers received additional resources of about 1.5 per cent of GDP (family allowances and adjustment for fiscal drag) and a reduction in working hours.

A year later, on 14 February 1984, came a new agreement more thoroughly applying the principle of wage pre-determination. A law set the overall increase of wages for 1984, a ceiling of 10 per cent on publicly administered prices, and a rent freeze.

1.3 Did it work?

The incomes policy experiment of 1983–84 matched some of the conditions of Tarantelli's original proposal. A programmed inflation rate was announced. The link between wage increases and past inflation was first attenuated in 1983 by a lower degree of indexation. It was practically severed in 1984, when the wage rises due to the *scala mobile* were calibrated not to past inflation but to the target inflation rate. In 1984 public administered prices evolved coherently. However, part of the proposal was left out. In the 1984 agreement there was no real wage insurance clause. The agreement was not signed by the largest union. In order to abrogate the law in which it was enacted, the same union promoted the unsuccessful referendum of 1985.

These two last elements were highly significant. They could well have undercut the impact of the incomes policy on inflation expectations.

The inflation rate did fall from 16.5 per cent in 1982 to 10.8 per cent in 1984. However, as empirical analyses by the Bank of Italy suggested, this was due mainly to prudent monetary policy. The GDP growth rate fell below potential. But incomes policy also contributed by attenuating wage indexation and lowering inflation expectations. The degree of indexation of wages to prices was reduced from 68 per cent in 1982 to 44 per cent in 1984. It was estimated that, for 1984, incomes policy lowered inflationary expectations by about 1.5 percentage points and reduced the speed at which past inflation was embedded in expectations.

It remains an open question whether the contribution would have been larger had all the actors accepted the *scambio politico* in full. One's impression, however, is that incomes policy contributed so little to disinflation basically because of the low degree of neo-corporatism in industrial relations. The mid-1980s were still characterized by strong ideological resistance, the so called *residuo ideologico*. It would take another 10 years to get rid of this heavy handicap.

1.4 An interpretation of the disinflation process in the longer term (1980–1998)

From its peak of 20 per cent at the start of the 1980s, inflation declined and averaged 10 per cent for the decade as a whole. The rate stood at 6 per cent in 1991 and by 1997, the crucial year for qualification for the euro, it was down to 2 per cent. Since then Italian inflation has been running at just above 2 per cent.

This victory was achieved slowly, laboriously. Disinflation was not steady, and in 1994–95 the country ran a serious risk of rekindling inflation. If this had occurred, Italy could not have joined the Economic and Monetary Union.

Although the inflationary charge of the wage escalator mechanism had been defused in 1984, it was not until 1993 that Italy instituted a comprehensive, consistent incomes policy. In the interim, the anti-inflation drive had certainly not come from fiscal policy. Indeed, budgetary policy had worked in the opposite direction, consistently running deficits of over 10 per cent of GDP, while the public debt soared from 76 to over 120 per cent of GDP before peaking at 124 per cent a year later. High interest rates (real long-term rates were in the order of 5 per cent) and the appreciation of the real effective exchange rate of the lira (by 11 per cent between 1985 and June of 1992) carried the burden of disinflation. The Bank of Italy's monetary and exchange rate policy succeeded in its intent, and with a gradualism that allowed average annual economic growth of 2.4 per cent.

Despite the two dramatic devaluations of the lira which followed, in September 1992 and again in March 1995, the downward trend in inflation proceeded. The year 1993 initiated a period of very moderate wage growth that still continues today, with unemployment high until 1998 (at 11.3 per cent) and then falling to its present rate of 8 per cent.

Meanwhile, the disequilibria of public finances were attenuated. The budget was nearly in balance in 2000, albeit temporarily. The public debt ratio was reduced to its present level of 106 per cent of GDP.

The orientation of monetary policy remained prudent. Short-term interest rates were kept at warning levels until the very eve of the launch of the euro at the start of 1999. Inflation expectations were rooted out, as is confirmed by the moderate slope of the yield curve. In the crucial months between the summer of 1994 and the spring of 1995 the Bank of Italy enacted a restrictive monetary policy which began, in a preventive fashion, with the raising of the discount rate on 11 August 1994. This policy was successful. The acceleration of prices which the Bank of Italy had already foreseen in the summer, was slowed and then reversed.

Starting in 1993 incomes policy, fiscal policy and monetary policy thus worked together to curb inflation. The continuity of disinflation relied mainly on the central bank's management of interest rates and the exchange rate. If this was not exactly the 'monetary constitution' that Governor Ciampi had called for in 1981, it was nevertheless a framework of consistency and complementarity among these three essential macroeconomic policy instruments.

The 'collinearity' of the trends in these policy variables makes it difficult, and perhaps irrelevant, to single out the specific contribution of each to disinflation.

My particular job and my own personal experience of the events just now described may account for an understandable tendency of mine to overestimate the importance of anti-inflationary monetary policy, not only vis-à-vis fiscal policy but also with respect to the incomes policy, broadly based on the contributions of Ezio Tarantelli.

However, there is at least one reason, one structural change, that explains the greater anti-inflationary effectiveness of Italian monetary policy and its lower cost in terms of output and employment in the 1990s by comparison with the '70s and 1980s, when Ezio was shaping his thought and developing his practical proposals, until his voice was silenced by the most vicious sort of violence. Ezio's thought and policy proposals referred to a world – especially in Italy – governed by a labour standard as defined by Sir John Hicks: 'the world we now live in is one in which the monetary system has become relatively elastic, so that it can accommodate itself to changes in wages, rather than the other way about. Instead of actual wages having to adjust themselves to an equilibrium level, monetary policy adjusts the equilibrium level of money wages so as to make it conform to the actual level. It is hardly an exaggeration to say that instead of being on a Gold Standard, we are on a Labour Standard' (Hicks, 1955, p. 196).

At the end of the century, however, finance developed enormously. Financial assets tended everywhere to surpass the stock of real assets, physical capital. The greatly expanded financial markets became increasingly self-referential *à la* Keynes. Even workers have become *rentiers*. They save, and their wealth consists largely of financial assets as well as housing and consumer durables. Not only the investment decisions of capitalists under uncertainty but also the decisions of working people – on wages, consumption, saving, portfolio composition – depend increasingly on conjectures about the future, on forecasts, on individuals' expectations, on their calculations and the prevailing Keynesian conventions.

Aside from the necessity of being more alert with regard to inflation – because wages are less indexed, because the monetary component of wealth is substantial – workers are now inflation-adverse, more than in the past, or unlike the past. They are even against inflation fuelled or preceded by wage increases, because the loss on capital account from the reduction in both the nominal and the real value of financial wealth can be greater than the gain in labour income. The conversion of wage-workers into *rentiers* dissolves rigidities and prevents inflationary wage pressures. It leads towards a transcending of Hicks's labour standard. Inflation again becomes easier to tame using monetary instruments.

The process by which workers save and invest in financial assets to become *rentiers* has occurred in Italy as well. It came later than in other countries that preceded Italy in economic development. Here, it began just as Ezio Tarantelli was producing his best analytical work, which was rooted in the labour-standard framework.

It can be seen in the statistics which were collected by the Bank of Italy from 1987 onwards. Let me cite the essential data. The share of total household saving accounted for by households headed by workers or pensioners rose to 70 per cent. Some 30 per cent of the overall flow of savings in Italy is accounted for by payroll workers and pensioners and their families, who invest 40 per cent of that flow in financial assets and no longer all in real estate. These households' financial wealth makes up nearly three quarters of the total stock of Italian households' financial assets. Between 1987 and 2002 the average financial wealth of employee households rose from €21,000 to €52,000 and that of pensioner households from €20,000 to €124,000, while that of self-employed households rose from €36,000 to €131,000.

1.5 'Doing good'

As an intellectual and as a scholar, Ezio Tarantelli gave the best of himself, made his deepest personal commitment, to solving what was then Italy's main economic problem, namely inflation.

Today, and for many years now, Italian society has been grappling with a profoundly different problem: stagnation.

Often, thinking of his extraordinary, original economist's mind, I wonder what Ezio would have suggested to get the Italian economy growing again. Rather than ask questions that have no answer, let me simply and directly describe the stuff of Ezio Tarantelli as an economist.

I can use the two simple words employed by Keynes, which he in turn took from his mentor, the philosopher George Moore: 'Doing good' (Keynes, 1972). For all of society, in the general interest, at least try to allay the shortcomings, the injustice of the economy in an imperfect world. A world in which necessity still prevails over freedom (Robinson, 1970). A world in which the market economy can promise but not guarantee material progress, a fair distribution of income and wealth, and real and monetary stability.

Today, economics risks being little more than the extenuating, repetitive application of new methods and algorithms to well-known paradigms. Moreover, the positive, analytical tendency is more and more sharply severed from the prescriptive, normative tendency addressed to economic policy, to problem solving, to doing good.

For us 'practitioners', this orientation of economic science is rather frustrating. We complain of the declining practical usefulness of the discipline. The prescriptions of many economists, if not exactly anodyne, are largely predictable.

In this Ezio Tarantelli can still serve, truly, as a shining counter-example. Analysis, per se, is easy; what is hard is devising a policy proposal. Ezio always directed his analytical efforts to policy prescription, and for that very reason analysis itself became difficult, challenging. He was a problem solver.

He was not just an adviser to policy-makers. He helped to set the policy course of one of Italy's leading trade union confederations. But he went beyond mere suggestions; he was in the front line in publicly defending that course. He did so with passion. No one could have imagined the personal risk he was taking.

He was amused when I jestingly compared him with Ferdinando Galiani: 'This science which the modern French in their infinite ignorance called 'economic' when they should have called it 'political' is a great deal harder than it appears … Anyone who thinks he has understood it when he has understood its theory only, is a fool … because its theoretical truths are so easy, so flat, so commonplace, almost useless, that any schoolboy can imagine them. But applying them requires an immense, profound, and extremely detailed knowledge of *that* country to which one wishes to give counsel' (Galiani, 1773, p. 69).

Yet academe attracted him. Together in 1971 we persuaded Governor Guido Carli to make a first exception to the Bank of Italy's practice and let us teach at the university, in our spare time from our engagement with the Research Department. Then I did everything I could to dissuade him from the academic road, to win him away from the university community that was wooing him, both in Italy and abroad, just as the Bank of Italy did not want to lose him.

His shining example remains. It is perhaps all the more precious today, quite apart from the merits of his work and his suggestions. These, as I have shown, depended on the context. They were context-bound because he intended them to have an impact on *that* context. Generous, creative, relevant, Ezio Tarantelli was a true economist and an unforgettable friend.

References

Galiani, F. (1773), 'Sull'annona di Genova', now republished in *Scritti di politica economica*, Lanciano: Carabba, 1999.

Hicks, J. (1955), 'Inflation and the wage structure', in *Money, Interest, and Wages*, Oxford: Blackwell, 1982.

Keynes, J.M. (1972), 'My early beliefs', in *Essays in Biography*, London: Macmillan.

Robinson, J. (1970), *Freedom and Necessity*, London: Allen & Unwin.

2 The 1960s and Ezio's Awakening to the Social Problems of Italy*

Mario Sarcinelli**

University of Rome 'La Sapienza', Italy

Voices of the UNEMPLOYED

In this land
No man has hired us.
Our life is unwelcome, our death
Unmentioned in 'The Times'.

Choruses from 'The Rock'
by Thomas Stearns Eliot

2.1 Some biographical notes

Although Ezio came from a good Abruzzese family, the difficulties his father encountered in finding work had forced him to earn his living from a very early age as an interpreter for the CIT travel agency and as a guide for foreign tourists at Villa Adriana and in Rome; his extensive knowledge of foreign languages had this practical origin, since he had studied only French at school.[1] After graduating in 1965, Ezio was taken on by the Bank of Italy a few months later as eligible for a Stringher scholarship.

Aware of the limited knowledge acquired in his Italian university studies, Ezio stayed behind his desk for only a very short time; he took leave from the Bank and went to Cambridge (UK) in 1965–66[2] to study the accumulation of capital, with Joan Robinson as his tutor. He returned to the Bank of Italy in June and was put to work in the Economic Research Department. His thirst for knowledge led him to leave again early in September, with very little money, to go to Cambridge

---

* Abridged version of a paper written in Italian and published in *Moneta e Credito*, **233**:23–44, 2006.

** I am very grateful to my friends Carole J. Beebe Tarantelli, Orazio Carabini, Mauro Marè, Giuseppe Mascetti, Guido M. Rey and Alessandro Roncaglia for kindly reading an earlier version of this work; as is normal in the circumstances, I remain entirely responsible for any errors and omissions and for the opinions expressed.

[1] I owe this biographical information to Carole J. Beebe Tarantelli, to whom I extend warm thanks.

[2] With a scholarship from the Ministry of Education.

(Mass.) and to stay there for the academic years 1966–67[3] and 1967–68,[4] above all with the intention of studying econometric methods. It was there that he met Carole, later to become his wife, who gave him generous moral and material support and with whom he established a profound intellectual relationship. Ezio had an open personality, always ready for a discussion and for an exchange of views, but he was also provocative. In January 1967, for example, he clearly wanted to show that he felt himself a member of Europe's left-wing élite and waved *The Accumulation of Capital* in front of Robert Solow. These were the years in which he established a close friendship with Franco Modigliani. In 1967 Paolo Baffi, and above all the Bank's Personnel Department, were unwilling to grant Ezio another period of leave to return to MIT; I promised to intercede on his behalf and in the end he obtained permission to go.[5] However, the difficulties he had had to overcome to leave Italy did not make him more prudent or disciplined; he turned up at the Bank a month and a half late.[6]

He was certainly a man tempered by the difficulties he had faced, but he also had the courage to go beyond the limit to which others were subject, spurred on by his ambition and awareness of his capabilities. From the middle of 1968 and for the whole of 1969 Ezio was in Italy and lived through the student uprisings, the bitter strikes of Italy's hot autumn, the tragedies that afflicted a divided, frightened and hesitant country.

2.2 The demand for a policy of structural reforms

Although as a former member of the Research Department I devoted a great deal of attention to the central bank's reading of the 1960s (Sarcinelli, 1965; Ciocca et al., 1975; Rey and Peluffo, 1995; Rey, 2003) and to the assessment of this that can be made on the basis of Guido Carli's memoirs (1993), it is not from the Bank of Italy's annual reports that a vivid picture can be obtained of the moods and passions of the young, especially of those who made up the new proletariat of the large cities of northern Italy, often with a low level of education and specialization

[3] He had been granted a scholarship by the University of Rome, supplemented by an allowance from the Bank of Italy in return for a commitment to study and remain in contact with the persons responsible for the research project on the modus operandi of monetary policy.

[4] In view of his brilliant results in his statistics, monetary economics, macroeconomics and development exams, the Economics Department of Boston College awarded him a stipend of $2,300 and exonerated him from the payment of $1,800 of tuition fees.

[5] Carole remembers the nervous walk Ezio and I took along Via Nazionale while she waited the outcome of our meeting in her Fiat 600. This time, however, the leave the Bank of Italy granted did not count towards his length of service.

[6] Carole has told me that he embarked on a Hellenic Lines cargo ship that went half way round the Mediterranean and was held up in Athens to carry out repairs, so that it reached Italy very late. Somewhere in the archives of the Bank of Italy's Personnel Department there should be a declaration concerning this unusual delay.

and employed on the assembly lines that Fordism had brought to large plants; it is therefore to historians that we must turn for help.

As Guido Crainz (2003) has put it:

> Consider the new working class that was emerging and whose nucleus consisted of the young. The pattern of purchases may have been individual and family-based, the consumption society may have had a great potential for 'integrating' the subordinate classes, but the economic boom triggered, or at any rate encouraged, a revival of collective protagonism that unhinged the scenario consolidated in the fifties. The conflicts that began to develop in the factories had recurrent causes: extremely hard working conditions, long hours (often extended arbitrarily by employers), discrimination, lack of rights, company profits out of proportion with wages. ... The refusal of the 'ethic of sacrifice' intertwined with the refusal of traditional forms of subordination and the rejection of anachronistic hierarchical and social distinctions; hence the accumulation of collective hopes and values in opposition to the existing order. (ibid., p. 20)

The call was for structural reforms, even if it was not always clear what was to be reformed or how.

Considered ex post, these unsatisfied requests become 'missed opportunities'. In contrast with the view taken by Michele Salvati (2000), they are to be interpreted in a psychological and sociological sense; regardless of whether they were utopian or realistic, they fuelled the individual or collective imagination all the more, the greater was the sense of frustration or just discontent with the present situation. And the most important of these missed opportunities was economic planning.

This may not have been a valid option, i.e. capable of respecting the principles of the market economy and at the same time of ensuring, by means of an incomes policy, a fairer distribution of the benefits of growth and worker representation in the management of the economy. Personally, I have never had much faith in the success of planning, which requires a strong, competent and respected public administration on the one hand and a powerful sense of social discipline on the other; even today both these conditions are largely lacking. Nonetheless, the advocacy of economic planning and its repeated reincarnation in ever different forms (Carabba, 1977) led to its being considered in the political and trade union imagination as perhaps the greatest missed opportunity.

Industrial conflict culminated in the hottest of 'hot' autumns, that of 1969. The growth in industrial employment had been rapid and there were about 6,850,000 industrial workers that year; the number of hours lost through strikes reached a peak of more than 230 million, nearly five times as many as in the previous year. The grounds for the disputes, over which the trade unions often lost control, were not only demands for large increases in pay but also the desire for greater respect for workers' dignity. The break between trade unions and workers did not only occur at Fiat and Pirelli, where the first unitary workers' committee was born, but also in the disputes at Battipaglia. Demands for equal pay increases for all gathered strength, as at Fiat, and shop stewards, elected or appointed by the workers and not the trade unions, gained new power.

2.3 The demand for a policy of empowerment

It was not only the working class that was looking for a role that went beyond that of consumer; students also perceived that the time was ripe, that relations between pupils and teachers were at best paternalistic and at worst authoritarian, that culture, as in the now obligatory middle school, remained or it was feared would remain for an élite, with the result that it did not counter the tendency for students to drop out (School at Barbiana, 1967). The law setting up the University of Calabria was passed in 1966, but universities were tending to multiply in a variety of ways, owing to the rapid increase in the number of students and above all to satisfy local ambitions; there thus began a process of lowering university studies to high-school level, often with adverse effects on research.

As early as 1964 there had been a series of agitations, strikes and occupations at schools and universities, certainly not out of high spirits but as a reaction to a state of discontent or as criticism of decisions taken by the educational authorities. Early in 1965 some marginal episodes gave rise more to concern than to alarm; they were clear enough signals of the cultural backwardness and social segmentation of the Italian school system, more than radical unrest on the part of young people in search of allies for their own 'revolution'. In 1965 tension rose to a high level at the University of Rome owing to the face-off between students of opposing factions and the support given to that of the far right by the rector and the police. The following year a socialist student, Paolo Rossi, was killed, triggering the occupation and counter-occupation of university faculties and the resignation of the rector. Moreover, in 1966, at the beginning of the academic year and while an agreement was being reached in the negotiations with the engineering workers, small groups of politically motivated students began to be seen in trade union demonstrations; during the strikes at Fiat in 1968 the confluence of the demands of workers and students became clear; in the previous year the University of Turin had provided a foretaste of the Italian 1968 insurrection. In many universities the students had come to believe that, like the workers, they were victims of class injustice, which led to the former converging spontaneously towards the latter.

The confrontation degenerated almost everywhere into fights not only with the police but also between groups of students of opposite political factions. Some illuminated minds recognized, however, that unyielding confrontation had no sense; Federico Caffè accepted some student requests early in 1968 and declared: 'I am not a "revolutionary", I act according to conscience'.

Guido Crainz, far from hostile to the student movements, wrote:

> ... even if today the blueprint appears crude and partial ... it provided students with a reading of every aspect of society that was continuously confirmed. It allowed a young generation of intellectuals ... to focus attention and civil sensibility on [old distortions and more recent deformations] and to propose generous, albeit ingenuous, transformation projects. (Crainz, 2003, p. 238)

2.4 A final roundup

Where was Ezio in the meantime? In the front of my mind throughout this brief incursion into the 1960s; he lived through 1968 and 1969 with passion for the French May, with moderation for events in Italy, with prudence for the defence of civil rights and the ending of the Vietnam War in the United States.[7] Assigned in the Bank of Italy's Economic Research Department to the group charged with building the econometric model of the Italian economy, with responsibility for the part dealing with productivity and wages, early in 1970 Ezio returned to America, this time on a mission on behalf of the Bank, married Carole and returned to Rome in July. From 1971 to 1975 Giancarlo Mazzocchi gave him a teaching appointment,[8] which he carried out on Saturdays at the Università Cattolica. In the meantime, towards the end of February 1973, he had become an assistant lecturer in the department headed by Professor Caffè in Rome, renouncing his employment at the Bank of Italy and becoming a consultant to the central bank.

Evidence of Ezio's interests and activity at the Bank of Italy is to be found in two fundamental papers (1970, 1971), which open the volume devoted to Ezio's economic writings edited in 1988 by his friends Renato Filosa and Guido Rey (Tarantelli, 1988). This initial work was followed by a copious and consistent stream of articles aimed at putting forward an original interpretation of Italian reality using the instruments acquired in America. According to Filosa and Rey, although reference continued to be made to potential income,

> ... his approach took over only the name of the aggregate and mechanical model developed by the North-American school. In fact his model was based on the interdependence of the markets for goods, labour and money. In these articles the preferences of the policymaker with regard to inflation and the external constraint were present. What took on decisive importance was the political exchange between the social partners in the definition of the trade-off between inflation and unemployment, external deficit and growth on the one hand and public expenditure and taxation on the other. (Tarantelli, 1988, p. XIV)

In order to organize this political exchange, it was necessary to ensure the coherence of the trade unions and their unification.

Furthermore, in his 'Introduction' to *La forza delle idee*, Bruno Chiarini wrote: 'Equipping itself with technical instruments of analysis and forecasting ... [constituted] in reality a sine qua non for the orientation of trade unions towards responsible and cooperative behaviour, towards political exchange with the government' (Tarantelli, 1995, p. XXIII). Ezio's work on this front earned him the esteem and support of the Confederazione Italiana Sindacati Lavoratori (CISL) in the creation of the Istituto di Studi ed Economia del Lavoro (ISEL), of which he became the

---

7 That he was a realist and anti-dogmatic can be seen in his judgement on the Great Helmsman when Chairman Mao unleashed the Red Brigades in defence of his Chinese revolution: 'Mao Tse-tung has become senile'.

8 Giancarlo Mazzocchi, attacked by Ezio during a seminar, proposed that he hold a course on 'Labour policy and social legislation' in order to learn more about their respective ideas.

chairman. In supporting the initiative, Eraldo Crea noted with a touch of irony: 'A trade union is like a hornet; it flies against the laws of aerodynamics and *you* want to understand why it flies!' The hornet trade union still flies, perhaps a bit lower; the inquirer into its flight was shot dead in the car park of the University of Rome on 27 March 1985. Those who killed him were probably unaware that in his *Odes* (viii.28) Horace wrote:

Dignum laude virum Musa vetat mori.

References

Barabba, M. (1977), *Un ventennio di programmazione: 1954–1974*, Rome-Bari: Editori Laterza.

Carli, G. (in collaboration with P. Peluffo) (1993), *Cinquant'anni di vita italiana*, Rome-Bari: Editori Laterza.

Ciocca, P., R. Filosa and G.M. Rey (1975), 'Integration and development of the Italian economy: 1951–71: a re-examination', *Banca Nazionale del Lavoro Quarterly Review*, **114**:284–320

Crainz, G. (2003), Il Paese mancato – Dal miracolo economico agli anni ottanta, Rome: Donzelli Editore.

Rey, G.M. (2003), *Il paradosso dell'economia italiana*, Rome: Aracne Editrice.

Rey, G.M. and P. Peluffo (eds) (1995), *Dialogo tra un professore e la Banca d'Italia*, Florence: Vallecchi.

Salvati, M. (2000), *Occasioni mancate – Economia e politica in Italia dagli anni '60 a oggi,* Rome-Bari: Editori Laterza.

Sarcinelli, M. (1965), 'La creazione di liquidità e la politica della banca centrale in Italia dal 1958 al 1964', in F. di Fenizio (ed.), *Letture di politica monetaria e finanziaria*, Milan: Banca Popolare di Milano, pp. 1051–1119.

School at Barbiana (1967), *Lettera a una professoressa,* Florence: Libreria editrice fiorentina.

Tarantelli, E. (1970), 'Produttività del lavoro, salari e inflazione: schema teorico e verifica empirica per l'industria italiana', *Quaderni di ricerche*, no. 5, Rome: Ente per gli studi monetari, bancari e finanziari 'Luigi Einaudi'.

Tarantelli, E. (1971), 'Costo del lavoro e margini di profitto industriale nel 1970', in Banca d'Italia, *Contributi alla ricerca economica*, no. 1, Rome, pp. 251–79.

Tarantelli, E. (1988), *L'utopia dei deboli è la paura dei forti: Saggi, relazioni ed altri scritti accademici*, G.M. Rey and R. Filosa (eds), Dipartimento di economia pubblica, Facoltà di economia e commercio dell'Università di Roma 'La Sapienza', Milan: Franco Angeli.

Tarantelli, E. (1995), *La forza delle idee: Scritti di economia e politica*, with a 'Remembrance' by F. Modigliani, an 'Introduction' by B. Chiarini, and 'Attualità dell'insegnamento' by G.M. Rey, Rome: Editoriale Lavoro, and Rome-Bari: Laterza.

PART II

THE IMPLEMENTATION OF TARANTELLI'S PROPOSALS

3 Employment Growth in Italy in the 1990s: Institutional Arrangements and Market Forces

Andrea Brandolini, Piero Casadio, Piero Cipollone, Marco Magnani, Alfonso Rosolia and Roberto Torrini

Bank of Italy, Economic Research Department, Italy

3.1 Introduction*

This story begins on 17th September 1992. On that day, the lira had to withdraw from the EMS, after few days of violent speculative attacks. The currency crisis epitomised the severity of the economic situation of Italy. The risk of a ruinous financial crisis was tangible. The following day the Amato Cabinet approved the most severe consolidation package in the country's post-war history (Rossi, 2003). In a context of weak world demand, the drastic readjustment of the public budget exacerbated the economic slowdown: GDP growth dropped to 0.8 per cent in 1992 and turned negative, to –0.9 per cent, in 1993. The repercussions on the labour market were dramatic. Between the first quarter of 1992, at the peak of the cycle, and the third quarter of 1993, at the bottom of the recession, the number of full-time equivalent employed plunged by 861,000, or 3.3 per cent. The fall in employment continued until 1995, well after the economy had started to recover.

These facts set the stage for the incomes policy agreement of 2nd July 1993. Since the Second World War, Italian industrial relations had been characterised by a high level of conflict, and had seen alternate phases of ruthless supremacy of either employers or workers (Regalia et al., 1978; Regalia and Regini, 1996; Magnani, 1996, 1997). Some change seemed to occur at the end of the 1970s, at the time of the unprecedented *de facto* sharing of government responsibility by the communist party, as the idea that wage increases are by themselves a factor of economic growth whatever the economic conditions lost ground among trade unions. But the clearest discontinuity is historically marked by the agreements of the early 1990s[1] – a discontinuity that owes much to the teaching of Ezio Tarantelli.

---

* We are indebted for very helpful comments to Tony Atkinson, Nicola Rossi, Salvatore Rossi, Ignazio Visco on a previous version of this chapter. We thank Angelina Cheche, Federico Giorgi, Federica Lagna and Raffaella Nizzi for excellent research assistance. This chapter draws extensively on our past work at the Economic Research Department of the Bank of Italy. However, the opinions presented here are solely ours, and they do not necessarily reflect the views of the Bank of Italy.

[1] The 1993 agreement ended a long confrontation between social partners that had started in 1990 when Confindustria, the main employers' association, had unilaterally reneged on the wage indexation agreement. In July 1992 a provisional trilateral accord abolished indexation and set a short-term wage freeze. Waiting for a full reform, any firm-level pay

The abolition of the half-a-century-old wage indexation mechanism (*scala mobile*) and the agreement on the tasks to be assigned to the two tiers of the new bargaining system (the protection of wage purchasing power for industry-wide national contracts, and the setting of performance-related pay rises for company-level contracts) are the most known changes introduced in 1993. These features were instrumental in the following years in abating the inflation rate and halting any wage–price spiral, in the face of significant external pressures on prices. But it would be diminishing to value these agreements exclusively for their anti-inflationary role. They had the ambition – as originally thought by Tarantelli ten years earlier – to set a frame for co-ordinated and co-operative relations between social partners.

The incomes policy agreements of the early 1990s have indeed succeeded in the attainment of two important macroeconomic objectives. First, as already mentioned, they contributed to reduce the inflation rate and to maintain it at the lowest levels since the late 1960s, broadly in line with those of other European countries. Second, they made it possible a major transformation of the Italian labour market with little resurgence of industrial conflicts, allowing employment to increase even in years of moderate growth of the economic activity. While proving effective in governing the emergency, the new frame was unable to bring to completion the reform of industrial relations, particularly for the failure to redistribute the rents reaped by industries protected from external and domestic competition, as well as to bring about a long-needed reform of the welfare system with the aim to meet the needs of a flexible labour market.

These summary observations suggest that the assessment of the first consistent episode of incomes policies in Italy is a complex exercise. In this chapter we provide some elements for this evaluation by drawing a comprehensive picture of the evolution of the Italian labour market since the recession of the early 1990s.[2] We begin, in the next section, with a discussion of Tarantelli's legacy, as many of the issues examined here were at the centre of his economic and political thinking. We then focus on the recent employment cycle: we submit, in Section 3.3, that the significant increase of the labour input at a time of modest economic growth originated in a fall of the price of labour relative to that of capital, and we investigate the underlying factors in Sections 3.4. In Section 3.5 we examine the impact of these developments on individual outcomes in the labour market.[3] We conclude by summarising the main points and offering our tentative assessment of the Italian experience of incomes policies in the last decade.

---

rise was suspended until the end of 1993, and compensated by a one-off undifferentiated payment equal to 0.7 per cent of the average wage in January 1993. The final agreement was reached in July 1993. The sense of drama is well conveyed by the decision of Bruno Trentin, the leader of the largest trade union (CGIL), to resign immediately after signing the 1992 accord (for a brief account see Ginsborg, 1998, pp. 897–8).

[2] See also Sestito (2002), Potestio (2005), Contini and Trivellato (2005) and Tronti (2006), among others.

[3] Except for occasional references, in this chapter we do not systematically deal with the implications of recent labour market developments for the North-South divide and the gender gap, two issues that would deserve specific discussion.

3.2 The legacy of Ezio Tarantelli

In the early 1980s, the indexation mechanism, known as *scala mobile*, was such that, in each quarter, about 80 per cent of past inflation was transferred to wage dynamics.[4] Some intervention was needed to prevent a wage–price spiral. The standard recipe was a discipline of nominal wage claims through monetary policy, on the grounds that it had worked in other countries. Tarantelli was among the few to realise that monetary policy could not be as effective in Italy as it had been in the Federal Republic of Germany and other countries, because of a substantially different institutional setting (see, for instance, Tarantelli, 1981a, 1986a). It took many more years before the idea that institutions matter became popular and econometricians began to regress the inflation rate on the degree of centralisation of wage bargaining (see Calmfors and Driffill, 1988, for an early example, and Flanagan, 1999, for a recent survey).

Tarantelli's tenet was that the inflation process of the 1970s had been the outcome of the distributive conflict exploded at the end of the 1960s and grown harsher after the first oil shock. This conflict could be settled by a tough monetary policy only where relatively small changes of the unemployment rate were sufficient to discipline wage claims. Where strong centralised unions could resist real wage cuts, fighting inflation by monetary policy could imply a very high cost in terms of output and employment. The successful anti-inflationary policies implemented in the Nordic countries, in Austria and in the Federal Republic of Germany were, by contrast, examples of co-operative games played by central banks and unions to tame inflation. The pre-condition was to put the distributive conflict

---

[4] *Scala mobile* was introduced in Italy soon after the Second World War. A substantial reform was carried out in 1951 and set rules that remained basically unchanged until 1975. In the 1951 system, each percentage point increase of the trade-union cost-of-living index (the so called *indice sindacale del costo della vita*) caused contractual wages to rise, with a lag, by predetermined fixed amounts which differed by occupation, sex, age and geographical area (e.g. Dell'Aringa, 1974; Robotti, 1973, 1975). At the beginning of 1975, trade unions and employers' organisations agreed to radically change the system, with the declared objective to reduce wage differentials: after a transition period ending in 1977, the differentiated fixed amounts were to be replaced by a single amount equal across all employees (*punto unico di scala mobile*) of value substantially higher than before. The 1975 agreements were also seen by social partners as a way to increase the centralisation of wage bargaining (Barca and Magnani, 1989). On the macroeconomics of the new wage indexation mechanism see Modigliani and Padoa Schioppa (1977). The actual protection guaranteed to earnings was extensively discussed by Faustini (1976), Spaventa (1976, 1977), Filosa and Visco (1977a, 1977b, 1980), and Visco (1979). Visco (1984) and Bodo and Visco (1987) estimated that during the 1970s and early 1980s nominal hourly earnings in the manufacturing sector were completely indexed to past price changes, as a result not only of *scala mobile* but also of the bargaining process. On the other hand, the operation of *punto unico* in the presence of double-digit inflation rates imparted, until the mid 1980s, a strong egalitarian bias to the evolution of the earnings structure, which was only partially compensated by decentralised negotiation (see Erickson and Ichino, 1995, Brandolini et al., 2002, Manacorda, 2004).

at the centre of the political arena, assigning the government a role in conciliating the opposite interests of workers and employers: wage moderation did not need to imply a reduction of disposable income of households, provided that fiscal policies were used to supply education, health and housing services. Incomes policies were the tool to achieve this 'political exchange', and the announcement of coherent and co-ordinated targets agreed by all social actors was seen as a device to lend them credibility and to guide agents' expectations in the whole economy.

The success of the scheme leant crucially on the mutual trust of the actors involved: employers' associations, trade unions and government. Drawing basically on the experience of Nordic and Central European countries, Tarantelli (1986b) identified three essential dimensions of neo-corporatism: the degree to which unions are willing to settle the distributive conflict in the political arena; the degree of centralisation of the bargaining process, seen as a measure of the ability of the system to prevent free riding behaviour; the probability that the actors enter co-operative solutions in an early stage of the game. He then showed that these indicators were good predictors of the macroeconomic performance, as measured by the Okun's index, in a panel of OECD countries during the period 1968–1983 (e.g. Tarantelli, 1986a).

It is within this framework that Tarantelli proposed, well ahead of the developments of the 1990s, to exchange flexible work arrangements with higher employment (1984a), a decent unemployment benefit with a less stringent employment protection (1982), the diffusion of part time with a reduction in the working time (1984b). But his most effective contribution was the idea of predetermining pay rises to guide price expectations. At the end of 1980, the inflation rate had peaked at about 20 per cent, after two years of rapid increase. This price acceleration stemmed from both domestic (e.g. the growth of the tariffs of public utilities which had been kept at very low levels in earlier years because of political and social pressures) and external factors (e.g. the second oil shock), but it also reflected the working of *scala mobile*. Closing the inflation gap with other countries was the policy priority, and a possible solution was seen in a reduction of the degree of wage indexation by netting the inflation rate from increases due to oil prices or currency depreciation. This solution had however drawbacks: the inflation rate would have persisted, even in the absence of additional external shocks, owing to the high inertia of the indexation scheme, or if pay settlements at the contractual round were not coherent with productivity developments. Moreover, expectations could be inconsistent with the monetary policy announced by the central bank. Tarantelli (1981b) understood that the main problem was in the backward-looking nature of *scala mobile*, and proposed to predetermine inflation-related pay rises in order to guide future price developments along the path agreed by social partners. A safeguard clause was to ensure that workers would have been compensated for any unexpected cut in the real wage.

After two years of intense debate and an economic recession, Tarantelli's proposal inspired the tripartite agreement of 22nd January 1983, known as 'Lodo Scotti' after the name of the Labour Minister. The agreement was the first example in Italy of a 'political exchange' along the lines described by Tarantelli: trade unions accepted to cut the degree of indexation by about 15 percentage points (the fraction of the inflation rate attributable to changes in indirect taxes, oil prices and the lira exchange rate) in exchange of a reduction in the hours of work, an increase in family allowances and a restitution of the fiscal drag. A year later, on 14th February 1984, a new more ambitious agreement, centred on the predetermination of wage rises due to the indexation mechanism, was reached. Politically backed by the socialist premier, it met with fierce opposition from the majority of the main trade union (CGIL), supported by the communist party. The opposition was eventually defeated in a referendum held in 1985 on whether the agreement should be rejected.

The incomes policy experiment of 1984 conformed in part to Tarantelli's original proposal: it announced the target inflation rate in accordance with the guidelines of monetary policy; public tariffs evolved coherently, at least in 1984; the dependence of pay rises from past inflation was almost severed in 1984, as the change of *scala mobile* linked wage increases to the target inflation rate. On the other hand, the agreement did not embody any safeguard clause against unexpected inflation. And it was rejected by a significant part of trade unions, failing to ensure the support of all social partners. Did the experiment succeed? The inflation rate did drop from 16.5 per cent in 1982 to 10.8 in 1984. Incomes policies contributed: the changes to *scala mobile* reduced the degree of indexation from 68 per cent in 1982 to 44 in 1984. The expected inflation rate was cut in 1984 by about 1.5 percentage points, and the speed at which past inflation was embedded in future expectations was also reduced. Empirical analyses later conducted at the Bank of Italy confirm that to some extent the fall was due to the incomes policy experiment, even though estimates differ in size (Guiso and Magnani, 1985; Gressani et al., 1988). It is an open question whether this experiment could have achieved more, had it been implemented along the more general lines of Tarantelli's original proposal.

3.3 The labour market in the 1990s[5]

The recession of the early 1990s was the most severe since the Second World War in terms of job losses, and the subsequent employment recovery did not start until 1995 (Fig. 3.1). During the crisis of the early 1960s, which ended to Italy's 'economic miracle', total employment declined by 640,000 full-time equivalent units (3.2 per cent) from 1962 to 1966; in the more recent episode, the cumulative fall reached 1,080,000 units (4.6 per cent) from 1991 to 1995. A reason for the high drop in employment in the early 1990s is that it was not cushioned by job creation in public administration, nor in State owned companies.[6] Moreover, layoffs were

[5] In March 2006 Istat released national accounts based on substantially revised methodologies. As the publication of revised data is to date largely incomplete, in this chapter we use pre-revision series for the sake of consistency. Moreover, we do not adjust the figures from the labour force survey prior to 2004 to account for the major break caused by Istat's methodological revision implemented in that year.

[6] Public employment ceased to increase after 40 years of steady growth: the number of full-time equivalent employees in public administration, education and health services

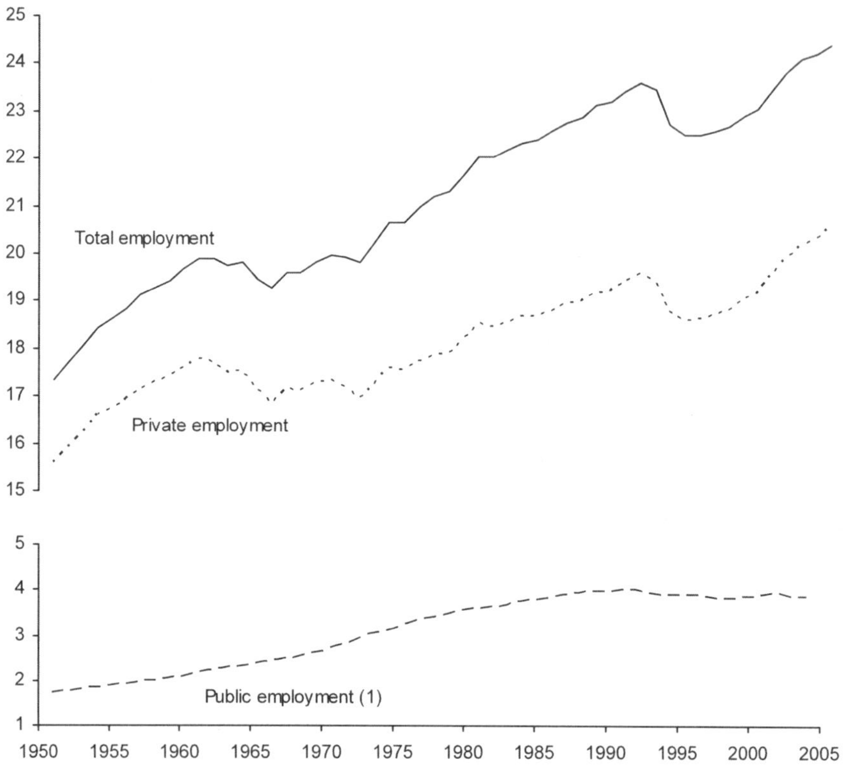

Fig. 3.1. Employment in post-war Italy (full-time equivalent employed, millions)

Source: Authors' elaboration on data from Istat, National Accounts, and Golinelli (1996).

Note: (1) As proxied by employees in: public administration, defence services and compulsory social security services; education; health and other social services. Some of these employees are actually employed in private firms.

(which also include some employed in private firms in the same sectors), which had gone up by 913,000 in the 1970s and 451,000 in the 1980s, dropped by 141,000 between 1990 and 2000. At the same time, the contribution to job creation by State owned companies (public utilities and companies controlled by the industrial conglomerate IRI) rapidly faded away, as a consequence of the shrinking State aids imposed by stricter EU rules and public budget cuts, reinforcing a trend started in the mid-1980s. Most of these companies engaged in painful restructuring processes, a pre-condition for subsequent privatisation. As a consequence of these changes, between 1991 and 1996 the number of employees of State owned or controlled companies fell by 257,000 units (21.4 per cent), according to national accounts data (Istat, 1997).

arguably easier than in the 1970s and 1980s owing to the change in the regulation of collective dismissals passed in 1991,[7] as shown by the high ratio of dismissals to average employment in the early 1990s (Fig. 3.2).

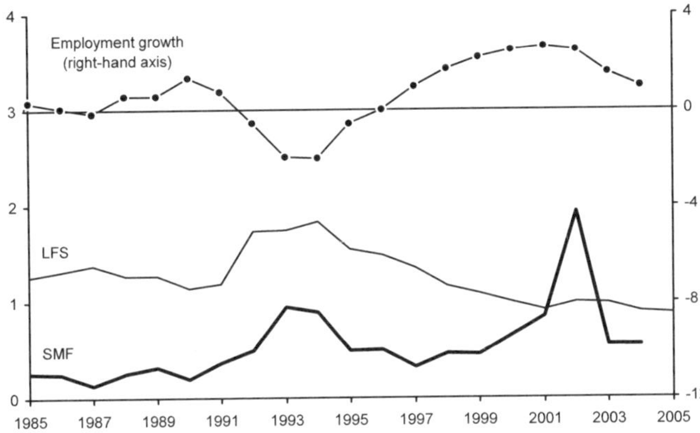

Fig. 3.2. Dismissal rate and employment growth (per cent)

Source: Authors' elaboration on data from Istat, National Accounts and Labour Force Survey (LFS), and Federmeccanica (2006 and previous years), Survey of Metalworking Firms (SMF).

Note: The dismissal rate is defined as the ratio of the number of dismissed persons to average employment in the year. In the LFS the number of dismissals is proxied by the number of non-employed persons reporting that they lost a job due to dismissal in the year preceding the interview, which underestimates the true number because it does not include fired workers who found a new job. In the SMF firms with less than 50 employees are excluded; the peak in 2002 is due to layoffs in few firms of the automobile sector. Employment growth is measured as the annual change in the number of employees in the business sector.

---

[7] Employment protection rules were introduced in 1970 by Law 300, known as 'Statuto dei lavoratori', after the so called 'hot autumn' of 1969, when large scale strikes all over the country forced the government to pass pro-labour reforms. According to these rules firings are only allowed on a just cause basis and workers can appeal to the court against them. If a dismissal is ruled to be unfair, the firm has to pay a severance payment, higher for firms with more than 15 employees. Firms above this threshold are also obliged to reinstate the unfairly dismissed workers. In 1991 Law 223 laid down a procedure for collective dismissals (i.e. involving five or more workers for reasons inherent in production) in firms with more than 15 employees, which reduced the uncertainty surrounding the final outcome of the firing process, *de facto* reducing firing costs for larger firms (e.g. Bertola and Ichino, 1995, pp. 387–8). Garibaldi et al. (2004) and Schivardi and Torrini (2005) find a negative, but small, effect of the more stringent employment protection in firms with more than 15 employees on the probability of growing for firms below this threshold and on the average size of Italian firms. Boeri and Jimeno (2005) estimate that workers employed in firms above the threshold are less likely to be fired. On the other hand, Schivardi and Torrini (2005) show that the overall worker turnover is higher for firms above the threshold, as they tend to use more intensively short-term contracts.

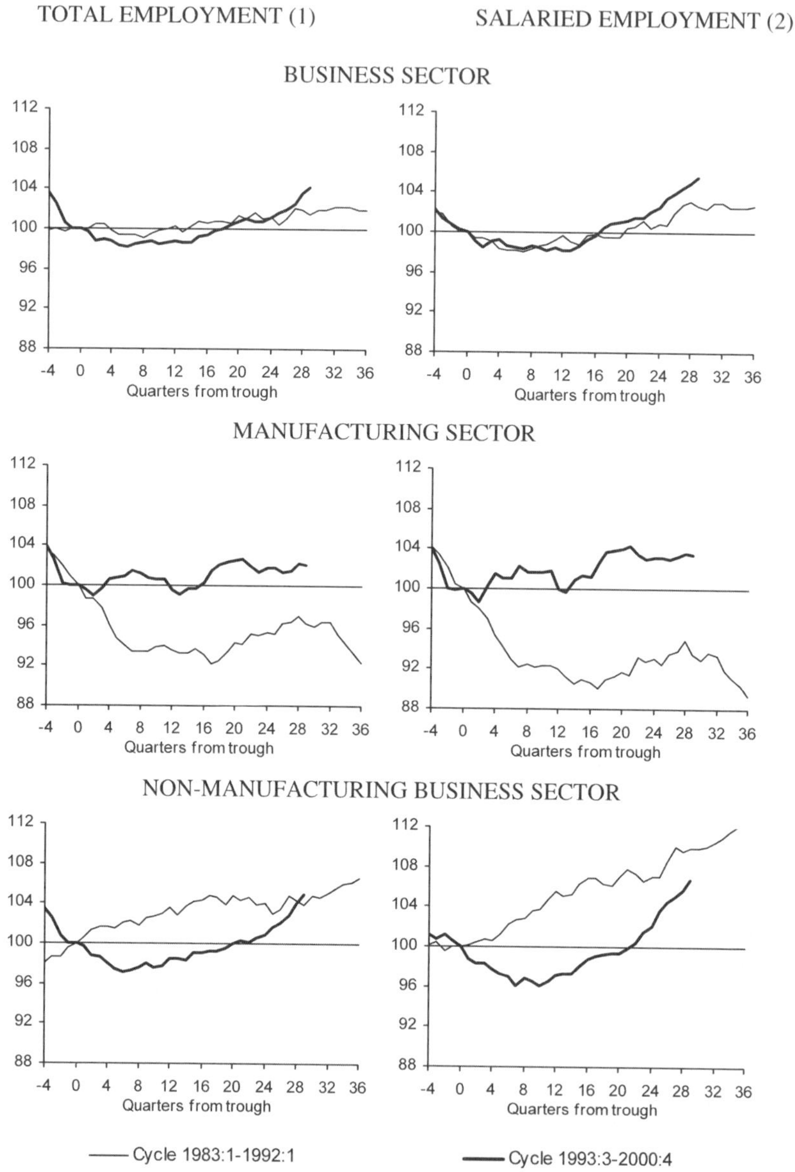

Fig. 3.3. Employment in the last two cycles (index: value in the trough = 100)

Source: Authors' elaboration on data from Istat, National Accounts.

Notes: Each series is re-scaled so to equal to 100 the value in the trough. (1) Full-time equivalent workers. (2) Full-time equivalent employees.

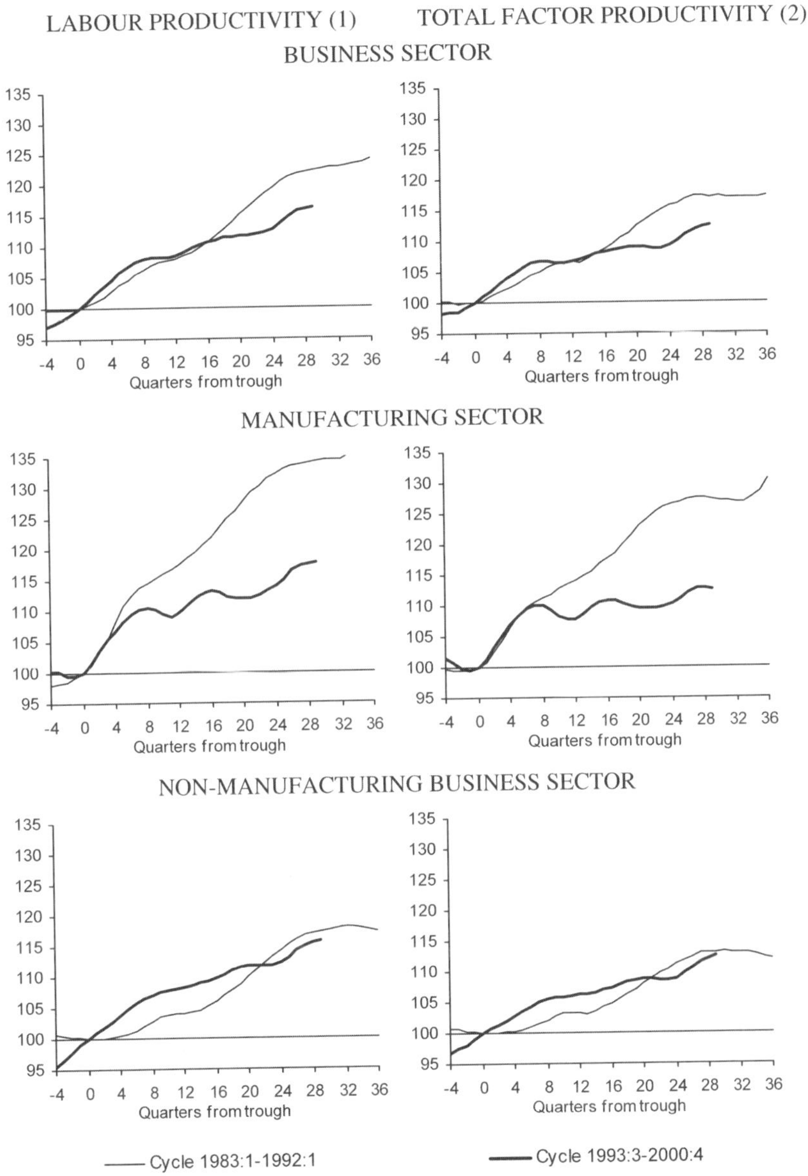

Fig. 3.4. Productivity in the last two cycles (index: value in the trough = 100)

Source: Authors' elaboration on data from Istat, National Accounts.

Notes: Each series is re-scaled so to equal to 100 the value in the trough. (1) Value added at factor costs (net of rental of buildings) per full-time equivalent worker. (2) Index of the difference between the rate of growth in value added at factor costs (net of rental of buildings) and the rates of growth in labour input and capital stock, weighted according to their respective shares in value added.

As the recession of the early 1990s was different, so was the subsequent recovery. To highlight its peculiarities eliminating cyclical effects, we compare the 1990s expansion with the earlier one.[8] On an annual basis, the average GDP growth was 2.2 per cent, noticeably below the 2.7 per cent registered during the previous expansion. Yet, employment gains were broadly comparable: 0.6 and 0.7 per cent, respectively.[9] What differed sharply was net job creation in the business sector: 0.6 per cent per year since 1993 as against 0.2 per cent in the 1980s, or 0.7 and 0.3 per cent considering only salaried employment (Fig. 3.3, top panels). Employment kept falling for several quarters after the turning point of the economic cycle.

After an initial acceleration, total factor productivity slowed down significantly, and at the cyclical peak at the end of 2000 it had gone up by 12 per cent since the trough in 1993, against 16 per cent in the previous cycle (Fig. 3.4, right-hand top panel). Also capital intensity augmented less, and its contribution to the growth of output per worker fell from 6 to 3 percentage points (Fig. 3.5, right-hand top panel). As a result, labour productivity rose by 15 per cent during the 1990s cycle, much less than the 22 per cent recorded in the 1980s (Fig. 3.4, left-hand top panel).[10] In spite of the slowdown, labour productivity outperformed the real cost of labour, especially in the first half of the expansion (compare the left-hand top

[8] We adopt here the standard classification of business cycles as discussed by Altissimo et al. (2000), and updated in ISAE (2003). The 1980s expansion starts in the first quarter of 1983 and ends in the first quarter of 1991. As regards the 1990s, we ignore the brief recession of 1996 and we take the period from the third quarter of 1993 to the fourth quarter of 2000 as a single expansion. Notice that the more recent cycle is seven quarters shorter than the previous one.

[9] Throughout the chapter we focus on employment and we pay very little attention to the dynamics of the unemployment rate. One reason is that the unemployment rate is in Italy an unsatisfactory measure of cyclical conditions and of the unused amount of labour available in the economy, as discussed by Viviano (2003), Battistin et al. (2005), and Brandolini et al. (2006).

[10] The growth of labour productivity is approximated by the difference between Δy and Δl, which in turn is equal to $\alpha(\Delta k - \Delta l) + \theta$, where y, l and k denote the logarithms of real value added, labour input and net capital stock, respectively, α is the capital share in value added and θ is total factor productivity growth. On the estimation of total factor productivity in Italy see Brandolini and Cipollone (2001a), where a correction for the quality of the labour input is also examined. Bassanetti et al. (2005) estimated total factor productivity accounting for the quality of capital goods and the impact of information and communication technologies. Our estimates are based on the official measure of net capital stock instead of the more appropriate, but not readily available, measure of productive capital (e.g. Oliner and Sichel, 2000, pp. 6–7). Comparing our findings to those of Bassanetti et al. (2005), who used a measure of productive capital, shows that the general picture is broadly unaffected: the observed slowdown in total factor productivity, in particular, does not depend on the concept of capital utilised.

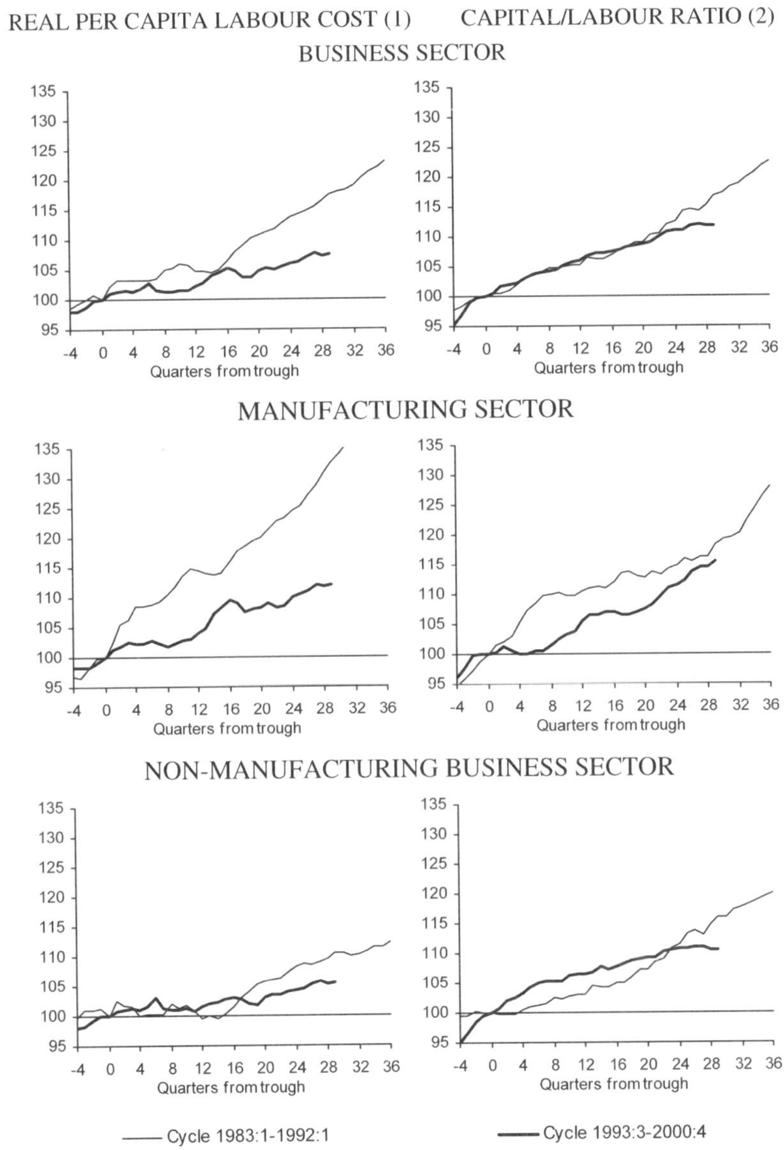

Fig. 3.5. Labour cost and capital intensity in the last two cycles (index: value in the trough = 100)

Source: Authors' elaboration on data from Istat, National Accounts.

Notes: Each series is re-scaled so to equal to 100 the value in the trough. (1) Employees compensation per full-time equivalent salaried worker divided by the deflator of value added at factor costs (net of rental of buildings). Unadjusted for the introduction of IRAP. (2) Net capital at 1995 prices (net of the stock of dwellings) per full-time equivalent worker.

panels in Figs 3.4 and 3.5),[11] and the gross capital share in value added rose to the highest levels in decades.

The business sector is a composite aggregate, comprising agriculture, manufacturing, energy production and distribution, construction, trade, hotels and restaurants, transport and communications, financial intermediation, and business activities. It is beyond the scope of this chapter to delve into the different sectoral dynamics, but it is nonetheless worth examining the corresponding patterns in the manufacturing sector. We single out this sector not only for its economic relevance, but also because of its high exposure to international competition. In the mid panels of Figs 3.3–3.5, we replicate for manufacturing the charts just discussed for the business sector. For completeness' sake, we also present in the bottom panels the analogous charts for the whole of the other business industries. During the 1990s expansion, the manufacturing share in total private employment has remained around 30 per cent (38 per cent for salaried employment), showing a slight tendency to diminish.

Differences in employment patterns in the manufacturing sector are even more striking than those discussed for the business sector as a whole. The expansion of the 1980s opened with an intense process of restructuring that led to net job losses for 371,000 units (6.6 per cent) between the first quarter of 1983 and the first quarter of 1985 (Barca and Magnani, 1989). Subsequent recovery was partial and temporary. By contrast, employment exhibited a moderate tendency to rise in the 1990s cycle. On average, the number of full-time equivalent employed units grew by 0.3 per cent per year from trough to peak, and that of employees by 0.5 per cent; in the previous expansion they had fallen by 0.9 and 1.2 per cent, respectively. The rise in the labour input was accompanied by a larger increase in the endowment of capital goods, but capital intensity increased less than in the 1980s, and so did its contribution to the growth of labour productivity (0.6 vs. 0.9 per cent per year). Also total factor productivity levelled off, after an initial improvement, and its dynamics lagged behind that recorded in the earlier expansion (1.4 vs. 2.6 per cent per year). Thus, both factors contributed to curb labour productivity growth, causing it to drop to 2.0 per cent per year in the 1990s, from 3.5 in the earlier expansion. As for the business sector as a whole, it grew more rapidly than the real cost of labour, allowing the capital share to rise slightly.

To sum up, the evolution of the Italian labour market in the 1990s was markedly different from that in the previous decade: net job creation was entirely sus-

[11] The real cost of labour is the average compensation of a full-time equivalent salaried worker divided by the deflator of value added at factor costs (net of rental of buildings). The gross capital share is the difference between the value added at factor costs (net of rental of buildings, gross of depreciation) and the compensation of labour (including that provided by the self-employed) as a ratio to the value added. We did not correct for the discontinuity caused in 1998 by the replacement of some social security contributions with the new regional tax on productive activities (IRAP). However, the impact on main trends would be minimal. It should be noticed that during the 1990s, the value added deflator – which is used here to obtain the cost of labour in real terms – grew much less than the consumer price index, opening a wedge between the production wage and the consumption wage.

tained by labour demand in the business sector and occurred in the face of slower output growth. Capital deepening appears to have decelerated, as a consequence of the adoption of relatively less capital intensive technologies, and the development of activities, especially in the service sector, where the labour input is prevalent; the pace of growth of both labour and multifactor productivity dropped considerably.[12] Our reading of the available evidence is that these changes were brought about by an evolution of the relative price of labour and capital that was more favourable to labour than in the expansion of the 1980s.[13] This seems to hold for the business and manufacturing sectors alike. Two factors contributed to such variation of relative factor prices: much slower growth of the real cost of labour, and greater flexibility in staff adjustment and the organisation of production and working hours. It is to these factors that we turn our attention in the next section.

3.4 Wage moderation and flexibility

The price of labour evolved more favourably in the 1990s than in the previous decade for several reasons. Monetary wage moderation stemmed from the new bargaining structure and from the changing composition of the work force. On the other hand, a substantial reduction in the cost of adjusting the labour input was brought about by a more flexible organisation of production and working times, and a relaxation of existing constraints to staff adjustment. These changes too were permitted by the new climate in industrial relations.

3.4.1 The new bargaining system[14]

The July 1993 agreement between social partners set up a hierarchy of specialised bargaining levels: national contracts were devoted to maintaining the purchasing

[12] Bassanetti et al. (2006) found that also France has been experiencing a similar pattern in recent years.

[13] It could be argued that the driving force of the employment recovery was an 'exogenous' recomposition of aggregate demand towards goods and services requiring relatively more labour for their production (e.g. the growing demand for personal care services brought about by the rapidly increasing share of the elderly population). As a crude test of this hypothesis, we conducted a simple shift-share exercise. Using the maximum sectoral disaggregation allowed by the national accounts, we computed the employment level in the non-farm business sector under the assumptions that the composition of real production (at factor cost) had remained constant at the 1994–95 values, while total production and sectoral labour productivities had evolved along their historical paths. The resulting counterfactual employment series closely tracks the historical pattern until 1999 and then lags behind it in following years. According to this calculation, the reallocation of production would explain less than a fifth of the increase in employment between 1995 and 2001.

[14] This section draws on Casadio (2003) and Casadio et al. (2005).

power of wages, while firm-level contracts were devoted to the distribution of productivity gains. The length of national contracts was set at two years for wage determination and at four years for the regulatory aspects. Pay rises were linked to the government's target inflation – a new, forward-looking policy tool – but an ex post compensation for the difference between this rate and the actual inflation rate in the two preceding years was envisaged to safeguard workers' purchasing power.[15] Company-level contracts should grant flexible wage increases reflecting firms' performance and productivity improvements. In the industrial sector, the contractual base pay, which incorporates the former cost-of-living adjustment, corresponds to around 80 per cent of gross earnings; in market services, this proportion is higher.

Target inflation understated actual inflation except in 1997–98 (Fig. 3.6). The cumulative change in the price level implied by the target inflation rates (a year

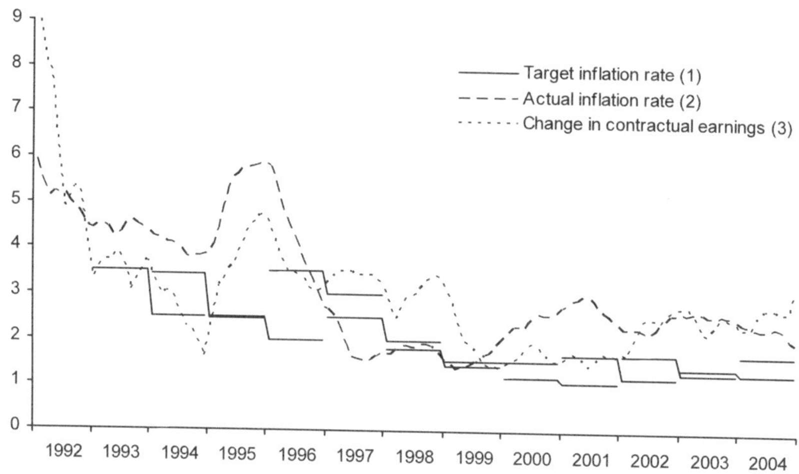

Fig. 3.6. Actual inflation, target inflation and contractual earnings in the business sector (per cent)

Source: Authors' elaboration on data from Istat and Ministero dell'Economia e delle Finanze (2003 and previous years).

Notes: (1) Government's target for following two years. For instance, the last broken line refers to the target set in July 2002 for 2003 and 2004. (2) Three-term moving average of the 12-month variation in the cost-of-living index. (3) Three-term moving average of the 12-month variation in the index of contractual earnings.

[15] According to the agreement, the ex post compensation should be adjusted to eliminate the effects of changes in the terms of trade due, for example, to a devaluation. The lack of a clear formulation of this clause has remained a source of conflict. In addition, nothing was specified about tax variations. In the period between the expiry of a contract and its renewal, employees receive an automatic wage increase equal to one-third of the target inflation rate after three months and half that rate after other three months.

ahead) between 1992 and 2004 would have been about 12 percentage points below the actual change (Table 3.1). Due to the ex post compensation mechanism, the business sector per capita contractual wage recouped about 8 points of this difference. The two-year length of wage settlements under national contracts worked in favour of wage moderation up to 1995, and again in 2000–01 as the nominal wage inertia prevented the temporary upward pressure from oil prices from being embodied in wages and, then, in firms' costs. On the other hand, its potentially destabilising effects showed up when workers tried to recoup past losses in real wages as in 1997.[16]

Table 3.1. Inflation and wage cumulative growth in the business sector in the 1990s (index: value in 1992 = 100)

	1994	1996	1998	2000	2002	2004
Actual inflation (1)	109	119	123	128	135	142
Target inflation (2)	107	114	119	122	126	130
Per capita contractual wage (3)	106	114	122	126	131	138
Per capita gross earnings (4)	109	119	126	134	141	149
Real per capita contractual wage (5)	98	96	99	98	97	97
Real per capita gross earnings (6)	100	100	102	104	105	105
Percentage ratio of contractual wage to total earnings	87	86	86	84	83	83
Memorandum items:						
Real per capita cost of labour (7)	104	105	107	110	110	111
Labour productivity (8)	108	112	115	120	119	119

Source: Authors' elaboration on data from Istat and Ministero dell'Economia e delle Finanze (2003 and previous years).

Notes: (1) Cost-of-living index, yearly average. (2) Cumulative rise of price level implicit in government's target inflation rate a year ahead. (3) Index of contractual earnings, yearly average. It implies that all the other wage components but the national contractual minima are kept constant. (4) Employees' gross wages and salaries per full-time equivalent salaried worker. (5) Per capita contractual wage divided by the cost-of-living index. (6) Per capita gross earnings divided by the cost-of-living index. (7) Compensation of employees per full-time equivalent salaried worker divided by the deflator of value added at factor cost (net of rental of buildings). (8) Value added at factor cost (net of rental of buildings) per full-time equivalent worker.

[16] Temporary deviations of contractual earnings from target inflation occurred. In 1992–94 the suspension of the former wage bargaining structure sharply reduced the rate of growth of per capita wages from above 9 per cent to below 2 per cent. In 1995–96 the first national bargaining round since the incomes policy agreements saw an acceleration of contractual earnings above the target inflation, which was however coherent with the new rules, as only the cumulative target inflation for 1995–96 and a partial ex post compensation for the real losses in 1992–94 were included. A considerable potential for conflict materialised in 1997 owing to the high unexpected inflation of the previous two years. The diffusion of firm-level contracts with flexible wage premia in 1995–96, and a target inflation set at a level higher than actual inflation helped to ease these tensions.

Econometric analysis confirms the visual impression from Fig. 3.6 that the government's inflation target has been effective in reducing inflation expectations and in fostering co-ordination of the different sectors' contractual wages. Fabiani et al. (1997) observed that the forecasts of the quarterly econometric model of the Bank of Italy, based on a standard Phillips curve estimated for the period 1970–1991, overestimated wage dynamics between 1992 and 1995; they provided evidence for a change in the wage determination regime, and showed that the elasticity of wages to previous-quarter inflation had drastically decreased. More recently, Destefanis et al. (2005) found that the behaviour of wage setters has become more forward-looking after the incomes policy agreements, and that expectations are influenced by target inflation, if weakly. Notice that Guiso and Magnani (1985) had similarly detected that the predetermination of indexation-related pay rises had reduced inflation expectations in 1984.

Until the end of the 1980s, a very small fraction of workers, concentrated in large industrial firms, were covered by firm-level contracts which usually paid premia set in fixed amounts. With the purpose of linking more closely wages to firm performance, the 1993 agreement envisaged a larger diffusion of company-level contracts characterised by flexible performance-related wage premia. The progress has however been limited. The coverage of firm-level contracts has increased moderately in the 1990s. In 1995–96, in firms with 10 employees or more they covered about 40 per cent of employees, or 3.2 millions, around a half of them being concentrated in industry (Rossi and Sestito, 2000). According to the Bank of Italy's Survey on Investment in Manufacturing (SIM), the coverage in manufacturing firms with 50 employees was higher, about 66 per cent of the work force in the period 1996–99; this proportion has steadily declined thereafter, to 46 per cent in 2004 (Table 3.2). Coverage is positively correlated with the firm size and markedly lower in the South. All in all, additional wage bonuses cover only a fraction of the work force, and even in manufacturing firms with more than 50 employees, where their adoption has been larger, they are not paid continuously.

Table 3.2. Share of employees receiving firm-level bonuses in manufacturing firms with 50 employees or more (per cent)

	1995	1996	1997	1998	1999	2000	2001	2002	2003	2004
Firm size										
50–199 employees	26.0	28.4	37.3	37.8	37.6	51.3	41.6	38.5	38.8	32.7
200–499 employees	31.6	47.4	49.1	51.6	49.1	51.2	48.3	46.1	53.5	48.1
500 employees or more	26.8	68.1	71.4	62.2	70.9	65.9	70.9	61.0	64.0	61.1
Firm location										
North-West	20.3	71.2	72.3	64.3	75.0	64.9	57.8	57.7	59.1	53.1
North-East	47.3	46.4	66.4	64.6	50.2	57.7	50.8	48.1	50.9	45.3
Centre	67.6	55.4	63.0	37.3	53.7	36.1	64.6	34.0	46.4	40.7
South	14.7	60.2	40.1	45.3	39.1	31.8	32.7	34.4	26.9	20.6
Total	27.0	66.2	69.3	60.9	68.1	57.3	54.2	46.0	51.6	46.1

Source: Authors' elaboration on data from Bank of Italy, Survey on Investment in Manufacturing.

The increase in total wages due to firm-level bonuses – both unilaterally paid or contracted upon – averaged one percentage point from 1995 to 2004 (Table 3.3). It is a relatively small number, which implies that the distribution of productivity gains to workers is partial.[17] The impact on regional wage differentials has also been small (Casadio, 1999).

In brief, the new bargaining system appears to have been successful in moderating wage claims and curbing inflation expectations. These results have been obtained by setting at the national level wage increases consistent, on average, with inflation targets. They have been reinforced by the partial coverage of pay rises agreed at the company level.

Table 3.3. Average contribution of firm-level bonuses to firm's wage growth in manufacturing firms with 50 employees or more (percentage points)

	1995	1996	1997	1998	1999	2000	2001	2002	2003	2004
Firm size										
50–199 employees	0.4	0.6	0.6	0.7	0.5	0.8	0.7	1.0	1.1	
200–499 employees	0.6	0.8	0.7	0.9	0.7	0.9	0.9	1.3	1.4	
500 employees or more	0.3	1.5	0.7	1.2	0.8	0.8	0.8	1.9	2.0	
Firm location										
North-West	0.2	1.6	0.7	1.2	0.7	0.8	0.7	1.8	1.8	
North-East	0.7	1.0	1.0	0.9	0.6	1.0	0.9	1.3	1.4	
Centre	0.7	1.0	0.7	0.9	1.2	0.7	0.8	0.9	1.6	
South	0.1	0.5	0.7	0.8	0.7	0.6	0.6	0.9	0.7	
Total	0.3	1.4	0.7	1.1	0.8	0.8	0.8	1.3	1.3	1.1

Source: Authors' elaboration on data from Bank of Italy, Survey on Investment in Manufacturing.

[17] Performance-related premia have been widely adopted, but their cumulative amount has remained low. According to Istat (2000), in 1995–96 about a quarter of employees in industry and a fifth in market services received performance-related pays. According to the SIM, at the end of 1999, 75 per cent of workers in firms with 50 employees or more were covered by contracts with variable wage bonus (note that these bonuses were not necessarily paid in the year) and was below 14 per cent in firms with 20 to 49 employees at the end of 2001. A firm-level contract with performance-related pay could signal collaborative labour relations which favour the adoption of a more flexible organisation of work (e.g. Cainelli et al., 2002). Using SIM data, Casadio and D'Aurizio (2001) show that these firm-level contracts are indeed associated with a more intensive utilisation of temporary contracts and with standard working time variability with respect to fluctuations in production.

3.4.2 Social security contributions and incentives

The containment of the labour cost also benefited from some reduction in social security contributions. According to national accounts, in the business sector the ratio of employers' social security contributions to gross earnings fell from 44.0 per cent in 1993 to 37.4 in 2001. This is a large reduction. In part, it reflects the rise of irregular employment, which by definition evades social contributions, from 16.3 to 18 per cent of total salaried employment (Istat, 2005a). But in large part it is the result of the cut of social security rates by almost two percentage points between 1998 and 2000 and of the replacement in 1998 of some employers contributions with IRAP, the new regional tax levied on value added. The actual reduction of the fiscal burden would be lower if labour were attributed back its share of IRAP.

Also public resources allocated to hiring incentives increased, gradually offsetting after 1994 the phasing-out of contribution relief for firms in the South imposed by the European rules on competition (Fig. 3.7). An important example of employment subsidy is the tax credit introduced by the Budget Law for 2001 (Cipollone and Guelfi, 2003, 2006a). It was a general and automatic incentive to all firms hiring workers on a permanent basis, under certain eligibility conditions for both workers and firms. The tax credit could be claimed against any kind of taxes (e.g. income tax, social security contributions, value-added tax), could be passed on to different fiscal years, and could be cumulated with other existing subsidies.

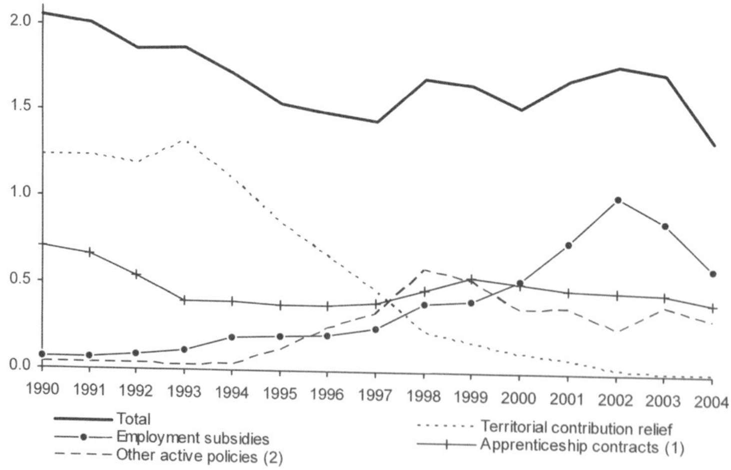

Fig. 3.7. Expenditure for active labour market policies (percentage ratios to total employees' compensation)

Source: Authors' elaboration on data from Istat, National Accounts, and Ministero del Lavoro e delle Politiche Sociali (2003, 2005); there is a break in 2000 due to methodological revisions.

Notes: (1) Includes work-and-training contracts. (2) Includes labour market training, direct job creation, incentives for self-employment, and other measures.

The contribution provided by this subsidy was generous. On average, in the non-farm business sector the reduction amounted to about 30 per cent in the South and 16 per cent in the central and northern regions.[18]

3.4.3 Changing composition of the work force

As mentioned, job losses were very high in the recession of the early 1990s. Both dismissals and quits for early retirement rose considerably relative to average employment. This caused major changes in the composition of the work force, when employment started to recover. In general, these changes helped to moderate wage growth.

The tenure of employees in the business sector declined from 1993 to 2001, although the trend reversed in the following two years. According to data from the Istat's Labour Force Survey (LFS), between 1993 and 2001 the share of persons who had been employed in their job for less than a year rose from 25 to 33 per cent in the age class 15–24, from 10 to 15 in the age class 25–34, and from 6 to 9 in the age class 35–44 (Fig. 3.8). The substitution of older/more experienced workers with younger/less experienced workers contributed to curb wage dynamics. A rough measure of the relative wage of new entrants can be obtained by comparing the after-tax earnings of the young workers (aged 15–30) with those of the adult workers (aged 31–50) and of the entire work force. On the basis of data from the Bank of Italy's Survey of Household Income and Wealth (SHIW; see Brandolini et al., 2002, for a description), between 1989 and 2000, the mean earnings of young workers declined by about ten percentage points with respect to both the the decline in the wage differential by age is due to the drop of entry wage levels in the first half of the 1990s; these lower entry levels do not seem to be compensated by faster wage growth later, a result which is fairly homogeneous across cohorts (Rosolia and Torrini, 2005).

[18] Every firm hiring workers with a permanent contract was given a tax credit of about 413 euros (620 euros for workers in the South) per month and per worker from the moment of hiring until the end of December 2003. The tax credit applied to all new hires taking place from October 2000, provided that there was a rise of the overall level of permanent employment. Workers were eligible if older than 24 years and not working with an open-end contract in the 24 months before hiring. In 2000 the tax credit implied a reduction in per capita labour cost ranging from 9.3 per cent in the banking sector in the Centre-North to almost 60 per cent in the agricultural sector in the South. These estimates understate the effect because the underlying figures for the labour cost refer to an average worker instead of a newly hired worker, whose wage is usually below the average. An opposite effect derives from the fact that national accounts also include estimates of the labour cost in the underground economy, which is very likely smaller than the legal labour cost for a new entrant. However, the latter effect should only attenuate underestimation. Cipollone et al. (2004) calculated that the introduction of the tax credit may have raised labour force participation by between one and two percentage points in 2001 and 2002, mainly among males aged 35–54 with low schooling level. They suggested that the subsidy might have encouraged the choice to leave underground economy.

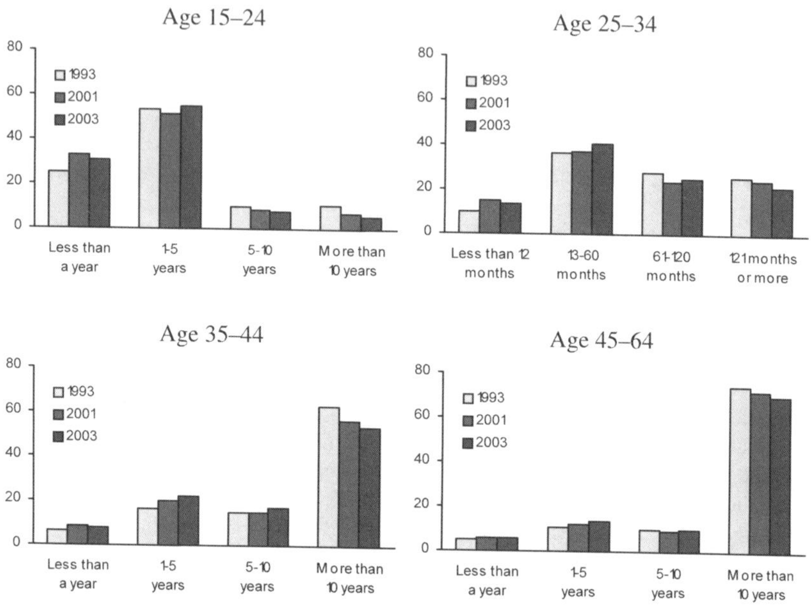

Fig. 3.8. Tenure of employees in the non-farm business sector (per cent)

Source: Authors' elaboration on data from Istat, Labour Force Survey.

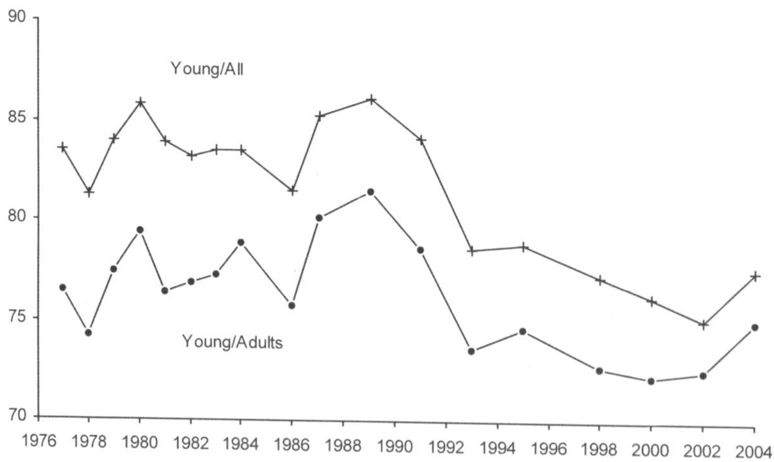

Fig. 3.9. Earnings differentials for young workers (per cent)

Source: Authors' elaboration on data from Bank of Italy, Survey of Household Income and Wealth, historical archive (Version 4.0, January 2006).

The actual drop of relative earnings of younger workers is likely underestimated, as only employees were considered. The 1990s saw the spreading, particularly among younger workers, of jobs as independent contractor known as *rapporti di collaborazione coordinata e continuativa* (e.g. Berton et al., 2005). Most of these workers are labelled 'quasi-employees' as they are virtually indistinguishable from standard salaried workers, except for being remunerated less and paid lower social security contributions, and for not benefiting from employment protection legislation.[19] Their inclusion in our calculation would further depress the relative wage of new entrants.

Quasi-employees are part of the much wider pool of self-employed workers, whose work arrangements typically guarantee high levels of flexibility. Relative to other industrial countries, Italy shows a disproportionate share of self-employment in the labour force, about 33 per cent of all persons employed in the business sector in the 1990s according to national accounts data (31 per cent excluding agriculture). This large share is not due to sectoral composition and seems rather to depend on some institutional characteristics of the country (Torrini, 2005a). The incidence of self-employment has slightly dropped in the last 15 years, but it has shown no sizeable sign of convergence towards other OECD economies. A decline in the number of traditional self-employed has been more than offset by a rise in the number of free-lance workers and independent contractors, who provide the system with additional flexibility both in terms of costs and working arrangements. According to LFS data, from 1993 to 2003 persons working on their own account, like shopkeepers and craftsmen, in the non-farm business sector fell by 262,000; professionals, including independent contractors and other non-standard workers, increased by 432,000.

The greater reliance on fixed-term contracts also contributed to restrain the growth of the labour cost. Our estimates based on SHIW data show that in 2000 the hourly post-tax earnings of temporary workers fell short of those of other workers, after controlling for individual characteristics, by 6 per cent for those employed for a period comprised between 4 and 11 months, and by 19 per cent for those working year-round.

3.4.4 Working hours

According to our estimates, based on methods described by Casadio and D'Aurizio (2000), in the manufacturing sector per capita worked hours increased by 11 per cent from 1985 to 1995, while contractual working time slightly de-

---

[19] Altieri and Oteri (2000, pp. 93–4) documented that nearly half of quasi-employees receives, usually monthly, a fixed compensation, while around a fifth is paid per hour, a sixth on a percentage basis, and a tenth by piece-rates. According to Istat (2005b), in 2004 independent contractors whose main occupation was on a *collaborazione-coordinata-e-continuativa* basis accounted for 1.7 per cent of total employment; more than half had working arrangements similar to those of an employee (single client, fixed time schedule, work in the client's premises).

clined. In the following years worked hours stayed close to this level, high by historical standards, in spite of an increase in part-time work (Fig. 3.10).

Also the organisation of working time has changed. First, there has been a marked rise of work on multiple shifts. In metalworking industries, the share of production workers working on three shifts or other non-standard arrangements more than doubled from 9 per cent in 1992 to 21 in 1999, remaining around 19–20 per cent in 2002–04 (Federmeccanica, 2006 and previous years). Second, the computation of working time defined in national contracts changed. Traditionally, the contractual hours of work were rigidly set at about 39–40 hours per each week, and compensation over several weeks was excluded. Working 37 and 43 hours in two subsequent weeks caused the firm to pay the overtime premium for 3 hours, even if the average hours worked per week were 40. The national contract signed in the chemical sector in 1998 extended from the week to the year the reference period for computing standard hours of work. This innovative practice was encouraged by Law 196 of 1997 (the so called 'Pacchetto Treu') that recommended an extension of the reference period in order to adjust working time schedules to the cyclical pattern of production. It was also introduced a mechanism – the so called 'bank of the hours' – that allows workers to use accumulated overtime hours as a buffer to fulfil their personal needs (Casadio and D'Aurizio, 2001). These changes show up in a stabilisation of overtime hours.

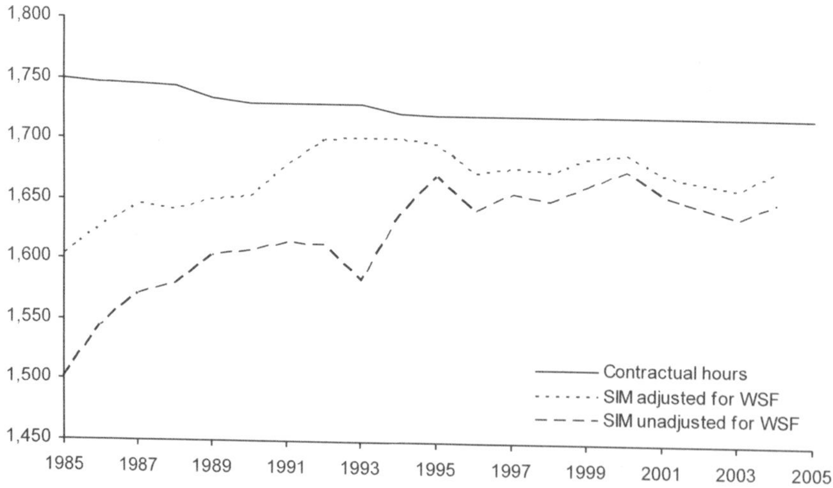

Fig. 3.10. Per capita annual hours worked in manufacturing

Source: Authors' elaboration on data from Istat and from Bank of Italy, Survey on Investment in Manufacturing, as elaborated by Casadio and D'Aurizio (2000).

Note: In the 'SIM adjusted for WSF' series the total number of hours worked is divided by the total number of employees *excluding* those not at work and receiving benefits from the Wage Supplementation Fund (WSF); in the 'SIM unadjusted for WSF' series the denominator is the total number of employees *including* those not at work and receiving benefits from the WSF.

3.4.5 Fixed-term contracts and part-time work

Temporary contracts have been used as a device to bypass the regulation of individual dismissals. The basic legislation of fixed-term contracts was passed in 1962 and remained virtually unchanged until the reform of 2001. Since 1977, however, some regulatory changes introduced exceptions that led to relaxing the limits to the application of fixed-term contracts and to expanding their diffusion. A major change was the introduction of the work-and-training contract (*contratto di formazione e lavoro*), a fixed-term contract with reduced social contributions aimed at young workers.[20] In the 1990s significant changes were made possible by national collective contracts, which already in 1993–94 started to raise the ceilings on the use of fixed-term work (Fig. 3.11). As a consequence, temporary contracts quickly took off. On the basis of the LFS data, their share in the flows of newly hired workers went from 28 per cent in 1993 to 40 per cent in 2003, while their incidence on the stock of employees grew from 6 to 10 per cent (Fig. 3.12).

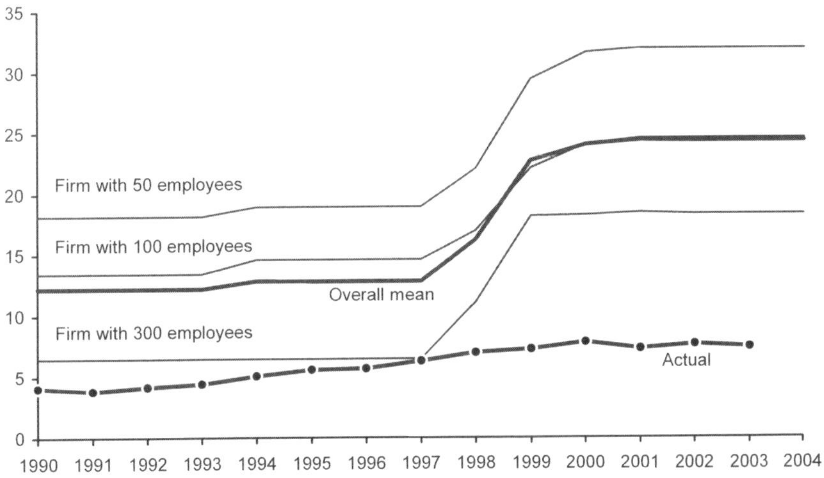

Fig. 3.11. Ceilings on the use of fixed-term work set by national contracts in industry (percentage ratios to salaried employment in previous year)

Source: Authors' elaboration on information drawn from National sectoral contracts and Istat, Labour Force Survey. The ceilings allow for temporary agency work since 1998.

[20] There is mixed evidence on the influence of work-and-training contracts on the hiring probability of young eligible workers. Contini et al. (2002) exploit the variation of the incentives across regions and over time and do not find any significant impact. Tattara and Valentini (2005) instead find a positive impact by using a matching estimator on data for Veneto.

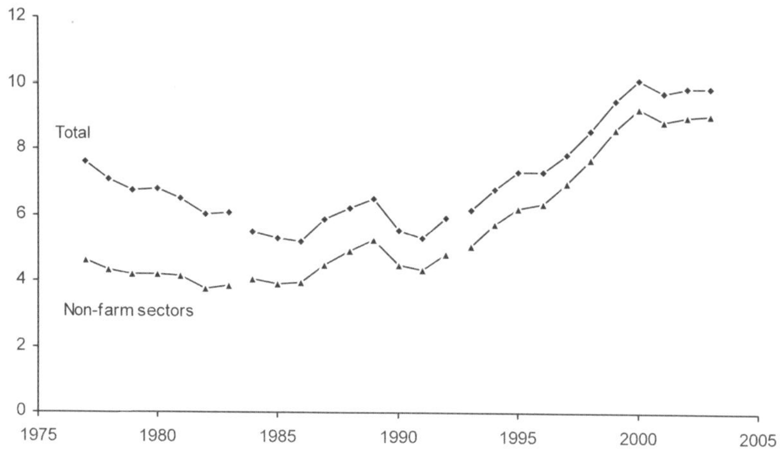

Fig. 3.12. Share of fixed-term workers in salaried employment (per cent)

Source: Authors' elaboration on data from Istat, Labour Force Survey. Interruptions in the lines indicate major statistical breaks. For the period 1977–83, fixed-term workers are identified with persons having a seasonal or occasional job.

How did this kind of increased flexibility change the relative prices? Cipollone and Guelfi (2006b) set up an econometric model to estimate the value that employers attribute to flexibility and applied it to a panel of firms in the metalworking sector in the 1990s. They found that the possibility of employing on a temporary basis one per cent of the newly hired workers amounted to a reduction of about two per cent of the wage of a permanent worker at the average tenure. By extending these estimates for the metalworking sector to the whole economy, the rise by 12 points in the share of fixed-term contracts in new hires over the period 1993–2003 would have been equivalent to a cut of about 24 per cent in the wage bill of newly hired workers. These are very rough estimates, but they suggest that the increased flexibility has originated a far from negligible reduction in the 'overall' cost of the labour input, i.e. including 'adjustment costs'.

The spreading of part-time work reflects the firms' need of greater flexibility in the utilisation of the labour input, but it is also driven by supply considerations, for it allows employees, typically women, a better allocation of their working time. Until 1984 part-time contracts were permitted but not explicitly regulated by the law; their provisions were set out directly by firms and workers, through individual negotiation or, more recently, collective agreements. Regular statistics did not exist, but scattered evidence suggests that their diffusion was marginal (see Istituto italiano per la promozione del lavoro a tempo parziale, 1980). Part-time work was first recognised and regulated in 1984 by Law 863, where it was defined with reference to the standard working time fixed in collective agreements (Addabbo, 1997). The share of part-time workers in total employment remained fairly modest until early 1990s, but it has been steadily increasing ever since (Fig. 3.13), as national contracts have accommodated this tendency by raising the ceilings on the use of part-time work and by relaxing the restrictions on its application.

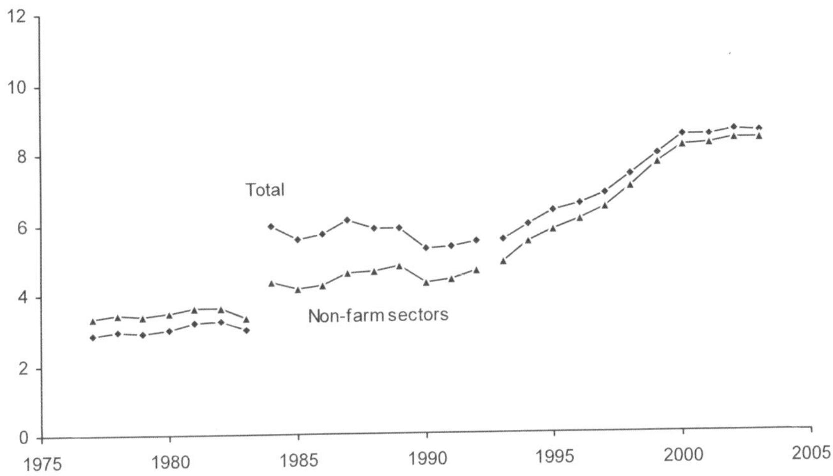

Fig. 3.13. Share of part-time workers in total employment (per cent)

Source: Authors' elaboration on data from Istat, Labour Force Survey. Interruptions in the lines indicate major statistical breaks. For the period 1977–83, part-time workers are identified with persons declaring a standard working time of less than 25 hours per week.

3.4.6 The job matching process

An alternative way to gauge the effect of flexibility is to look at the efficiency of the process of matching unemployed people with vacant jobs. A preliminary indication is provided by Fig. 3.14 that presents the series of the total hires of salaried workers from 1970 onward, expressed as a ratio to the stock of employment at the beginning of the period (for details on the construction of the series see Brandolini and Cipollone, 2001b). In spite of the quarter-to-quarter volatility, these series tell a rather coherent story, which holds for both yearly and quarterly flows (even if the latter are evidently smaller). In the second half of the 1980s, the rise in employment was accompanied by a moderately growing number of hires; after the peak reached around 1991, the flow into employment dropped dramatically in 1993. In 1994 it recovered an upward trend that has continued almost till the end of the decade, when the entry rate stabilised.

The evidence just discussed, albeit coarse, seems to suggest that a possible structural change has occurred in the 1990s. This may stem from two different factors, not necessarily mutually exclusive. First, the input of the 'matching' technology probably increased in the second half of the 1990s. Participation rates of the population aged 15 to 64 years went up from 57 to 60 per cent between 1995 and 2000; moreover, the pool of potential workers grew also among persons classified outside of the labour force (Viviano, 2003; Brandolini et al., 2006). Second, it may be that labour market reforms succeeded in improving the efficiency of the matching mechanism, so that for given inputs (i.e. number of job searchers and vacancies) the number of successful matches increased. To weigh these two factors,

Brandolini and Cipollone (2001b) estimated a Cobb–Douglas specification of the job matching function including a time varying (quadratic) term to allow for possible shifts of the efficiency of the matching process. Vacancies were proxied by a transformation of the share of industrial firms experiencing labour shortage, as measured by ISAE surveys.

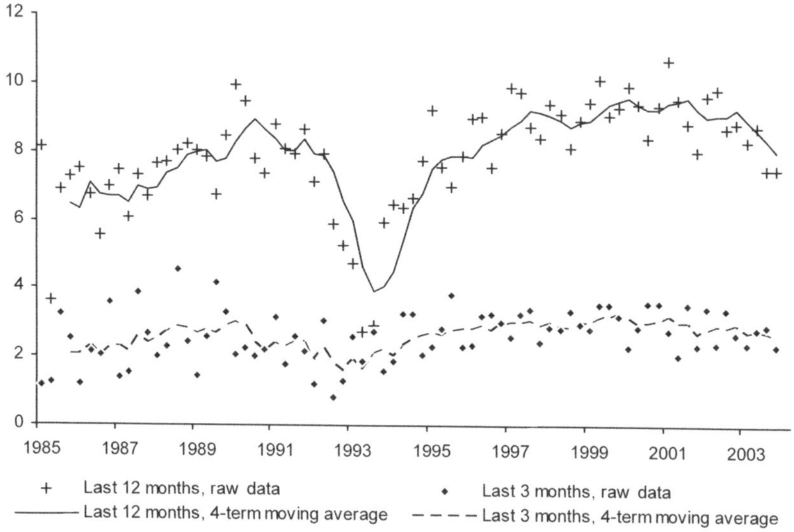

Fig. 3.14. Inflows into salaried employment (percentage ratios to current employment)

Source: Authors' elaboration on data from Istat, Labour Force Survey. The inflows are estimated from recall questions, and are computed as the difference between the variation in salaried employment in a year or a quarter and the exits from salaried employment in the same period.

The estimates of this matching function seem to provide a reasonable description of the flows into employment, with both demand and supply sides being important. The significant quadratic time trend suggests that the efficiency of the matching process deteriorated throughout the 1980s and then improved over the 1990s. Though the magnitude of temporal changes varies across different statistical specifications, all estimates agree in fixing the turning point in the early 1990s. It is worth noticing that the extent to which the efficiency of the matching technology fell over the 1980s – between 2.5 and 5 per cent per year, according to the estimates – is close to that found by Blanchard and Diamond (1989) for the United States over the period 1968–81. The improvement in the 1990s was rapid, in the order of 3 to 5 per cent per year, and it largely compensated the worsening in the previous decade. This pattern conforms with the observed lessening of labour market regulation.

3.5 The burden of flexibility

Non-standard forms of employment have granted firms greater flexibility in the adjustment of the labour input, and have increased employment opportunities. On the other hand, persons employed in temporary jobs, and to a lesser extent part-time jobs, face more uncertain job prospects and may fail to earn an adequate income. As suggested by the figures reported above on the labour outcomes of young workers, there is a legitimate concern that the burden of greater flexibility is largely borne by some groups in the work force.

Evidence of a segmented labour market was found for 1995 by Cipollone (2001). Subsequent estimates for 1998 showed some blurring of the boundaries between the two segments together with a polarisation of the labour force between workers with high probability of being in the primary segment and workers with high probability of being in the secondary one. The analysis focused on a demographic group with a strong attachment to the labour market – adult male breadwinners employed in the non-farm business sector – and found a significant probability of being in the secondary sector for about a third of the group, for the most part poorly educated production workers in small firms in manufacturing, construction and trade. The spreading of non-standard employment might have worsened the situation as more people are trapped in a sequence of temporary occupations, with few chances of upgrading to the good jobs.

On the basis of the LFS data, the probability of finding a permanent job within a year oscillated around 5 per cent for persons in working age from 1994 to 2002 (Table 3.4). The modest improvement towards the end of the period was driven by favourable cyclical conditions in 1999 and 2000, and the working of the tax credit for permanent hires in 2001 and part of 2002. The probability of getting a permanent position was much higher for persons already holding a fixed-term job, around 36 per cent, but the time pattern was the same. Chances were better for persons in the age group 15–29, but this tended to reflect the higher educational levels. The one-year transition probability to a permanent job rises to 8 per cent for a person with at least a high school diploma, but it falls to 4 per cent for somebody who has completed at most lower secondary school. These figures are simple statistical frequencies and are affected by compositional changes. If we control for individual characteristics (age, sex, marital status, educational achievement, occupational sector, region) and we account for the cycle by taking two years where economic growth was comparable, 1995 and 2000, the probability of moving from a temporary to a permanent job within twelve months drops by 5 percentage points, or 13 per cent of the average transition probability in 2000. Moreover, a period of one year may be too short to assess the extent to which people are caught in unstable jobs. Using data from the Longitudinal Survey of Italian Households, Barbieri and Scherer (2005) find that the proportion of persons who at 35 years of age had a work history of precariousness has increased considerably for the cohorts born in 1963–1967 relatively to the older cohorts born in 1958–1962 and 1948–1957.

Table 3.4. Probability of moving to a permanent job within a year (per cent)

Initial status	1994	1995	1996	1997	1998	1999	2000	2001	2002	Mean
	Persons aged 15–64 with at most a lower secondary school degree									
Fixed-term job	31.2	36.3	31.6	29.3	28.8	31.5	34.5	39.6	31.7	32.8
Self-employment	4.6	4.3	3.7	3.9	4.2	4.7	4.5	5.2	5.3	4.5
Non-employment	2.7	2.8	2.9	2.5	2.8	2.5	2.4	2.7	2.2	2.6
All three statuses	3.9	4.1	3.9	3.6	3.9	4.0	4.1	4.6	4.0	4.0
	Persons aged 15–64 with at least an upper secondary school degree									
Fixed-term job	35.5	47.3	39.1	36.1	37.1	37.0	41.4	42.3	39.8	39.8
Self-employment	7.0	6.1	6.0	5.7	5.6	6.1	5.6	6.4	5.7	6.0
Non-employment	5.7	5.4	5.4	4.6	5.2	5.2	5.0	5.6	5.3	5.3
All three statuses	7.7	8.2	7.6	6.8	7.4	7.7	8.2	9.2	8.3	7.9
	All persons aged 15–64									
Fixed-term job	32.9	40.9	34.9	32.4	32.6	34.2	38.0	41.1	35.9	36.2
Self-employment	5.3	4.9	4.5	4.6	4.7	5.3	5.0	5.7	5.5	5.1
Non-employment	3.4	3.4	3.5	3.1	3.4	3.3	3.2	3.6	3.1	3.3
All three statuses	4.8	5.2	4.9	4.6	5.0	5.2	5.5	6.2	5.6	5.2

Source: Authors' elaboration on data from Istat, Labour Force Survey (April wave).

A non-standard job does not necessarily imply low pay. Following the international practice, the low paid may be identified with the employees earning less than two thirds of the median earnings of full-time employees. The SHIW data on take-home earnings show that the proportion of low-paid employees declined from 17 per cent in 1977 to 12 per cent in 1983 and remained fairly stable until 1991; the upward trend of the 1990s brought the share back to 17–18 per cent from 1998 to 2004 (Fig. 3.15; the large year-to-year variations reflect in part the small sample size). The spread of part-time work explains most of the rise of low pay during the 1990s, as its incidence among full-time employees has varied between 11 and 12 per cent. As in other advanced economies, young people, women and generally persons who are not household heads, the less educated and manual workers, employees in agriculture and trade and lodging are disproportionately represented among the low-paid jobs. Most importantly, the trend from 1991 to 2004 has differed across these groups: for instance, the share of low-paid full-time employees rose by 4 percentage points among the young (aged 30 or less) and by 2 points among adult persons (aged 31–50), but remained virtually unchanged among older workers. Lastly, the probability of staying in a low-pay status after two years was high in the 1990s (50 per cent for men and 57 for women), and about half of it depended on personal characteristics (Cappellari, 2002, 2006).[21]

[21] Persistence in the low-pay status was high in the 1980s as well, according to estimates by Contini et al. (1998) and Lucifora (1998).

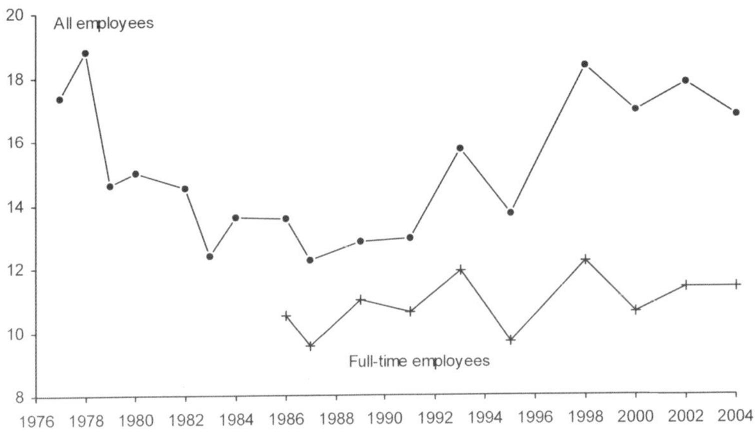

Fig. 3.15. Share of low-paid workers, 1977–2004 (per cent)

Source: Authors' elaboration on data from Bank of Italy, Survey of Household Income and Wealth, historical archive (Version 4.0, January 2006).

Unless the low-paid is the household's head, the probability of being in poverty is less closely correlated with low pay than with the amount of employment in the household (Brandolini et al., 2002). This result is borne out by the analysis of the relationship between condition in the labour market and household income. Using the SHIW data, households can be classified according to the number of household members who are in employment, and the share of hours worked in traditional and non-standard jobs (i.e. fixed-term contracts, temporary agency work, *collaborazioni coordinate e continuative*, and part-time jobs). In 2004 households comprising only traditional workers accounted for about half of the total; 7 per cent of the households included only non-standard workers, and 10 per cent had both types of workers; the remaining third of the households had no member in employment (Table 3.5). In 2000–04, the probability of being low-income was far higher for the households entirely dependent on non-standard, especially fixed-term, work than for the households with some traditional employment. Between 2000 and 2004, the incidence of income insufficiency rose among traditional single-earner's households, and declined among households of pensioners without employed members.

On the one hand, these findings highlight the role of employment in reducing poverty risk: not only this risk is significantly lower among households with two or more employed members, but also the great majority of the households fully dependent on non-standard work are above the poverty line. On the other hand, they expose the inadequacy of the Italian social safety net: the high probability of being low-income for the households of non-standard workers reflect both the lack of wage subsidies for the low-paid, and the poor coverage of the unemployment benefits; the fact that the bulk of households with no income from labour or pension is in poverty reveals the absence of a basic income scheme. According to

Table 3.5. Household low-income condition and labour status (per cent)

Composition of household employment (1)	Share in total population			Share in low-income households			Low-income ratio		
	2000	2002	2004	2000	2002	2004	2000	2002	2004
Only traditional jobs	47.4	49.4	48.9	28.5	32.7	36.9	7.5	8.1	9.0
1 employed	28.3	29.7	30.9	25.5	30.5	33.6	11.2	12.5	13.1
2 or more employed	19.1	19.7	18.1	3.0	2.2	3.3	2.0	1.4	2.2
Traditional and non-standard jobs	10.4	10.3	10.0	2.1	3.8	4.2	2.5	4.5	5.1
Less than a 1/3 in non-standard jobs	6.3	5.6	5.7	1.2	2.7	1.8	2.4	5.9	3.9
1 employed (2)	-	-	-	-	-	-	-	-	-
2 or more employed	5.8	5.3	5.3	1.2	2.6	1.4	2.5	6.1	3.1
More than a 1/3 in non-standard jobs	4.1	4.7	4.3	0.9	1.0	2.4	2.7	2.7	6.7
1 employed (2)	-	-	-	-	-	-	-	-	-
2 or more employed	4.0	4.5	4.3	0.8	1.0	2.4	2.5	2.8	6.8
Only non-standard jobs	7.5	6.5	6.7	19.1	15.7	16.7	31.7	29.6	30.0
Only fixed-term jobs	4.3	3.4	3.0	15.2	11.6	10.2	43.7	42.3	40.4
1 employed	3.7	2.8	2.6	13.9	9.4	8.9	46.3	41.5	42.0
2 or more employed (2)	-	-	-	-	-	-	-	-	-
Other non-standard jobs	3.2	3.1	3.7	3.9	4.0	6.5	15.4	15.8	21.4
1 employed	2.5	2.5	3.1	3.0	3.9	6.0	15.0	18.9	23.6
2 or more employed (2)	-	-	-	-	-	-	-	-	-
None in employment	34.7	33.9	34.3	50.2	47.9	42.2	18.0	17.3	14.8
None receiving pension income	1.7	1.7	1.1	12.3	12.3	7.0	88.4	86.0	76.8
Receiving pension income	33.0	32.1	33.2	37.9	35.6	35.2	14.3	13.5	12.7
Total	100.0	100.0	100.0	100.0	100.0	100.0	12.4	12.2	12.0

Source: authors' elaboration on data from Bank of Italy, Survey of Household Income and Wealth, historical archive (Version 4.0, January 2006).

Notes: (1) Non-standard work includes fixed-term contracts, temporary agency work, *collaborazioni coordinate e continuative*, and part-time jobs (i.e. less than 18 worked hours per week). Remaining jobs are classified as traditional. Job positions are aggregated, for persons and households, on the basis of hours of work. (2) Figures are not reported because observations are fewer than 100.

the latest statistics on social protection (Eurostat, 2006), in 2003 social benefits for family, unemployment, housing and social exclusion amounted in Italy to only 1.5 per cent of GDP, the lowest value across European countries and less than a third of the EU average. On the basis of data drawn from the European Community Household Panel, taking the average over the period 1994–2001, only 17 per cent of the Italian job-searchers who had lost their job in the previous twelve months reported to receive unemployment benefits, compared with twice as many in Greece and Portugal, and over 80 per cent in Austria, Belgium, Denmark, Finland and Germany (Boeri and Brandolini, 2004, p. 479).

These results lead us to three observations. First, the figures on transition probabilities and low pay may not suggest a general deterioration, but point at a worsening of the situation for some population sub-groups: the burden of flexibility has not been shared equally. Second, the long-standing deficiencies of Italian social protection are made even more acute by the need to cushion the effects of an increased job instability and for a much larger stock of 'flexible' workers. Third, the analysis of segmentation must be seen in the context of a disappointing performance of real labour incomes. We have reported above about the modest rise of real wages since the early 1990s, according to national accounts. If we take the SHIW data, the mean after-tax monthly earnings of a full-time employee was in 2004 only 4 per cent above its value in 1991, while the median was virtually unchanged. Job instability is much more difficult to face when real wages, and the economy, are not growing.

3.6 Epilogue: back to Tarantelli

The agreements of the early 1990s set the stage for substantial changes in the Italian labour market during the following decade. The process is still ongoing, as witnessed by the recent approval of Law 30 of 2003 (so called 'Legge Biagi'). These developments owe much to the intellectual contribution of Ezio Tarantelli, which centred around the attempt of building a system of regulated industrial relations in a country where the distributive conflict had been historically acute, and sometimes disruptive. The implementation of his proposals in the early 1980s was limited to the predetermination of the indexed component of nominal wage increases and had some success in curbing inflation. But the underlying idea of a 'political exchange' – i.e. making wage bargaining compatible with the objective of stable growth through an expansion of public services, so that wage moderation would not need to imply a reduction of households well-being – remained largely unaccomplished.

In the aftermath of the 1992 crisis the gist of Tarantelli's intuition re-emerged in a new political context within a 'codetermination' framework, where industry-wide national wages were linked to target inflation and room was made for additional pay rises at the company level conditional on firm's performance. As in the 1980s, the existence of powerful and highly representative unions was a prerequisite of the success of the attempt. The agreements were successful in producing a remarkable moderation of the price of labour in two ways: first, by leading to national wage increases consistent, on average, with inflation targets; second, by easing the conditions for a significant rise in the degree of flexibility in the use of labour input. This last channel was of paramount importance in reducing labour 'adjustment costs' which, by their nature, are not embodied in monetary wages: changes in the organisation of production and working hours, the rapid expansion of non-standard contracts, the resulting new composition of the work force, and the improvement of the job matching process played a major role in the process. The overall effect was a decrease in the relative price of labour, despite the reduction of the user cost of capital driven by the fall in interest rates. After an initial drop, employment grew more than in the previous cycle, even in the face of weaker economic growth, sustained by labour demand in the business sector.

From trough to peak, employment went up by 708,000 full-time equivalent units. But outcomes differed across industries.

In the manufacturing sector, the reduction in the adjustment costs of the labour input was substantial, as shown by the implicit value of fixed-term contracts estimated for the metalworking industries. Nominal wages kept a moderate pace, but the subdued increase of output prices, checked by the rising competitive pressure on the world markets, combined with the weak development of productivity to raise unit labour costs; the capital share in value added declined to historically low levels (Fig. 3.16). In spite of the improvements in the usage and cost of labour, the intensified international competition made structural problems of Italian industry much more severe, with negative effects on the growth of output and exports, and eventually employment.

There is no simple single story for the rest of the business sector, not least for its composite nature. In some sectors (e.g. energy, transport, telecommunications), the restructuring originated at the beginning of the 1990s by the privatisation process, and the reduced cost of labour could have prompted a virtuous circle of efficiency gains, price reduction, and production expansion. Efficiency gains were indeed achieved, as total factor productivity grew more than in any other industry (Bassanetti et al., 2005). But in many cases the former State-owned companies retained, after privatisation, substantial market power. Because of the lack of an appropriate regulatory frame oriented to competitiveness, rents were mainly transferred from the employees to shareholders, both public and private, rather than to consumers and downstream producers through price reductions (Torrini, 2005b). The progress towards higher competition was also slow in other sectors, such as retail trade and professional services: this hindered employment and productivity gains (Viviano, 2006; Schivardi and Viviano, 2006) in sectors where efficiency

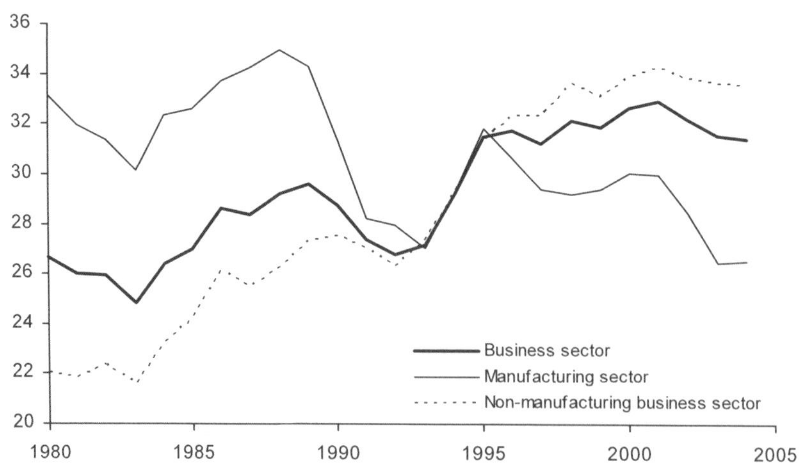

Fig. 3.16. Capital share (per cent)

Source: Authors' elaboration on data from Istat, National Accounts.

improvements already lagged behind (Barca and Visco, 1993). As a consequence, consumption prices, the terms of reference for nominal pay rises, kept rising more rapidly than producer prices in industries exposed to international competition, contributing to erode their competitiveness.

In conclusion, the incomes policies of the 1990s have achieved important results for the macroeconomic stability and the functioning of the labour market, but as in the 1980s their success has been partial. As just seen, they have failed to govern the distribution of the costs and benefits of the adjustment across sectors and social partners. But they have also failed to protect the individuals who mainly bear the burden of the adjustment: the less educated and manual workers, young people and women, who are more likely to be trapped in temporary occupations and are over-represented in low-paid jobs. Despite ambitious attempts, like the plan drafted by the Onofri Commission (1997), Italian welfare institutions are still waiting for a long-needed comprehensive reform. It is an outdated and inadequate social protection system to cope with the greater individual insecurity associated with a more flexible labour market. Today's proposals to reform the Italian welfare state may be different from those of the past but, twenty years after, one of the basic constituents of the 'political exchange' conceived by Tarantelli has yet to be realised.

References

Addabbo, T. (1997), 'Part-time work in Italy', in H.-P. Blossfeld and C. Hakim (eds), *Between Equalization and Marginalization. Women Working Part-Time in Europe and the United States of America*, Oxford: Oxford University Press, pp. 113–32.

Altieri, G. and C. Oteri (2000), 'Atipici, ma quanto?', in G. Altieri and M. Carrieri (eds), *Il popolo del 10%. Il boom del lavoro atipico*, Rome: Donzelli, pp. 62–115.

Altissimo, F., G.P. Oneto and D.J. Marchetti (2000), 'The Italian business cycle: coincident and leading indicators and some stylized facts', *Giornale degli economisti e Annali di economia*, **60**(n.s.):147–220.

Barbieri, P. and S. Scherer (2005), 'Le conseguenze sociali della flessibilizzazione del mercato del lavoro in Italia', *Stato e mercato*, **74**:291-321.

Barca, F. and M. Magnani (1989), *L'industria tra capitale e lavoro: piccole e grandi imprese dall'autunno caldo alla ristrutturazione*, Bologna: Il Mulino.

Barca, F. and I. Visco (1993), 'L'economia italiana nella prospettiva europea: terziario protetto e dinamica dei redditi nominali', in S. Micossi and I. Visco (eds), *Inflazione, concorrenza e sviluppo: l'economia italiana e la sfida dell'integrazione europea. Saggi in ricordo di Stefano Vona*, Bologna: Il Mulino, pp. 21–91.

Bassanetti, A., M. Iommi, C. Jona-Lasinio and F. Zollino (2005), 'La crescita dell'economia italiana negli anni novanta tra ritardo tecnologico e rallentamento della produttività', *Temi di Discussione 539*, Banca d'Italia.

Bassanetti, A., J. Döpke, R. Torrini and R. Zizza (2006), 'Capital, labour and productivity: what role do they play in the potential GDP weakness of France, Germany and Italy?', in O. de Bandt, H. Herrmann and G. Parigi (eds), *Convergence or Divergence in Europe? Growth and Business Cycles in France, Germany and Italy*, Berlin: Springer, pp. 119–56.

Battistin, E., E. Rettore and U. Trivellato (2005), 'Choosing among alternative classification criteria to measure the labour force state', *Institute for Fiscal Studies Working Paper 05/18*, October.

Bertola, G. and A. Ichino (1995), 'Crossing the river: a comparative perspective on Italian employment dynamics', *Economic Policy*, **21**:359–415.

Berton, F., L. Pacelli and G. Segre (2005), 'Il lavoro parasubordinato in Italia: tra autonomia del lavoratore e precarietà del lavoro', *Rivista italiana degli economisti*, **10**:57–99.

Blanchard, O.J. and P. Diamond (1989), 'The Beveridge curve', *Brookings Papers on Economic Activity*, **1**:1–76.

Bodo, G. and I. Visco (1987), 'La disoccupazione in Italia: un'analisi con il modello econometrico della Banca d'Italia', in Banca d'Italia, *Contributi all'analisi economica del Servizio Studi*, **3**:7–74, Rome: Banca d'Italia.

Boeri, T. and A. Brandolini (2004), 'The age of discontent: Italian households at the beginning of the decade', *Giornale degli economisti e annali di economia*, **63**(n.s.):155–93.

Boeri, T. and J. Jimeno (2005), 'The effects of employment protection: learning from variable enforcement', *European Economic Review*, **49**:2057–77.

Brandolini, A. and P. Cipollone (2001a), 'Multifactor productivity and labour quality in Italy, 1981–2000', *Temi di discussione 422*, Banca d'Italia. In Italian: in S. Rossi (ed.), *La Nuova Economia. I fatti dietro il mito*, Bologna: Il Mulino, 2003, pp. 71–91.

Brandolini, A. and P. Cipollone (2001b), 'Evidence on mismatch in Italy, 1970-2000'. Banca d'Italia, background paper for the European Central Bank's Third Structural Issues Report on 'Labour Market Mismatches in the Euro Area Countries', August.

Brandolini, A., P. Cipollone and P. Sestito (2002), 'Earnings dispersion, low pay and household poverty in Italy, 1977–1998', in D. Cohen, T. Piketty and G. Saint-Paul (eds), *The Economics of Rising Inequalities*, Oxford: Oxford University Press, pp. 225–64.

Brandolini, A., P. Cipollone and E. Viviano (2006), 'Does the ILO definition capture all unemployment?', *Journal of the European Economic Association*, **4**:153–79.

Cainelli, G., R. Fabbri and P. Pini (2002), 'Performance-related pay or pay for participation? The case of Emilia-Romagna', *Human Systems Management*, **21**:43–62.

Calmfors, L. and J. Driffill (1988), 'Bargaining structure, corporatism and macroeconomic performance', *Economic Policy*, **6**:13–62.

Cappellari, L. (2002), 'Do the 'working poor' stay poor? An analysis of low pay transitions in Italy', *Oxford Bulletin of Economics and Statistics*, **64**:87–110.

Cappellari, L. (2006), 'Earnings mobility among Italian low-paid workers', *Journal of Population Economics*, in press.

Casadio, P. (1999), 'Diffusione dei premi di risultato e differenziali retributivi territoriali nell'industria', *Lavoro e relazioni industriali*, **1**:57–81.

Casadio P. (2003), 'Wage formation in the Italian private sector after the 1992–93 income policy agreements', in G. Fagan, F.P. Mongelli and J. Morgan (eds), *Institutions and Wage Formation in the New Europe*, Cheltenham, UK: Edward Elgar, p. 112–33.

Casadio, P. and L. D'Aurizio (2000), 'Orari di lavoro pro capite, flessibilità e efficienza produttiva dell'industria manifatturiera italiana tra il 1985 e il 1998', *Rivista italiana degli economisti*, **5**:413–47.

Casadio, P. and L. D'Aurizio (2001), 'Flessibilità oraria, occupazionale e retributiva nell'industria italiana: complementi o sostituti?', *Economia e lavoro*, **35**:71–91.

Casadio, P., M. Lamelas and G. Rodano (2005), 'Cambiamento istituzionale, salari e flessibilità: l'esperienza della concertazione in Italia', *Rivista internazionale di scienze sociali*, **113**:185–214.

Cipollone, P. (2001), 'Is the Italian labour market segmented?', *Temi di discussione 400*, Banca d'Italia.

Cipollone, P. and A. Guelfi (2003), 'Tax credit policy and firms' behaviour. The case of subsidies to open-end labour contracts in Italy', *Temi di discussione 471*, Banca d'Italia.

Cipollone, P. and A. Guelfi (2006a), 'Financial support to permanent jobs. The Italian case', *Politica economica*, **32**:51–64.

Cipollone, P. and A. Guelfi (2006b), 'The value of flexible contracts: evidence from an Italian panels of industrial firms', *Temi di discussione 583*, Banca d'Italia.

Cipollone, P., C. Di Maria and A. Guelfi (2004), 'Hiring incentives and labour force participation in Italy', *Giornale degli economisti e Annali di economia*, **63**(n.s.):161–203.

Contini, B and U. Trivellato (2005), 'Dinamiche e persistenze nel mercato del lavoro italiano: una sintesi', in B. Contini and U. Trivellato (eds), *Eppur si muove. Dinamiche e persistenze nel mercato del lavoro italiano*, Bologna: Il Mulino, pp. 13–84.

Contini, B., M. Filippi and C. Villosio (1998), 'Earnings mobility in the Italian economy', in R. Asplund, P.J. Sloane and I. Theodossiou (eds), *Low Pay and Earnings Mobility in Europe*, Cheltenham, UK: Edward Elgar, pp. 15–31.

Contini, B., F. Cornaglia, C. Malpele and E. Rettore (2002), 'Measuring the impact of the Italian CFL programme on the job opportunities for the young', *LABOR Working Papers 11*, LABORatorio R. Revelli, Centre for Employment Studies.

Dell'Aringa, C. (1974), 'Scala mobile e salari reali', *Rivista internazionale di scienze sociali*, **82**:211-231.

Destefanis, S., G. Mastromatteo and G. Verga (2005), 'Wages and monetary policy in Italy before and after the wage agreements', *Rivista internazionale di scienze sociali*, **113**:289–318.

Erickson, C.L. and A. Ichino (1995), 'Wage differentials in Italy: market forces, institutions, and inflation', in R.B. Freeman and L.F. Katz (eds), *Differences and Changes in Wage Structures*, Chicago: University of Chicago Press, pp. 265–305.

Eurostat (2006), *European Social Statistics – Social Protection. Expenditure and Receipts. Data 1995–2003*, Luxembourg: Office for Official Publications of the European Communities.

Fabiani, S., A. Locarno, G. Oneto and P. Sestito (1997), 'NAIRU: incomes policy and inflation', *OECD Working Paper 187*. In Italian: 'Risultati e problemi di un quinquennio di politica dei redditi: una prima valutazione quantitativa', *Temi di discussione 329*, Banca d'Italia, 1998.

Faustini, G. (1976), 'Indicizzazione dei salari e inflazione in Italia', *Moneta e credito*, **29**:282–99. In English: 'Wage Indexing and Inflation in Italy', *Banca Nazionale del Lavoro Quarterly Review*, **29**:364–77.

Federmeccanica (2006), *28° Indagine sulla situazione dell'industria metalmeccanica. Anno 2004*. Available at: http://www.federmeccanica.it/pubb/f02a.html.

Filosa, R. and I. Visco (1977a), 'L'unificazione del valore del punto di contingenza e il grado di indicizzazione delle retribuzioni', *Moneta e credito*, **30**:55–83.

Filosa, R. and I. Visco (1977b), 'Copertura delle retribuzioni e inflazione a tasso variabile', *Moneta e credito*, **30**:327–37.

Filosa, R. and I. Visco (1980), 'Costo del lavoro, indicizzazione e perequazione delle retribuzioni negli anni '70', in G. Nardozzi (ed.), *I difficili anni '70. I problemi della politica economica italiana 1973/1979*, Milan: Etas Libri, pp. 107–39.

Flanagan, R.J. (1999), 'Macroeconomic performance and collective bargaining: an international perspective', *Journal of Economic Literature*, **37**:1150–75.

Garibaldi, P., L. Pacelli and A. Borgarello (2004), 'Employment protection legislation and the size of firms', *Giornale degli economisti e Annali di economia*, **63**(n.s.):33–68.

Ginsborg, P. (1998), *Storia d'Italia 1943–1996. Famiglia, società, Stato*, Turin: Einaudi.

Golinelli, R. (1996), 'La banca dati su dischetto per la contabilità nazionale in Italia in base 1990 (1951–1995)', Prometeia, mimeo.

Gressani, D., L. Guiso and I. Visco (1988), 'Disinflation in Italy: an analysis with the econometric model of the Bank of Italy', *Journal of Policy Modeling*, **10**:163–203.

Guiso, L. and M. Magnani (1985), '1981–1984 – Perché l'inflazione è calata?', Banca d'Italia, background paper for the *Annual Report for the year 1984*.

ISAE (2003), 'La cronologia del ciclo italiano', in *Rapporto trimestrale – Gennaio 2003*, pp. 53–5, Rome: ISAE.

Istat (1997), *Conti economici e finanziari dei settori istituzionali. Anni 1980-96*, floppy disk, Rome: Istat.

Istat (2000), 'La flessibilità del mercato del lavoro nel periodo 1995–96', *Informazioni*, 34, Rome: Istat.

Istat (2005a), 'La misura dell'occupazione non regolare nelle stime di contabilità nazionale. Anni 1980–2004', *Statistiche in breve*, 16 December, Rome: Istat.

Istat (2005b), 'Collaborazioni coordinate e continuative nella rilevazione sulle forze di lavoro. I, II, III e IV trimestre 2004', *Statistiche in breve*, 21 March, Rome: Istat.

Istituto italiano per la promozione del lavoro a tempo parziale (1980), *Il lavoro part-time. Realtà sociale e aspetti giuridico-sindacali*, Milan: Etas libri.

Lucifora, C. (1998), 'Working poor? An analysis of low-wage employment in Italy', in R. Asplund, P.J. Sloane and I. Theodossiou (eds), *Low Pay and Earnings Mobility in Europe*, Cheltenham: Edward Elgar, pp. 185–208.

Magnani, M. (1996), 'Le istituzioni della contrattazione salariale in Germania e in Italia: consenso ed efficienza in una prospettiva storica', in *La Germania Unita. L'economia tedesca di fronte all'unificazione*, Padua: Cedam, pp. 275–320.

Magnani, M. (1997), 'Alla ricerca di regole nelle relazioni industriali: breve storia di due fallimenti', in F. Barca (ed.), *Storia del capitalismo italiano: dal dopoguerra a oggi*, Rome: Donzelli, pp. 501–44.

Manacorda, M. (2004), 'Can the scala mobile explain the fall and rise of earnings inequality in Italy? A semiparametric analysis, 1977–1993', *Journal of Labor Economics*, **22**:585–613.

Ministero dell'Economia e delle Finanze (2003), *Documento di programmazione economico-finanziaria per gli anni 2004–2007*, Rome: Ministero dell'Economia e delle Finanze.

Ministero del Lavoro e delle Politiche Sociali (2003), *Monitoraggio delle politiche occupazionali e del lavoro. 2003. Nota di aggiornamento*, Rome: Ministero del Lavoro e delle Politiche Sociali.

Ministero del Lavoro e delle Politiche Sociali (2005), *Aggiornamento del quadro informativo sulle politiche del lavoro*, Rome: Ministero del Lavoro e delle Politiche Sociali.

Modigliani, F. and T. Padoa Schioppa (1977), 'La politica economica in una economia con salari indicizzati al 100 o più', *Moneta e credito*, **30**:3–53.

Oliner, S.D. and D.E. Sichel (2000), 'The resurgence of growth in the late 1990s: is information technology the story?', *Journal of Economic Perspectives*, **14**:3–22.

Onofri Commission (Commissione per l'analisi delle compatibilità macroeconomiche della spesa sociale) (1997), *Relazione finale*, February.

Potestio, P. (2005), 'L'occupazione in Italia dal 1970 al 2003', *Rivista di politica economica*, **95**(3–4):245–322.

Regalia, I., M. Regini and E. Reyneri (1978), 'Labour conflicts and industrial relations in Italy', in C. Crouch and A. Pizzorno (eds), *The Resurgence of Class Conflict in Western Europe since 1968*, vol. I. National Studies, Basingstoke: Macmillan, pp. 101–58.

Regalia, I. and M. Regini (1996), 'Sindacato e relazioni industriali', in *Storia dell'Italia repubblicana. Volume III. L'Italia nella crisi mondiale. L'ultimo ventennio. I. Economia e società*, pp. 777–836. Turin: Einaudi.

Robotti, L. (1973), 'Incidenza dell'indennità di contingenza nella dinamica salariale in Italia: 1951–1970', *Rassegna di statistiche del lavoro*, **25**(Supplemento I):7–21.

Robotti, L. (1975), 'Scala mobile e inflazione', *Ricerche economiche*, **29**:23–44.

Rossi, S. (2003), *La politica economica italiana 1968–2003*, Rome-Bari: Laterza.

Rossi, F. and P. Sestito (2000), 'Contrattazione aziendale, struttura negoziale e determinazione decentrata del salario', *Rivista di politica economica*, **90**(10–11):129–84.

Rosolia, A. and R. Torrini (2005), 'Il divario generazionale', Banca d'Italia, background paper for the *Annual Report for the year 2004*.

Schivardi, F. and R. Torrini (2005), 'Identifying the effects of firing restrictions through size-contingent differences in regulation', *CEPR Working Paper 5303*.

Schivardi, F. and E. Viviano (2006), 'Entry barriers in Italian retail trade', Banca d'Italia, background paper for the *Annual Report for the year 2005*.

Sestito, P. (2002), *Il mercato del lavoro in Italia. Com'è. Come sta cambiando*, Rome-Bari: Laterza.

Spaventa, L. (1976), 'Salario protetto dal meccanismo di scala mobile a 'punto pieno'', *Moneta e credito*, **29**:387–402.

Spaventa, L. (1977), 'Ancora sul grado di copertura del salario: un'estensione dell'analisi', *Moneta e credito*, **30**:217–27.

Tarantelli, E. (1981a), 'Le politiche di rientro dall'inflazione nei paesi industrializzati e il ruolo economico del sindacato', *Laboratorio politico*, **4**. Reprinted in E. Tarantelli, *L'utopia dei deboli è la paura dei forti*, Milan: Angeli, 1988, pp. 697–720.

Tarantelli, E. (1981b), 'Se l'inflazione non cala paghino le imprese', *La Repubblica*, 8 April. Reprinted in E. Tarantelli, *La forza delle idee*, Rome-Bari: Laterza, 1995, pp. 113–15.

Tarantelli, E. (1982), 'Tra scambio politico e scambio 'masochista': una proposta per il sindacato'. *Prospettive del mercato del lavoro*, July. Reprinted in E. Tarantelli, *La forza delle idee*, Rome-Bari: Laterza, 1995, pp. 39–46.

Tarantelli, E. (1984a), 'Lavorare meno lavorare tutti'. *La Repubblica*, 17–18 June. Reprinted in E. Tarantelli, *La forza delle idee*, Rome-Bari: Laterza, 1995, pp. 167–9.

Tarantelli, E. (1984b), 'Lavorare meno per occupare di più'. *Forum Isel*, October. Reprinted in E. Tarantelli, *La forza delle idee*, Rome-Bari: Laterza, 1995, pp. 61–4.

Tarantelli, E. (1986a), 'The regulation of inflation and unemployment', *Industrial Relations*, **1**. Reprinted, in Italian, in E. Tarantelli, *L'utopia dei deboli è la paura dei forti*, pp. 768–88, Milan: Angeli, 1988.

Tarantelli, E. (1986b), *Economia politica del lavoro*, Turin: Utet.

Tattara, G. and M. Valentini (2005), 'Evaluating the Italian training on the job contract (CFL)', Università Cà Foscari di Venezia, mimeo.

Torrini, R. (2005a), 'Cross-country differences in self-employment rates: the role of institutions', *Labour Economics*, **12**:661–83.

Torrini, R. (2005b), 'Profit share and returns on capital stock in Italy: the role of privatisations behind the rise of the 1990s', *Discussion Paper 671*, London School of Economics, Centre for Economic Performance. In Italian: 'Quota dei profitti e redditività del capitale in Italia: un tentativo di interpretazione', *Politica economica*, **21**:7–41.

Tronti, L. (2006), 'The July protocol and economic growth: the chance missed', in this volume.

Viviano, E. (2003), 'Un'analisi critica delle definizioni di disoccupazione e partecipazione in Italia', *Politica economica*, **19**:161–90.

Viviano, E. (2006), 'Entry regulations and labor market outcomes: evidence from the Italian retail trade sector', *Temi di discussione 594*, Banca d'Italia.

Visco, I. (1979), 'L'indicizzazione delle retribuzioni in Italia: analisi settoriale e stime per il 1978–1979', *Rivista di politica economica*, **69**:807–38. In English: 'The indexation of earnings in Italy: sectoral analysis and estimates for 1978–79', *Rivista di politica economica. Selected Papers*, **13**:151–83.

Visco, I. (1984), 'Inflation expectations: the use of Italian survey data in the analysis of their formation and effects on wage changes'. Paper presented at the workshop on 'Price Dynamics and Economic Policy', Organisation for Economic Co-operation and Development, Paris, 6–7 September 1984.

4 The July Protocol and Economic Growth: The Chance Missed*

Leonello Tronti

ISTAT, Italy

4.1 The big chance

In the words of a successful book on Italian entrepreneurs, for Italian firms the 1990s were 'a big chance' (Mucchetti, 2003). For the firms operating in the industries once directly organised or, at least, strongly conditioned by the public hand, the chance was offered first by privatisations. Even more powerful and pervasive, though, was the reform of the wage-bargaining system. The abrogation of automatic cost-of-living allowances in 1992 and the introduction of a new wage fixing mechanism in the tri-partite Protocol of July 1993 gave Italian businesses a decade of extraordinarily moderate wage dynamics, despite a sharp decline in unemployment.

In order to understand what has happened, it may be useful to briefly recall the provisions of the Protocol, which instituted two separate, non-overlapping wage-bargaining levels. National, industry-wide agreements (first level), comprising a four-year contract on rules and standards and two two-year contracts on wages, is intended to safeguard the purchasing power of contractual wages. The wage increases fixed every two years apply to contractual minima and must be consistent with the programmed inflation rate, set by the Government as an economic policy target; if the actual inflation rate turns out to be higher, the Protocol allows for a recovery bargaining mechanism in the second two-year period. The second wage bargaining forum is that of local agreements (at the firm or geographical area level), designed to govern the distribution of gross wage increases above the inflation rate on the base of gains in productivity, profitability and/or quality. Consequently, gross wages can grow along with productivity, keeping labour's share unchanged, only if second-level agreements allocate all the gains in productivity

* The chapter, that does not necessarily reflect the opinions of Istat, is the sole responsibility of the author who, however, gratefully acknowledges useful comments and suggestions from Nicola Acocella, Mario Biagioli, Carlo Dell'Aringa, Sebastiano Fadda, Luigi Frey, Riccardo Leoni, Luisa Picozzi, Fabio Rapiti, Guido Rey, Salvatore Rossi and Anna Simonazzi. Previous versions were presented at a Seminar in honour of Ezio Tarantelli (Rome, 'La Sapienza' University, April 7, 2004), at the Aiel-Aisri Conference 'The July 1993 Agreement and the wage structure' (Bergamo University, June 18, 2004), and at the XIX National Labour Economics Conference (Modena and Reggio Emilia University, Modena, September 23–24, 2004).

obtained by the firms to labour income.[1] After 1993, however, first-level contractual wages failed to keep pace with inflation, and above all, gross wages failed to keep up with labour productivity. As a consequence, labour's share, which had been declining since the 1980s, fell still further.[2]

For this reason, despite modest economic growth, wage moderation has contributed to a substantial increase in profit levels. Adding to these employer-favourable income distribution conditions the spectacular decline in industrial conflict,[3] it is hard to deny that the 1990s offered Italian firms a probably unrepeatable opportunity. But have they managed to exploit that opportunity by modernizing the production system and facing the challenges posed by global markets and the euro? The concessions made by labour have been generous.[4] Can we say that Government and business responded to workers' sacrifices with policies and conduct that could usher in a new phase of social and economic development?

To raise these questions is in no way to ignore the extraordinary merits acquired by the Protocol in so many key areas: curbing inflation (even after the dramatic lira devaluation of September 1992), controlling the public debt, allowing for Italian adoption of the euro from the outset and the unprecedented job growth that followed the 1992–95 employment crisis. Such exceptional results, though, cannot veil the fact that they were not matched by any appreciable resumption of competitiveness and growth. The incompleteness or lack of reciprocity in incomes policy allowed Italian prices to rise faster than those of competitors, while wages had to play a deflationary role. And the opening of a wedge between prices and labour costs has allowed for the privatised firms in the sheltered sectors of the economy to collect a growing flow of rents, seriously undercutting the competitiveness of the tradable sector and overall economic growth.

The analytical path of the chapter is built on a series of stylised facts, starting from the consideration that, in an economy burdened by many oligopolistic segments and where money supply is largely exogenous, the level of profitability is determined by the distributive conflict as well as by firms' price policies. Profitability in turn forms the basis of private investment choices; and these (together with the public ones) shape both employment and productivity growth, which ultimately determine economic growth. It is important to note, however, that the analysis is not intended to check the robustness of this very general model, but to show how greatly the dynamics of the macroeconomic variables and, above all,

---

1 An increase in gross wages in line with that of labour productivity ensures the invariance of distributive shares, and is therefore known as the 'golden rule' of incomes policy as, other conditions being equal, it allows for the maximum wage increase compatible with the absence of pressures on firms' pricing policies (see, among many others, Brunetta et al., 1994; Cucchiarelli and Tronti, 1997).

2 The decline was common to many European countries, but in Italy has been more pronounced (see Blanchard and Giavazzi, 2003; Torrini, 2004; Zenezini, 2004).

3 See Istat (2003a).

4 This consideration is based on a comparison with the far faster growth of wages in France and the United Kingdom, where the macroeconomic performance has undoubtedly been better.

their interactions have changed since 1993, on the hypothesis that such changes can be traced to incomes policy and its interplay with privatisations.

The discussion is organised as follows. The chapter first presents an analysis of income distribution to productive factors before and after 1993, focussing on first and second-level wage growth and the labour share. In the light of labour productivity trends, wage moderation in the 1990s should be properly considered as a case of significant wage deflation, inducing a considerable fall in labour's income share. In an economy where numerous segments are still sheltered from international competitiveness, privatisation policies and the wage deflation have combined in favouring an escalation of rents. Consequently, quite unexpectedly for standard economics, wage moderation was combined with a perceptible competitive deterioration for the Italian economy, and both have been reflected in slow growth. To throw some light on this undesired result, the chapter analyses the relationship between profit and investment trends. The changes brought about after 1993 in the relationships among growth, profits, investment and employment show that employment expansion was accompanied by a clear deterioration in the quality of the new jobs created, in terms of both labour productivity and total factor productivity. The deterioration is discussed with reference to innovation, workplace re-organisation and the accumulation of relational goods. In this last perspective, the chapter also explores the possible causes of a weakening in the effectiveness of social pacts, showing that major shortcomings can be traced to the lack of commitment of Government and the social partners to preserving the credibility and fully implementing the objectives of the '93 Pact. The concluding remarks offer some indications on wage policy and social pacts, aimed at resolving the incompleteness of the July Protocol and putting the Italian economy on the 'high road' to competitiveness and economic development.

4.2 Income distribution to factors and wage growth

Through almost all of the second half of the last century, the Italian economy was characterised by a strong inflationary bias, which repeatedly forced it to regain competitiveness through currency devaluations.[5] After various phases of a tormented participation to the European Monetary System (in which a crucial role was played by the tripartite incomes policy accords adopted as the results of Ezio

[5] If between 1948 and 1968 the average annual rate of growth of consumer prices stayed relatively stably around 3 per cent, between 1968 and the first oil shock (1973) it almost doubled to 5.7 per cent. Between 1973 and 1983 Italy had to face the higher inflation period (an average yearly rate of more than 17 per cent); and afterwards, from 1983 to 1993, with the help of the tripartite policies conceived by Tarantelli, inflation was reduced to 6.3 per cent. After 1993, with the July Protocol and Italy joining the euro club, consumer prices slowed down to 3 (1993–99), and then to 2.6 per cent (1999–2003) (see Istat, 2000, and the following consumer prices press releases).

Tarantelli's efforts and, finally, of the sacrifice of his own life[6]), the July 1993 Pact imposed new macro and microeconomic constraints upon wage negotiations, in view of the single European currency.

Since then Italian wages have grown with extreme moderation, while firms' profits have increased very appreciably: from 1993 to 2001, while the gross profit share in net product[7] soared from 18 to 24 per cent, with an average gain of 0.7 points each year, the wage labour share (already declining since the 1980s) further fell by about half point per year from 60 to 56 per cent (Fig. 4.1). Once corrected for the self-employed (who are particularly numerous in Italy), the total reward for labour fell even more rapidly, from 82 to 76 per cent of net product.

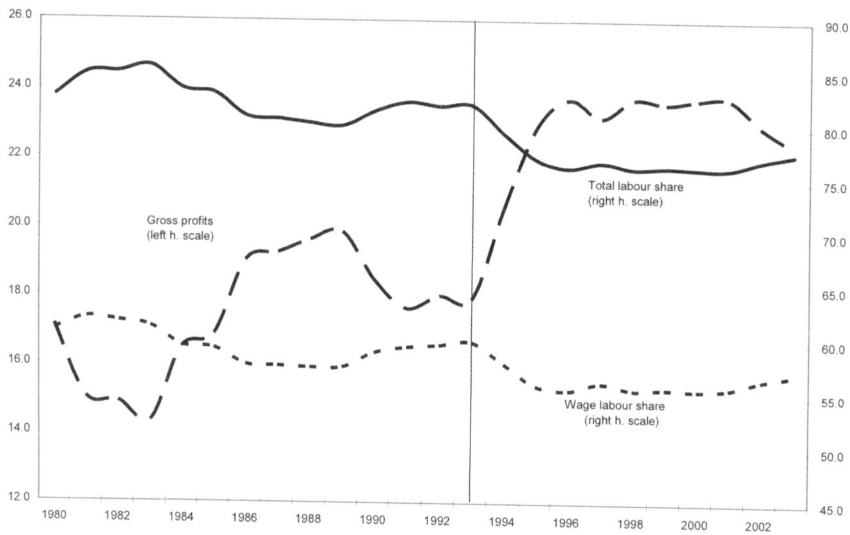

Fig. 4.1. Income distribution to factors before and after 1993 – Years 1980–2003 (percentage shares on net domestic product[8])

Source: Istat, National Accounts, and author's calculations.

[6] The major incomes policy episodes before the 1992 repealing of the automatic cost-of-living allowance and the 1993 Protocol came in 1982, 1984 and 1986.

[7] Net domestic product, which we can assume to constitute the matter of industrial conflict, is equal to the sum of three elements: i) gross wages and non-wage labour costs (wage labour income); ii) the labour income of the self-employed; and iii) gross profits. It is thus equal to GDP less capital depreciation and indirect net taxes. The average labour income of the self-employed is proxied here by average total labour cost in the corresponding industry. Gross profits, then, exclude both capital depreciation, net indirect taxation and the labour income of the self-employed.

[8] See footnote no. 7 for definitions.

Fig. 4.1 clearly shows that the impact on the income distribution to factors – some true and opposite level shifts in factor shares – was concentrated between 1993 and 1996, during the employment crisis and the wage negotiation freeze.[9] In the following years, after the purchasing power recovery of 1996–1997, the profit share resumed slight growth until 2001. Finally, in 2002–2003, with negative labour productivity growth, the trend changed again, causing a modest recouping of the labour share.

A more detailed look at wage dynamics shows that the preservation of real contractual wages, entrusted by the Protocol to the first bargaining level, has been 'problematic', to say the least[10] (Table 4.1). Only in the final period of the decade (2002–2003) did national industry-wide agreements succeed in defending the purchasing power of wages. In the other periods, first-level wages have not succeeded in keeping pace with inflation: neither in the first implementation period (with the employment crisis, the bargaining freeze and the inflation slowdown) when real contractual wages suffered a 0.3-point-per year fall, nor in the next four years, in spite of robust job growth and a strong fall in unemployment.

Table 4.1. First level wages and inflation – Years 1994–2003 (average yearly percentage rates of growth; consumer price index for manual and clerical worker families, including tobacco)

Periods	Contractual wages for full-time employees	Consumer prices	Real contractual wages
1994–2003	2,7	2,8	–0,1
A) 1994–1997	3,4	3,7	–0,3
B) 1998–2001	2,1	2,2	–0,1
C) 2002–2003	2,4	2,3	0,1
B–A	–1,2	–1,5	0,3
C–B	0,2	0,1	0,1

Source: Istat, Contractual wages and Consumer prices.

Within the set of rules introduced by the Protocol, however, a loss in the economic role of first-level wages would not have been worrisome if at the same time the industrial relations system had assured a widespread and lively second bargaining level, strong enough to distribute to wages all of the productivity gains. A stronger correlation at the microeconomic level between gross wages and labour productivity was, indeed, one of the major objectives of the Protocol signatories.

[9] In the private sector, the first national industry-wide collective agreements bargained under the new rules were signed at the end of 1994, while the first second-level local agreements were signed in the following six months. In the public sector, the new contracts deferred the initial effects on wages to the beginning of 1996.

[10] I take this word from Birindelli et al. (2003). See, on this, Istat (2001).

Unfortunately, however, this has never been the case. Local wage bargaining has never really taken off, and real gross wages have grown in the decade by an average 0.5 per cent per year, almost entirely attributable to the 1998–2001 period (Table 4.2). Moreover, if we consider take-home pay (net of withholding tax and employees' social contributions), the wage performance after 1993 unambiguously confirms Italian employees' common perception of impoverishment: overall growth in the decade has been just 0.8 per cent (less than one tenth of a point per cent per year), and the acceleration after 1997 only just managed to bring real wages in 2003 back to the value of 1990.

In an international perspective, the wage stagnation of Italian workers is striking. According to OECD estimates, between 1996 and 2002 Italy has had the slowest growth of real net wages not only of all 15 EU members, but even of all the new acceding countries (save only Cyprus, where growth has been negative) (Istat, 2004a).

Table 4.2. Gross and net real wages and labour productivity – Years 1993–2003 (average yearly percentage rates of growth; consumer price index for manual and clerical worker families, including tobacco; value added deflator at factor costs; v.a. at f.c. at 1995 prices)

Periods	Deflationed with consumer prices		Deflationed with value added deflator	Labour productivity
	Gross	Net of labour income taxes and social conts[(a)]		
1994–2003	0,5	0,1	0,6	1,0
A) 1994–1997	0,1	–0,7	0,0	2,1
B) 1998–2001	0,9	0,5	1,4	0,8
C) 2002–2003	0,5	0,9	–0,1	–0,5
B–A	0,8	1,2	1,3	–1,3
C–B	–0,4	0,5	–1,5	–1,3

Source: Istat, National Accounts and Consumer prices.

Note: [(a)] Author's estimate on Istat data.

From the firms' point of view, we can better evaluate these trends (and confirm how they have offered an unrepeatable opportunity) by deflating gross wages with the value added deflator. This exercise shows that, between 1994 and 1997, product wages did not grow at all, while labour productivity was growing 2.1 per cent per year (last two columns in Table 4.2). In the next four years (1998–2001) labour productivity suffered a considerable slowdown and then, in the last two years, an actual reduction, so that the ratio between the two variables has considerably decreased: however, the absolute difference continued to widen until 2001, from € 18,400 to € 21,600 at 1995 prices.

The growing distance between the remuneration and the (partial) productivity of labour, at the origin of the labour share decline, is also mirrored in the elements of unit labour cost. In fact, thanks to a number of legislative measures to narrow the tax wedge on wages,[11] unit labour costs have risen even less than the wage rate. Therefore, the differential between the growth of labour productivity and that of labour costs in the period 1993–2001 came to about 9 percentage points, and the absolute distance, measured at 1995 prices, increased by one third, from € 10,900 to € 14,500 (Fig. 4.2).

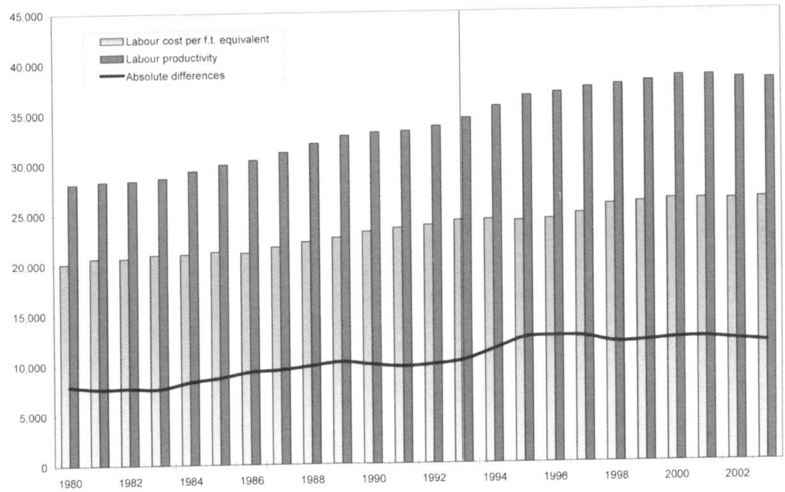

Fig. 4.2. Labour productivity and labour costs before and after 1993 – Years 1980–2003 (euro/eurolira at 1995 prices)

Source: Istat, National Accounts.

[11] The most substantial effect came from the introduction of Irap (*Imposta Regionale sulle Attività Produttive*, Regional Tax on Productive Activities), the new tax on value added that in 1998 replaced the mandatory contribution to the National Health Service and a series of other, minor levies. The change, however, has consisted mainly in shifting a fiscal burden, previously improperly located among social contributions, rather than a real reduction of the tax burden on business, and its net effects are still in doubt. After 1998, however, non-wage labour costs paid by the employer underwent many smaller reductions, leading to a decrease in the average effective rate from 38.7 to 37.4 per cent of gross wages. In an international perspective these rates may seem quite high; but the measurement of the tax wedge is highly sensitive to the way in which the Tfr (*Trattamento di fine rapporto*, Separation allowance) is considered. This, in fact, cannot be indisputably classified as a non-wage labour cost, as it is not a compensation for any risk but rather a deferred wage component. All employees are entitled to the allowance in all cases of separation (firing, resignation, retirement), and, after a certain tenure, they can also draw on it without separating. As its average incidence on gross wages is about 7.4 per cent, counting it as a wage cost cuts down the average effective tax wedge to 27.9 per cent of gross wage ((37.4–7.4)/(100+7.4)). In Fig. 4.2, in order to limit the distortions in the measurement of value added and of its components caused by the introduction of Irap, labour productivity is calculated with reference to value added at factor prices.

4.3 Wage moderation and competitiveness

To sum up, since 1993 Italy has displayed extremely, indeed uniquely moderate wage growth, not only among the large but among all European countries.[12] Wage moderation significantly slowed the rise in unit labour costs, further frozen after 1998 by the measures to narrow the tax wedge. Fig. 4.3 compares price dynamics, as measured by the value added deflator, with the growth of unit labour costs and with the parallel fall in the labour share.

The comparison shows that, after 1993, while prices underwent a significant deceleration (the yearly growth rate falling from an average 10 per cent between 1980 and 1993 to 2.7 per cent afterwards), the slowdown in unit labour costs was even more pronounced (from 9.7 to 2 per cent), producing the decline in labour's share.[13]

The scenario in which labour costs are curbed more sharply than prices opens an extremely favourable period for profits.[14] The opportunity is visually represented by the size of the wedge separating output prices from unit labour costs: after 1993 that wedge grows bigger without interruption up to 2001, initially (up to 1997) with average annual increments of 5.5 percentage points, and subsequently still 2.8 points.

[12] See also Istat (2003b) and figures at p. 177.

[13] Between 1994 and 2001 the labour share declined at an average pace of 0.7 points per year (with a deceleration between 1994–97, when the average reduction was 1.3 points per year, and 1998–2001, when it was only 0.1 points). As mentioned, in the last two years, in the face of a fall in labour productivity, the labour share has shown an increase that essentially reflects the downward rigidity of wages. In order to gain a better comprehension of the relationships among the three variables presented in Fig. 4.3, we can note that the labour share (*Sl*) is defined as follows:

$$Sl = \frac{(N_d + N_i)\cdot w}{Y \cdot p} = \frac{N \cdot w}{Y \cdot p} = ulc \cdot p^{-1}$$

where N_d is wage employment, N_i non-wage employment, w per capita labour cost, Y net product, p prices, N total (wage and non-wage) employment, and ulc unit labour cost. We then can express the labour share as the ratio of unit labour cost to prices. So, in terms of changes we have:

$$\delta Sl = \delta ulc + \delta p^{-1} + (\delta ulc \cdot \delta p^{-1})$$

hence, assuming the interaction term is negligible, we obtain the stability condition:

$$\delta Sl \approx 0 \Leftrightarrow \delta ulc \approx \delta p \qquad \delta Sl \leq 0 \Leftrightarrow \delta ulc \leq \delta p$$

The share will remain stable if and only if unit labour cost and prices change at the same rate: if unit labour cost grows less than prices, the share will fall.

[14] See the data presented in Istat (2004b).

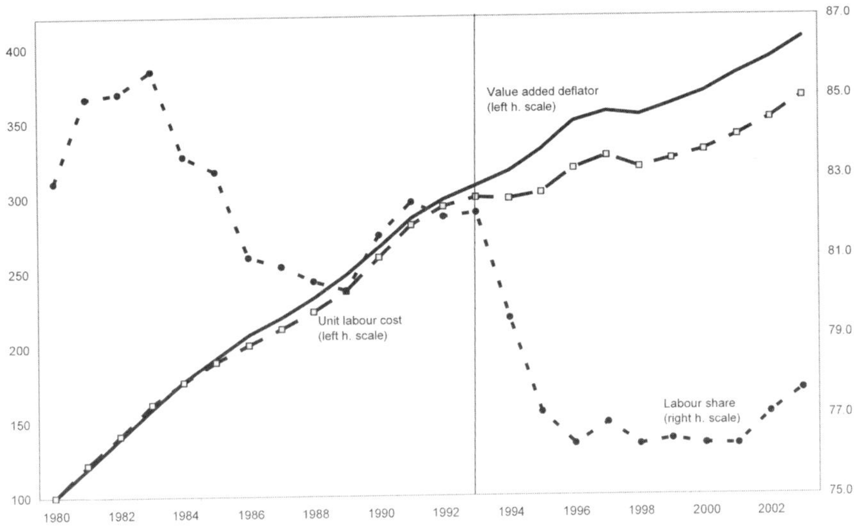

Fig. 4.3. Prices, unit labour cost and the labour share before and after 1993 – Years 1980–2003 (for the v.a. deflator and unit labour cost, index numbers in base 1980 = 100; v.a. at factor costs; labour share corrected for the self-employed)

Source: Istat, National Accounts, and author's calculations.

Table 4.3 shows the levels and the changes of different profitability indicators, before and after 1993. The average profit rate for the Italian economy[15] after 1993 increases 1.1 percentage points, while the average mark-up grows by 8.1 percentage points and its speed of growth jumps from 0.2 to 0.7 percentage points per year. In 2002–2003 profitability is hit by the productivity fall; nonetheless, in the final year the level of the mark-up is still 7 points higher than in 1993. Similar observations can be made for the other profit indicators; in particular, the return in the following year to the outlays for investments and labour costs shows, after 1993, an increase of 7.9 percentage points (reaching 28 per cent); and its average speed of growth goes from 0.1 to 0.7 percentage points per year.

In the light of this income distribution scenario, it is impossible not to judge as profoundly unsatisfactory Italy's comparative performance on inflation, productivity, and competitiveness – evidenced, in particular, by the heavy loss of export market shares. Between 1998 and 2003 the incidence of Italian exports falls from 14.5 to 13.5 per cent of flows within the euro area, and from 4.3 to 10.6 per cent of the exports outside the area. More recently, notwithstanding the acceleration in world trade, Italian exports contracted by 4 per cent in 2003 after a 1.4 per cent fall in 2002.

[15] It may be useful to note that what we are measuring here is the profitability of the entire economic system, not just of the business sector. For this reason, the exclusion from the scope of the measurement of the public sector or of private non-profit institutions, which play important roles in regulating the system, would be inappropriate.

Table 4.3. Profitability before and after 1993. Years 1980–2003 (whole economy, values at 1995 prices; average percentage values and average annual increases in percentage points)

Periods	Profit rate [(a)]	Mark-up	Gross profits [(b)] as a ratio to: Fixed gross investments	Labour costs	Investments plus labour costs
			AVERAGE PERCENTAGE VALUES		
A) 1980–1992	4,3	121,2	67,5	28,8	20,2
B) 1993–2003	5,4	129,2	89,7	40,9	28,0
B–A	1,1	8,1	22,2	12,1	7,9
C) 1993–1997	5,2	127,7	90,0	37,9	26,7
D) 1998–2001	5,7	131,1	93,0	44,3	30,0
E) 2002–2003	5,3	129,3	82,3	41,4	27,5
D–C	0,5	3,3	3,0	6,4	3,3
E–D	–0,4	–1,8	–10,7	–2,9	–2,5
			AVERAGE ANNUAL INCREASES IN PERCENTAGE POINTS		
A) 1980–1992	0,3	0,2	0,3	0,2	0,1
B) 1993–2003	0,1	0,7	1,4	1,1	0,7
B–A	–0,2	0,5	1,1	0,9	0,5
C) 1993–1997	0,4	2,1	7,3	3,3	2,3
D) 1998–2001	0,0	0,2	–1,8	0,6	0,1
E) 2002–2003	–0,3	–1,2	–3,7	–2,1	–1,3
D–C	–0,4	–1,9	–9,1	–2,7	–2,2
E–D	–0,2	–1,4	–1,9	–2,7	–1,4

Source: Istat, National Accounts, and author's calculations.

Notes: (a) Gross profits as a percentage share of net capital at substitution prices. (b) For the definition, see footnote no. 7. Gross fixed investments and total labour costs (employee compensation) of the preceding years, at constant 1995 prices.

In the absence of wage pressures, at the macroeconomic level the persistence of Italy's inflation differential signals the inadequacy of the incomes policy experiment enacted with the July Protocol: the problem is not at all that of moderating wage growth but rather *the unwillingness or inability to extend such discipline to the other types of income*. In the prisoner's dilemma of incomes policy, prices, tariffs and profits unload onto wages the burden of competitiveness. For this reason, the kind of incomes policy implemented in Italy after 1993 should properly be called a case of *wage deflation*, not simple wage moderation. The differential between the growth rates of labour costs and of labour productivity (in average equal to –1.1 percentage points per year) gives a rough but immediate measure of the wage deflation contribution to curbing other prices inflation in the 1993–2003 period.

A distributive mechanism of this kind, however, turns out to be perverse for economic growth. In an economy still burdened by many industries structurally sheltered from domestic and international competition, wage moderation not accompanied by low prices permits them to accumulate considerable rents. Fig. 4.4 shows the relevance of this undesirable outcome, paradoxical at a time when the Italian economy has undergone large-scale privatisations, supposed to enhance the competitiveness of the economic system.[16] The evolution of rents in the main economic sectors of the Italian economy between 1980 and 2003 spotlights two major aspects. First, considering the whole economy, after 1993 the share of rents in value added grows by an average of 0.4 percentage points per year, producing a flow of resources to business (and to the golden shares often still owned by the Government) of around € 65 billion per year at 1995 prices. This growth is driven by extraordinary rent increments in the primary sector, considerable ones in the financial and business service sector and, to a lesser extent, in the other private services; while in manufacturing and personal and social services rents stay unchanged, and in construction they actually diminish. Second, the different speeds at which the various industries accumulate rents produce rapid convergence on quite high levels (in 2003, between 9 and 22 per cent of value added), even though the initial values in 1993 were scattered over a much larger interval and some were nil or even negative.

At a greater level of detail, the biggest increases in rents came in agriculture (where, not coincidentally, the typical exodus that started in the '30s appears to have come to an end), in the production of electricity, gas and water, in business services and in the social and personal services other than education and health;

[16] On the basis of international literature (see, in particular, Griffith and Harisson, 2004), I consider here as rents the profits exceeding the 'normal' rate of profit in a competitive market. The procedure to estimate rents used by Griffith and Harisson is based on the mark-up of value added with respect to the sum of labour and capital costs. In particular, they estimate capital cost as a user cost of the capital stock, and they assume it to be equal to a constant proportion (10 per cent). In this way, they calculate for the Italian private non-agricultural sector the highest rents of all countries considered in their paper (14 EU countries plus the United States): more than 1.4 between 1985 and 2000, against an average 1.26. Furthermore, the Italian indicator, reaching 1.5 at the end of the period, also shows the fastest increase. Such an indicator, however, overestimates Italian rents because the authors do not take into account the labour income of the self-employed, who in Italy are particularly numerous. When this factor is considered, the cost of labour is higher and capital cost and rents are reduced. I, therefore, propose a slightly different measure of rents, based on the following formula:

rents = value added – [(*labour cost + labour income of the self-employed*) + *capital cost*]

In this measure capital cost, corrected for the labour income of the self-employed, is assumed equal to 7.5 per cent of capital stock at substitution prices. The capital cost calculated this way is, on average, around 3.5 percentage points of capital stock higher than depreciation. In the private non-agricultural sector alone in the period 1985–2000 (the time and sector coverage of Griffith and Harisson), my estimate of the average value of the Italian rents is 1.2, and the value in the final year 1.23.

smaller rents, but still significantly larger than the average, go to non-energy mining and to transport and communications. At the other end, fishing shows a perceptible rent reduction, and the same goes for many manufacturing industries (leather, paper, printing and publishing, fuel production, mechanical machinery, apparel, means of transport, other manufacturing industries), for construction and for education. However, the heaviest losses are concentrated in some manufacturing, tradable industries: energy mining, food, beverages and tobacco, non-metallic mineral products, electrical and electronic machines.

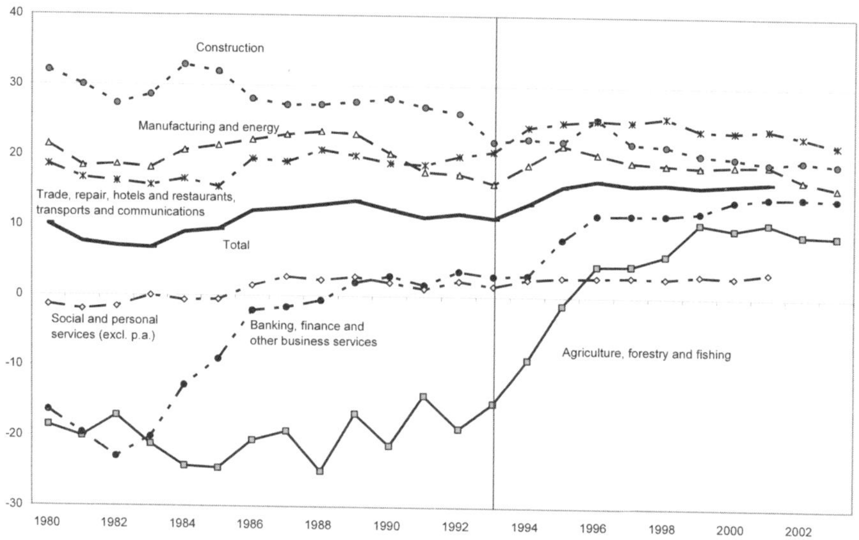

Fig. 4.4. Rent accumulation in the economic sectors of Italian economy before and after 1993[17] – Years 1980–2003 (percentage shares in value added; the total excludes public administration, defence and social insurance)

Source: Istat, National Accounts, and author's calculations.

The increase in rents after 1993 shows that privatisations have not only failed to stimulate efficiency in the industries sheltered from international competition but quite paradoxically reduced it. Consequently, manufacturing and other industries exposed to international competition have found themselves even more compressed between the hammer of international price competition and the anvil of price and tariff increases in the domestic market, and have been forced to play out yet again, on a new stage, a traditional, perverse script of Italian economic history.

Wage deflation has not only been useless: it has been harmful. Confronted with the euro and the growing internationalisation of trade, the Italian economy should have chosen one of two alternative paths: either an export-led growth strategy, based on the compression of domestic demand so as to regain some advantage in export prices; or the opposite, a demand-led strategy, based on the expansion of

[17] For the estimation of rents, see footnote no. 16.

high-quality consumption to improve products and production processes. But the distortions in income distribution have forced the economy to take the worst of both worlds: on the one hand being unable to control price and rent growth in the sheltered sectors (and, consequently, letting the burden on the tradable sector grow heavier); on the other, substantially depressing the major component of domestic demand.

4.4 High profits, booming employment, low investments: how to lose competitiveness

The principles of good economic governance, as well as reciprocity and joint responsibility between the social partners, which are indispensable to the success of social pacts, would have required employers, in response to the extraordinary resource inflow to firms and under the control and co-ordination of the Government, to make good use of their accumulated profits by promoting a growth strategy based on workplace reorganisation and export competitiveness.

In fact, in the face of increasingly stringent international constraints due to new competitors with extremely low labour costs,[18] the only growth strategy viable to an advanced economy like the Italian is the so-called 'high road to competitiveness'. This result, by the way, is so evident that it had been already indicated by the second part of the Protocol itself[19] (and subsequently proposed again, albeit a little too formally, by the so-called 'Christmas Pact' of 1998). The 'high road to competitiveness', moreover, was proposed for the entire European Union by the 2000 Lisbon Council (and, beforehand, by the Delors White Paper: European Commission, 1993). The 'high road' is the knowledge-based economy and growth spurred by learning: the road of employers that, through the creation of high trust-high performance labour relationships and the diffusion of good organisational practices, reshape workplaces so as to support the accumulation of skills and competence, update relational goods and, in a word, transform firms into learning organisations[20]. It is not at all just one option among many: in the euro scenario in which Italy is now located, deprived of the safety valve of competitive devaluations, and even more so after the entry into the Union of the new accession countries, the high road to competitiveness is the only possible choice for Italian firms

[18] In some EU-25 countries the hourly labour cost of workers with comparable education can be as low as a third or even a fifth of the Italian. Outside the EU, it can fall to a tenth or, for manual workers, even a twentieth.

[19] On the shortcomings created by the failure to implement the second part of the July Protocol, see the appeal by Ciampi (1996) and the subsequent investigations in Antonelli and De Liso (2004).

[20] The international literature on these aspects is vast. Here it suffices to recall, with reference to the specific case of Italian firms, the works by Cristini et al. (2003), Leoni (2006) and Pini (2004). I make reference also to a paper of mine on the development of the knowledge markets (Tronti, 2003).

– the only choice that can yield a recovery of international competitiveness and growth.

However, despite the extremely favourable framework designed by the July Protocol and the good intentions contained in it as in all the bi- and trilateral social pacts that followed,[21] the Italian economy has not yet taken the high road. On the contrary, for some time there have been worrying signals of malaise, unprecedently severe since the end of World War II. There is simply no way to avoid the fact that the 'big chance' of the 1990s has been unforgivably wasted.

Undoubtedly, with a lag, employers did react to the exceptional improvement in profitability: after 1996 the economy initiated an extraordinary employment cycle, expanding the workforce by more than 10 per cent (about 2.3 million additional people employed), raising the overall employment rate by about 6 percentage points. For women, employment growth neared 20 per cent (more than 1.4 million), and their employment rate rose by 8 points. Such a boom is all more striking as it was associated with very modest growth of output, reflecting a strong increase in the employment content of economic growth and an appreciable increase in the labour market's responsiveness to the economic cycle (Istat, 2003b).

This employment performance, however, was not grounded in any comparable strengthening of the investment function. Following the fall of the 1980s (from 27 to 21 per cent of GDP), after 1993 investment showed some sign of recovery: but this acceleration (bringing it just over 22 per cent in 2003) proved largely insufficient to put the economy back on an appreciable growth path (Fig. 4.5).

Fig. 4.5. Gross fixed investment before and after 1993 – Critical ratios – Years 1980–2003 (percentage ratios to net domestic product and gross profits[22])

Source: Istat, National Accounts, and author's calculations.

[21] At national level, the 'Pact for Employment' of 1996, the 'Christmas Pact' of 1998 and the 'Pact for Italy' of 2001.

[22] See footnote no. 7 for definitions.

The first signal of insufficiency is that, whereas in 1992 investment had been about 76 per cent of profits, by 2003, despite an intense reorganisation of the capital market, numerous privatisations and the reforms of collective bargaining and the labour market, they had fallen back to 64 per cent. Further evidence of the insufficiency of investment comes from the comparison of the changes in both profitability and investment per full-time equivalent (fte) (Fig. 4.6). If, after 1993 and until 1997, the operating surplus per fte rose in real terms by around 6 per cent per year, investment went up by only 3 per cent. After 1998, there was some realignment, but not at all enough to close a gap that, in real terms, has more than doubled with respect to the 1980–1992 period.

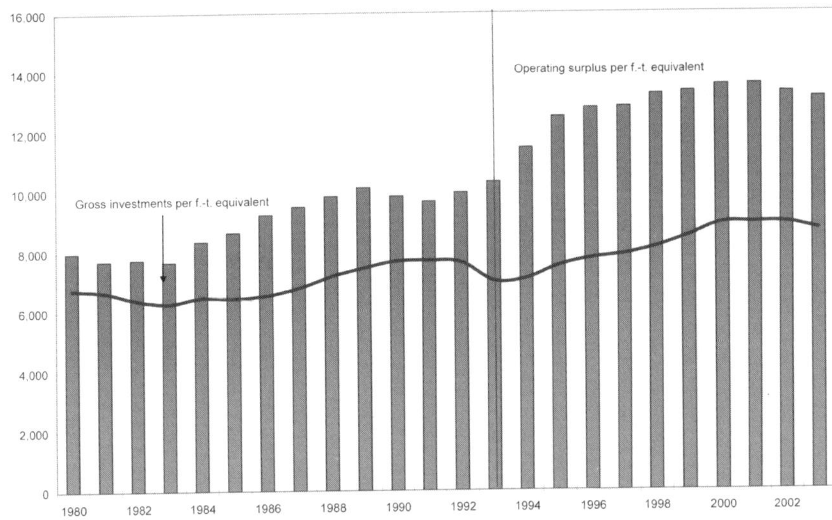

Fig. 4.6. Profitability and investment per full-time equivalent (fte) before and after 1993 – Years 1980–2003 (operating surplus includes capital depreciation and excludes the labour income of the self-employed; eurolira/euro at 1995 prices)

Source: Istat, National Accounts, and author's calculations.

4.5 Growthless employment

To summarize the amplitude of the changes in the reactions of profits to economic growth as well as of investment to profits, after 1993, notwithstanding a certain slowdown,[23] each percentage point of growth is matched by a 3.6 per cent increase in gross profits (with a peak of 6.5 points in 1993–1997)[24] (Fig. 4.7).

[23] In the period 1993–2003, the average yearly growth rate of the Italian GDP fell to 1.7 per cent from 2 per cent in 1980–1992.

[24] In the 1980s the average ratio between the two rates was a little over 1.5.

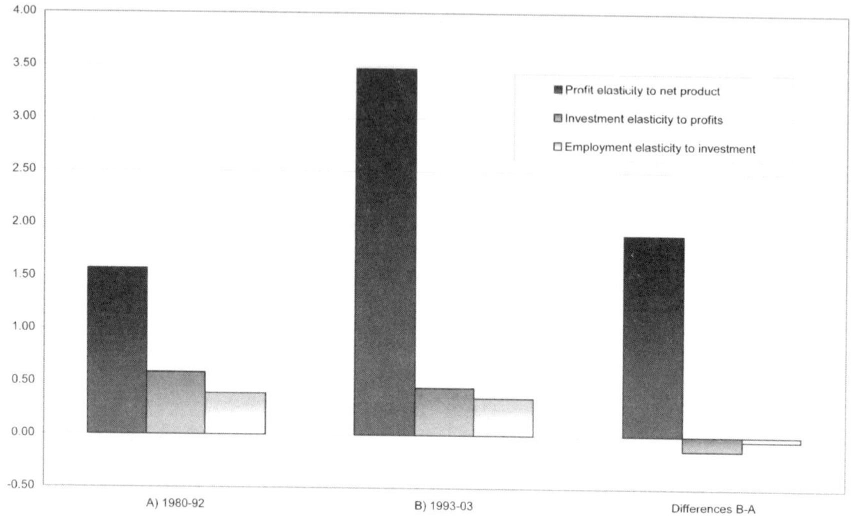

Fig. 4.7. The path growth-profit-investment-employment before and after 1993 – Periods 1980–93 and 1993–2003 (ratios between yearly percentage rates of change)

Source: Istat, National Accounts, and author's calculations.

Yet despite the privatisations, this striking improvement in profitability brought no enhancement of the economy's ability to transform profit into investment. On the contrary: the apparent elasticity of investment to profits, which had been 0.6 in the period 1980–1992, fell to 0.4 after 1993[25].

Why the failure of profitability to spur investment and change for the 'high road'? Authoritative economists argue that excessive wage moderation has enabled sheltered (newly privatised) corporations to reap growing margins without making any real investment in innovation or organisational and technological change (among others, Sylos Labini, 2003). The assertion that low wages can hinder innovation is certainly not new; it was put forth strongly, at a different moment in Italian economic history, by Ezio Tarantelli (who, nevertheless, was one of the leading advocates of Italian social pacts); and long before, by such ideologically distant economists as Alfred Marshall and John Maynard Keynes.[26]

The risks involved in wage moderation without sufficient domestic or international competition have been highlighted by Blanchard and Giavazzi (2003), who construct a general equilibrium model to assess the effects of jointly de-regulating the product and the labour markets. Not surprisingly, the model shows that where

[25] The average value of the period 1993–2003 conceals large variations over time: in the first sub-period (1993–97) the apparent elasticity was near zero, due to the 1993 slump in investments; in the second (1998–2001) it rose rapidly to 1.7, and in the third (2002–2003) it fell back to 0.2. These ample oscillations confirm the traditional frailty of the Italian economy investment function.

[26] The convergence is recalled by Roncaglia (2001).

a country reforms the labour market (with the same wage compression effects of the Protocol) without adequately reforming the product market so to assure competitive pressure on prices and profit margins, the result will be a decline in labour's share and high prices: i.e. a reduction of the workers' purchasing power. Even if the Blanchard and Giavazzi model does not show it, it is clear that, in a phase of sharpening international competition, high prices will cause a loss of competitiveness that will further compress growth. The country will thus be in Italy's situation, with exports and growth hampered by rent-pulled inflation and domestic demand compressed by wage deflation.

Moving on to the investment-employment relationship, the extraordinary results that followed the employment crisis of 1992–95 cannot be attributed to a recovery in the volume of investment as much as to the dramatic increase in the elasticity of employment with respect to investment, especially after 1997: 0.5 in 1998–2003, after –0.05 in 1993–1997 (with the employment crisis), and 0.35 in 1980–1992 (before the Protocol). Nevertheless, even the brilliant employment cycle of the second half of the 1990s cannot be simply taken at face value. The increasing elasticity of employment, in fact, highlights the weakening trend of the investment needed to create jobs; and after 2001 this slowdown turns into an actual decrease. This result casts some legitimate doubt upon the quality of the jobs created after 1997.[27]

As a matter of fact, after that year (and in coincidence with the European Employment Strategy and the reform of employment arrangements known as the 'Treu package') the profits accumulated by employers in the years of the bargaining freeze and of the start of the new wage-determination mechanism are (at least partially) reinvested. The effect is evident between 1998 and 2001, when each percentage point of profit growth is matched by a 1.7-point increase in investment. The parallel, strong increase in the elasticity of employment to investment, however, makes it clear that firms were not investing to improve workplaces and products in order to face the sharpening international competition, but merely increasing employment in relatively low-productivity jobs.[28]

This signal finds macroeconomic confirmation in the slowing of productivity growth as employment expands. Fig. 4.8 shows that the expansion of employment in the period of full application of the new wage fixing mechanism is accompanied by a sharp deceleration in productivity. In 1998, for the first time employment growth exceeded productivity growth; this negative differential widened steadily from then onwards, and in 2002, when productivity fell by 0.9 per cent, was more than 2.5 percentage points.

[27] Chapter 4 of the Istat Report on 2003 is dedicated to the quality of the jobs created in the employment cycle and, in particular, to the weakened link between employment and GDP growth (Istat, 2004c).

[28] On this, see especially Istat, 2004d.

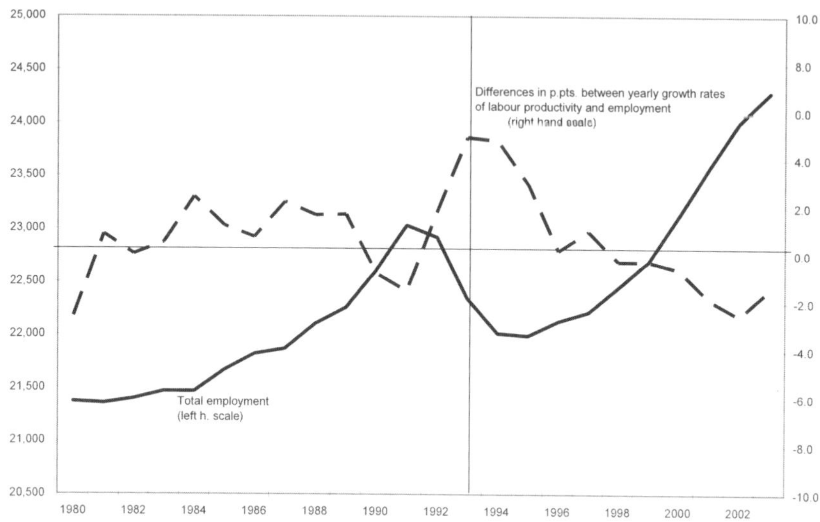

Fig. 4.8. Employment and productivity before and after 1993 – Years 1980–2003 (domestic employment in thousands and yearly differences between the rates of growth of productivity and of employment in full-time equivalents)

Source: Istat, National Accounts, and author's calculations.

4.6 Productivity, innovation and relational goods

We can now provide a deeper analysis of the Italian case by examining how the links of profitability to productivity and to employment changed after 1993, as well as those of labour productivity to employment and to investment. Fig. 4.9 shows the magnitude of the increase in the change in profitability relative to changes in labour productivity or in employment. The figure highlights two fundamental areas, both revolving around labour productivity, that are critical to macroeconomic performance.

The first finding is the appearance of a clear trade-off between employment growth and productivity growth. This is an empirical result reported by many authors, generally with reference to long-term international comparisons between the US and European economies.[29] The explanation of the trade-off involves the heterogeneity of physical and human capital: Blanchard (2004) for instance, addressing the second kind of heterogeneity, maintains that in the past higher minimum wages kept European employers from hiring lower productivity workers, thus

[29] On evidence of the employment-productivity trade-off comparing the US and Europe, see also Sestini and Tronti (2002).

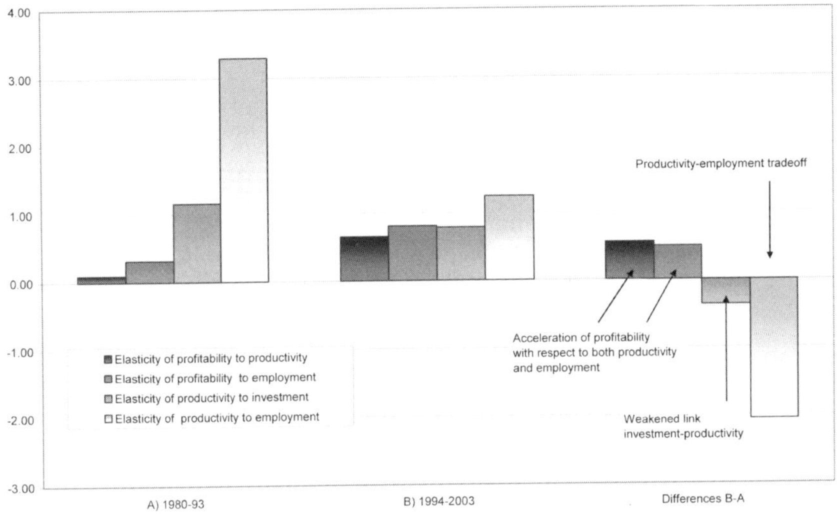

Fig. 4.9. Apparent relationships of profitability to labour productivity and to employment, and of labour productivity to employment and to investment before and after 1993 – Years 1980–93 e 1993–2003 (ratios between average percentage rates of change; profitability measured as the ratio of gross profits to the sum of gross fixed investment and total labour cost of the preceding years, at constant prices; domestic employment)

Source: Istat, National Accounts, and author's calculations.

keeping the unemployment rate and average labour productivity artificially high.[30] However, it is difficult to attribute productivity differentials only to the workers' side, as they most likely emerge from different quality combinations of labour and capital services.

In a Ricardian perspective, the wage deflation has progressively allowed for the survival of jobs with decreasing marginal productivity. If these jobs are also characterised by sufficient profitability, as the simultaneous increase in the apparent elasticity of profitability to both employment and productivity would suggest, employers will concentrate a growing share of their employment creation strategies in that direction, consequently depressing average labour productivity growth. Average productivity, however, slows down not only when the share of low-productivity jobs goes up, but also when an increasing share of employment is accounted for by firms with stagnant or declining productivity, regardless of its initial level. The employment-productivity trade-off, in fact, is also implied by Baumol's 'unbalanced growth' model (1967) when the markets for the products of the dynamic sector (manufacturing) are saturated: employment growth can occur, but

[30] However, the relevance of Ricardian effects in a labour demand model with non-homogeneous human (and physical) capital, as opposed to the Vulgate of 'Okun law', was already noted by De Cecco (1972) and Tarantelli (1970, 1974), with reference to the Italian case.

it will come in the stagnant sector (services, utilities), significantly slowing aggregate growth. The larger the aggregate employment increase, the stronger the slowdown effect.[31]

The second critical area refers to the declining impact of investment on productivity: after 1993 the apparent elasticity of productivity to investment shows steady erosion. Whereas between 1980 and 1993 every percentage point increase in investment brought a 1.2-point rise in productivity, after 1993 this average elasticity diminishes by a third, falling from around one point in 1994–1997 to 0.6 points in 1998–2003. This result highlights the deterioration in the quality of investment and suggests that in recent years (at least at the margin) investment has been direct to the creation of low- or stagnant-productivity jobs.

The decreasing impact of investment on productivity is also reflected in the recent negative trend of total factor productivity (Istat, 2004e):[32] between 1999 and 2003 the overall contribution of TFP to value added growth is negative (–0.2 per cent per year), with significant falls in agriculture (–2.7 per cent), construction (–1.3 per cent) and manufacturing (–0.5 per cent). Despite an investment performance that while not brilliant is not disastrous either (see Fig. 4.5), this result would indicate not only a slowdown in technical progress, but rather (or also) a deterioration of *relational goods* in the firms or in the markets.

The term 'relational goods' designates the assets and services produced by personal relationships that allow each worker to increase the services of his/her human capital (Fondazione Giacomo Brodolini, 1997).[33] Further to its intensity and to the technology at its disposal, the services that human capital can provide depend crucially on the quality of inter-personal relationships, in the workplace but also outside it: different cultures, values, technologies and institutions mould different links, connections and relationships between persons in the units that form the object of economic analysis – be they families, firms, territories, industries or whole economies; and this differentiates their capacity to promote and value knowledge, skills and competence. This process can happen because relational goods operate essentially by spreading both trust and information in the human

[31] A recent exercise by Istat (2004d) shows that the labour productivity decline suffered by the Italian non-agricultural business sector between 1998 and 2001 is, in fact, a composition effect due to employment growth in industries with low and stagnant productivity: without this change in the employment mix, productivity growth would have been slow but nevertheless positive.

[32] Even not discarding its euristic value, I cannot deny my dissatisfaction with an indicator whose construction makes a tautological use of distributive shares as proxies of product elasticities to factors. As this chapter amply shows, in fact, distributive shares follow paths conditioned by historical, social, political and institutional causes, that range quite far from what an efficient (or competitive) income distribution criterion would require.

[33] This is a stricter definition of *relational goods* than the one commonly used in the economic literature on the link between rationality and relational behaviours (see the volume edited by Sacco and Zamagni, 2002). In particular, I use a definition directly linked with the effects of inter-personal relationships on the production and distribution processes. Such an approach, even if confined to much shorter time periods, draws from the fundamental work of Putnam (1993) on the economic development of Italian regions.

capital networks that produce and accumulate them. From this standpoint, the relational goods endowment of each economic unit is a fundamental aspect of its growth potential. A social environment sufficiently endowed with relational goods can allocate, connect and manage human capital more productively, and therefore generate a higher self-sustaining growth path; meanwhile, in a social environment deprived of relational goods, the mere creation of potential human capital by the public actor (typically through education and training) may not be sufficient either to ensure its transformation into effective human capital or to generate and reward the personal effort necessary to economic development.

Furthermore, with the new information and communication 'relational technologies', in addition to the problem of the traditional relational deprivation of some social environments and geographical areas, workers and firms have to face the problem of managing a real 'relational gap': existing relational goods assets, based on previous technologies, may be at least temporarily 'crowded out' by the relational potential of new technologies. The production system, therefore, starting from their elementary units (workplaces), has to convert and reorganise in order to make the best use of the relational potential of the new technologies while limiting the losses in the networks sustained by older techniques. From this point of view, policies for the transformation of firms into learning organisations should not be restricted to promoting knowledge accumulation or even exchange in the workplace but should also attack the problem of updating previous relational networks and creating new ones through new technologies. Obviously, one of the areas most deeply affected by such a change is that of industrial relations.

4.7 The weakening of social pacts

In this perspective, further insight into the Italian performance may well come from an investigation of the endurance of the industrial relations system – undoubtedly one of the major relational goods of the economy – despite the poor results of the Protocol in terms of growth.[34] Trilateral incomes policy, in fact, tends to be socially costly, as it may weaken the actors that implement it. This happens for two reasons: first because it requires of collective actors a very substantial effort of co-ordination, which limits the scope for the initiatives of the agents represented (firms, workers, Government-owned companies etc.); second because, once the actors' behaviours are set on a 'virtuous' path, precisely those disequilibria get corrected whose reduction is the most appealing reward for the 'social partners' to bargain, so that the incentive for corporatist agreements progressively diminishes. Given the Protocol's indisputable effectiveness to date, it is natural and reasonable to wonder whether the Italian industrial relations system has fallen victim to it, to the point of making any tripartite effort to embark on the high road and spur growth no longer attractive, even impracticable.

[34] A discussion of a pillar of the Italian system of industrial relations, the 1970 Labour Rights Act, as a fundamental relational good is provided by Tronti (2001).

According to Tarantelli (1986), there are three prerequisites for the success of social pacts; and taken together, they define the 'degree of neo-corporatism' of an industrial relations system. They are:

1. The 'neo-cooptation' of trade unions and employers' associations – but, it is worth noting, also of governments – into the tripartite regulation of economic policy. This is a relational prerequisite that involves both the reputation and the credibility of social actors, as it implies: i) on the one hand, their genuine commitment to implement the economic policy measures that can ensure the targets explicitly agreed upon; ii) on the other, the actors' capability to fulfil and make their counterparties fulfil the obligations agreed to and, therefore, their credibility with respect to the subjects represented as well as to the other signatories.
2. The 'centralisation' of collective bargaining, i.e. the need for the pacts to be undertaken by sufficiently 'encompassing' organisations, so as to avoid both free-riding behaviours (by minority workers' groups with strong powers of interdiction as well as by firms with oligopolistic positions) and pattern bargaining. This prerequisite is usually assured through a bargaining architecture in which wage agreements are made chiefly at the national, industry, or even regional levels, and signed simultaneously. The centralisation has also to deal with the asymmetry between workers' and employers' associations: that is, while trade unions generally exert solid control on the contractual behaviour of associates, employers' associations have only very weak control on their members' inflationary pricing behaviour. For this reason, surveillance on employers has to be implemented by means other than mere agreements (antitrust policies, fiscal policies, penalty clauses etc.).
3. The 'neo-regulation' of industrial conflict, that is the industrial relations system being endowed with effective instruments for preventing conflict from taking destructive forms, or such as to compromise the commitments undertaken. This means not only an adequate institutional framework (regulation of the right to strike, regulation of union representation, arbitration and conciliation procedures), but also the absence of 'ideological residuals' on both sides of the industrial relations arena – that is the sharing of a genuine 'social partnership' spirit by both social actors and the government as well, so as to enable the common goals to prevail over diverging immediate interests.

We can then try to analyse the Italian industrial relations system in the light of these fundamental pre-requisites, to see whether its 'degree of neo-corporatism' has diminished since 1993 and this may not be a reason for the Protocol's ineffectiveness in fostering growth and competitiveness. Let us examine the prerequisites one by one.

First, as for 'neo-regulation' of industrial conflict, the picture is clear. Since the early 1990s, the number of man-hours lost to strikes have literally crumbled to average values about one tenth of the previous levels (Istat, 2003a); and the recent conflicts over the proposed changes to Art. 18 of the Labour Rights Act and other disputes have not even approached the intensity of the '60s and the '70s. One may be sure that in the Italian industrial relations system there are still various 'ideological residuals', which do not impede social pacts in principle but every now and then do induce one actor to try to use them against the other.[35] On the other hand, the development of conciliation and arbitration procedures is still insufficient, and users of essential public services may suffer great inconvenience from strikes, even if the matter is amply regulated. However, all in all the framework of conflict regulation is unquestionably robust and efficient.

Second, the hypothesis that the 'centralisation' of collective bargaining has become insufficient is definitely more disputable. Certainly, the debate on the reform of the Protocol has repeatedly pointed out that the failure of the second bargaining level to take off continues to impede wider wage differentials between firms and, above all, between regions. But centralisation has lost some strength as to the agreements' synchrony, especially within the public sector. And if the rules of the Protocol have proved strong enough to avoid any pattern bargaining spiral on the workers' side, they have not succeeded in preventing the employers and the Government itself (as a ruler of public service prices and tariffs) to let prices and margins grow beyond the agreed targets.

The main suspicions, however, focus on the third prerequisite. In fact, even in the climate of general wage moderation and low conflict (or perhaps precisely because of this climate), after the 1998 'Christmas Pact' the actors have displayed an increasingly visible dearth of 'neo-cooptation'. The shortfall is evidenced by failures to abide or make the other actors abide by the agreement, or even to preserve its meaning, joint responsibility and the behaviour necessary for its success also with respect to growth and competitiveness. In particular, if we look for inadequacies in fulfilling obligations, the greatest failures have been by employers and the Government, as they have proven unable to control prices, profit margins, and tariffs under the single currency, in accordance with the collectively bargained incomes policy targets. They have not been able to correspond to the unions' compliance with the programmed inflation rate, thus depriving this variable of its meaning and value as a realistic economic policy target – a target whose failed achievement immediately indicts at least one of the parties for defaulting.[36]

The trade unions, by contrast, must bear responsibility for: i) not having been able to compel the other signatories to comply with the pact; and, ii), not having committed themselves (and not having demanded for the employers' commitment) to the construction of a system of rules and representation throughout the country

[35] I am not referring here only to anti-capitalist ideologies that pervade some trade union fringes, but also to the (equally noxious) anti-wage 'neo-liberal' ideologies that permeate some employers and government milieus; such a stance makes the microeconomic point of view prevail over the general interest, threatening substantial losses of welfare and growth potential.

[36] The creation of a growing differential between programmed and actual inflation dates back to 2001. In order to keep pace with the second, national collective agreements tend to negotiate wage dynamics significantly stronger than the first, thus seriously damaging the functioning of the 'forward looking wage policy' designed by the Protocol. In 2004 contractual wage growth came 1.2 percentage points over the programmed inflation rate and 0.7 points over the actual rate. The trend continued in the first half of 2005, when contractual wages grew by 3.5 per cent against a less than 2 per cent increase in consumer prices.

to allow for the takeoff of the second bargaining level and the defence of labour's share. The lapsing of the necessary surveillance on the other actors, and the repeated conflicts between the right-wing Governments (in alliance with some unions) and the largest Italian labour union (the left-wing CGIL, the Italian General Confederation of Labour) have compromised both the full discharge of obligations and the unfolding of the potential for taking the high road that were inherent in the Protocol.[37] Moreover, the progressive weakening of the fear that the unions were not 'co-opted' enough in the pact – perhaps precisely because of their feeble surveillance over the other actors' compliance – eventually led Government and employers to nourish the illusion that the consent of all the unions was no longer needed, and the Italian economy could be ruled without it. This belief showed up, for instance, in the mentioned campaign to abolish Article 18 of the Labour Rights Act.[38] The campaign was weak technically, as the hypothesis that Article 18 discouraged small firms below the application threshold from increasing their staff could never be demonstrated[39]; and it was biased by a very substantial 'ideological residual' along a strategic perspective distant indeed from the goal of efficient reshaping of workplaces and the high road to competitiveness.

4.8 Incomes policy and zero growth: starting over?

What indications can be drawn by these results? Does the July 1993 edifice have to be demolished? This is not on the agenda (even if it shows more than one crack), thanks to the agreement's solid achievements in curbing inflation and fostering employment. If it cannot be abandoned, however, the Protocol should certainly be revisited with a new spirit and urgency.

It is indispensable, first of all, for all actors to agree that while the Protocol may be a *necessary* instrument it is surely not *sufficient* for a policy governing *all incomes*. Consequently, if the Italian social actors are unable to agree upon such an all-incomes policy, the Protocol alone may well prove to be not just useless but actually harmful to growth: as long as labour market reform precedes or dominates competitiveness-enhancing product market reform, there will be adverse repercussions for labour's share in value added and for prices – hence for domestic demand and growth. On the contrary, only if product market reform precedes and prevails over labour market reform can moderate wage growth keep up with prices and the economy benefit from the resilience of domestic demand and the competitive advantage of parallel moderation of prices and wages.

[37] It may be useful to recall that the original design of the Protocol included, in accordance with the lines drawn at his time by Tarantelli, the power to sanction firms/industries that made price increases above target inflation by discretionary increases in social contributions or taxes (the so-called *tax-based incomes policy*). Such sanctions, however, have not only never been applied but have never even been called for or threatened.

[38] The Article entitles the employee dismissed without just cause by a firm with 15 or more employees to reinstatement, rather than only to severance compensation.

[39] See, among others, Tronti (2001).

In the Italian case, the privatisations enacted since the 1980s have not only failed to build the competitive environment necessary for the economy to keep the pace with European integration and globalisation; paradoxically they have allowed a very substantial increase in rents in the industries sheltered from international (and also domestic) competition. Because of incomplete and asymmetric implementation of the Protocol, in the prisoner's dilemma of incomes policy prices, tariffs and margins have put the entire burden of competitive adjustment on wages, with the disappointing result of generating a wage deflation accompanied by relatively high price inflation and a net decline in export competitiveness. The measures for privatisation alone have not only failed to prevent some industries (energy production and distribution, transport and communications, business services and also agriculture), from exploiting both their market positions and wage moderation: they have even often supported them in doing so, by allowing the new privatised firms to abandon their traditional social-service mission for private profit-maximisation. In the short run, this may have eased public finances, thanks to the boosting dividends collected by the Government, owner of some of these firms' golden share. But, in a longer run, it certainly has worsened the economic conditions for the families as well as for the firms engaged in international competition.

Consequently, as the need for some effective rent-reducing and competition-increasing measures in the sheltered industries has become more and more urgent, the public actor, organised labour and the representatives of firms *in the tradable industries* should undertake strict surveillance of these firms' inflationary behaviour. Opportunism with regard to common targets, represented by the target inflation rate (or, better, by specific rates programmed at the industry level) should be penalised by discretionary increases in taxes and social contributions or by other dissuading measures. Until this is done, product markets will continue to allow for rent accumulation, wage moderation will continue to dominate product market deregulation, and growth will continue to be penalised.

For this reason, in the short run it is indispensable for the social actors to reinterpret the July Protocol: wage growth should be revived so as to ensure the recovery of domestic demand and the resilience of labour's share in income and value added. Moreover, even if creating a conflict between the micro- and the macroeconomic levels, wage growth has to be recognised as a fundamental stimulus to technological and organisational innovation. The social actors, therefore, should explicitly agree to distribute the entire gain in productivity to employees. A move in this direction will provide an incentive for both employers and workers to deal with workplace reorganisation (which, in any case, needs specific policies).

In order to attain this goal, the social partners must work for the substantial development of the second bargaining level, to reward innovation and productivity, in the perspective recently opened by the craftsmen's organisations. But the industrial relations system also needs to be more pragmatic, using the first level to distribute a more or less ample share of productivity gains in the sectors where the second level finds it hard to gain ground. Where the second level of bargaining is inadequate, in fact, the first level cannot but grow in importance (at least provisionally): either social actors engage in the construction of local industrial relations systems that prove to be differentiating, efficient in rewarding innovation and distributing productivity gains, and present throughout the nation, or inevitably the task of macroeconomic correction should be restored to the national level, regulating industry by industry not only the defence of the purchasing power, but also the growth of real wages in line with productivity.

In conclusion, the social actors should not dismantle the 1993 Protocol, but rather bring it to completion. If in 1993 the idea of assigning social pacts to promote economic growth and reshape workplaces, as well as curbing inflation and increasing employment, was one for the future, today it is a pressing necessity. This objective demands unquestionable joint responsibility of all the social partners and the resolute debunking of the false belief (strongly opposed already by Adam Smith) that low wages, as such, are a good thing.

References

Antonelli, G. and N. De Liso (eds.) (2004), *European Economic Integration and Italian Labour Policies*, Aldershot, UK: Ashgate,

Baumol, W.J. (1967), 'Macroeconomics of unbalanced growth: the anatomy of urban crisis', *American Economic Review*, **57**:415–26

Birindelli, L., G. D'Aloia and A. Megale (2003), *La politica dei redditi negli anni '90: Potere d'acquisto, contrattazione e produttività in Italia e in Europa*, Rome: Ediesse.

Blanchard, O. (2004), 'The economic future of Europe', *NBER Working Paper 10310.*

Blanchard, O. and F. Giavazzi (2003), 'Macroeconomic effects of regulation and deregulation in goods and labor markets', *Quarterly Journal of Economics*, **118**(3):879–90.

Brunetta, R., A. Cucchiarelli, P. Naddeo and L. Tronti (1994), *Politica dei redditi e struttura della contrattazione*, Rome: Ediesse-Edizioni Lavoro.

Ciampi, C.A. (1996), *Un metodo per governare*, Bologna: Il Mulino.

Cristini, A., A. Gaj, S. Labory and R. Leoni (2003), 'Flat hierarchical structure, bundles of new work practices and firm performance', *Rivista Italiana degli Economisti*, **8**(2):313–41.

Cucchiarelli, A. and L. Tronti (1997), 'Produttività e distribuzione del reddito: equità ed efficienza in un modello a due settori', in M. Biagioli (ed.), *L'analisi economica delle relazioni industriali. Modelli teorici e studi empirici sull'esperienza italiana*, Naples: ESI.

De Cecco, M. (1972), 'Una interpretazione ricardiana della forza-lavoro in Italia', *Note economiche*, **1**:5–47.

European Commission (1993), *White Paper. Growth, Competitiveness and Employment: The Challenges and Ways Forward into the 21st Century*, Luxembourg: Office for Official Publications of European Communities.

Fondazione Giacomo Brodolini (1997), 'Sviluppo economico e beni relazionali', *Economia & lavoro*, 1-2.

Griffith, R. and R. Harisson (2004), 'The link between product market reform and macroeconomic performance', *European Economy Economic Papers, 209.*

Istat (2000), *Il valore della lira dal 1861 al 1999*, Rome: Collana Informazioni.

Istat (2001),'Contrattazione di primo livello e potere d'acquisto delle retribuzioni', in: Istat, *Rapporto Annuale. La situazione del Paese nel 2000*, Rome: Poligrafico dello Stato, pp. 222–30.

Istat (2003a), 'Salari, inflazione e conflitti di lavoro', in: Istat, *Rapporto Annuale. La situazione del Paese nel 2002*, Rome: Poligrafico dello Stato, pp. 231–37.

Istat (2003b), 'Quadro strutturale e ciclico', in: Istat, *Rapporto Annuale. La situazione del Paese nel 2002*, Rome: Poligrafico dello Stato, pp. 165–77.

Istat (2004a), 'Le retribuzioni nette nei paesi Ocse', in: Istat, *Rapporto Annuale. La situazione del Paese nel 2003*, Rome: Poligrafico dello Stato, pp. 252–53.

Istat (2004b), Il reddito disponibile del settore istituzionale 'famiglie', in: Istat, *Rapporto Annuale. La situazione del Paese nel 2003*, Rome: Poligrafico dello Stato, pp. 319–24.

Istat (2004c), Dinamiche dell'occupazione, qualità del lavoro e comportamenti individuali, in: Istat, *Rapporto Annuale. La situazione del Paese nel 2003*, Rome: Poligrafico dello Stato, pp. 207–307.

Istat (2004d), Crescita dell'occupazione e rallentamento della produttività del lavoro, in: Istat, *Rapporto Annuale. La situazione del Paese nel 2003*, Rome: Poligrafico dello Stato, pp. 216–22.

Istat (2004e), Il contributo dei fattori produttivi alla crescita economica, in: Istat, *Rapporto Annuale. La situazione del Paese nel 2003*, Rome, pp. 123–24.

Leoni, R. (ed.) (2006), *Economia dell'innovazione. Disegni organizzativi, pratiche di gestione delle risorse umane e performance d'impresa*, Milan: Franco Angeli (forthcoming).

Mucchetti, M. (2003), *Licenziare i padroni?*, Milan: Feltrinelli.

Pini, P. (ed.) (2004), *Innovazione, relazioni industriali e risultati d'impresa. Un'analisi per il sistema industriale di Reggio Emilia*, Milan: Franco Angeli.

Putnam, R. (1993), *Making Democracy Work: Civic Traditions in Modern Italy*, Princeton: Princeton University Press.

Roncaglia, A. (2001), *La ricchezza delle idee. Storia del pensiero economico*, Rome-Bari: Laterza.

Sacco, P.L. and S. Zamagni (eds) (2002), *Complessità relazionale e comportamento economico. Materiali per un nuovo paradigma di razionalità*, Bologna: Il Mulino.

Sestini, R. and L. Tronti (2002), 'Escaping the stagnancy trap. Unbalanced growth and employment in the services', in R. Balducci and S. Staffolani (eds), *Income distribution, growth and employment*, Naples: ESI, pp. 171–208.

Sylos Labini, P. (2003), *Berlusconi e gli anticorpi*, Rome-Bari: Laterza.

Tarantelli, E. (1970), 'Produttività del lavoro, salari e inflazione', in *Quaderni di Ricerche L. Einaudi*, Rome, now in E. Tarantelli (1988), *L'utopia dei deboli è la paura dei forti. Saggi relazioni e altri scritti accademici*, edited by R. Filosa and G.M. Rey, Milan: Franco Angeli.

Tarantelli, E. (1974), *Studi di economia del lavoro*, Milan: Giuffrè.

Tarantelli, E. (1986), *Economia Politica del Lavoro*, Turin: Utet.

Torrini, R. (2004), 'Profitti e redditività del capitale in Italia: un tentativo di interpretazione', paper presented at the Conference 'Distribution and Growth in Italy' organised by the journal *Politica Economica*, Bologna, June 4.

Tronti, L. (2001), 'Lo Statuto: elementi fondamentali di una valutazione economica', *Economia & Lavoro*, **35**(2):53–69.

Tronti, L. (2003), 'Capitale umano e nuova economia. Riorganizzazione dei sistemi formativi e sviluppo dei mercati delle conoscenze', *Lavori diritti mercati*, **1**.

Zenezini, M. (2004), 'Il problema salariale in Italia', *Economia & Lavoro*, **2**:147–81.

5 The '93 July Agreement in Italy: Bargaining Power, Efficiency Wages or Both?

Annalisa Cristini and Riccardo Leoni

University of Bergamo, Italy

5.1 Introduction*

In Italy the decentralised bargaining was instituted in 1993, within the so-called July Agreement which signed a broader change of positions in the industrial relations, summarized in the slogan *from conflict to participation.* The protocol primary objective was the inflation restrain that was to be achieved essentially by abolishing the wage indexation mechanism. In addition, in order to allow non inflationary wage increases, the protocol modified the existing collective agreement by introducing a second level bargaining. According to this new two-step process, wages are firstly collectively negotiated by each category union at the national level; successively, at the firm-level, a wage premium, strictly linked to some form of profit/gain sharing (hereafter, profit sharing, for simplicity), may be further agreed. The Pact explicitly recognises that the second level bargaining could be of advantage to the whole productive system through an improvement of firm efficiency and profitability.[1] For matters concerning the wage, the national collective agreement is renegotiated every two years, whereas the second level bargaining takes place every four years; according to the protocol, during this four-year span both parts should engage in procedures of information, consultation or negotiation aimed at managing the social effects of technical innovations, firm reorganisation and restructuring.

With respect to the usual union-firm bargaining, the decentralised negotiation spelled out in the July Agreement presents an important novelty as the explicit profit sharing element introduces efficiency wage considerations in the firm level

* The authors are grateful to Eleonora Bazzana for her precious and accurate research assistance. The project has received financial support from Research Funds of the University of Bergamo (Annalisa Cristini: project 2003; Riccardo Leoni: project 2004). The authors thank Paolo Garonna and Richard Freeman for the helpful discussion on a previous version of the chapter.

[1] 'The parts recognize (...) the specific and innovative institution of the firm level bargaining and the advantages that this may bring to the whole productive system through an improvement of the firms' efficiency and operating results ...' (from the July Agreement).

bargaining.[2] Moreover, since the specific implementation of both the incentive programs and the profit sharing scheme are left to each firm, the enhancing productivity effect is likely to be firm specific so that the returns from adopting the decentralised bargaining are expected to vary across firms.

Since the many firms' management may have been using various incentive schemes even before the July Agreement plainly stated in favour of them and the national unions confederations sustained their adoption across firms, an important question regards to what extent the support of the unions towards such mechanisms have changed their effectiveness.

Our first objective is to provide an estimable wage equation[3] and to this end we model the final wage by combining the usual wage bargaining model with efficiency wages along the lines initially suggested by Summers (1988) and later formalized by Martin and Garino (2000), and Mauleon and Vannetelbosch (2003); moreover, following Muysken and van Veen (1996) and Mulino (2000), we account for the presence of a two-stage bargaining and differentiate between the first-level bargaining wage equation and the second-level bargaining wage equation.

In particular we ask three main questions: i) Is the first-stage sector-wide wage affected by profit sharing elements? ii) Is there evidence of profit sharing at the second-level bargaining and, if so, how large is it relative to the first level wage? iii) Is the wage premium affected by the specific profit sharing scheme adopted by the firm? Specifically, iiia) does it make any difference to the final wage whether the unions' representatives take active part or not in the design of the profit sharing scheme? And iiib) does the evidence support the idea that a mechanism that relates the pay to employee performance assessments is always a better productivity enhancing means than 'unconditioned' profit sharing?

5.2 A model of decentralised bargaining and efficiency wages

We set up a model where the firm's i real revenue at time t is $A_{it}F_{it}=A_{it}\left(e_{it}N_{it}\right)^{\alpha}$, where A is any factor that improves the real revenue like productivity shifts and demand shocks, e is effort, N is employment. Effort is a positive function of the paid real wage, W, relative to the alternative real wage Ω, and rises with the productivity enhancing effect of paying higher wages, captured by β, hence: $e=\left(W/\Omega\right)^{\beta}$ and $(\partial e/\partial W)(W/e)=\beta$. For $\beta=0$, $e=1$ and efficiency

[2] 'The firm level wage increases should be strictly related to the results achieved by the realization of programs, agreed by the parts, whose objectives may be productivity increases, quality increases and other competitive elements with the inclusion of productivity margins, in excess of those already recognised in the national contract, as well as results linked to the firm economic condition' (from the July Agreement).

[3] The cited literature on decentralized bargaining and efficiency wages is mostly concerned with theory.

wages are absent. We assume that both parts, when bargaining the wage at the sector level, take into account the effort induced by the bargained wage and assume that level of effort to be the minimum one, i.e. the level obtained in firms that show the lowest productivity response to paying higher wages (Muysken and van Veen, 1996), hence at the sector level $\beta = \underline{\beta}$ and $e = \underline{e}$.

$\overline{W}_{st}$ defines the real wage bargained at the national level for each sector s; employment is assumed to be unilaterally decided by the employer confederation in order to maximise the average firm's profit.[4] Let γ_s be the union power at the sector level and R the reservation wage. Hence, for each sector we have:

$$\overline{W}_{st} = \underset{W}{\arg\max} \left[\left(W_{st} - R_t \right) \right]^{\gamma_s/(1-\gamma_s)} \left[A_{st} F_{st} - W_{st} N_{st} \right]$$

$$\text{subject to } A_{st} \frac{\partial F_{st}}{\partial N_{st}} = W_{st}$$

The wage solving the constrained maximisation satisfies expression (5.1) below according to which the wage bargained at the sector level is a mark up on the reservation wage and the mark up is increasing in union power and in $\underline{\beta}$ (see Appendix):[5]

$$\overline{W}_{st} = R_t + \frac{\gamma_s}{(1-\gamma_s)(1-\underline{\beta})} \frac{A_{st} F_{st} - W_{st} N_{st}}{N_{st}} \tag{5.1}$$

The second step bargaining is formalised in an analogous way but with different fall-backs; had the decentralised wage agreement to fail, the sector wage applies and consequently the firm's fall back is:

$$\overline{\Pi}_{it} = A_{it} \left(\left(\frac{\overline{W}_{st}}{R_t} \right)^{\beta_i} N_{it} \right)^{\alpha} - \overline{W}_{st} N_{it}$$

At the second level bargaining, whether the firm pays a wage premium or not depends on the firm's 'ability to pay' the premium, ability which arises if the incentive mechanism is effective; precisely, according to the agreement, the amount

[4] Unions and employers also bargain over wage differentials across skills so that workforce composition is also unilaterally decided by the firm together with total employment.

[5] Alternatively equation (5.1) can be expressed in the following way:

$$\overline{W}_{st} = R_t + \frac{\gamma_s}{\gamma_s + (1-\gamma_s)(1-\underline{\beta})} \frac{A_{st} F_{st} - R_t N_{st}}{N_{st}}$$

of wage premium depends on the additional productivity. Again, this implies that the second level wage is agreed only if the payment of the premium does not force a reduction of employment; this assumption, which we write as: $\partial N / \partial W|_{\bar{W}_{st}} = 0$, amounts to assuming that the second stage bargaining is 'strongly' efficient (Mc Donald and Solow, 1981).[6] The final wage is therefore the solution of the following maximization:

$$\max_{W} \left[N_{it} \left(W_{it} - \bar{W}_{st} \right) \right]^{\gamma/(1-\gamma)_i} \left[\left(A_{it} F_{it} - W_{it} N_{it} \right) - \bar{\Pi}_{it} \right]$$

where γ is union power at the decentralised level. The first order condition yields (see Appendix):

$$W_{it} = \bar{W}_{st} + \frac{\gamma}{(1-\gamma)(1-m\beta)} \frac{\left(\Pi_{it} - \bar{\Pi}_{it} \right)}{N_{it}} \tag{5.2}$$

where $m = \alpha(AF/WN) = |\eta| / |\eta| - 1$ is the price mark-up over marginal cost and η is the elasticity of demand.[7]

The wage drift is therefore a share of the *additional profitability* due to the increased effort; the share is larger the higher the union power, the higher the mark-up and the higher the elasticity of effort to the relative wage.[8]

---

6 The same assumption is made by Margolis and Salvanes (2001).

7 Recall that, as assumed in first stage bargaining, the representative average firm is on its labour demand curve; however, this may not be the case for the individual firm.

8 Notice that, since the pay-out of the wage premium is conditional on the event of the *additional productivity*, in principle any firm could sign the decentralised contract. However, 20 per cent of firms in our sample (and 30 per cent at the national level; see Casadio and D'Aurizio, 2001) have not signed the decentralised contract. Data refer to year 1999, and to firms with at least 50 employees. We can think of various reasons that may justify firms' preference not to sign the decentralised contracts:

a. the management is myopic and does not foresee the potential productivity improvement;
b. the firm is satisfied with the existing labour effort;
c. transaction costs are higher than the potential additional productivity;
d. the decentralised wage contract is an insufficient mechanism to induce additional productivity and should be complemented with other factors/conditions which are too costly to implement.

5.3 Empirical model, methodological issues and data

The empirical counterparts of equations (5.1) and (5.2) must account, first of all, for the wage dynamics; in particular, we expect the wage to show considerable inertia and the profit variable to affect the wage with some lags; at this regard recall that the collective sector-wide wage contracts are set every two years – although negotiations may be lengthy so that the actual arrangements are finally struck beyond two years from the previous ones. As far as decentralised bargaining is concerned, according to the July Agreement, matters regarding earnings should also be negotiated every two years. In order to capture all possible lags, the precise specification of the lag distribution of the dependent variable and of the regressor of interest is decided empirically on the basis of first and second order residuals auto-correlation tests.

Specifically regarding equation (5.1), we let time dummies, industry dummies and lags of the dependent variable to capture elements that may affect the reservation wage; the estimated equation is the following:

$$\bar{W}_{st} = z_s + z_t + pdl\left[\ \bar{W}_{st-1}\right] + pdl\left[\left(\frac{\Pi}{N}\right)_{st}\right] + \varepsilon_{it} \tag{5.3}$$

where *pdl* indicates polynomial distributed lag and ε_{it} is the error term.

Notice that the sector-wide profit per employee is an indicator of 'the sector profitability conditions' which are explicitly mentioned in the collective national wage agreements.

The estimation of the firm, second-level wage equation, defined in equation (5.2), encounters an additional problem since $\bar{\Pi}_{it}$, the profit the firm would have gained had not signed the second level contract, is not observable. In order to obtain an estimable wage equation, we make use of two alternative proxies for this counterfactual. In one case $\bar{\Pi}_{it}$ is simply proxied by the average profit of firms, belonging to the same sector, that have not adopted the pay for performance decentralised contract. In a second case, $\bar{\Pi}_{it}$ is the profit per employee of a 'companion' firm identified on the basis of a propensity score – the conditional probability of adopting the pay for performance decentralized contract – and matched according to the nearest neighbour method.

As it is clear from equation (5.2), the first level sector-wide minimum wage is controlled for in the second stage bargaining. However, from the estimation point of view, the lagged dependent variable, adjusted by the inclusion of sector and year dummies (z_s and z_t) results to be suitable to capture both the nationally set contractual wage and the inertia related to firm-level wage. Notice finally that the extent of autocorrelation in the deviation of firm profits per employee from the counterfactual value, may be less important than for the level of profits per employee; again however, we will consider this aspect empirically.

The estimated equations, in the two cases, are the following:

$$W_{it} = z_s + z_t + \lambda\ W_{it-1} + \alpha_1 \left(\left(\frac{\Pi}{N} \right)_{it} - \left(\frac{\bar{\Pi}}{N} \right)_{st|no\,dec} \right) + \varepsilon_{it} \tag{5.4.1}$$

$$W_{it} = z_s + z_t + \lambda\ W_{it-1} + \alpha_2 \left(\left(\frac{\Pi}{N} \right)_{it} - \left(\frac{\bar{\Pi}}{N} \right)_{jt|match} \right) + \varepsilon_{it} \tag{5.4.2}$$

Both for the first-level and the second-level wage equations, the estimation strategy must account for the following methodological issues. Profits are endogenous for two reasons: first of all, there is a precise negative accounting relationship between operating profits and wages: as wages rise profits decline, *ceteris paribus*. Secondly, in presence of efficiency wages, an opposite force comes into play since a rise in the relative wage rises effort hence labour productivity and the rate of profit, *ceteris paribus*. If not accounted for the first correlation biases the profit coefficient downward while the second one may produce an upward bias.

Firm's profits are also correlated with various firm characteristics; some of these are observable and controlled for but others are unobservable (e.g. quality of management) or not present in firm level data (personal characteristics of managers and employees – for example: experience, age).

To assess the extent of these issues, we compare pooled OLS with first difference GMM estimates which take care of unobservable fixed effects, profit endogeneity and lagged dependent variable.

Our main interest is to estimate the extent of profit sharing; since the structural parameters of interest γ, β and m cannot be identified, the effectiveness of efficiency enhancing factors as well as the unions' representatives bargaining power, are assessed by confronting various sub-samples of firms. In particular, using some of the questions present in the questionnaire, we identify, among the firms that signed a decentralised contract explicitly including a pay-for-performance clause, the following sub-groups (see Table 5.1):

a) Firms that adopt formal performance assessments[9] explicitly aimed at determining the wage premium. As long as the wage premium is linked to the actual performance and such a link is formally assessed, we expect motivation and hence effort, to be relatively higher.
b) Firms that negotiate the incentive mechanism with the firm unions' representatives. Since incentive systems are normally designed by the management, this sub-sample of firms is likely to be representative of companies with a relatively high union power.

[9] Formal performance assessment procedures may regard the output of the effort (such as quantities and qualities of products, services or processes) or the input of the effort (such as learning of superior organizational behaviours or technical competences). While the former has a short run perspective, the latter has a long run one. Unfortunately, in our empirical analysis we cannot make a distinction between these two categories.

Table 5.1. Distribution of firms by groups

	Percentage of all firms	Percentage of firms with decentralised contract
Performance assessment	75.2	72.9
Negotiation of the incentive scheme	49.0	50.3
Extended adoption of decentralised contract	37.8	39.1
Performance assessment and negotistion of the incentive scheme	37.1	38.0
Of which adopting extending decentralised bargaining	63.5	
Pay for performance decentralised bargaining	86.5	100.0
Total firms	100.0	

c) Firms that since July 1993 have been more keen to negotiate with the unions' representatives a broader set of aspects regarding the firm's life. As long as these firms represent those in which the management and the unions' representatives act in a collaborative way, we expect efficiency enhancing mechanisms to be, here, relatively more effective.
d) Firms that both formally assess employee performance and negotiate the incentive mechanisms with the firm unions' representatives. Such firms, where a formal performance-premium link exists and where unions' representatives have the power to bargain its design with the management, could indeed be a significant example of those concerted situations referred to in the previous group.

The dataset is composed of 100 manufacturing firms with at least 50 employees, located in Northern Italy (province of Bergamo). For each firm we have balance sheet data from 1990 to 1999 and information from a detailed survey conducted in 1999 on various aspects of the firm's organisation, workplace practices and industrial relations. Indeed we use some of these information to define the above sub samples.

As described in Table 5.2 the widest adoption of decentralised bargaining takes place in the large firms of the metalworking sector; a large majority of chemical firms also adopted the decentralised bargaining while it was more limited in the textile sector and in firms with less than 100 employees. Although half of the firms that engaged both in a second step bargaining and in formal assessment procedures belongs to the metalworking sector, the chemical industry shows, once again, the highest frequency together with firms counting between 200 and 500 employees. On the other hand, incentive schemes are typically negotiated in the metalworking sector; quite interestingly, the textile industry, from several years under the threat of production de-localisations, is also likely to include the negotiation of incentive schemes in the decentralised bargaining agreement. Likewise small-medium firms (with less then 200 employees) tend to utilize the latter mechanisms whereas medium-large firms prefer the tool of performance assessment.

Table 5.2. Distribution of groups of firms by firm size and sector

	Pay for performance decentralised bargaining		Pay for performance decentralised bargaining and performance assessment		Pay for performance decentralised bargaining and negotiation of incentive mechanisms		Pay for performance decentralised bargaining and extended adoption of the decentralised contract		Total
	no	yes	no	yes	no	yes	no	yes	
Size									
50-99	32.5	16.7	25.0	6.4	22.3	16.3	35.5	13.5	14.0
100–199	58.8	36.9	44.8	35.8	34.4	43.9	64.5	37.6	39.4
200–499	8.8	30.0	18.2	39.7	33.3	21.5	0	30.8	30.9
>500	0	16.4	12.1	18.2	10.0	18.3	0	18.1	15.7
Total	100.0	100.0	100.0	100.0	100.0	100.0	100.0	100.0	100.0
Sector									
Metal-working	57.3	47.6	51.2	46.1	51.7	45.4	36.8	42.9	48.2
Chemical	7.6	21.7	14.9	26.3	25.7	14.3	10.5	21.1	21.6
Textile	34.3	14.5	25.8	11.5	16.8	17.5	47.4	15.0	17.3
Other	3.5	16.1	8.1	16.2	5.8	22.8	5.3	21.0	12.9
Total	100.0	100.0	100.0	100.0	100.0	100.0	100.0	100.0	100.0

5.4 Results

The estimation of the first-level contractual wage is reported in Table 5.3. The dependent variable is the sector contractual wage normalised using sector production price indices. Columns 1–3 present the results obtained by pooling the observations and using OLS, columns 4–7 employ first differences GMM. As expected, the bargained wage shows a strong inertia; the profit per employee is significant only if lagged two periods, a feature that will be confirmed also using GMM and that may be related to the biannual bargaining. The profit sharing coefficient is 0.03 and essentially invariant if a second lag on the dependent variable is added.

This coefficient turns out to be downwards biased: when using first differences and GMM, hence controlling for unobservable fixed effect and the endogeneity of the regressor and of the lagged dependent variable, the coefficient rises to 0.07 as reported in columns 6 and 7. Notice that tests for the residuals first and second order autocorrelations, which guarantee, together with the Sargan test for overidentifying restrictions, the validity of the instrument set, are correct[10] only if the profit per employee enters with two lags, which confirms the result using OLS. Notice also that, because of the lags, the actual estimation of the preferred specification in column 6 is from 1993; the length of the sample is therefore insufficient to compare the wage dynamics before and after July 1993. In column 7 we check if the first renegotiation, which took place in 1997, signed a significant change in the extent of rent sharing. We let the rent sharing coefficient vary from 1997 onwards but the results seem to exclude a significant change after 1997.

Tables 5.4 and 5.5 report the estimated regressions for the second level wage. Here wages are at the firm level and, again, normalised using sector production prices. In Table 5.4, for each firm i belonging to sector s, the counterfactual profit per employee, from which deviations are computed, is taken to be the average profit per employee of the firms in sector s that have not adopted a pay for performance decentralised contract. In Table 5.4a observations are pooled, OLS are used and the estimation covers the period 1990–99. Tables 5.4b and 5.4c use GMM first differences and differ only for the sample period: 1990–99 in 5.4b and 1994–99 in the last table. In all tables each column refers to a specific sub group of firms; in this case estimation always include the inverse Mill's ratio even if in most cases they happen to be collinear with other regressors and hence excluded from the estimation.

By comparing the first column, which considers the sub-group that adopted the pay for performance decentralised bargaining, across Tables 5.4a–5.4c, it is clear that OLS produce a severe downward bias of the rent sharing coefficient, as for the first level wage; the coefficient rises from 0.03, if estimated using OLS, to 0.09 using first difference GMM on the period 1990–99 to 0.10 in first difference GMM from 1994 to 1999. On the contrary, by changing the estimation from OLS to first differences GMM, the lagged dependent variable looses statistical significance; the residual autocorrelation tests however are correct once the first lag of the endogenous variables included in the instrument set is sufficiently long.

By comparing across the identified groups of firms, in Tables 5.4b and 5.4c, we observe that signing a decentralised pay for performance agreement does not guarantee to the wage earners a significant rent sharing. In particular we find that for the sub groups defined either on the basis of performance assessment procedures – but independently of the parts that take part in the design of the incentive scheme (column 2), or on the basis of the parts designing the incentive mechanism – but independently of the presence of a formal performance-premium link (column 3), the rent sharing coefficient is low and not statistically significant. We

[10] We expect a significant first order autocorrelation, since we use first difference transformation, but absence of second order autocorrelation.

Table 5.3. First-level bargaining, dependent variable: sector wage $\bar{W}_{st}$, all firms, 1990–99

Regressors ↓	OLS pooled			GMM first differences			
	1	2	3	4	5	6•	7••
$\left(\frac{\Pi}{N}\right)_{s,t-1}$	–0.007 (0.30)			0.125 0.00)***	0.128 (0.00)***		
$\left(\frac{\Pi}{N}\right)_{s,t-2}$		0.033 (0.01)***	0.026 (0.03)**			0.069 (0.00)***	0.068 (0.00)***
$d_{97-99}\left(\frac{\Pi}{N}\right)_{s,t-2}$							–0.012 (0.86)
$\bar{W}_{s,t-1}$	0.746 (0.00)***	0.674 (0.00)***	0.635 (0.00)***	0.256 (0.08)	0.743 (0.00)***	0.907 (0.00)***	0.902 (0.00)***
$\Delta\bar{W}_{s,t-1}$			0.155 (0.00)***		–0.512 (0.02)**	–0.790 (0.00)***	–0.778 (0.00)***
Obs (nr. Firms)	694	593	593	485 (88)	485 (88)	485 (88)	485 (88)
Adj R	0.92	0.92	0.92				
Sargan (P–val)				$X^2(20)$ 28.10 (0.14)	$X^2(20)$ 20.80 (0.41)	$X^2(20)$ 23.46 (0.27)	$X^2(19)$ 23.70 (0.21)
Ar1 (P-val)				–0.98 (0.33)	1.14 (0.25)	2.19 (0.03)**	2.07 (0.04)**
Ar2 (P-val)				4.54 (0.00)***	–0.66 (0.51)	–1.43 (0.15)	–1.35 (0.18)

Notes:
All estimations include time trend, year dummies and three industry dummies. Instruments: industry dummies, trend, time dummies, $(\Pi/N)_{s,t-2}$, $W_{i,t-1}$, GMM $\bar{W}_s$ from $t-4$ backwards. *P* value in parenthesis. Significant at the level: *** = 10%, ** = 5%, * = 1%.

• Because of lags, the actual estimation is from 1993.

•• Instruments include $d_{97-99}(\Pi/N)_{s,t-2}$.

Table 5.4a. Second-level bargaining, Counterfactual: profit per employee of firms of the same sector that have not adopted a pay for performance (pfp) decentralised contract. OLS Pooled 1990–99

	Pay for performance decentralized contract	Pay for performance decentralized contract and performance assessment	Pay for performance decentralized contract and bargaining of the incentive scheme	Pay for performance decentralized contract, performance assessment and bargaining of the incentive scheme••	Pay for performance decentralized contract and extended adoption of the decentralized contract•
$\left(\frac{\Pi}{N}\right)_{it} - \left(\frac{\Pi}{N}\right)_{st\mid nodec}$	0.027 (0.00)***	0.030 (0.01)***	0.036 (0.00)***	0.054 (0.00)***	0.026 (0.12)
W_{t-1}	0.828 (0.00)***	0.744 (0.00)***	0.767 (0.00)***	0.724 (0.00)***	0.788 (0.00)***
Inverse Mill's ratio	1.83 (0.34)	–3.738 (0.14)			
Obs (nr. Firms)	524	274	274	150	194
Adj R	0.83	0.82	0.77	0.79	0.72

Table 5.4b. Second-level bargaining, Counterfactual: profit per employee of firms of the same sector that have not adopted the decentralised contract. GMM First differences 1990–99

	Pay for performance decentralized contract	Pay for performance decentralized contract and performance assessment	Pay for performance decentralized contract and bargaining of the incentive scheme	Pay for performance decentralized contract, performance assessment and bargaining of the incentive scheme••	Pay for performance decentralized contract and extended adoption of the decentralized contract•
$\left(\frac{\Pi}{N}\right)_{it} - \left(\frac{\Pi}{N}\right)_{st\mid nodec}$	0.090 (0.04)**	0.046 (0.26)	0.004 (0.93)	0.088(0.04)**	0.085 (0.01)***
W_{t-1}	0.225 (0.25)	0.172 (0.40)	0.276 (0.10)*	0.107 (0.54)	0.017 (0.92)
Obs (nr. Firms)	451 (67)	236 (35)	237 (34)	129 (19)	167 (25)
Sargan (P-val)	$X^2(27)$ 24.38 (0.61)	$X^2(27)$ 31.70 (0.24)	$X^2(27)$ 20.01 (0.83)	$X^2(27)$ 27.20 (0.45)	$X^2(31)$ 29.87 (0.52)
Ar1 (P-val)	–2.52 (0.01)***	–2.38 (0.02)**	–2.83 (0.00)***	–1.79 (0.07)*	–2.02 (0.04)**
Ar2 (P-val)	0.10 (0.92)	–0.17 (0.86)	0.00 (0.99)	–0.89 (0.37)	–0.28 (0.78)

Notes:
All estimations include time trend, year dummies and three industry dummies. Instruments: size dummies, industry dummies, time dummies, Inverse Mills ratio, GMM W_t from $t-3$ to $t-5$; GMM deviation of profit per employee from $t-4$ to $t-5$. Significant at the level: *** = 10%, ** = 5%, * = 1%.

• Because of lags, the actual estimation is from 1993.

•• Instruments include $d_{97-99}(\Pi/N)_{s,t-2}$.

Table 5.4c. Second-level bargaining, Counterfactual: profit per employee of firms of the same sector that have not adopted the decentralised contract. GMM First differences 1994–99

	Pay for performance decentralized contract	Pay for performance decentralized contract and performance assessment	Pay for performance decentralized contract and bargaining of the incentive scheme	Pay for performance decentralized contract, performance assessment and bargaining of the incentive scheme••	Pay for performance decentralized contract and extended adoption of the decentralized contract•
$\left(\frac{\Pi}{N}\right)_{it} - \left(\frac{\Pi}{N}\right)_{st\|no\,dec}$	0.102 (0.02)**	0.060 (0.19)	0.011 (0.83)	0.098 (0.04)**	0.081 (0.02)**
W_{t-1}	0.157 (0.44)	0.148 (0.49)	0.242 (0.19)	0.068 (0.73)	0.045 (0.83)
Obs (nr. Firms)	354 (67)	185 (35)	182 (34)	100 (19)	131 (25)
Sargan P-val	$X^2(26)$ 22.97 (0.63)	$X^2(26)$ 27.63 (0.38)	$X^2(26)$ 17.33 (0.90)	$X^2(26)$ 23.06 (0.63)	$X^2(33)$ 29.73 (0.63)
Ar1 P-val	–2.20 (0.03)**	–2.27 (0.02)**	–2.56 (0.01)***	–1.64 (0.10)*	–1.96 (0.05)**
Ar2 P-val	–0.42 (0.68)	–0.27 (0.78)	–0.10 (0.92)	–1.06 (0.29)	–0.47 (0.64)

Notes:
All estimations include time trend, year dummies and three industry dummies. Instruments as above except where indicated. Significant at the level: *** = 10%, ** = 5%, * = 1%.

• GMM $\overline{W}_s$ from $t-3$ to $t-6$.

•• GMM deviation of profit per employee from $t-4$ to $t-7$.

interpret this result as indicating that the efficiency enhancing effect is not sufficiently activated in these contexts nor the union's representatives strength succeeds in grasping part of the rent. On the contrary, those firms that extended the decentralised firm-level contract to other aspects of the firm's life (last column) show a statistically significant coefficient which rises from OLS to first differences GMM to around 0.08. Similar results are obtained for those firms that couple performance assessments and negotiation of the specific incentive scheme with the unions' representatives .[11]

Tables 5.5a and 5.5b report the results for the second level wage again using first differences GMM but employing a propensity score matching technique to obtain the counterfactual profit per employee. The two tables employ two different propensity scores, that is the probability of the 'treatment' before the actual treatment takes place, where the treatment, in this case, refers to the adoption of a pay for performance decentralised contract. Since the actual decentralised contract comes into play in 1993, the propensity score is computed in 1992. In one case the probability of treatment depends only on firm's size and sector; in a second case it also depends on the level of the average wage in the years before 1992, measured using three year moving average over the years 1990–92 (see Table 5.6). The propensity score matching is penalised by the sample size: in 1992 we have on the whole 59 firms that adopted the decentralised contract and 8 that did not; the balancing property being satisfied, the number of treated firms and the number of controls in the two cases are the following:

Inferior bound of propensity score	Pay for performance decentralised contract			
	Probit *a*		Probit *b*	
	yes	no	No	Yes
0	-	-	2	10
0.4	-	-	0	1
0.6	6	19	4	5
0.8	2	40	2	43
Total	8	59	8	59

Table 5.5a uses propensity score from Probit (a) and Table 5.5b uses propensity score from Probit (b). On the whole the results are qualitatively similar to those of Tables 5.4 although the rent sharing coefficients are smaller in size.

[11] Instruments' time lags had to be increased by one period in these two cases in order to correct residual first order autocorrelation test and/or the sign of the lagged dependent variable.

Table 5.5a. Second-level bargaining, Counterfactual: profit per employee of companion firm identified using propensity score matching (1) in Table 5.6. GMM First differences 1994-99

	Pay for performance decentralized contract	Pay for performance decentralized contract and performance assessment	Pay for performance decentralized contract and bargaining of the incentive scheme	Pay for performance decentralized contract, performance assessment and bargaining of the incentive scheme••	Pay for performance decentralized contract and extended adoption of the decentralized contract•
$\left(\frac{\Pi}{N}\right)_{it} - \left(\frac{\Pi}{N}\right)_{jt\vert match}$	0.050 (0.07)*	0.038 (0.13)	0.039 (0.14)	0.045 (0.04)**	0.070 (0.00)***
W_{t-1}	0.200 (0.33)	0.197 (0.40)	0.117 (0.57)	0.134 (0.51)	0.041 (0.81)
Obs (nr. Firms)	266 (53)	146 (28)	150 (29)	88 (16)	114 (21)
Sargan P-val	$X^2(32)$ 22.16 (0.90)	$X^2(29)$ 22.94 (0.78)	$X^2(32)$ 32.80 (0.43)	$X^2(29)$ 34.79 (0.21)	$X^2(29)$ 27.96 (0.52)
Ar1 P-val	–2.43 (0.01)***	–2.23 (0.03)**	–2.01 (0.04)**	–2.06 (0.04)**	–2.20 (0.03)**
Ar2 P-val	–0.26 (0.80)	–0.32 (0.75)	–0.87 (0.38)	–0.65 (0.51)	–0.55 (0.58)

Notes:
All estimations include time trend, year dummies and three industry dummies. Instruments: size dummies, industry dummies, time dummies, Inverse Mills ratio, GMM W_t from $t-3$ to $t-5$; GMM deviations of profit per employee from $t-2$ to $t-5$. Significant at the level: *** = 10%, ** = 5%, * = 1%.

•• GMM W_t- from $t-2$ to $t-4$ and GMM deviations of profit per employee from $t-3$ to $t-4$.

• GMM W_t from $t-2$ to $t-5$ and GMM deviations of profit per employee from $t-3$ to $t-4$.

Table 5.5b. Second-level bargaining. Counterfactual: profit per employee of companion firm identified using propensity score matching (b) in Table 5.6. GMM First differences 1994-99

	Pay for performance decentralized contract	Pay for performance decentralized contract and performance assessment	Pay for performance decentralized contract and bargaining of the incentive scheme	Pay for performance decentralized contract, performance assessment and bargaining of the incentive scheme♦♦	Pay for performance decentralized contract and extended adoption of the decentralized contract♦
$\left(\frac{\Pi}{N}\right)_{it} - \left(\frac{\Pi}{N}\right)_{jt\mid match}$	0.045 (0.01)***	0.022 (0.12)	0.037 (0.02)**	0.134 (0.36)	0.049 (0.01)***
W_{t-1}	0.004 (0.62)	0.059 (0.57)	0.082 (0.44)	0.024 (0.30)	0.139 (0.92)
Obs (nr. Firms)	238 (45)	133 (24)	146 (27)	80 (14)	91 (16)
Sargan P-val	$X^2(52)$ 55.12 (0.36)	$X^2(52)$ 48.89 (0.60)	$X^2(52)$ 61.89 (0.16)	$X^2(25)$ 20.04 (0.74)	$X^2(30)$ 29.76 (0.48)
Ar1 P-val	–6.35 (0.00)***	–5.38 (0.00)***	–5.20 (0.00)***	–4.11 (0.00)***	–4.22 (0.00)***
Ar2 P-val	–0.54 (0.59)	–0.64 (0.52)	–1.11 (0.26)	–0.58 (0.56)	–0.48 (0.63)

Notes:
All estimations include time trend, year dummies and three industry dummies. Instruments: size dummies, industry dummies, time dummies, Inverse Mills ratio, GMM W_t from $t-2$ backwards; GMM deviations of profit per employee from $t-2$ backwards. Significant at the level: *** = 10%, ** = 5%, * = 1%.

♦♦ GMM W_t- from $t-2$ to $t-4$ and GMM deviations of profit per employee from $t-3$ to $t-4$.

♦ GMM W_t from $t-2$ to $t-5$ and GMM deviations of profit per employee from $t-3$ to $t-4$.

Table 5.6. Propensity score probits

	Coefficient (p value)	
	(a)	(b)
Size: less than100 employees	–1.21 (0.05)**	–1.27 (0.10)*
Size: between 100 and 199 employees	–0.02 (0.15)	–0.64 (0.32)
Sector: metalworking and mechanical	–0.89 (0.13)	–5.82
Sector: textile	–0.91(0.18)	–6.02 (0.00)**
Moving average wage 1992–99		–0.26 (0.95)
Constant	2.54 (0.00) ***	7.39 (0.00)**
Nr. of observations	67	55
Pseudo R^2	0.14	0.23

Note: Significant at the level: *** = 10%, ** = 5%, * = 1%.

Since all equations are estimated in levels, the sizes of the coefficients are not readily comparable; Table 5.7 reports the corresponding wage elasticity (computed at the mean) and the wage change, as a percentage of the average wage, due to a change of one standard deviation of the profit per employee (for the first level bargaining) or due to one standard deviation increase of the profit per employee deviations from the counterfactual (for the second level bargaining).

Although the estimated wage elasticity is normally larger in the first level bargaining, being 3 per cent with respect to around 1.5 per cent in the second level bargaining, if we consider the variability of the profit per employee (or of its deviation from the counterfactual in the second level bargaining), the extent of rent sharing is actually larger at the second level bargaining. This ranges from 3 per cent to 6 per cent of the average wage in response to a standard deviation increase of the deviation of profit per employee from its benchmark, compared to a 1 per cent increase of the average sector wage in response to one standard deviation increase of the average sector-wide profit per employee.

In firms that adopt an 'extended version' of the decentralised contract, wages can share a part of the additional profit per employee and such a share amounts to around 6 per cent of the average wage; this percentage turns out to be slightly higher for those firms that both negotiate the incentive scheme and assess employees' performance.

On the whole our results confirm that where unions' representatives can guarantee and justify the incentive scheme to the workforce or, which is analogous, where collaborative industrial relations are present within the firm, the adoption of the decentralised contract produces a significant impact on the wage and, we expect, also on the profit per employee.

Table 5.7. Wage elasticity and wage changes in response to profit per employee changes

First level bargaining		Elasticity of the sector contractual wage to sector-wide profit per employee (computed at mean values)	Sector-wide contractual wage change, in percentage of average sector contractual wage, due to one standard deviation increase of the sector-wide profit per employee
All firms		0.03	1.01
Second level bargaining		Elasticity of the wage to deviation of profit per employee from counterfactual profit per employee (computed at mean values)	Wage change, in percentage of average wage, due to one standard deviation increase of the deviation of profit per employee from counterfactual profit per employee.
Firms with pay for performance decentralised contract			
Counterfactual profit per employee proxied by profit per employee of firms in the same sector without decentralised bargaining		0.016	6.24
Counterfactual profit per employee proxied by the profit per employee of the companion form matched using propensity score and nearest neighbour matching	(a)	0.019	3.58
	(b)	0.015	2.93
Firms with pay for performance decentralised contract and extend adoption of the decentralised contract			
Counterfactual profit per employee proxied by profit per employee of firms in the same sector without decentralised bargaining		0.013	5.72
Counterfactual profit per employee proxied by the profit per employee of the companion form matched using propensity score and nearest neighbour matching	(a)	0.030	6.06
	(b)	0.014	4.65

Firms with pay for performance decentralised contract and bargaining of the incentive scheme			
Counterfactual profit per employee proxied by profit per employee of firms in the same sector without decentralised bargaining		ns	ns
Counterfactual profit per employee proxied by the profit per employee of the companion form matched using propensity score and nearest neighbour matching	(a)	ns	ns
	(b)	0.014	2.83
Firms with pay for performance decentralised contract, performance assessment and bargaining of the incentive scheme			
Counterfactual profit per employee proxied by profit per employee of firms in the same sector without decentralised bargaining		0.010	6.95
Counterfactual profit per employee proxied by the profit per employee of the companion form matched using propensity score and nearest neighbour matching	(a)	0.017	4.05
	(b)	ns	ns

Note: ns = non statistically significant. (a) and (b) refer to table 5.6.

To compare the state of industrial relations in the previously identified sub groups, Fig. 5.1 plots the distribution of firms according to the degree of agreement regarding the following statement: 'Unions' representatives help finding the best way to improve the firm's performance'. The question is part of the questionnaire surveying the view of the respondent who is usually the personnel manager or the owner of the firm.

Managers whose firm use employee performance assessments mostly disagree on the statement; on the contrary managers whose firms adopt employee performance assessment *and* bargain the incentive scheme, mostly agree with the statement; likewise managers of firms that, after 1993, are more keen to negotiate with the unions' representatives on various matter are also quite likely to agree on the statement. The fact that these two groups of firms are also those where the second level rent sharing is larger and significant, confirms that efficiency is reinforced by the presence both good incentive scheme and good industrial relations.

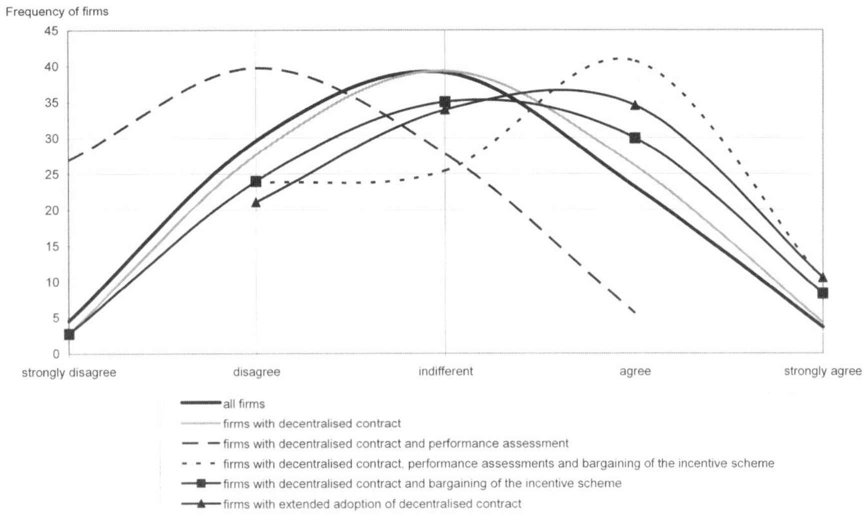

Fig. 5.1. Unions' representatives help finding the best way to improve firm's performance

5.5 Conclusions

On the assumption of a two-level bargaining and efficiency wages, we have derived two estimable wage equations, one for the first level sector wage and one for the final firm level wage set at the second stage bargaining. The existing theoretical literature on wage determination in presence of bargaining and efficiency wages finds that the wage premium obtained when bargaining and efficiency wages interact is higher than the premium obtained in presence of bargaining alone. We show that the second level rent sharing depends on the additional profit obtainable if more effective productivity incentive mechanisms are adopted.

The so called July Agreement signed by the Italian social parties and government in 1993, introduced a decentralised firm level bargaining to favour efficiency which marked an important change in the wage determination and in industrial relations; for this reason we use it to test the theoretical result of the reinforcing wage effect of bargaining and efficiency wages.

We derive a first-level sector-wide wage equation and a second level wage equation and estimate both of them on a sample of Italian firms located in Northern Italy for which survey data on industrial relations and various organisational aspects are available, together with balance sheets from 1990 to 1999. The main findings are the following.

The rent sharing accruing to the sector contractual wage at the first level bargaining is computed on the sector-wide profit per employee; according to our estimates the elasticity of the sector wage to the sector profit per employee is 3 per cent, which corresponds to an increase of the average sector wage of 1 per cent in response to one standard deviation rise of the profit per employee.

At the second-level bargaining the rent sharing is on the additional profit per employee obtainable as long as more effective incentive schemes are adopted, given union power and the firm market share. According to our estimates, for firms that signed the pay for performance decentralised contract the elasticity of the firm wage to the additional profit per employee ranges between 1.5 per cent and 2 per cent, slightly rising after 1993. However, one standard deviation rise of the measured additional profit induces an increase of the average wage which ranges between 3 per cent and 6 per cent, hence considerably larger that the response of the first level wage.

At the second level bargaining the extent of rent sharing appears to differ across firms. At this regard we identify two subgroups where the rent sharing is relatively higher and significant: one in which the decentralised contract is extensively adopted, that is union's representatives negotiate on various aspects of the firm's life, and the other one where unions' representatives take part in the design of the incentive scheme and performance assessments guarantee a link between the effort and the wage premium. In these two groups, we estimate that a 5 per cent to 7 per cent of the wage is due to rent sharing on the additional profit per employee. On the contrary, the adoption of performance assessments, independently of the unions' participation or, analogously, the unions' bargaining of the incentive scheme regardless of the presence employees performance assessments do not seem to produce sufficient additional profit to be shared by the employees under the form of higher wages.

Appendix

First stage bargaining

In the first stage bargaining all variables are referred to the sector. The first stage wage $\overline{W}_{st}$ is obtained by solving the following constrained maximisation:

$$\max_{W} \left[(W_{st} - R_t)\right]^{\gamma_s/(1-\gamma_s)} \left[A_{st}F_{st} - W_{st}N_{st}\right]$$

$$\text{subject to } A_{st}\frac{\partial F_{st}}{\partial N_{st}} = W_{st}$$

First notice that $\partial F_{st}/\partial W_{st} = \alpha F_{st}\left[(\partial e/\partial W)/e\right]$ which, using the constraint $(\alpha A_{st}F_{st})/N_{st} = W_{st}$ can be written as:

$$\frac{\partial F_{st}}{\partial W_{st}} = \frac{\beta N_{st}}{A_{st}} \qquad (5.\text{A1})$$

This is precisely the effect that counterbalances the usual negative impact of the wage in the firm's profits.

Finally, the first stage wage $\bar{W}_{st}$ is obtained by substituting (5.A1) in the first order condition below:

$$\frac{\gamma_s}{1-\gamma_s}\left(\frac{A_{st}F_{st}-W_{st}N_{st}}{W_{st}-R_t}\right)+\left(A_{st}\frac{\partial F_{st}}{\partial W_{st}}-N_{st}\right)=0$$

Second stage bargaining

The second stage bargaining takes place at the firm level and takes as given the wage agreed at the first stage and the profit fall-back. Again, assume Nash bargaining, hence the final wage solves:

$$\max_{W}\ (W_{it}-\bar{W}_{st})^{\frac{\gamma}{1-\gamma}}\left[(A_{it}F_{it}-W_{it}N_{it})-\bar{\Pi}_{st}\right]$$

From the first order condition obtain:

$$\frac{\gamma}{1-\gamma}\frac{(A_{it}F_{it}-W_{it}N_{it})-\bar{\Pi}_{st}}{N_{it}-A_{it}\dfrac{\partial F_{it}}{\partial W_{it}}}=W_{it}-\bar{W}_{st}$$

By substituting for $\partial F_{it}/\partial W_{it}$ obtain:

$$\frac{\gamma}{1-\gamma}\frac{(A_{it}F_{it}-W_{it}N_{it})-\bar{\Pi}_{st}}{N_{it}\left(1-\alpha\dfrac{A_{it}F_{it}}{W_{it}N_{it}}\beta\right)}=W_{it}-\bar{W}_{st}$$

there $(A_{it}F_{it})/(W_{it}N_{it})$ is the inverse of the labour share.

Notice also that from profit maximizing:

$$P_{it}=\frac{\tilde{W}_{it}}{\dfrac{\partial F_{it}}{\partial N_{it}}}\left(1-\frac{1}{|\eta|}\right)^{-1}$$

where $\tilde{W}$ is the nominal wage and η the elasticity of demand.

Substituting for $\partial F_{it}/\partial N_{it}=\alpha\left[(A_{it}F_{it})/N_{it}\right]$ yields:

$$\alpha\frac{P_{it}A_{it}F_{it}}{\tilde{W}_{it}N_{it}}=\left(1-\frac{1}{|\eta|}\right)^{-1}$$

which may be written as:

$$\alpha \frac{A_{it} F_{it}}{W_{it} N_{it}} = m$$

where W is the real wage and m is the mark-up.

References

Black, S. and L. Lynch (2001), 'How to compete: the impact of workplace practices and information technology on productivity', *Review of Economics and Statistics,* **83**(3):434–45.

Black, S. and L. Lynch (2004), 'What's driving the new economy? The benefits of workplace innovation', *Economic Journal,* **114**:97–116.

Blanchflower, D., A. Oswald and P. Sanfey (1996) 'Wages, profits and rent sharing' *Quarterly Journal of Economics,* **111**:227–51.

Casadio, P. and L. D'Aurizio (2001), 'Flessibilità oraria, occupazionale e retributiva nell'industria italiana: complementi o sostituti?' [*Hourly, employment and wage flexibilities in the Italian industry: complements or substitutes?*], *Economia & Lavoro,* **35**(3):71–91.

Cristini, A., A. Gaj, S. Labory and R. Leoni (2003), 'Flat hierarchical structure, bundles of new work practices and firm performance', *Rivista Italiana degli Economisti,* **8**(2):137–65.

Greenan, N. (2003), 'Organisational change, technology, employment and skills: an empirical study of French manufacturing', *Cambridge Journal of Economics,* **27**:287–316.

Ichniowski, C., K. Shaw and G. Prennushi (1997), 'The effects of HRM systems on productivity: a study of steel finishing lines', *American Economic Review,* **87**:291–313.

Kato, T. and M. Morishima (2002), 'The productivity effects of participatory employment practices: evidence from new Japanese panel data', *Industrial Relations,* **4**(4):487–520.

Konings, J. and P. Walsh (1994), 'Evidence of efficiency wage payments in UK firm level panel data', *Economic Journal,* **11**:442–70.

Margolis, D. and K. Salvanes (2001), 'Do firms really share rents with their workers?', *IZA DP 330.*

Martin, C. and G. Garino (2000), 'Efficiency wages and union-firm barganing', *Economics Letters,* **69**:181–85.

Mauleon, A. and V. Vannetelbosch (2003), 'Efficiency wages and union-firm bargaining with private information' *Spanish Economic Review,* **5**(4), 307–16.

Mc Donald, I. and R. Solow (1981), 'Wage bargaining and employment', *American Economic Review,* **71**:896–908.

Mulino, M. (2000), 'Salari di efficienza e livelli multipli di contrattazione'[*Efficiency wages and multiple level of bargaining*], *Rivista di Politica Economica,* **5**:1–28.

Muysken, J. and T. van Veen (1996), 'Efficiency wages and local wage bargaining', *Scandinavian Journal of Economics,* **98**(1):119–27.

Nickell, S. (1996), 'Competition and corporate performance', *Journal of Political Economy,* **104**(4):724–46.

Pini, P. (ed.) (2000), *Premi di partecipazione o premio di risultato? La contrattazione aziendale in Emilia-Romagna dopo il 1993* [Participation or result premium? The firm-level bargaining in Emilia-Romagna after 1993], CLUEB, Bologna.

Stewart, M.B. (1990), 'Union wage differentials, product market influences and the division of rents', *Economic Journal*, **100**:1122–37.

Summers, L. (1988), 'Relative wages, efficiency wages and Keynesian unemployment' *American Economic Review*, **78**:383–8.

PART III

SOCIAL PACTS IN EUROPE

6 Wage Bargaining Institutions in Europe. A Happy Marriage or Preparing for Divorce?

Jelle Visser

University of Amsterdam, The Netherlands

6.1 Introduction

In July 1980, in the wake of the second oil crisis, the Organisation for Economic Co-operation and Development organized a special meeting with trade union officials to discuss two issues about which strong disagreement had arisen: fighting inflation and free collective bargaining. According to the OECD experts, combating inflation 'calls for tight fiscal and non-accommodating policies, notwithstanding the high level of unemployment persisting in a number of countries even before the second oil price shock'. They are confident that 'the resulting worsening of unemployment will be temporary – a side effect of restrictive policies, not their objective' (p. 4).[1] The union officials agree that inflation needs to bc fought, but reject the deflationary cure proposed by the OECD as 'unnecessarily costly, inefficient and indirect' (p. 5). Instead they advocate competition in energy markets and pressure on the OPEC cartel. It seems to me that history has proven the unions right and the OECD experts wrong: the worsening of unemployment resulting from restrictive policies will be far from temporary, develop into long-term unemployment for many, or withdrawal from the labour market, two developments which proof extremely hard to reverse even twenty years later.

The issue of free collective bargaining also divided the discussants. There is agreement that the stagflation of the 1970s – the combination of rising inflation and rising unemployment – had narrowed the space for free collective bargaining and compelled many governments to intervene in wage setting. Both direct and indirect state intervention in wage negotiations – the first by suspending negotiations, imposing a freeze or ceilings; the second by participating in negotiations ('tripartism') and sponsoring central coordination – reached a peak in the late 1970s (Fig. 6.1). The participants feared that 'genuinely free collective bargaining could be limited to "fair weather" periods' (p. 17). The OECD policy makers believe, however, that after restrictive policies will have delivered lower inflationary expectations, and 'with more slack in the labour market, union demands will be more subdued' and 'therefore lessening the potential conflict between bargaining and economic policy' (p. 18). On this point, history will proof the OECD experts

[1] Report of the meeting of trade union experts and OECD experts from the Economics and Statistics Department and Directorate for Social Affairs, Manpower and Education, 30th June – 2nd July 1980, Paris: OECD, *mimeo*, p. 4.

right: the non-accommodating monetary policies of the 1980s and 1990s, resulting in significantly higher levels of unemployment, forced wage restraint on union and thus prepared the conditions for a return to 'free' wage bargaining.

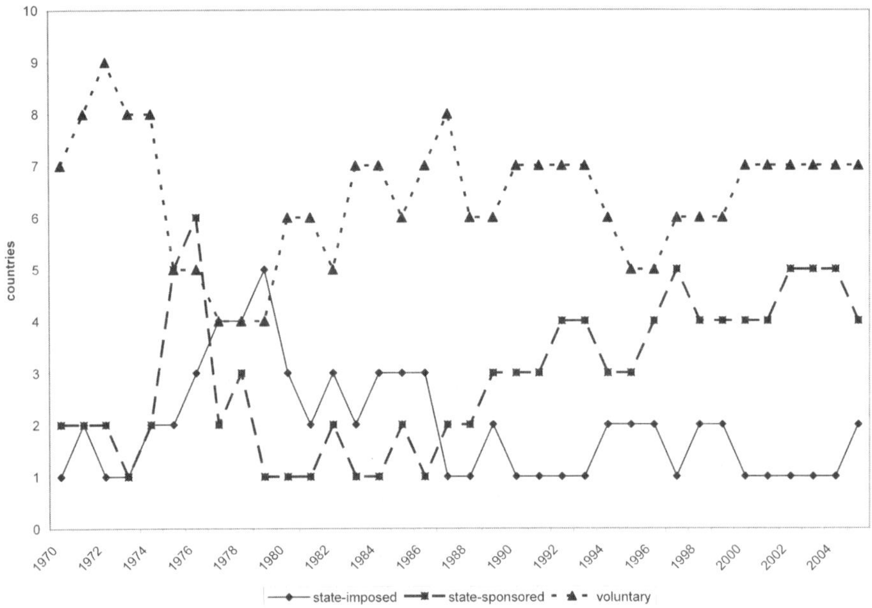

Fig. 6.1. Coordination of wage bargaining, 14 countries

Yet, as can be seen from Fig. 6.1, state intervention, in particular in the indirect form, did not disappear and in the context of preparing the Economic and Monetary Union in Europe tripartism and state-sponsored coordination became used in many countries. But had tripartism generally been seen as having failed in the late 1970s – examples can be cited from Italy and Britain (Regini, 1984), Ireland (Hardiman, 1988), and Belgium and the Netherlands (van Ruysseveld and Visser, 1996) – it appeared more promising twenty years later. What was rarely effective in the 1970s or early 1980s – a central wage norm or incomes policy guideline in a less than fully centralised system of wage bargaining – became apparently feasible in the 1990s: soft coordination takes over from hard centralisation, or so it seemed in many of the New Social Pacts (Fajertag and Pochet, 2000). The 'marriage of opposites' between centralisation and decentralisation, to use an expression of Tarantelli (1986a: 216), emerges as the new compromise of the 1990s. Will it last or end in divorce?

In this chapter, written as a reappraisal of Ezio Tarantelli's work, I intend to review the development of wage bargaining institutions in Europe since 1980 with that question in mind: has a new institutional compromise emerged in the field of collective bargaining over wages, mixing the advantages of coordination and decentralisation, or is the current situation unstable and should we expect a disintegration of centralising institutions?

In this review I limit myself to a part of Europe and cover developments during the past quarter century in fourteen countries – four from the North (Sweden, Finland, Norway and Denmark), five from the Centre (Germany, Austria, Switzerland, the Netherlands and Belgium), two from the West (Britain and Ireland), and three from the South (France, Spain and Italy). These countries reflect considerable variation in state traditions in industrial relations (Crouch, 1993), economic coordination (Hall and Soskice, 2001) and welfare state development (Esping-Andersen, 1990). The exclusion of the new democracies and transition economies of Central and Eastern Europe can be defended on the ground that there the issue is a different one: *not change but creation* of wage bargaining institutions based on democratic organisation, class conflict and market rules. Moreover, we do not have comparable data for these 25 years and the data that we have should be evaluated from a different perspective.

The second limitation is the restriction to wage bargaining institutions and the role of trade unions. I leave aside social and employment protection, training and skill-supply, product market and corporate governance institutions and policies, all of which are important in the final analysis. I impose this limit because the topic is already very complex, it fits best what I know, and – last and least – wage bargaining institutions were focal in Tarantelli's analysis. Employers' policies will be considered in the final part where I analyse stability and change.

The chapter is divided in three parts. Part 1 begins with restating Tarantelli's approach to macroeconomic stabilisation and the role of wage bargaining institutions. Next, I discuss the patterns and variation in the institutional make-up of wage bargaining since 1980. In the final part, I discuss the stability of Tarantelli's 'marriage of opposites' and speculate about its future.

6.2 Tarantelli's first-best and second-best approach

At home and abroad, Ezio Tarantelli participated passionately in the debate over wage bargaining, unemployment and inflation.[2] He judged the OECD strategy *second best*, though probably unavoidable under conditions of high inflation *and* decentralised wage bargaining. When wage bargainers are unable or unwilling to voluntarily restrain wages, inflationary expectations can only be broken by a monetary cure creating higher unemployment (Tarantelli, 1986a, p. 52). However, the *first best* strategy, because less costly for employment, is based on a negotiated announcement by the unions, agreed with the government and with employers, to lower wage increases, thus breaking inflationary expectations and allowing mone-

[2] He took part in another OECD expert conference, *Collective Bargaining and Economic Policies: Dialogue and Consensus*, Paris, 18–20 July 2003, for which he wrote a contribution a version of which appeared in *Laboratorio politico*, a journal of the Communist Left. In it he defended his 'first best' approach to disinflation by way of a negotiated incomes policy.

tary authorities to support growth. This strategy is however only available *if* the unions find the will to use wages as a target for inflation, rather than the other way around, *if* the system of setting wages is sufficiently centralised to prevent free riding, and *if* there is also an accepted and efficient system of settling disputes (Tarantelli, 1986b).[3]

Oddly, Tarantelli lobbied tirelessly for a negotiated incomes policy among policy makers and union leaders in his own country, in spite of Italy's low rating on any of the institutional conditions associated with his first-best strategy. The story has been told elsewhere (Fiorito, 2003; Brandolini et al., 2006). He wanted the unions to understand that they were key to bringing down high inflation – at one point, in 1980, running at over 20 per cent! – by non-monetarist means, by accepting the replacement of the 'backward looking' automatic indexation of wages to prices ('*scala mobile*') by a 'pre-determined pay rise' which then could guide economic agents' expectations about future price developments. His ideas inspired the Social Pact ('Lodo Scotti') of January 1983 and the failed central agreement and government decree of February 1984. Outside Italy, the idea of a 'predetermined' inflation target was picked up by policy makers in France and Spain. In Italy, Tarantelli's ideas resonated in the central agreement of July 1992, which abolished indexation, and the 'Ciampi Pact' of July 1993, which revised the Italian bipolar system of collective bargaining into a two-tier system with a hierarchy between industry and company bargaining.

These agreements could not have been predicted on the basis of the usual institutional and political preconditions mentioned in the literature on neo-corporatism: i.e., centralisation and concentration of unions and/or employers' associations; authoritative joint councils or similar bodies that bring representatives of capital and labour together and conciliate conflicting interests and views; pro-Labour governments or governments based on broad coalitions that promote the involvement of private interest groups in public policy. Little of this applied to Italy. Hence, an explanation problem exists (see Baccaro, 2003; Regini, 1997). In the event, explanations offered for the agreements of 1992–93 include: the changed international economic situation after the decisions of Maastricht in December 1991; the political crisis and demise of the main popular political parties following *mani pulite*; the determination to take Italy in the EMU; the enhanced autonomy from politics and greater unity of the trade unions (Ferrera and Gualmini, 2004).

These explanations based on what were *emergency* conditions do raise doubts regarding the *stability* of the institutional solutions of 1992–93. Will governments and employers remain interested in negotiated incomes policies and accept that unions be given a voice in decisions over key aspects of government policy once

[3] What is first- or second-best depends on the actor's perspective and preference. Tarantelli took a public policy perspective with a strong but *conditional* preference for full employment. His first-best strategy, a negotiated income policy, is probably second-best for the unions because of the concessions involved, the uncertainty of the future payoffs, and the organsational strain of convincing and disciplining their members. Their first-best strategy would have been an *unconditional* public policy commitment to full employment.

inflation has been beaten and the country is safely landed in the EMU?[4] Will such policies survive an antagonistic government, disunity in the union movement, or a renewed outbreak of distributional conflict between employers and unions? How much and what type of institution building is necessary for sustainable, inflation-proof incomes-policies oriented towards goals such as growth, job creation and social cohesion? These questions are rather acute in the present situation in Italy, where macroeconomic policy making seems rather far removed from the 'spirit' of 1993 and the inflation disadvantage with Germany has cumulated to 12 percentage points since entry in the EMU (ISTAT data, *Corriere della Sera*, 20 July 2005). Should we interpret Italy as a case where lessons about how to handle distributional conflicts were learned the hard way, but have since been forgotten?

In Tarantelli's view three institutions were required for a negotiated incomes policy: the capacity and willingness of unions to enter into cooperative solutions with employers and/or governments; the capacity of central organisations to prevent or repress free riding of local and sectional actors; and mechanisms for settling or containing distributive conflict (Tarantelli, 1986a, pp. 76–9). Although there were occasional attempts to reach a cooperative solution, for instance during the government of National Unity (1976–78) and again in 1983–84, they never lasted very long and were contested in both the political and industrial arena. Marino Regini has shown that the combination of poor delivery on promises and the inability to manage the resulting representation crises, compounded by political rivalry and organisational fragmentation in the Italian and British union movement, proved deadly for such experiments of 'political exchange' in Italy and the United Kingdom (Regini, 1984).

On all dimensions – centralisation; union concentration; coordination and concertation – Italy was always ranked at or near the bottom of the various indicators of corporatism (Table 6.1). Colin Crouch argues that 'a strategy of neo-corporatist concertation is available only where labour market organizations – unions and employers' associations – are capable of centrally coordinated action and are under pressure to do so without externalising costs which have to be born in making adjustments' (Crouch, 2000, p. 279). If correct, then there was no place for such a strategy in Italy.

Table 6.1 is based on a comparison of different rankings of union centralisation, bargaining coordination and corporatism that I did some years ago for the ILO (Visser, 2001a). These studies cover the 1970s and early 1980s, the time of Tarantelli's engagement in the debate. They tell us what international scholars thought where Italy stood when its adventures with a negotiated incomes policy

[4] Fiorito (2003, p. 294) answers 'no' and argues that it is the 'paradox of corporatism' that once they have done the job of driving inflation from the expectations of economic agents, centralised bargaining and neo-corporatist concertation become unnecessary and their costs more conspicuous. Hancké and Rhodes (2005) defend the thesis that in the post-EMU situation incomes policy pacts are no longer necessary and therefore no longer the priority of governments and employers *if* wage setting is sufficiently articulated in industry- and company-based policies of skill-formation and productivity-development.

Table 6.1. Rankings of centralisation, co-ordination and corporatism

	Union cohesion & centralisation				centralisation of bargaining		corporatism & unions		corporatism & consociationalism			super-rank	CoV.
	(1)	(2)	(3)	(4)	(5)	(6)	(7)	(8)	(9)	(10)	(11)		
Sweden	5	2	2	3	3	5	4	4	3	4,5	3,5	3	0,299
Finland	5	4,5	(8)	5	5	8	7	4	7	8	8	7	0,256
Norway	5	3	3	2	2	4	4	2	4	4,5	2	2	0,378
Denmark	7	4,5	6	4	4	7	4	4	5	7	5	5	0,247
Germany	8	7	4	6	6	2	2	8	6	2	7	6	0,450
Austria	1	1	1	1	1	1	1	1	1	1	1	1	0,000
Switzerland	10	9	10	12	(9)	6	(7)	9	9	6	6	9	0,233
Netherlands	2	8	5	7	8	3	7	6	2	3	3,5	4	0,474
Belgium	3	6	(7)	8	7	9	9	7	8	9	9	8	0,243
France	9	12	12	9	10	11	10	10	10	11	11	10	0,099
Italy	11,5	11	9	11	12	12	12	12	12	12	10	12	0,089
UK	11,5	10	10,5	10	11	10	11	11	11	10	12	11	0,064

Columns:

(1) Schmitter, 1981: centralisation of unions, data 1970s.
(2) Cameron, 1984: centralisation and power of unions, data 1970s.
(3) Visser, 1990: centralisation and cohesion of unions, average. 1970-85 (ranks of Finland and Belgium added, based on same methodology.
(4) Calmfors and Driffill, 1988: centralisation and co-ordination of unions, data 1970s and 1980s.
(5) Blyth, 1979: centralisation of collective bargaining, data of 1970s.
(6) Bruno and Sachs, 1985: centralisation and co-ordination of unions and employers, data late 1970s.
(7) Tarantelli, 1986b: centralisation of bargaining, regulation of conflict, and degree of consensus, data 1970s.
(8) Schmitter, 1981: corporatism; centralisation, monopoly and involvement of unions, data 1970s.
(9) Lehmbruch, 1984: organisation of unions and involvement of unions in public policy formation, data 1970s.
(10) Crouch, 1985: corporatism; state and societal interaction, data 1970s and 1980s.
(11) Lijphart and Crepaz, 1991: corporatism and consociationalism, data 1980s.

Source: adapted from Visser, 2001a.

began. I have adjusted the rankings in the original study to 12 countries in this chapter (all except Ireland and Spain, for which no or too few rankings exist).

There is little disagreement among scholars about the extremes: Austria and Sweden are always at or near the top; Italy, France and the UK always at or near the bottom. As one can see from Tarantelli's own ranking (in column 7), he shared an international opinion about the absence of the institutions for neo-corporatist incomes policy in Italy. His ranking gave much weight to cooperation and conflict resolution, *behavioural* features that later, in a seminal contribution of David Soskice (1990), were featured as coordination rather than centralisation. It is therefore hardly surprising that Tarantelli put Austria, Germany and Japan (he did not consider Switzerland) before the three Scandinavian countries.[5] As shown by the larger coefficient of variation across rankings, there is more doubt among scholars about the position of Germany and the Netherlands. The ranking of these countries depends very strongly on which dimension is being considered: organisational cohesion; centralisation within organisations (unions); bargaining coordination; conflict resolution or political concertation.

Lane Kenworthy (2001) has done a marvellous job in reviewing these 'first generation' indicators of wage setting and criticised their rather impressionistic nature, time invariance and mixing up of different dimensions of agency, behaviour and structure. He gives a much better press to some of the newer 'second generation' studies, based on more conceptual and measurement precision, as well as capturing some of the variation over time. These studies include the measures of union centralisation of Golden et al. (1999), the index of bargaining centralisation of Iversen (1999), the measures of centralisation and coordination of wage bargaining of Traxler et al. (2001), and Kenworthy's own scale for measuring bargaining coordination, now also reflected in recent work of the OECD (2004) and the European Commission (Visser, 2004).

6.3 Wage bargaining institutions

Inspired by comparative studies such as Bruno and Sachs (1985), Tarantelli (1986b) and Calmfors and Driffill (1988), we now have hundred or more studies of wage bargaining institutions ('corporatism') and socio-economic performance. For recent overviews I refer to Aidt and Tzannatos (2002), Calmfors et al. (2001), EC (2005), Flanagan (1999, 2003), OECD (2004), Traxler et al. (2001). The results are somewhat disappointing, however:

---

[5] Unfortunately, Soskice's scores on 'economy-wide coordination' (Soskice, 1990, p. 55) included too few of the countries of this chapter to be represented in Table 1. He put Japan, Austria and Switzerland, but not Germany, before Norway and Sweden (and did not include Denmark, Finland or Ireland). Soskice emphasised employers' behaviour, whereas Tarantelli, like most scholars at that time, focused almost exclusively on trade unions. How this caused their different ranking of Germany is unclear. In international studies covering all OECD countries, the ranking of Japan, Germany, Switzerland and the Netherlands proved most unstable (Siaroff, 2001).

- Union density (or coverage), taken as a proxy for union bargaining power, tends to be associated with higher levels of unemployment and wages, or is insignificant.
- The impact of bargaining centralisation is unstable and depends strongly on which countries are included, how centralisation is measured and what other institutions and policies are taken into consideration.
- The effects of centralised and intermediate-level (sectoral) bargaining tend to depend on the type of monetary policy, with sectoral bargaining producing more restraint if combined with a non-accommodating monetary policy.
- How sectoral and firm-level bargaining perform relative to each other is unclear, with company bargaining producing more restraint if product markets are competitive and at low levels of union density.
- Bargaining coordination improves outcomes or mitigates the negative effects of high union density, but these effects are smaller in the 1990s than in the 1970s and 1980s, and the measures for coordination are rather crude and impressionistic.
- Studies focusing on the interaction between economic shocks and labour market institutions tend to confirm that high union density or bargaining coverage increase the probability that transitory effects of economic shocks will turn into persistent unemployment, whereas coordination tends to mitigate this effect (Blanchard and Wolffers, 2000; Nickell et al., 2003), but these results are unstable across studies (EC, 2005).
- Most studies agree (Aidt and Tzannatos, 2002; Blau and Kahn, 1999; Iversen, 1999; OECD, 1997, 2004; Rowthorn, 1992) that unions tend to reduce wage inequality and that this compression effect is strongest in countries where union density and bargaining coverage are high, and bargaining is centralised or coordinated, but this has not been checked with recent data. Some authors suggest that this has worsened the already limited employment opportunities of people with few skills, but this has not been tested in rigorous analysis (OECD, 2004, pp. 141–2).

Bob Flanagan (2003, p. 178) notes that the 'sensitivity of empirical results to small changes in the institutional characterization of a small sample of industrialized countries is a disturbing characteristic of much of the literature'. Results depend very strongly on which countries, variables and years are included, and there is large scope for measurement error and omitted variables. In a recent evaluation of ten years Jobs Strategy, the OECD (2004, p. 133) admits that 'the overall fragility of the evidence linking collective bargaining to macroeconomic performance suggest that great caution should be exercised when attempting to draw guidance for making policy choices from this research'.[6] This caution also regards the use

[6] Ten years before, with the launching of the Jobs Strategy, the OECD was less cautious and advised its members to encourage decentralisation and differentiation of wage bargaining in response to local conditions and skill differences; reduce the scope and level of minimum wages; abandon wage-to-price-indexation; and phase out the administrative extension of sectoral agreements (OECD, 1994). Member states had been reluctant to fol-

of indicators, many of which, according to Flanagan (1999, p. 1172), 'do not measure the concepts stressed by theory'. He is most critical of the composite and often ill-defined index of corporatism, because one can never be sure which part of the index drives the action in a correlation.

The key debate of recent years concerns the difference between *centralisation* and *coordination*. Whilst centralisation refers to the level at which wage settlements are usually negotiated and to the enforceability of these agreements, coordination reflects the degree to which pay negotiations conducted in different bargaining units are synchronised and take into account the effects on each other and on the economy as a whole. While centralisation has been equalled with formal structures, organisational hierarchies and legal rules, coordination is often associated with softer forms of guidance and influence. As is pointed out by Kenworthy (2001), coordination is fundamentally a behavioural concept, whilst centralisation is rather a structural property of the system. This creates two difficulties for designing and measuring an index of coordination.

Firstly, bargaining coordination can be generated by qualitatively rather different arrangements and its ranking is therefore far from straightforward. Franz Traxler and his colleagues (2001, p. 117) list three modes of 'voluntary' coordination, e.g. inter-associational, intra-associational and pattern setting, and two modes in which the state plays a direct ('state-imposed') or indirect ('state-sponsored') role. The case of direct state intervention is rather special. Traxler et al. (2001, p. 297) observe that intervention is most frequently associated with the *failure* of coordination by other means. This leaves four modes of voluntary coordination, however induced or motivated. In 2005 half of our 14 countries engaged in one or the other form of associational coordination, including pattern setting (Austria, Germany, Switzerland, Spain, Sweden, Denmark, Norway), four rely on state-sponsored coordination and tripartism (Ireland, Finland, Netherlands, Italy); two on state-imposed coordination (Belgium and France), and one does without coordination of pay bargaining (United Kingdom) (see also Fig. 6.1). Taking into consideration whether voluntary or sponsored coordination is supported by one or both sides (intra- or inter-associational), pattern setting is regular or irregular and covers all or part of the economy, it is possible to rank coordination on a scale from 1 to 5 (see Table 6.2). If the understanding of wage coordination is that it is a solution to the collective action problem of securing wage restraint against the temptation of free riding (Soskice, 1990), then both mutual assurances and relative size should matter.

Secondly, since it is rather difficult to collect information on behavioural intentions and near to impossible to rank intentions across economies if we had such information (Kenworthy, 2001: 79), many authors, following Soskice, have ranked countries according to the *observed* degree of coordination of wage outcomes. The problem of that approach is that it tends to be rather subjective, difficult to verify

low this advice, however, as was admitted in the first evaluation (OECD, 1999; see also Armingeon and Beyeler, 2004)

Table 6.2. Bargaining coordination, unions and employers, 2000 or later

Kenworthy and OECD circa 2000	Soskice circa 1990	Visser (revised from Traxler et al. 2001) 2000-3
1 = fragmented company bargaining (UK)	1 = zero employer, union or government coordination (UK)	1 = no coordination (UK)
	1.5 = tacit government coordination through large firms (FR)	1.5 = intra-organisational, one sided (unions or employers), low coverage
2 = company and sector bargaining, unarticulated, weak government coordination (FR)	2 = informal coordination, mostly within employers camp, some role unions (IT)	2 = informal, one-sided, high coverage (FR)
		2.5 = intra-organisational, both sides, low coverage, irregular pattern setting
3 = sector bargaining, irregular pattern setting, moderate coordination major players (SE, ES), (Kenw. also: DK, IT)	3 = informal coordination, large firms and employers, medium role unions (NL)	3 = irregular pattern setting, high coverage and monopoly (IT, ES), or regular pattern setting and low coverage and monopoly (CH)
	3.5 = strong inter-industry coordination, strong role employers, medium to strong role unions (DE)	3.5 = intra-organisational, both sides, high coverage and monopoly, regular pattern setting (DE, SE, DK)
4 = sector bargaining, regular pattern setting, intra-peak coordination, government intervention, central agreements w/o peace clause (AT, DE, CH, BE, NL, EI), (OECD also DK, IT) (Kenw. also FI, NO)	4 = coordination centralised and powerful employers organitations and/or unions (SE, NO, CH)	4 = inter-organisational coordination in preparing negotiations or issuing guidelines (AT, NL)
		4.5 = inter-organisational coordination with binding agreements, medium to low coverage and monopoly one side (FI, NO, BE, EI)
5 = central bargaining with peace obligation, and/or government imposition and/or intra-peak coordination with full union monopoly (OECD: FI, N, and (half the time) B).	5 = all encompassing union (AT) or employers, with pliant unions (JA)	5 = inter-organisational coordination, with binding agreements, medium to high coverage and monopoly both sides (SE in 1980)

Sources: Visser, 2004; Kenworthy, 2001; OECD, 2004; Soskice, 1990; Traxler et al., 2001.

and prone to measurement error, since it allows no control of the indicators independently of the behaviour observed.[7] It would be possible to eradicate such subjectivism by taking the actual movement of wages as the basis for the measure of the degree of coordination, but that would make coordination as an explanatory institutional variable in the explanation of union behaviour useless because tautological (ibid.).

In my coding of coordination, I combine data on the nature of the intra- or inter-associational relationships and the coverage of such relationships. Similarly, I follow the mixed *organisational* approach, as suggested by Clegg (1976) and Windmuller (1975), combining information on the observed level of bargaining with data on the size and structure of bargaining units and agents, and the type and enforceability of agreements, strike controls and articulation of lower-level bargaining (Visser, 1990). Table 6.3 explicates my coding for the 14 countries of this study from 1980 to 2003, taking into account three levels of bargaining: central, sectoral (and/or regional), and company (or establishment). Although relying on different – behavioural v. organizational – data, this mixed way of gauging coordination and centralisation produces highly comparable indexes. They measure the same property (the capacity and willingness of unions to coordinate wages) in different ways and can thus be used almost interchangeably.[8]

Limiting myself to the role of unions and wage bargaining, I shall now review the five usual suspects: union density, bargaining coverage, union concentration, bargaining centralisation and coordination. First I clarify what I think these indicators stand for, then propose a measure and compare European labour markets during the past 25 years.

6.3.1 Union membership and density

Union density, i.e. union membership relative to those eligible to join, is the commonly used measure for evaluating the position of trade unions in labour markets and society (Bain and Price, 1980). It indicates the *regular* support that unions are capable of mobilising in their key constituency of workers and salaried employees and thus measures the 'associational power' of labour (Wright, 2000). There are several ways to gauge the extent of support for unions, e.g., financial contributions; willingness to fulfil tasks in the union and supply 'unpaid' labour; voting for union candidates in workplace elections; public opinion data; participa-

7 Kenworthy (2001, p. 77) notes that the Layard et al. (1991), Hall-Franzese (1999) and OECD (1997) coordination indicators 'appear to follow Soskice's measurement strategy, but it is difficult to know for certain because no explicit rationale is provided for their coding schemes. Plainly, there is potential for significant measurement error in such indicators'.

8 Taking all years together, the Spearman correlation coefficient between my index of centralisation and coordination for the 14 countries of this study is .88 and the main deviant case is Switzerland (low on union centralisation but relatively high on employer coordination).

Table 6.3. Wage bargaining: levels, enforcement, conflict control and articulation, by country and year: 1980–2003

Weights (a)	(b)	(c)	Description	Country	Years
1.0	.0	.0	confederation(s) monopolize wage bargaining, agreements are enforced confederal control over strike decisions Industry unions implement agreements	Norway	1988–89
.8	.0	.2	confederation(s) negotiate (or implement) enforceable central agreement confederal control over strike decisions local bargaining possible	Denmark Sweden	1985 1980–82; 1985–86, 1989–90
.5	.3	.2	confederation(s) negotiate central agreements with some enforceability industrial unions conduct wage bargaining within limits confederal and union control over strike decisions, limited scope local bargaining	Finland Netherlands Norway	1981–82, 1984–88, 1990, 1996–99, 01– 2002–4 1980, 1983, 1985, 1996–97, 03
.5	.0	.5	confederation(s) negotiate central agreements with some enforceability (or, failing that, defer to state intervention) industrial and local unions conduct wage bargaining within limits limited control over local unions and strike decisions	Belgium Ireland Italy Spain	1980– 1980, 1987–99 1983–84, 1992–93 1980–83, 1985–86
.2	.6	.2	confederation(s) negotiate non–enforceable central agreement, set targets and/or synchronise claims industry unions conduct bargaining, agreements are enforceable local bargaining limited	Austria Netherlands Norway	1980–92 1983–93 1981–82, 1984, 1986–87.
.2	.4	.4	confederation(s) negotiate non–enforceable central agreement, set targets and/or synchronise claims industry unions conduct bargaining, with general opening clauses union control over local bargaining and strike decisions	Austria Denmark Netherlands Norway Sweden	1993– 1980–84, 1986–7 1994– 1990–5, 1998–02 1983–84, 1987–88, 1991–92
.1	.7	2	minor involvement confederation(s) (claims, ballots, strike control) industry unions conduct bargaining, agreements are enforceable local bargaining limited	Finland Netherlands	1980, 1983, 1989, 1991–95, 2000 1980–82

Table 6.3. continued

Weights (a)	(b)	(c)	Description	Country	Years
.1	.5	4	minor involvement confederation(s) (claims, ballots, strike control) industry unions conduct bargaining, with general opening bargaining local bargaining circumscribed by higher level agreement	Denmark Italy Spain	1988–94, 1999– 1994– 1997–
.1	.0	9	minor involvement confederation(s) in bargaining (ballots, strike control) unclear hierarchy between industry and local bargaining limited control over local strike decisions	France Italy Spain	1980– 1980–82 1984
.0	.9	.1	no involvement or control confederation(s) industry union monopolise bargaining, agreements are enforceable control over local strike decisions	Germany	1980–1997
.0	.7	.3	no involvement or control confederation(s) industry unions conduct bargaining with room for local bargaining (or local bargaining dominates but strictly under peace obligation and mediation rules), agreements are enforceable, control over local strike decisions	Denmark Germany Sweden Switzerland	1995–98 1998– 1993– 1980–
.0	.3	.7	no involvement or control confederation(s) unclear or unstable hierarchy between industry and local bargaining, agreements are not enforces and limited control over local strike decisions	Italy Spain	1985–91 1987–1996
.0	.1	.9	local bargaining, limited enforceabity and control over local strike decisions	Ireland UK	1981–86 1979–

Weights: (a) central level (entire economy or private sector); (b) sectoral or industrial branch level; (c) company or establishment level

Source: Visser, own data, database of wage bargaining process, agreements and organisational data 1980-2003.

tion in union strike calls, but membership sums up most of this and it is together with electoral data easiest to collect and compare. A large membership tends to bring organisational and financial independence, allows the payment of professional staff, and devote energy and ideas to causes that *go beyond the survival* of the organisation. It conveys to workers the self-assuring idea that they may count on others and supports the group sanctioning mechanism needed to uphold the norm of membership (Booth, 1985; Visser, 2002).

In most econometric treatments union density is taken as an indicator of union bargaining power or wage pushfullness (see Flanagan, 1999). The idea is that the issuing of threats in bargaining games will be more credible when the identification with the union is strong and the pool of non-union workers and potential strikebreakers is small. However, as far back as early debates in French syndicalism, union leaders were aware that large memberships meant moderation.[9] In his book *Unions and Capitalism*, Charles Lindblom makes the point that union size is a double-edged sword: it increases the bargaining power of unions but it also 'makes obvious to all union leadership their actual responsibility for the welfare of the economy even if they do not wish to act responsible' (Lindblom, 1949, p. 196). Mancur Olson has popularised this point, arguing that large unions will be internally diverse and that their leaders will have *organisational* reasons to be prudent, because 'the members of an encompassing union own so much of the society that they have an important incentive to be actively concerned about how productive it is; they are in the same position as a partner in a firm that has only a few partners' (Olson, 1982, p. 48), though he left doubt whether this was a blessing or a pain, suggesting that large organisations may also slow down decision making and represent stronger veto power (see Schwerin, 1984).

Peter Lange (1984) speculates that a large membership size gives workers more trust in the cooperation of fellow workers and thus enables 'workers to extend the time-horizon over which they maximize by making them a bit more inclined to run the risk of paying costs in the present as part of conditional strategies intended to improve their own longer-term outcomes' (Lange, 1984, p. 106). Such trust would, in his view, be encouraged if the union used 'mechanisms of verification', like membership ballots and referendums that 'allow workers throughout the union movement to gain some sense of how many of their fellow workers are inclined to cooperate' (ibidem, p. 108). In sum, union size not only enhances bargaining power but also increases the probability that the union exercises strategic capacity.[10] Holden and Raum (1991) propose a model in which the incentive for bargaining coordination among employers increases with union density, reasoning that a larger union can potentially inflict more harm on firms. It is for this reason problematic to equal union density with wage pushfullness and we cannot make

---

[9] Albert Levy, treasurer (!) of the French *Confédération Générale du Travail* (CGT), believed that it was better for unions to have fewer but highly motivated members, 'car le lourde modération entre avec le grand nombre (cited in Visser, 1989, p. 53)'.

[10] A union has strategic capacity if its actions have predictable and discernable effects on the welfare and actions of other actors (Iversen, 1999, p. 94) and no strategic capacity if its decisions are unaffected by others.

such predictions without taking into account the interaction with other variables, in particular union structure and coordination.

We have now reasonably reliable and comparable union membership and density statistics, often from different (administrative and survey) sources.[11] The union density rates in Table 6.4 (left panel) are calculated for employed workers and without retired workers, students, the self-employed and others without employee status, for this gives the best comparison with labour market and household survey data and the best index of the standing of the unions in the labour market.[12] The picture that emerges is one of *considerable and even increasing variation across countries amidst a general tendency of decline*, in recent years also affecting unions in countries like Sweden, Finland and Denmark. Union decline is observed in both liberal, coordinated and mixed market economies, in countries with (Austria, Netherlands) and without (UK, France) corporatist features of organisation and policy-making, and in countries with (Ireland) and without (Germany) social pacts. This suggests that there is a rather general process behind this decline, which is *endogenous* to labour market changes (rise of service employment, fixed-term and part-time contracts, unemployment, outsourcing, privatisation, etc.) but with a different timing, magnitude and impact across countries, and mediated by nationally differing institutions such as union involvement in the administration of unemployment insurance, union presence in the workplace and the recognition of trade unions by firms and in the national political arena (Checchi and Visser, 2005; Ebbinghaus and Visser, 1999; Western, 1997).

Three more common developments are striking: the concentration of union membership in the public or publicly financed and regulated sector; the aging of union members; and feminisation. These three developments are found in all countries, but the concentration of union membership in the public sector is strongest where the decline of manufacturing employment and unionism has been very pronounced, as for instance in Britain, France, and the Netherlands. Female membership is strongly tied to the rise of services and new professions, partly overlapping with the public sector. Ageing is related to the instability of youth labour markets, education and later entry into the labour force and also the decline of industry and manual work.

As was pointed out before, it is not possible to make general predictions for union wage behaviour on the basis of membership or density data. However, the decline in density tends to increase the uncertainty of unions and their dependence on the decisions and support of other actors in the political and industrial arena. Many unions and union federations are in financial dire straits and the central organisations in particular have been forced to scale down staff, finances and activities, with possible negative consequences for their coordinating role. Interlocutors

[11] See Visser et al., 2004 (http://www.oecd.org) for an overview of methods and sources, and annual figures from 1960–2001/2,

[12] In 2001, in these fourteen countries an average of 17 per cent of the total membership had retired from the labour market, 1–2 per cent were self-employed and 7 per cent unemployed. These proportions vary across countries (Ebbinghaus and Visser, 2000).

Table 6.4. Union density and bargaining coverage 1980–2003

	Union density				employer density[b)]	bargaining coverage rate			
	1980–3	1990–3	2000–3	trend	2000–3	1980–3	1990–3	2000–3	trend
Sweden	79	82	78	stable?	55	80+	83	92**	up
Finland	69	76	74	stable?	60	95	95	95*	stable
Norway	58	58	53	down	55	70+	75	75**	stable
Denmark	80	76	72	down	52	70+	73	76**	stable
Germany**	35[a]	31[a]/34	24	down	63	70+	70+*	60+*/**	down
Austria	55	45	36	down	100[c)]	98	98	98*	stable
Switzerland	30	23	18	down	40	50+	50+	40+	down
Netherlands	33	25	23	down	85	85	82	86*	stable
Belgium	53	54	55	stable	72	95	95	95*	stable
France	18	10	8	down	74	85	92	95*	up
Spain	9	15	16	up	70	60+	70+	80+*	up
Italy	48	39	34	down	51	80+	80+	80+*	stable
UK	49	38	29	down	40	71	47	35	down
Ireland	57	50	36	down	60	..	,,	..	un-known
mean	49	45	40	down	41	77	76	74	stable
st.dev.	(20.5)	(22.8)	(22.9)		(22.8)	(11.1)	(14.5)	(18.0)	

Sources: Union membership and density: own data; employer density: Visser (2004); bargaining coverage: EC (2004); national reports (*EIROnline*); OECD (2004); for Denmark 2000-3: Scheuer (2004); for Germany, recent years (1995-): IAB and WSI data.

Notes: Adjusted rates (see text).
[a)] West Germany; [b)] private sector; [c)] compulsory membership
* Including non-organized firms bound by agreements through administrative extension (France, Spain, Belgium, the Netherlands, Finland, Germany; and Austria through compulsory membership) or court decisions (Italy)
** Including non organized firms not bound by a sectoral agreement but nonetheless applying the agreement (Sweden, Denmark, Germany).

may take continued membership decline as a sign that unions have become dispensable or may be more readily forced into concessions. If lower density rates and more dependence on others means less bargaining power, uncertainty may nonetheless produce more assertive policies and instability.

6.3.2 Bargaining coverage

Bargaining coverage denotes the share of employed wage and salary earners whose terms of employment are affected by collective agreements negotiated between unions and employers. It is an indicator of the degree of *joint regulation* of labour markets (Traxler et al., 2001, p. 194). Collective agreements vary in regulatory effect (Clegg, 1976); some will affect only wage floors, others detail standard pay rates or do not have wage clause at all but only procedures stipulating how wages may be changed. Company agreements tend to be more detailed than industry agreements and industry agreements in Sweden are much more detailed than in France. The variation is quite endless and has further increased with the diffusion of 'opening', 'hardship', 'opt-out' and 'inability to pay' clauses in sectoral agreements (see below). The common denominator of all these agreements is that they are procedural safety nets and guarantee some degree of union control. Usually, collective agreements overrule individual employment contracts.

We can measure bargaining coverage fully comparable with union density statistics as the share of employees working in firms covered by collective agreements. Measurement errors may stem from definitional problems (what is a contract?); double counting (especially problematic in the case of multi-level agreements); and registration failures (membership or agreements that have expired, or are only registered for the year when the agreement was reached). In general, coverage statistics are more problematic than membership statistics if only because the double check with survey data is less available (on an annual basis such data is now only available in the UK). Data based on household surveys is probably less reliable as workers may not know that they are covered, a problem that can be especially large in the case of industry-wide and pluri-annual agreements.[13] Finally, coverage statistics must be adjusted and take out those sectors or groups that have no (legal) access to collective bargaining (for instance, civil servants, police, military) (Traxler, 1994).

The coverage rates shown in Table 6.4 (right panel) should therefore be used with more caution than the union density rates and they are less detailed. In some countries, it is only possible to indicate the lower boundaries (OECD, 2004, Table 3.3). In all countries coverage rates exceed density rates; in some countries (France, Spain, Italy, the Netherlands, Germany, Austria and Belgium) by a wide margin.[14] This reflects the greater extent of employer organisation in these countries and the possibility to extend union-negotiated agreements non-organised employers by public law (Traxler and Behrens, 2002). This data tell us something about the degree of recognition and support for union-negotiated employment contracts among employers and public policy makers, often based on rules and prin-

[13] According to Steen Scheuer, who conducted several surveys on union membership and contract coverage in Denmark, 'there is a remarkable lack of interest in collective agreements' and 'only few employees know or have read their own collective agreement' (Scheuer 2004, p. 99).

[14] There is hardly a correlation between the two measures. Taking all years together, the Spearman correlation coefficient between density and coverage rates in the 14 countries of this study is .28 and weakening over time.

ciples that cannot be changed without significant legal and political conflict. Bargaining coverage rates, therefore, *proxy the degree of institutionalisation* of collective bargaining and trade unions in labour markets.

Unlike union density rates, bargaining coverage rates are remarkably stable and not trended downwards. This reflects the continuation of multi-employer bargaining, usually with an added layer of company bargaining. There are only three cases of decline: the United Kingdom, Switzerland and Germany. The UK and Switzerland are the only cases in which less than half of all employees are currently covered by collective bargaining. In the UK this is related to the collapse of multi-employer (sectoral) bargaining and employer organisation; in Switzerland more likely to the function loss of the sectoral agreement, which in many cases no longer contains a wage clause. In Germany the erosion is due to the withdrawal of small firms and those in Eastern Germany from employers associations and multi-employer agreements. Bargaining coverage in the private sector was more or less stable – around 70 per cent or more – in West Germany before unification and is currently estimated at 59 per cent in Western and 36 per cent in Eastern Germany according to the IAB Panel Database for 2004. However, half of these non-organised firms nonetheless orient themselves toward the sectoral agreement and follow its basic features on pay and working time. This pushes the German coverage rate up by 10–15 percentage points. This practice of applying the agreement 'by invitation' of the unions is quite widespread in Scandinavia and reflects the power of the unions to some extent. Such quasi-voluntary wage following behaviour thus retains an element of coordination and confirms that firms may want more autonomy but nonetheless apply the union contract if that gains them an implicit 'peace offer' from the unions and lowers the risk of conflict.

The standardised coverage rates shown in Table 6.4 are aggregated for agreements at all levels with an attempt to avoid double counting. In general coverage rates vary like union density rates: higher in the public sector (though some categories, like the military, the police or high ranking civil servants may be excluded); in large firms; in older sectors (manufacturing, banking, etc.), among workers with stable contracts and those in manual occupations. The same variation is also generally found for the coverage of workplace representation and works councils. Bargaining coverage and works council coverage overlap to a great extent, but whilst collective agreements cover employees in small firms in the case of multi-employer bargaining, the law usually exempts small firms from the obligation to create a structure for employee representation and consultation. Where there is no bargaining, there are usually no councils either and works council hardly adds to the union coverage rate based on collective agreements. For instance, in Germany only between two and three per cent of the firms not covered by collective agreements had a works council in 2002. Together these firms employed some seven per cent of German employees (these included some large firms like IBM with an anti-union policy.

The importance of mandated and elected works councils as a *second channel* of representation in addition to the union lies in the *internal extension* of the agreements negotiated by the union, that is, in the legal mandate to monitor and apply legal and negotiated standards to *all* employees in the firm, including non-union members. In *single channel* representation, workplace representation is based on union membership and the extension of standards and rights to non-members may depend on their willingness to join the union. In actual practice, the differences tend to be small, however. Union-based councils in for instance Italy represent also non-members, whereas mandated councils in Germany or the Netherlands, elected by members and non-members alike, tend to be highly unionised (Rogers and Streeck, 1995). Local union representatives and works councils have become increasingly important for the adjustment of sectoral agreements and additional company bargaining, even if the law formally denies them a role in pay bargaining. This development has taken place 'beyond the law' and is now formalised in delegation and opening clauses.

6.3.3 Union structure and concentration

Union structure defines the opportunity structure for competition and coalition building among trade unions and is an important element in predicting the possibilities of coordination and centralisation of union bargaining. The key indicator is concentration or the extent to which members are grouped in few large unions rather than in numerous small ones. The argument that size matters draws on arguments that unions which encompass large chunks of the economy do not face the same incentives as small occupational, enterprise or even industry unions. Large unions cannot, like small unions or workplace representatives, expect to hide behind others or externalise the costs of their actions.

Union concentration can be approached in similar ways as economic concentration of firms or political parties, using the so-called Herfindahl-index which weights large unions more than small and denotes the probability that two randomly selected union members belong to the same organization (Iversen, 1999, p. 53; Visser, 1990, p. 172; Wallerstein and Western, 2000, p. 372). In the political party literature the inverse of this index is called the 'effective' number of parties and by analogy we speak of the effective number of unions. Table 6.5 shows the changes in union concentration at the central (entire economy) and intermediate (sector) level: N_{peaks} refers to the effective number of peak associations or national union confederations (left panel); $N_{affiliates}$ to the effective number of national unions affiliated with the largest confederation (middle panel); N_{all} to effective number of all unions by multiplying N_{peaks} x $N_{affiliates}$ (right panel).

The first number reflects the degree of unity in the labour movement and the dominance of a large central organisation and it also takes into account the share of unionised workers represented by unaffiliated unions or minority federations. It is a useful measure for assessing the degree of coordination if unions would negotiate wages or issue guidelines at the central level (across industries). There appears to be little variation over time, but across countries the differences are pronounced. There are four countries (Austria, Germany, the UK and Ireland) where most unions and union members find a common house, but in the other countries they are divided over two or more, and in one case, France, over many peak associations. The decline of the traditional Social Democrat (and Communist)

Table 6.5. Union concentration – across and within industries, 1980–2003

	central level			intermediate sectoral level					
	effective number of confederations			effective number of unions (largest confederation)			effective number of unions (all confederations)		
	1980–83	1990–93	2000–03	1980–83	1990–93	2000–03	1980–83	1990–93	2000–03
Sweden	2,2	2,2	2,4	7	6	6	16	14	15
Finland	2,3	2,8	2,8	12	11	10	27	30	27
Norway	2,1	2,6	3,1	12	8	7	25	20	22
Denmark	1,9	2,0	2,0	7	8	7	14	15	14
Germany	1,5	1,5	1,4	6	6	6	9	9	8
Austria	1,0	1,0	1,0	9	9	8	9	9	8
Switzerland	4,1	4,3	4,8	6	6	6	25	26	28
Netherlands	2,5	2,4	2,0	9	6	4	23	15	7
Belgium	2,3	2,3	2,3	9	10	10	21	24	22
France	5,6	7,1	6,1	10	8	8	56	59	51
Spain	2,6	2,8	2,7	8	9	8	22	26	21
Italy	3,1	3,4	3,5	9	10	10	29	32	34
UK	1,3	1,5	1,4	17	15	11	22	21	15
Ireland	1,2	1,1	1,1	6	5	4	7	5	4
mean	2,4	2,6	2,6	9,1	8,2	7,4	21,7	21,7	19,8
st.dev	(1,2)	(1,6)	(1,4)	(2,9)	(2,5)	(2,2)	(12,0)	(13,5)	(12,5)

Source: J. Visser (calculated from Ebbinghaus and Visser, 2000, CD-Rom, with updates for 2000–2003).

confederations, with manual and industrial membership, for instance in Scandinavia, Italy or France, is also reflected in these figures. They were in the past the main sponsors of wage coordination and their decline suggests that the organizational support for economy-wide coordination may have decreased.

Moving one level down, we calculate the effective number of unions in similar ways. The effective number of unions affiliated with the largest confederation may be thought of as the effective number of bargaining *units* (Iversen, 1999, p. 53). It will be a reasonably accurate approximation of the number of bargaining *agents* if unions affiliated with different confederations but in the same firm or industry form cartels and bargain jointly. This is usually the case in Scandinavia (for unions representing different occupational groups), in Belgium, the Netherlands, Italy and Spain (for unions representing different political or religious orientations). If they do not, N_{all} will be the better measure and this applies to France in most years and sectors.

At the intermediate or sectoral level, the main trend is towards union concentration. This is partly caused by differing growth rates (the rise of the public service unions, the decline of manufacturing unions) but union mergers and take-overs of smaller unions play a big role as well. This tendency has been particularly pronounced in countries where membership has stagnated or declined (UK, Netherlands, Ireland, Switzerland). The new 'conglomerate unions' often straddle the borders of many industries and have become little peak associations themselves, internally diverse and with decentralised decision-making in matters of wage bargaining (Streeck and Visser, 1997). This implies that the assumption of one (effective) union = one bargaining unit is becoming less realistic.

Cross-national differences in union concentration are massive but have narrowed – the UK is now much less an outlier than it once was when there were still hundreds of unions around. France beats all other countries in terms of union fragmentation, at some distance followed by Italy, Switzerland and Finland. Unions are most concentrated in Austria and Germany, in the Netherlands, Denmark and Ireland. In some of these countries there is a large union trumping all others in size and bargaining influence. There appears to be no relationship between country size and union concentration, although there should be less space for viable sectoral specialisation in small countries and more pressure toward concentration.

A large union may set a wage trend which other unions are only glad to follow. The union may then act as 'substitute peak association' by assuming responsibility for the national economy or the export sector at large, as did the IG-Metall for many years in Germany (Streeck, 1994). Thus, concentration can be a substitute for centralisation (Golden, 1993; Visser, 1990; Wallerstein and Western, 2000), just as centralisation through federation building is a response to fragmentation stopping short of amalgamation or merger. For example, the strong powers and wide ranging tasks of the Norwegian labour federation LO have been associated with the large number of small unions spread out over a large territory, whereas the dominance of some very large unions in a much more concentrated space prevented such a development in the Danish LO (Galenson, 1949, 1952). This may explain the weak association between centralisation and concentration, an empirical result that puzzled Traxler et al. (2001).[15]

6.3.4 Union bargaining centralisation

Centralisation refers to the level(s) at which decisions are taken, and to the authority or enforceability of those decisions (Traxler et al., 2001; Visser, 1990). A centralisation indicator should tell us how decisions taken by bargainers at any level are affected by decisions at one or more higher levels, or in the parlance of game theory how it changes the inside options or disagreement payoffs of bargainers at any level (Naylor, 2003). This requires the consideration of both union structure and union authority.

If each union negotiates only one contract, if there is no overlap in jurisdiction and all bargaining happens at one level, than centralisation equals concentration and is the inverse of the effective number of unions (Iversen, 1999, p. 53). However, this is not a realistic approximation of actual wage bargaining and the first point to consider is *multi-level bargaining*. If collective bargaining takes place at different levels, we need to assign a weight to each of these levels based on its importance for the overall outcome. In essence we need to know the number of levels and the authority vested in each level as it affects the next (lower) level(s). We can assign weights using information on the enforceability of agreements, strike control and actual participation of central organisations and union officials in bargaining processes at lower levels, as was done in Table 6.3. Enforceability depends upon the capacity of bargaining agents to implement the agreements they negotiate and presupposes a degree of control over the methods of conflict, for instance through the imposition of sanctions or the denial of support in case of conflict. This control need not and does not usually come entirely from within the union, but may be buttressed by employer sanctions and court action.

The second point to consider is that at each level there is usually more than one bargaining agent or unit. It is at this point that we must combine our data on union concentration with the information on the relative importance of levels. This renders a measure of centralisation which reflects the relative weight of each level of bargaining and the concentration or fragmentation of bargaining units or agents at that level (Iversen, 1999, p. 53).

Studying the centralisation data in Table 6.6 (left panel), a decentralisation trend is observed in Scandinavia, very strongly in Sweden and to a lesser extent in Norway and Denmark. The Swedish bargaining system was unique in its degree of centralisation in 1980, but has now become quite average, close to Germany and Denmark. There are two countries in which wage bargaining has become more centralized in recent times: Ireland most definitely, but also in Finland. The cases of Belgium and the Netherlands are less clear-cut; in the Netherlands is it rather

[15] Taking all years together, the Spearman correlation coefficient between my index of centralisation and concentration for the 14 countries of this study is .51.

Table 6.6. Union centralisation and bargaining coordination, 1980–2003

	Centralisation (indicator Iversen revised)				Coordination (indicator Kenworthy revised)			
	1980–83	1990–93	2000–03	Δ	1980–83	1990–93	2000–03	Δ
Sweden	66	48	35	down	5	4	3,5	down
Finland	44	35	50	up	4	3,5	5	up
Norway	46	36	41	down	4,5	4	4	stable
Denmark	41	38	37	down	3	3,5	4	up?
Germany	38	39	36	stable	4	4	4	stable
Austria	52	52	51	stable	4	4	4	stable
Switzerland	22	22	21	stable	3	3	3	stable
Netherlands	34	42	45	up	3,5	4	4	up?
Belgium	46	56	56	up	3,5	4	4,5	up
France	16	15	16	stable	2	2	2	stable
Spain	43	16	31	vari-able	4	2	3	vari-able
Italy	42	38	28	vari-able	2,5	3,5	3	vari-able
UK	12	12	13	stable	1	1	1	stable
Ireland	28	55	56	up	2,5	4,5	4,5	up
mean	38	36	37		3,3	3,3	3,4	
st.dev	(14,4)	(14,8)	(14,1)		(1,2)	(1,0)	(1,1)	

Source: Visser, own data, see text; and Table 6.3 (for centralisation) and Table 6.2 (for coordination)

concentration (union mergers) that drives the action, in Belgium, however, central level bargaining had remained very prominent. Ireland and Belgium have now the most centralised systems of union wage bargaining, though each significantly lower than Sweden in 1980 (or the Netherlands in 1970). They are followed by Austria, on account of central union power and monopoly to synchronise wage bargaining, then Finland and somewhat further down, the Netherlands and Norway, Denmark, Sweden, Germany, Spain and Italy. Finally, we have five countries (Austria, Germany, Switzerland, France and the UK) with little change since 1980, but at rather different levels of centralisation, and two (Spain and Italy) were there is much change but no clear trend covering these 25 years. In Spain, the wage pacts of the first half of the 1980s were followed by decentralisation and then some re-establishment of broadly aggregated sectoral bargaining with more discipline over the local level. In Italy the fragile pacts of the early 1980s were followed by a period of decentralisation, then a new period of central agreements and pact making, leading to the reform of sectoral bargaining with articulated company bargaining, but the re-appearance of conflict between the main union confederations and the relative decline of the largest confederation sets Italy on a downward trend in recent years.

6.3.5 Bargaining coordination

Coordination refers to the relationships between bargaining units or agents and the strength of such links. Coordination is based on relational networking, monitoring based on exchange of partly private information and reliance on collaborative rather than competitive relationships. Wage leadership and pattern setting are forms of indirect linking; cartels and single table bargaining and joint formulation and evaluation of demands constitute forms of direct linking or aggregation of bargaining units. Data on union concentration and union structure may help us to understand how and when coordination through direct and indirect linking is feasible. Thus, stable trend setting patterns will be observed only when there is a dominant union and a unitary or at any rate dominant peak federation. Cartels will be observed at intermediate levels of union confederations but only where political or ideological rivalry is muted.

However, the increasing number of union takeovers and mergers that crosscut occupational and industry borders do no longer warrant the assumption that fewer unions means fewer bargaining units and less inter-union disputes. In addition to data on union concentration we need therefore additional information on the demarcation of bargaining units, the existence of joint bargaining, the settlement of inter-union conflicts, and the coordination of bargaining within conglomerate unions,[16] in order to arrive at a meaningful institutional variable of union coordination in collective bargaining.

Soskice tried to uncover the different mechanisms that helped explain observed wage outcomes. He argued correctly that the argument about centralisation and wage outcomes developed by Calmfors and Driffill (1988) did not strictly depend on the level of bargaining but on the degree of coordination across bargaining units, and that only in the case of single-level bargaining at the central level, centralisation and coordination are the same. In decentralised or multi-level bargain-

[16] For instance, *FNV-Bondgenoten*, the largest private sector union, negotiates half of the 200 sectoral and two-thirds of the 800 company agreements in the Netherlands. Each year issuing a report with its major demands, weighing data, evaluations and forecasts of the Central Planning Bureau, the government, the central federation, and the Social-Economic Council, the union coordinates not through synchronisation but by setting targets and defining joint agenda's for its negotiators, allowing additional local issues to arise within a general approach to responsible wage development. Coordination is enhanced because negotiating union officials meet regularly, are appointed and can be moved to other tasks or districts, and all strike decisions are centralised. This example suggests that bargaining coordination without some degree of organisational centralisation may be rare.

ing there may be other mechanisms, more or less formalised. No such mechanisms were hidden in the data on decentralised bargaining in the UK, but in other countries Soskice detected various examples: a strong monopoly on either side (Austria, Japan): pattern setting by large unions, employers or large firms (Germany, to a lesser extent in the Netherlands); employers control over conflict expression (Switzerland)), some pattern setting by the state combined with other means (France, Italy).

The coordination scores in Table 6.6 (right panel) follow those of Soskice, Kenworthy and the OECD presented in Table 6.2, with some modifications because I have tried to ignore the degree of state intervention, simply noting that in all recent cases of central bargaining state sponsorship and threats of intervention have been prominent (Visser, 2004 p. 45).

About half of all EU Member States have maintained or re-introduced some form of explicit co-ordination at the national level. In Finland, Ireland and the Netherlands central-level coordination has occurred within the framework of tripartite cross-industry dialogue and agreements. The two-year national agreements in Belgium move within a framework set by law. In Denmark, sectoral agreements have since 2000 been supplemented by 'climate agreements' between the social partners, a similar development occurred in 2004 in Sweden and in Spain central agreements have set guidelines for wage conduct since 2001. In Italy, finally, tripartite negotiations in 2002 and 2003 have mostly concentrated on labour law reform, but also sought to influence the inflation targets set by the government, but in this case there was a deep split between the union confederations. Almost all of these agreements recommend a policy of wage moderation in order to sustain non-inflationary economic development and to improve national competitiveness. Implicit coordination, through pattern following, has remained the main form of coordination in Austria and Germany. Finally, there was little apparent union or employer coordination in these matters in the UK and France.

6.4 Wage bargaining institutions in Europe: how stable are they?

From the quantitative overview in the preceding pages we get a picture of considerable stability. Union density is declining, but structures of collective representation and bargaining appear rather stable. Nearly three out of four workers are covered by collective bargaining and the British example of concentrating all bargaining at the company level has not received a following (with the partial exception of Switzerland). The trend towards decentralisation of wage setting is not general and often checked by increased union concentration and coordination with employers or within the union movement itself. All but two countries – or only one, the UK, if we disregard state-imposed coordination in France – have retained or regained a form of coordination above the level of firms.

Two more observations are possible. In all (twelve) countries that have retained or even strengthened a form of central or sectoral wage bargaining or regulation, higher-level agreements or regulations *have widened the scope for adjustment at the company level* through general or conditional opening clauses under more or less control of national union representatives. But as important is the conclusion that all countries except Britain (and Switzerland) *have tried to maintain, strengthen or return to some form of coordinated wage setting*, sometimes reversing experiments with decentralised and uncoordinated bargaining. This does not, of course, mean that all countries have succeeded in raising the spectre of coordination. Some (e.g., France, Belgium) have resorted to pervasive and recurrent state intervention, with standardising and centralising effects that tend to conflict with other priorities, especially among employers. Others, like Germany or Sweden, have experienced that it is difficult to graft a tripartite practice on unions and employers steeped in autonomous bargaining.

Wolfgang Streeck and Kathy Thelen (2005) suggest that there is a fundamental asymmetry in these developments. Stepping up the degree of coordination in wage setting requires not only the willingness but also organisational and strategic capacities to overcome distributive conflict and collective action dilemmas. Decentralisation and non-cooperation are much less demanding and some of it may just happen by inaction and non-organisation. They identify several mechanisms for *gradual yet transformative change*, two of which are particularly relevant here: *drift* or neglect, when formal rules fall in disuse by not being updated, possibly because the actors cannot agree or mount the collective action required for maintenance and renewal; and *layering*, when new elements become added onto the old institution and then grow more rapidly, eventually changing the nature of the institution. The diffusion of opening clauses in sectoral agreements and re-assignment of bargaining rights to local representatives and works councils is an example of layering, just as the continuation of a practice of enforcing standardised agreements on an increasingly diverse community of firms and workers by legal and hierarchical means might be considered a lack of bringing existing institutions 'up to date'. Streeck and Thelen observe that neglect is often deliberate, just as layering may need active sponsors. Their key point is that the thresholds on collective action needed for an all-out attack on existing institutions or for their reform through negotiations with other actors tend to be much higher; hence, we will often see incremental change like drift and layering, which cumulatively and by stealth may result in a qualitative transformation.

Given the weakening of the trade unions, we should expect that the institutional stability of collective bargaining, and in particular of the sectoral and national agreement, depends less than before upon the power of the unions and more upon the capacity and willingness of employers to continue joint bargaining. Sweden's unions, with their exceptionally high membership levels, have been able to defend sectoral bargaining against the attack of some powerful employers, but they were forced to give up nationwide bargaining. The British case illustrates the more general point that collective bargaining structures and institutions above the level of firms become fragile when they rest solely on the power of unions *even when unions are or appear strong*, as was the case in the 1970s. Labour market institutions above the level of firms will be vulnerable even in the best of times, but especially when they do insufficiently address issues and problems of production, discipline, training and allocation important to employers (Thelen, 2001). Given their 'low degree of control and an unrealistically narrow scope' (Brown, 1993, p. 190), sectoral agreements in Britain did nothing to help employers and made abandonment of multi-employer bargaining with the unions a rather costless option for them. Ending a 'century-old tradition of official support for collective bargaining' (ibid.), Mrs. Thatcher gave this development a strong push in the direction of no bargaining.

The German situation suggests a different dilemma. Here, sectoral bargaining institutions are highly institutionalised, shared between unions and employers, addressing both wage and non-wage issues, and their operation is nested in congenial institutions in the company, like the works council, board representation and codetermination (Streeck, 1992). However, there tends to have arisen a conflict between actual or perceived regulatory tightness[17] of the sectoral agreements and the size of the bargaining units, especially after unification (but perhaps even without it). When bargaining units are very large[18] and cover large and small firms or regions with sharply different abilities to pay and market conditions, the pressure to break down agreements in smaller units will inevitably rise. If decentralisation or differentiation is blocked and it is not possible to make bargaining units effectively smaller for a larger range of issues, employers with the lowest capacity to sustain the costs of such agreements will withdraw and coverage decreases. The conflict between the macro institution and micro behaviour becomes larger with the 'uploading' of sectoral agreements with 'social policy' and 'work-family' issues, two developments related to welfare state retrenchment and EU regulation (Trampusch, 2004). Whilst small firms and weak sectors or regions might seem to benefit most from joint collective bargaining in terms of lower transaction costs and protection against union pressure, they are least capable to sustain the increasingly complex and costly qualitative or non-wage elements of the resulting agreements.

One way out, it seems, is the customisation of agreements, offering more choice to individual companies and workers. Streeck and Rehder (2003), for instance, interpret the formalisation through 'opening clauses' of what began as an informal development of not applying the agreement, with or without the consent and knowledge of union representatives, as a (late) attempt at re-institutionalisation of the German system. Elsewhere, I have described such attempts at rescuing the sectoral agreement by giving up some of its defining characteristics as a process of 'learning ahead of failure' (Visser, 2001b). With the diffusion of 'opt out' and 'delegation' clauses in sectoral agreements, firms gain the power, under certain conditions like the consent of the union or the works council, to suspend or selectively apply particular aspects of a legally binding sectoral agreement negotiated by their representatives. This may create the 'marriage of opposites' that em-

[17] It may be that the rigidity of German collective agreements is a 'carefully constructed myth' as is claimed by WSI-researches associated with the German unions, but if this is how German employers and politicians perceive them, and unions are unable to dispel such myths, they become part of reality.

[18] Industry bargaining in Germany takes place at the regional (state) level, but these agreements are close copies of each other and regional variation is small. Contractual rates set for the former East German *Länder* are still lower than the national average, but differences have narrowed, as has been a consistent union objective since 1989.

ployers seem to like – between on the one hand more autonomy in decision making over wages and working hours, reflecting different product and labour market constraints, and on the other hand a guarantee to keep distributional conflict out of the firm and retain the life-buoy of the sectoral agreement.

How successful this strategy of institutional renewal – reviving the sectoral agreement by giving up some of its distinctive features – will be, is hard to say. I hazard the prediction that much depends on whether or not the sectoral agreement remains relevant for wages and wage structures. A sectoral agreement without a wage clause will probably disintegrate, because well-organised union groups in more profitable companies will no longer have reasons to defend the sectoral agreement as an instrument to limit the competition arriving from the external labour market. Another major variable, it seems to me, is the strength of workplace representation and its integration in the union. Where representation is strong and integrated, unions can be more confident in accepting forms of decentralisation based on the loosening of the sectoral agreement. Where union workplace representation is fragile, does not reach many (small and medium-sized) firms, is not under full control of national unions or has fallen victim to competition between them, unions have more to fear from decentralisation.

This discussion shows that bargaining institutions are both means and ends and cannot be treated as just *exogenous*, as is usually done in econometric exercises. The fight over institutions is never only a fight over social and economic outcomes. A lot of union behaviour would be quite inexplicable if we treated the union as a bargaining instrument for higher wages or some other utility function only, as Alan Flanders has reminded us. In addition to economic achievement unions stand for the attempt to regulate labour markets in such ways so as to free workers from 'dependence on chance and arbitrary will of others' (Flanders, 1970, p. 240).

Moreover, the fact that labour market institutions such as unions and collective bargaining are contested does not imply that it is always a zero-sum conflict. The contested character of these institutions does neither rule out cooperation between contending actors nor outcomes in which some employers promote and maintain equalizing industry standards negotiated with and enforced by the unions as a strategic entry barrier against other firms. In some economic accounts this is an efficiency loss and the basis for rent seeking (Williamson, 1968), but that assumes that the market is already functioning efficiently. In Streeck's theory of 'beneficial constraints' there is the possibility that joint industry standards work as incentive structures for firms and workers, motivating them to upgrade their technology and skills and enhance the product quality of the sector (Streeck, 1992). These incentives are weakened if the 'external' bargaining structure (across firms) discourages coordination and become undone if the 'internal' bargaining structure (within firms) allows inefficient employers to side with works councils and workers faced with job losses in their attempts to lower or disregard the industry's wage and social standards on a massive scale. This requires that 'regime' or 'institution shopping' is restricted. A general 'opt out' to firms and workers, for instance allowing them to work very long hours, diminishes the incentive of firms to invest in short hours – high productivity solutions and is a sure guarantee that overtime will remain a 'thriving institution' (Flanders, 1964) needed by firms to compensate for inefficient work practices and by workers to top up their meagre income. Bad institutions work like drugs, as the British experience with the general opt-out clause (art 18(1)b) of the working time directive shows (Barnard et al., 2003). Having become used to long hours, many firms and workers cannot survive without them.

This brings me to my final question. How hard and binding must wage bargaining institutions be to become effective? Recent studies on wage bargaining tend to argue that the organizational and administrative centralisation of wage bargaining are *less* important in achieving beneficial outcomes in wage policies than a cooperative mood, common understanding and trust among the major players (Calmfors et al., 2001; O'Donnell, 2001; Culpepper, 2004). There is little doubt that a common understanding of the situation and a co-operative mood plaid a role in the success of coordinated incomes policies in countries like Ireland, Denmark and the Netherlands and that such qualities help produce good results within *any* bargaining structure. A norm-based incomes policy, based on jointly elaborated facts and a common understanding of the situation, and rooted in joint experiences of and investments in cooperation, has undoubtedly better survival chances than where such conditions are absent. But it is unlikely that such normative commitments are sufficient, 'unless the structure of pay-offs and surrounding conditions (...) are consistent with self-interest' (Lange 1984, p. 106).

Among the surrounding conditions are the rules and regulations that cannot be negotiated, at least not in the short-run. The crux of an institution is its binding or *obligatory* character, embodying the legitimate expectation that actors follow certain rules also when it is not expedient and in their immediate advantage (Streeck and Thelen, 2005). The older corporatist literature predicated such rule-following behaviour on particular organisational characteristics, with a strong and probably unwarranted bias towards centralisation and hierarchical control (Baccaro 2003, for a critique). Thus, wage coordination was thought to be facilitated by organisational structures and practices that allowed the unions 'to "insulate" bargaining from particularist demands and "coerce" their members to accept the terms of the bargain once reached' and helped them to prevent disruptive competition (Lange, 1984, p. 106). This approach was embedded in a view that union leaders, armed with professional advice and welcomed to the secrets and corridors of macroeconomic policy making, would be stronger motivated to endorse long-term, national and 'public-regarding' goals than their members.[19] As Peter Lange (1984) pointed out, both the reformist (corporatist) and radical (Marxist) wing in the labour movement tended to share the view that members and local bargainers had to be *forced or fooled* into supporting a policy of restraint. Baccaro (2003) has criticised the corporatist writers for their failure to consider mechanisms of democratic deliberation, accountability and legitimacy within organisations such as unions. These mechanisms may provide alternative means for achieving the intra- and inter-organisational cohesion and coordination needed for concerted policy making, better adapted to the greater diversity of firms, labour markets and employment

[19] Mancur Olson (1982), too, made strong assumptions about the relationship between leaders and members in interest organisations like unions: in 'exclusive groups' and 'distributional coalitions' members are assumed to control the leaders, in 'encompassing organisations' *vice versa*.

and life conditions, and to and enhanced capacity for decentralised decision making. Presumably, in a successful 'marriage of opposites' one needs both: non-negotiable commitments and engagement based on deliberation.

References

Aidt, T. and Z. Tzannatos (2002), *Union and Collective Bargaining, Economic Effects in a Global Environment*, Washington, DC: The World Bank.

Armingeon, K. and M. Beyeler (ed.) (2004), *The OECD and the Welfare State*, Cheltenham, UK: Edward Elgar.

Baccaro, L. (2003), 'What is alive and what is dead in the theory of corporatism', *British Journal of Industrial Relations*, **41**(4):683–706.

Bain, G.S. and R. Price (1980), *Profiles of Union Growth. A Statistical Portrait of Eight Countries*. Oxford: Blackwell.

Barnard, C., S. Deakin and R. Hobbs, 'Opting out of the 48-hour week: employer necessity or individual choice? An empirical study of the operation of article 18(1)(b) of the Working Time Directive in the UK', *Industrial Law Journal*, **32**(4):223–52.

Blau, F. and L. Kahn (1999), 'Institutions and laws in the labour market', in O. Ashenfelter, and D. Card (eds), *Handbook of Labor Economics*, Amsterdam: North-Holland, vol. 3, pp. 1399–461.

Blyth, C.A. (1979), 'The interaction between collective bargaining and government policies in selected member countries', *Collective Bargaining and Government Policies*, Paris: OECD, Organisation for Economic Co-operation and Development.

Brandolini, A., P. Casadio, P. Cipollone, M. Magnani, A. Rosolia and R. Torrini (2006), 'Employment growth in Italy in the 1990s: institutional arrangements and market forces', in this volume.

Brown, W. (1993), 'The contraction of collective bargaining in Britain', *British Journal of Industrial Relations*, **31**(2):189–200.

Bruno, M. and J. Sachs (1985), *Economics of Worldwide Stagflation*, Cambridge, MA: Harvard University Press.

Booth, A.L. (1985), 'The free rider problem and a social custom theory of trade union membership', *Quarterly Journal of Economics*, **100**:253–61.

Calmfors, L., A. Booth, M. Burda, D. Checchi, R. Naylor and J. Visser (2001), 'The role of collective bargaining in Europe', in T. Boeri, A. Brugiavini and L. Calmfors (eds), *The Role of the Unions in the Twenty-First Century*, Oxford: Oxford University Press, pp. 1–156.

Calmfors, L. and J. Driffill (1988), 'Bargaining structure, corporatism, and macroeconomic performance', *Economic Policy*, **6**:15–61.

Cameron, D.A. (1984), 'Social democracy, corporatism, labour quiescence and the representation of economic interest in advanced capitalist society', in J.H. Golthorpe (ed.), *Order and Conflict in Contemporary Capitalism. Studies in the Political Economy of Western European Nations*, Oxford: Clarendon Press, pp. 143–78.

Checchi, D. and J. Visser (2005), 'Pattern persistence in European trade union density – A longitudinal analysis 1950–1996', *European Sociological Review*, **21**(1):1–22.

Clegg, H.A. (1976), *Trade Unions Under Collective Bargaining. A Theory Based on Comparison of Six Countries*, Oxford: Blackwell.

Crouch, C.J. (1985), 'Conditions for trade union wage restraint', in L.N. Lindberg and C.S. Maier (eds), *The Politics of Inflation and Economic Stagnation*, Washington, DC: Brookings Institution, pp. 105–39.

Crouch, C.J. (1993), *Industrial Relations and European State Traditions*, Oxford: Oxford University Press.

Crouch, C.J. (2000), 'The euro and labour market and wage policies', in K. Dyson (ed), *European Strategies and the Euro*, Oxford: Oxford University Press, pp. 278–304.

Culpepper, P.D. (2004), 'Focal Points and power plays in institutional change: an empirical assessment', paper prepared for presentation at the Annual Meeting of the American Political Science Association, Chicago, IL, September 2-5 2004.

Ebbinghaus, B. and J. Visser (1999), 'When institutions matter: union growth and decline in Western Europe, 1950–1995', *European Sociological Review*, **15**:1–24.

Ebbinghaus, B. and J. Visser (2000), *Trade Unions in Western Europe Since 1945*, London: Palgrave-Macmillan.

Esping-Andersen, G. (1990), *Three Worlds of Welfare Capitalism*, Cambridge, UK: Polity Press.

European Commission (2005), 'Labour markets in the EU: economic analysis of recent performance and prospects', *The European Economy*, 1, special issue: 1–44.

Fajertag, G. and Ph. Pochet (eds) (2000), *Social Pacts in Europe. New Dynamics*, Brussels: European Trade Union Institute and Observatoire Social Européenne.

Ferrera, M. and E. Gualmini (2004), *Rescued by Europe? Social and Labour Market Reforms from Maastricht to Berlusconi*, Amsterdam: Amsterdam University Press.

Fiorito, R. (2003), 'The paradox of corporatism: Italy's case', in M. Baldassarri and B. Chiarini (eds), *Studies in Labour Markets and Industrial Relations*, London: Palgrave-Macmillan, pp. 277–97.

Flanagan, R.J. (1999), 'Macroeconomic performance and collective bargaining: an international perspective', *Journal of Economic Literature*, **37**(3):1150–75.

Flanagan, R.J. (2003), 'Collective bargaining and macroeconomic performance', in J.T. Addison and C. Schnabel (eds), *International Handbook of Trade Unions*, Cheltenham, UK and Northampton, MA (USA): Edward Elgar, pp. 172–96.

Flanders, A. (1964), *The Fawley Productivity Agreements*, London: Faber and Faber.

Flanders, A. (1970), *Management and Unions. The theory and reform of industrial relations*, London: Faber and Faber.

Galenson, W. (1949), *Labor in Norway*, Cambridge, MA: Harvard University Press.

Galenson, W. (1952), *The Danish System of Industrial Relations*, Cambridge, MA, Harvard University Press.

Golden, M. (1993), 'The dynamics of trade unionism and national economic performance', *Americal Political Science Review*, **87**:439–54.

Golden, M., M. Wallerstein and P. Lange (1999), 'Postwar trade-union organization and industrial relations', in P. Lange, H. Kitschelt, G.. Marks, and J. Stephens (eds), *Continuity and Change in Contemporary Capitalism*, Cambridge, UK: Cambridge University Press, pp. 194–230.

Hall, P.A. and D. Soskice (2001), 'An introduction to varieties of capitalism', in P.A. Hall and D. Soskice (eds), *Varieties of Capitalism. The Institutional Foundations of Comparative Advantage*, Oxford: Oxford University Press, pp. 1–68.

Hardiman, N. (1988), *Pay, Politics, and Economic Performance in Ireland 1970–1987*, Oxford: Clarendon Press.

Holden, S. and O. Raum (1991), 'Wage moderation and union structure', *Oxford Economic Papers*, **43**:409–23.
Iversen, T. (1999), *Contested Economic Institutions. The Politics of Macroeconomics and Wage Bargaining in Advanced Democracies*, Cambridge, MA: Cambridge University Press.
Kenworthy, L. (2001), 'Wage-setting institutions: a survey and assessment', *World Politics* **54**(October):57–98.
Lange, P. (1984), 'Unions, workers and wage regulation: the rational basis of consent', in J.H. Golthorpe (ed.), *Order and Conflict in Contemporary Capitalism. Studies in the Political Economy of Western European Nations*, Oxford: Clarendon Press, pp. 98–123.
Lehmbruch, G. (1984), 'Concertation and the structure of corporatist networks', in J.H. Golthorpe (ed.), *Order and Conflict in Contemporary Capitalism. Studies in the Political Economy of Western European Nations*, Oxford: Clarendon Press, pp. 60–80.
Lindblom, C.E. (1949), *Unions and Capitalism*, New Haven, CT: Yale University Press.
Lijphart, A. and M. Crepaz (1991), 'Corporatism and consensus democracy in eighteen countries: conceptual and empirical linkages', *British Journal of Political Science* **21**:235–56.
Naylor, R. (2003), 'Economic models of union behaviour', in J.T. Addison and C. Schnabel (eds), *International Handbook of Labour Economics*, Cheltenham, UK and Northampton, MA (USA): Edward Elgar, pp. 366–413.
O'Donnell, R. (2001), 'Towards post-corporatist concertation in Europe', in H. Wallace (ed.), *Interlocking Dimensions of European Integration*, London: Pinter.
OECD (1994), *The OECD Job Study: Facts, Analysis, Strategy*, Paris: Organisation for Economic Co-operation and Development.
OECD (1997), 'Economic performance and the structure of collective bargaining', *Employment Outlook 1997*, pp. 63–93.
OECD (1999), 'Implementing the OECD jobs strategy: assessing performance and policy', Report, Paris: Organisation for Economic Co-operation and Development.
OECD (2004), 'Wage-setting institutions and outcomes', *Employment Outlook 2004*, pp. 127–82.
Olson, M. J. (1982), *The Rise and Decline of Nations*, New Haven, CT: Yale University Press.
Regini, M. (1984), 'The Conditions for political exchange: how concertation emerged and collapsed in Italy and Great Britain', in J.H. Golthorpe (ed.), *Order and Conflict in Contemporary Capitalism. Studies in the Political Economy of Western European Nations*, Oxford: Clarendon Press, pp. 124–42.
Regini, M. (1997), 'Still engaging in corporatism? Recent Italian experience in comparative perspective', *European Journal of Industrial Relations*, **3**(3):259–78.
Rogers, J. and W. Streeck (eds) (1995), *Works Councils. Consultation, representation and cooperation in industrial relations*, Chicago, Ill.: The University of Chicago Press.
Rowthorn, B. (1992), 'Centralisation, employment, and wage dispersion', *The Economic Journal*, **102**:506–23.
Scheuer, S. (2004), 'Extra holiday entitlements in Denmark. Towards a transformation of collective bargaining?', in J. Lind, H. Knudsen and H. Jorgensen (eds), *Labour and Employment Regulation in Europe*, Brussels: P.I.E. - Peter Lang. 45.

Schmitter, Ph.C. (1981), 'Interest intermediation and regime governability in contemporary Western Europe and North America', in S. Berger (ed.), *Organizing Interests in Western Europe*, Cambridge, MA: Cambridge University Press, pp. 285–327.

Schwerin, D.S. (1984), 'Historic compromise and pluralist decline? Profits and Capital in Nordic Countries', in J.H. Golthorpe (ed.), *Order and Conflict in Contemporary Capitalism. Studies in the Political Economy of Western European Nations*, Oxford: Clarendon Press, pp. 231–56.

Siaroff, A. (1999), 'Corporatism in 24 industrial democracies: meaning and measurement', *European Journal of Political Research*, **36**:175–205.

Soskice, D.W. (1990), 'Wage determination: the changing role of institutions in advanced industrialised countries', *Oxford Review of Economic Policy*, **6**(4):36–61.

Streeck, W. (1992), *Social Institutions and Economic Performance: Studies of industrial relations in advanced capitalist economies*, London: Sage.

Streeck, W. (1994), 'Pay restraint without incomes policy: institutionalised monetarism and industrial unionism in Germany', in R. Boyer, R. Dore, and Z. Mars (eds), *The Return to incomes Policy*, London: Pinter, pp. 118–40.

Streeck, W. and J. Visser (1997), 'The rise of the conglomerate union', *European Journal of Industrial Relations*, **3**(3):305–32.

Streeck, W. and B. Rehder (2003), 'Das Flachentarifvertrag. Stabilität und Wandel', *Industrielle Beziehungen*, **10**(3):341–62.

Streeck, W. and K.L. Thelen (2005), 'Introduction: institutional change in advanced political economies', in W. Streeck, and K.L. Thelen (eds), *Beyond Continuity*, Oxford: Oxford University Press, pp. 1–39.

Tarantelli, E. (1983), 'La predeterminazione dell'inflazione nei paesi industrializzati e l'accordo sul costo del lavoro del 22 gennaio 1983', *Laboratorio politico*, January-February.

Tarantelli, E. (1986a), 'The regulation of inflation and unemployment', *Industrial Relations*, **25**:1–15.

Tarantelli, E. (1986b), *Economia politica del lavoro*, Turin: UTET.

Thelen, K.L. (2001), 'Varieties of labor policies in developed countries', in P.A. Hall and D. Soskice (eds), *Varieties of Capitalism. The institutional foundations of comparative advantage*, Oxford: Oxford University Press, pp. 71–103.

Trampusch, C. (2004), 'Sozialpolitik durch Tarifvertrag in den Niederlanden. Die Rolle der industrielle Beziehungen in der Liberalisierung des Wohlfahrtstaates', Coldogne, Max Planck Institute for the Study of Societies, *MPIfG Discussion Paper* 04/12.

Traxler, F. (1994), 'Collective bargaining: levels and coverage', *OECD Employment Outlook 1994*, pp. 167–94.

Traxler, F., S. Blaschke and B. Kitter (2001), *National Labour Relations in Internationalized Markets: A Comparative Study of Institutions, Change, and Performance*, Oxford: Oxford University Press.

Traxler, F. and M. Behrens (2002), 'Collective bargaining coverage and extension procedures', *Report*, Dublin: European Foundation for the Improvement of Living and Working Conditions.

Visser, J. (1989), *European Trade Unions in Figures, 1913–1985*, Deventer and Boston: Kluwer Law and Taxation.

Visser, J. (1990), 'In search of inclusive unionism', *Bulletin of Comparative Labour Relations*, **18**:5–278.

Visser, J. (2001a), 'Industrial relations and social dialogue', in P. Auer (ed.), *Changing Labour Markets in Europe. The role of institutions and policies*, Geneva: ILO, pp. 184–242.

Visser, J. (2001b), 'Industrial relations management of the consequences of success. Learning ahead of failure and organised decentralisation', *Report for the National Economic and Social Council of the Republic of Ireland*, Amsterdam: Amsterdam Institute for Avanced Labour Studies AIAS.

Visser, J. (2002), 'Why fewer European workers join unions – A social customs explanation of membership trends', *British Journal of Industrial Relations*, **40**(3):403–30.

Visser, J. (2004), 'Patterns and variations in European industrial relations', in J. Visser (ed.) (on behalf of European Commission, Department for Social Affairs, Employment and Equal Opportunities), *Industrial Relations in Europe* 2004, Luxembourg: Office for Official Publications of the European Communities, pp. 11–58.

Visser, J. (2005), 'Beneath the surface of stability: new and old methods of governance in European industrial relations', *European Journal of Industrial Relations*, **11**(3):287–306

Visser, J., S. Martin and P. Tergeist (2004), *Trade Union Members and Union Density*, Paris: OECD, http://www.oecd.org.

Wallerstein, M. and B. Western (2000), 'Unions in decline? What has changed and why?', *Annual Review of Political Science*, **3**:355–77.

Western, B. (1997), *Between Class and Market: Postwar Unionization in the Capitalist Democracies*, Princeton, NJ: Princeton University Press.

Williamson, O.E. (1968), 'Wage rates as barrier entry: the Pennington case in perspective', *Quarterly Journal of Economics*, **82**(1):85–115.

Windmuller, J.P. (1975), The authority of national trade union confederations: A comparative analysis', in D. Lipsky (ed.), *Union Power and Public Policy*, New York: IILR Press, pp. 91–107.

Wright, E.O. (2000), 'Working-class power, capitalist-class interests, and class compromise', *American Journal of Sociology*, **105**(4):957–1002.

PART IV

INDUSTRIAL RELATIONS AND MACROECONOMIC PERFORMANCE

7 Wage Setting Institutions and Economic Performance

Carlo Dell'Aringa

Catholic University of Milan, Italy

7.1 Introduction

In a comment written as an introduction to a work by Ezio Tarantelli published posthumously in 1986, two of his colleagues and friends, Lloyd Ulman and David Soskice, wrote: 'Further work, which must be left to others, will doubtless modify Tarantelli's approach, but it will also build on his pioneering effort in the analytical and quantitative assessment of what has been referred to as neocorporatist arrangements and policies' (Tarantelli, 1986, p. 1). The aim of this note is to develop this comment. Especial reference will be made to the 'further work' which has been carried out during the last twenty years, and to Ezio's 'pioneering effort', which still survives today.

7.2 First question: what is the relation between industrial relations and macroeconomic performance?

The article by Ezio Tarantelli (ET) was entitled 'The Regulation of Inflation and Unemployment' and contained the central nucleus of his neo-corporatist ideas. He tested empirically these ideas by estimating an univariate relationship, for 15 developed countries, between the well-known Okun's index (or 'misery index', i.e. the sum of the inflation rate and the unemployment rate) and the corresponding value, for each country, of a neo-corporatism index which measured some fundamental aspects of the industrial relations system. These aspects were: the 'cooption' of trade unions (roughly the degree of ideological and political consensus between unions and government), the centralisation of collective bargaining and the regulation of industrial conflict.

ET found a very high negative correlation between the misery index and the degree of 'neo-corporatism', for the periods he considered, 1968–73, 1974–79 and 1980–83 (see Fig. 7.1), and this brought him to conclude that, 'in the presence of a high degree of neo-corporatism ... unemployment would be a less necessary tool of stabilisation policy' (p. 14). The article was published in the winter 1986 volume of *Industrial Relations*, the journal of the Department of Industrial Relations of the University of California at Berkeley. Thirteen years later, in a review article, published in the *Journal of Economic Literature*, another of ET's colleagues

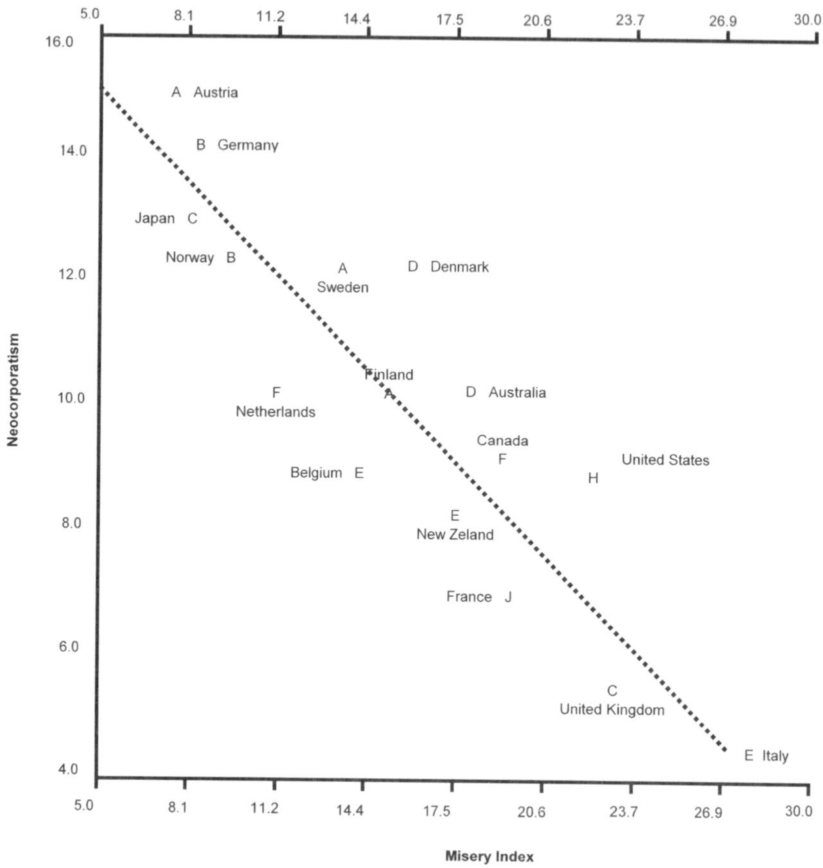

LEAST SQUARES
Misery index = 31.2 – 1.49 neo-corporativism
$\overline{R}^2 = 0.75$

Fig. 7.1. Neo-corporatism and Misery Index (1980–1983)

Source: Tarantelli (1986, p. 13)

and friends, Robert Flanagan, wrote of the theoretical contribution of neo-corporatists in the following way: 'Corporatism is an inherently multidimensional concept, for which precise definition is elusive' (p. 1155). As well as Ezio, Flanagan cites political scientists as Lehmbruch, Schmitter and Crouch, who provided definitions which were partially complementary, but partially different of the concept of 'neo-corporatism' and who, moreover, according to Flanagan, did not formally develop a coherent theory of this concept. The constituent elements of corporatism were identified by the political scientists as some features of both the industrial relations system and the system of political representation. Indicators of these features were later borrowed by social scientists who tried to test the neo-corporatist hypothesis by estimating relations similar to that estimated by ET.

But 'even when such correlations emerge', comments Flanagan, 'they are difficult to interpret, because it is not clear which dimensions of the corporatist indexes provide the statistical action. There have not been many efforts to study the influence of individual elements of the broad corporatism indexes separately ... The notion of corporatism suffers from uncertain theoretical foundations and a lack of attention to the micro-foundations of the economic and social processes that produce superior outcomes' (p. 1157). Flanagan's criticisms were harsh, though friendly (!), and seemed to imply that the neo-corporatist theory was too complex and insufficiently clear, combining economic elements with social and political ones in such a way as to make empirical testing difficult to carry out, and even difficult to interpret.

The economic literature which followed tried to overcome these limits and to some extent detached itself from the previous literature of political science. In the first place the government vanished almost completely from the analysis. Secondly with the aid of economic models, an attempt was made to make the 'story' simpler and based on more solid microeconomic foundations – at least this was the initial tendency.

The economic literature focalised almost exclusively on the characteristics of collective bargaining and on union strength, and a formal analysis was developed of the relation between a few simple features of the system of industrial relations and macroeconomic performance, deliberately ignoring aspects of a more political or sociological nature which were instead considered very important by scholars of corporatism. The theoretical framework developed by economists tended to exclude the idea that industrial relations had anything to do with inflation, and also to exclude any link between inflation and unemployment, apart from possible short-term interactions. The main problem of many industrialised countries as of the end of 1980s, was a continuously high level of unemployment. In many models developed during this period, inflationary pressure still has an important role, but in the end it is the equilibrium unemployment rate which provides the main indicator of macroeconomic performance. The 'misery index' too has almost completely disappeared from analysis.

In models developed within traditional economic theory, the aim of the unions is to raise real wages using their bargaining power, taking into account the negative effects (negative for the unions themselves too) of an increase in real wages on employment. In the empirical studies which have tried to apply this model, indicators such as union density or coverage of collective bargaining are considered as being indicators of union strength and therefore conducive to higher real wages. A very different relationship was hypothesised by ET, according to which strong unions and high coverage of collective bargaining were a constituent element of the degree of centralisation of the industrial relations system. In the economic literature of this period, the twin aspects of a wage setting system, coverage and density on the one hand, and centralisation on the other, are kept separate. The former, as indicators of union power, have negative effects on employment, while centralisation may contrast this effect by producing a positive one. The positive role of centralisation has been explained in several important theoretical studies, above all the well-known work by Calmfors and Driffill (1998). It is enough to remember the importance of the role plaid by the existence of external economies and by the elasticity of labour demand in this context. In this current of literature, the concept of centralisation was quickly replaced by that of co-ordination of collective bargaining (Soskice, 1990). What is important is not where bargaining takes place, whether centralised or decentralised, but rather to what extent it is co-ordinated, formally or informally.

The exact relation between centralisation (together with co-ordination) of bargaining, and macroeconomic performance, has been discussed both theoretically and empirically. The relation may be monotonic, signifying that more co-ordination implies wage restraints, or hump-shaped, as Calmfors and Driffill maintained in their article, meaning that good performance may be also achieved when wage restraints are the result of a high elasticity of the labour demand which unions must face when bargaining with a single employer. Within this theoretical framework, the worst situation from the point of view of wage pressure and the resulting higher unemployment, is represented by an intermediate level of co-ordination (corresponding more or less to bargaining at sectoral level, as it is done in many European countries, including Italy and Germany) which is able neither to internalise the negative effects of wage claims nor produce the positive effects of a more competitive and disciplined labour market. An enormous amount of research has attempted to verify the one (monotonic) or the other (hump-shaped), without reaching any precise conclusion.

Some of the most recent reviews of the literature go further and conclude that the very relationship between degree of co-ordination together with centralisation, and economic performance, seems to have vanished during the 1990s (Aidt and Tzannatos, 2002). This is the result found by a recent OECD study (OECD, 2004), which by means of cross-country comparisons repeated over time, fails to find, especially for more recent periods, any direct correlation either between macroeconomic performance and degree of centralisation-co-ordination (see Table 7.1), or even with the indicators of union power, i.e. density and coverage. Conclusions are incomplete because they refer to simple univariate correlations in which the only regressors are the variables of the system of industrial relations. The analysis is not particularly sophisticated, and the OECD itself recognises that this is a preliminary study, preparatory to more sophisticated analyses. However, the results suffice to show that countries with similar wage-setting institutions do achieve different macroeconomic performances.

More sophisticated analyses is exactly what has been done by a large body of economic literature. It shows, both theoretically and empirically, that the wage setting system is indeed important in affecting the performance of the labour market. The system of collective bargaining is however set against a wider background. In rather elaborated models of the functioning of the labour market, both dynamic aspects and the conditions of general economic equilibrium are taken into account (Nickell and Layard's model (1999) is perhaps the most important example). On the empirical front, these studies try to explain the different performances of the various countries not only on the basis of differences in the wage setting systems, but also on that of differences regarding other institutional aspects or political measures, referred both to the labour market and the overall economic system. Of these the most well known are the tax wedge, employment protection legislation, and unemployment benefits.

Table 7.1. The degree of bargaining centralisation/co-coordination (CC) and macroeconomic performance (averages 1990–2002)

	Unemployment rate	Misery index
High CC	7.4	11.3
Intermediate CC	7.1	8.6
Low CC	7.2	11.1

Source: OECD (2004).

More recently other aspects of an institutional nature have been included in the analyses to explain the differences between countries' rates of unemployment and/or employment. This is the case for example of systems of regulation of product markets (Nicoletti et al., 2001), or the share of employment in the public sector in total employment (Algan et al., 2002; Forni, 2004), or the development of risk capital markets (Phelps, 2004).

Lively debate has developed over the relative importance of each of these institutional aspects, and, among them, the variables of the wage setting system have not always proved to be the most important in influencing the macroeconomic performance.

It is important to note that while some welfare costs could be considered as the subject of bargaining and political trade-off in the original corporatist literature (wage restraints in exchange for more 'welfare'), now in the more recent economic literature some of these social costs (for example unemployment benefits) cause a decidedly negative effect on unemployment and employment. The reform of the welfare system (another example is pension reform) has become a political concern for those countries which aim to improve their macroeconomic performance. In this context unions, which generally tend to defend the 'status quo', do not play a positive role (Boeri, Brugiavini, Calmfors, 2001).

The most recent developments in economic literature have included studies which have tried to increase the explanatory power of the models used, hypothesising and empirically testing the possible interactions of the variables considered. Important contributions have been made by studies which hypothesise interactions between institutional variables and macroeconomic shocks (Blanchard and Wolfers, 2000), or between the taxation system and the wage setting system (Daveri and Tabellini, 2000), or between monetary policy and the wage setting system (Iversen, 1998), or again between the very variables which characterise the wage setting system, i.e. coverage, density, co-ordination (Belot and Van Ours, 2004).

Different results have been obtained. This diversity is most certainly due to the differences between the theoretical models of reference and the varying specification of the relations tested empirically. It is also due to the time periods considered; indeed, with the passage of time a higher number of observations have become available, and this has made it possible, in addition to the traditional cross-sections, to estimate the same relations over time, by taking into account variations both in macroeconomic outcomes and in institutional settings (see a recent interesting contribution by Nickell, 2004).

Results are also dependent on the rankings of the various countries as regards wage setting institutions. The level of co-ordination of collective bargaining existing in each country is the result of a subjective evaluation. Indeed, there is a lack of adequate quantitative indicators, so that results are highly sensitive to the different rankings of the countries examined. Sometimes it is sufficient for a couple of countries to shift position to change the results. Despite the great number of studies, each of which has attempted to establish its own ranking of countries, this is a sector in which further research could be useful. Some studies have tried to include further dimensions of the industrial relations theoretical framework. One example is the concept of vertical and horizontal co-ordination suggested by Traxler (2003). This concept has been elaborated to describe central organisations' ability to control the behaviour of their 'rank and file'. Of the indicators used, some refer to aspects such as 'peace obligation' or 'enforceability of agreements' which were also developed by ET in his index of neo-corporatism. But even the traditional concepts of centralisation and co-ordination are broken down in ever-more sophisticated ways. In the OECD work cited above (OECD, 2004), the indicators of both centralisation and co-ordination are really compound indices, composed of simple averages of primary indices. Each primary index is used to give a score to each country. These procedures are rather ad hoc and do not make sufficient reference to theoretical arguments able to describe the mechanisms involved – not to mention the problem of giving scores in these rankings to the countries where two-tier systems are in force, i.e. with two levels of bargaining, national and local. The relative weight of the two tiers is not easily identified or measured, because they act together and influence each other. The problem often coincides with the role played by wage drift, which may substitute or be in addition to the wage increases obtained at the higher level of bargaining.

In conclusion it can be said that over the last twenty years the economic literature has provided some very interesting results, but has left many questions unanswered. This brings us again to the same difficulties ET and other scholars of neo-corporatism faced. Economic analysis should have simplified issues the scholars of neo-corporatism had made 'complicated' by mixing economic factors with social and political factors. The complexity which left by the door came back in through the window, and the great abundance of theoretical and empirical analyses on this topic, and the quantity of institutional and political factors cited, leads us to repeat Flanagan's important observation, that 'any relationship between bargaining structure and macroeconomic outcomes is contingent on the particular economic and political environment of a country' (p. 1162). Economic literature has enabled us to make enormous progress, but to day's difficulties and problems, as well as some important intuitions, are rather similar to those faced and elaborated by ET and his colleagues 20 years ago.

7.3 Second question: why is collective bargaining becoming decentralised?

The second question refers to a problem which was tackled only marginally by ET. It concerns the role, positive, that collective bargaining can have even at a decentralised level. In his article cited above, ET speaks of this only in the conclusions, when he mentions the concept of 'decentralised neo-corporatism'. 'Although an oxymoron – he observes – decentralised corporatism is not an internally inconsistent theoretical concept' (p. 14). He did not have time to develop this intuition, though it is easy to imagine what he had in mind.

Taking this as a starting point, I would like to extend the analysis to include the role of collective bargaining in influencing pay dispersion and wage inequalities. While the empirical literature has not fully clarified what is the precise relationship between the degree of centralisation and coordination of collective bargaining and the performance of the labour market, there is at the same time much empirical literature which shows more or less unambiguously that in systems featuring high levels of centralisation and co-ordination, pay dispersion is lower and wage differentials are more compressed (Blau and Kahn, 1999, 2002; OECD, 1997; Wallerstein, 1999).

It is unclear whether compression of wage differentials can have negative effects on the levels of unemployment and employment. On the one hand textbooks teach that wage differentials must be left free to carry out their allocative function, otherwise there will be mismatches of varying kinds between labour demand and supply. On the other, in a number of studies it is shown that, in particular circumstances (for example when there are imperfections in the capital markets), a reduction in pay differentials can have positive effects on employment and even on growth (Acemoglu and Pischke, 1998; Agel, 1999).

The theoretical debate is still open and no final conclusion has been reached. Nevertheless, it is a matter of fact that in a growing number of countries the system of collective bargaining has been progressively decentralised (EEAG Report, 2004). There are probably several factors that can explain this process. One of these can be the increasing mismatches occurring between labour demand and labour supply, and the deterioration of the unemployment mix in many countries (in particular, skilled towards unskilled labour). This factor induced a number of countries to reconsider the balance of advantages and disadvantages of a centralised and coordinated system of collective bargaining and the merits and demerits of a national wage policy based on principles of solidarity and equality.

Another important factor to consider as a possible explanation of the process of decentralisation, is the idea that the pay structure and pay differentials can be seen both as useful incentive mechanisms and as a tool to develop participation and increase collaboration of workers inside the firm. This is probably what ET had in mind when he wrote of 'decentralised corporatism'.

The shift towards decentralisation has not always followed the same path. Different countries have taken different paths and three types can be distinguished.

In some countries the shift has been slow and smooth, and has not changed the existing system in a radical way. There has been an increase in scope and diffusion of collective bargaining at the company level. In some countries this has happened through decisions of individual companies that in specific circumstances, have left their employers' association or have decided to 'opt out' from the coverage of a multi-employer collective agreement. This is the case, for example, of Germany (Ochel, 2005). In other countries the unions took part in the process. Especially in countries where a two-tier system of collective bargaining is in place (bargaining occurs not only at a multi-employer level, but also at the company level) unions have favoured some form of decentralisation as long as this strengthened rather that weakened the existing system. This is, for example, the case of Italy (see Casadio, 2003). All these moves towards decentralisation have not proceeded at a very fast pace and there is not much empirical evidence on the final results in terms of an increased flexibility of relative wages. The implicit objective was to reconcile the advantages of coordinated bargaining with the advantages of decentralisation, that is to achieve the best of the two world: wage restraint at macro-level and flexibility of wages at the micro-level.

However, as far as the macro-level is concerned, one has to observe that if a gradual shift towards company-level bargaining moved the industrial relations system more towards an intermediate position in the ranking of countries according to their degree of centralisation and coordination, and if, at the same time, the hump-shaped hypothesis were true, there would be a reduction in incentives for wage restraint, and a consequent deterioration of the performance of the labour market.

On the other hand, if a high level of coordination of company bargaining were maintained, the positive effect expected from decentralisation on wage differentials would be uncertain. Recent research shows how in countries with a high level of national co-ordination, for example Belgium, Italy, company-level bargaining does not make a significant contribution to contrasting the compression of wage differentials determined by national labour agreements.

In Table 7.2 measures of inequalities (standard deviation (St. dev.) and coefficient of variation (CV)) have been calculated for wages of individual workers of four countries: Belgium, Italy, Spain, and UK. The data have been collected through the 'Structure of Earnings Survey' conducted by Eurostat in 1995. The table presents values for St. dev. and CV of wages, both for manual and non manual workers, separately by bargaining regime. MEB represents the group of workers covered by a multi-employer bargaining, while SEB represents the group of workers covered by a single-employer bargaining. There is an important difference among the four countries. In Belgium and Italy the bargaining system is two tier: all workers considered in the table are covered by a MEB, but only some of them are covered, in addition, also by a SEB. In Spain and UK workers are covered only by one type of contract: one type exclude the other.

Two extreme cases can be detected from the results described in Table 7.2. One is Belgium where, contrary to expectations, wages are less compressed when workers are covered only by a MEB. The other is UK, where wages are much more compressed exactly when workers are covered by a MEB. For Italy and Spain the results are more mixed and depend on which measure of inequality is considered.

On the whole the data show that where a strong national coordination of local bargaining exists, as it is the case of Belgium and, to some extent also in Italy, bargaining at company level does not necessarily increase wage inequalities and does not contrast the compression of wage differentials that might be determined by national wage agreements. These results are probably due to the forces of imitation and coordination that limit the role of SEB in widening inter-firm differentials and to the egalitarian character of wage policies that in an environment where values of equity, solidarity and uniformity are strong and diffused, are also followed by unions negotiating at the level of the single firm, or single establishment. Only in UK, workers covered by a MEB have less dispersed wages. These results seem to show that it is not easy to combine elements of centralisation and/or coordination with elements of decentralisation of collective bargaining in order to reap the benefits of both situations.

Table 7.2. Unconditional measures of wage inequalities

		Std dev			CV	
	All	MEB	SEB	All	MEB	SEV
ITALY						
All	0.439	0.427	0.445	0.153	0.151	0.148
Non Manual	0.465	0.459	0.451	0.147	0.147	0.137
Manual	0.295	0.305	0.246	0.110	0.114	0.089
BELGIUM						
All	0.428	0.465	0.375	0.067	0.074	0.059
Non Manual	0.433	0.473	0.383	0.066	0.072	0.058
Manual	0.260	0.246	0.242	0.043	0.041	0.039
SPAIN						
All	0.532	0.512	0.490	0.074	0.073	0.066
Non Manual	0.586	0.588	0.526	0.079	0.080	0.069
Manual	0.430	0.381	0.417	0.061	0.055	0.057
UK						
All	0.545	0.407	0.568	0.268	0.203	0.278
Non Manual	0.605	0.461	0.624	0.274	0.219	0.281
Manual	0.374	0.333	0.380	0.204	0.173	0.210

Source: Dell'Aringa and Pagani (2005).

Note: Rata refer to the Structure of Earnings Survey (Eurostat). The survey contains matched employer-employee information for the year 1995. MEB represents groups of workers covered only by a multi-employer collective bargaining. SEB is for workers covered by single-employer collective bargaining.

A completely different path has been followed by those countries in which the process of decentralisation of bargaining has been radical and also accompanied by massive de-unionisation. This is the case of a series of English-speaking countries: the United Kingdom, New Zealand and to some extent Australia. A radical shift from a multi-employer bargaining system to a single-employer bargaining system has taken place at the same time as a dramatic fall in union density and in the level of coverage of collective bargaining. It is certain that the use of performance-related pay schemes has increased significantly, and wage structures have become much more flexible. In these countries wage dispersion is greater and wage differentials are much less compressed than they are in continental Europe. In these countries there has been also a process of radical de-regulation in the field of employment protection legislation. In addition, other important reforms have been made, for example reform of product and service markets, and reform of public administration, with an emphasis on various forms of liberalisation and privatisation. Although these reforms are often believed to produce positive macroeconomic effects, it is hard to say what effects all this complex change has produced. Certainly in some of these countries, the unemployment rate reached relatively low levels when, at the same time, it was dramatically increasing in some of the largest countries of continental Europe, where the process of reforming the functioning of labour and product markets was much more slow. Nevertheless it is difficult to attribute this better performance to single specific aspects of the radical change which has taken place, so that we do not know precisely what it has been the role plaid by the process of decentralisation of the collective bargaining system.

Finally a third kind of path, perhaps more profitable, has been taken by some northern European countries. This is the path known as 'organised decentralisation' as it has been called by Traxler (1995). It refers to a system of collective bargaining where decisions are taken at the local level, but they must respect the general guidelines set by a national 'framework' agreement. Translated in terms of wage policy this system of 'organized decentralisation' implies that the national level of bargaining determines only the total 'margin' and leaves freedom to parties bargaining at company level to distribute this margin to individual workers. In this way, in some countries responsibility is divided between centralised and decentralised levels. At the former, which determines the total margin, responsibility is taken for keeping total wage demands under control. At the latter, where real wage increases of individual workers are determined, it is possible to fix both wage differentials in accordance with the conditions of local labour markets, and to use wages as incentives (for stimulating more effort and on-the-job-training), and for performance-related pay schemes at individual and collective level. Efforts in this direction have been made in Holland (Eironline Netherlands, 2002) and Denmark (Eironline Denmark, 2003), but it is perhaps in Sweden that this path towards decentralisation has been followed the most.

The means by which decentralisation is put into practice in Sweden are numerous and vary from industry to industry. In some industries the decentralisation process has gone even further: Table 7.3 shows how a significant proportion of workers are covered by national agreements which do not even specify the total margin to be distributed at local level. Not only wage increases for individual workers, but also average overall increases are defined at this latter level (see Table 7.3). This procedure is adopted in industries covering 7 per cent of workers in the private sector and is also adopted in the public sector, in a total of about 30 per cent of the whole. This type of bargaining applies above all to white-collar workers with higher education. In this respect it must be borne in mind that Sweden abandoned its traditional centralised system some time ago, with the specific aim of meeting the wishes of private firms and public administration, which complained that the centralised system had over-compressed wage differentials by education and skill level, thwarting workers' investment in human capital. It seems that in Sweden decentralisation of bargaining has produced an increase in wage dispersion and a widening in salary differentials, without compromising the role of bargaining at a national level to keep overall wage dynamics under control. In principle, this solution seems to offer the best opportunity for combining the benefits of co-ordination in terms of internalisation of various effects caused by wage pressures, together with the benefits of increased flexibility of relative wages.

Table 7.3. Types of collective agreement in Sweden, 2002

	Percentage of employees in each sector		
	Private sector	Central government	Local government
1. Local bargaining without nationally determined margin for wage increase	7	32	28
2. Local bargaining with nationally determined margin for wage increase if the local parties cannot agree	5		
3. Local bargaining with nationally determined margin for wage increase if the local parties cannot agree and some type of binding individual guarantee	8	68	
4. Local bargaining on distribution of nationally determined margin for wage increase without any type of individual guarantee	7		24
5. Local bargaining on the distribution of nationally determined margin for wage increase with a binding individual guarantee or an individual guarantee if the local parties cannot agree	45		48
6. Nationally agreed general wage increase plus local bargaining on the distribution of additional nationally determined margin	18		
7. Nationally agreed general wage	7		

Source: Avtalsrörelsen och lönebildningen (2002). Reproduced by EEAG, Cesifo, 2004

Note: Local government refers to regional authorities and municipalities.

There are some 'buts', which hold for all systems of wage determination emphasising the role of norms for wage increases. These can certainly carry out the important role of providing benchmarks for subsequent bargaining at local level, but the danger is that from being 'ceilings' beyond which decentralised increases cannot go, they become 'floors', i.e. minimum increases, after which local bargaining leads to additional increases. In Sweden, the system of organised decentralisation seems to work properly and norms are correctly interpreted as ceilings to be respected, but it is not necessarily true that it would work well elsewhere, in different economic, social and institutional contexts. For example, the attempt, to import this system into public sector bargaining in Italy, although only partial, did not bring the expected advantages either in terms of overall control of wage dynamics or in terms of increased flexibility in wage structures (Dell'Aringa et al., 2004). Also in this case the words of Flanagan sound most appropriate: the success of a specific collective bargaining system is 'contingent on the economic and political environment of a country'.

Moreover, not all countries with centralised systems of bargaining suffer the same skill mismatch problems experienced in Sweden. The flexibility of wage structures that is required to avoid mismatches may vary from country to country. Let's take the example of Germany, Italy and Spain. These are the countries which, together with France, experience the most serious employment problems in the whole of continental Europe. Germany and Spain have two of the highest rates of unemployment, while Italy has the lowest rate of employment in Europe. However, the employment problems of these three countries are essentially regional. They are the countries with the greatest regional disparities in unemployment and employment rates. If the unemployment and employment rates of the most developed regions of these countries are compared with rates of those countries which have undergone successful reform, such as Sweden, Denmark, Holland, and Ireland (countries which are also comparable with many regions of the previous four big countries), one finds no substantial differences. They show, more or less, the same good performance of the labour market.

It is not far from the truth to say that the problem regarding lack of jobs in Europe is concentrated in some backward regions of Italy, Germany, Spain, and possibly also France. If this is the problem, possible solutions should concentrate on this. However, over recent decades wage differentials between regional areas have gone in the opposite direction from that required (see Figs. 7.2 and 7.3). In Germany and Italy especially, wage differentials between geographic areas have decreased over time, while differences in unemployment and employment rates have increased. A greater flexibility in geographical wage structures requires a greater decentralisation of collective bargaining, which to be effective may require a reduced level of co-ordination, both formal and informal, at the national level. On the other hand, what the four largest nations of continental Europe need is perhaps greater co-ordination within the whole of the eurozone. Collective bargaining co-ordination has to take place at the same level as monetary policy-making to be effective in favouring wage restraint (Crouch, 2000). For this reason, sooner or later the need for some kind of co-ordination above the national level for the whole of the eurozone will arise. The geographical dimension is destined to take on increasing significance when identifying levels of bargaining and co-ordination. The traditional triple distinction of 'firm-sector-economy wide', which has so far characterised the organisation of collective bargaining in European countries and which has been the focus of analysis in the economic literature, perhaps needs to be and should be supplemented ever more by a new triple distinction, that of 'region-country-eurozone'.

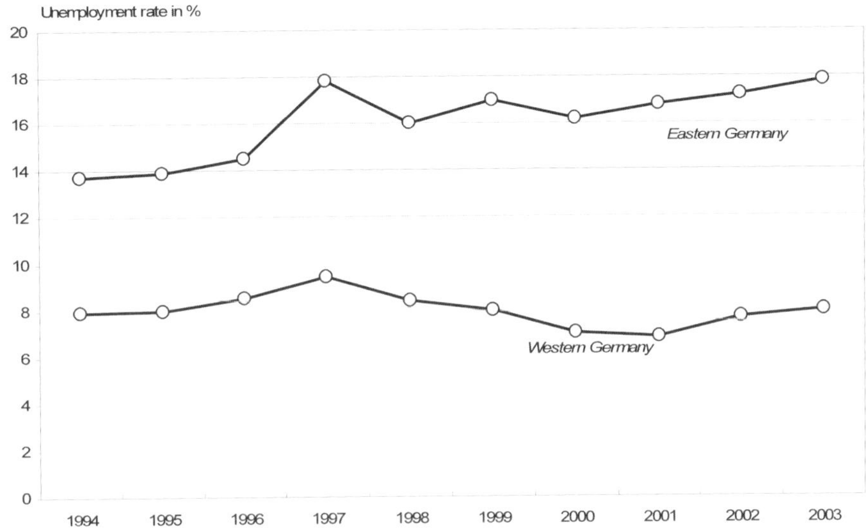

Fig. 7.2a. Unemployment rates in Eastern and Western German

Source: Federal Employment Service, Germany.

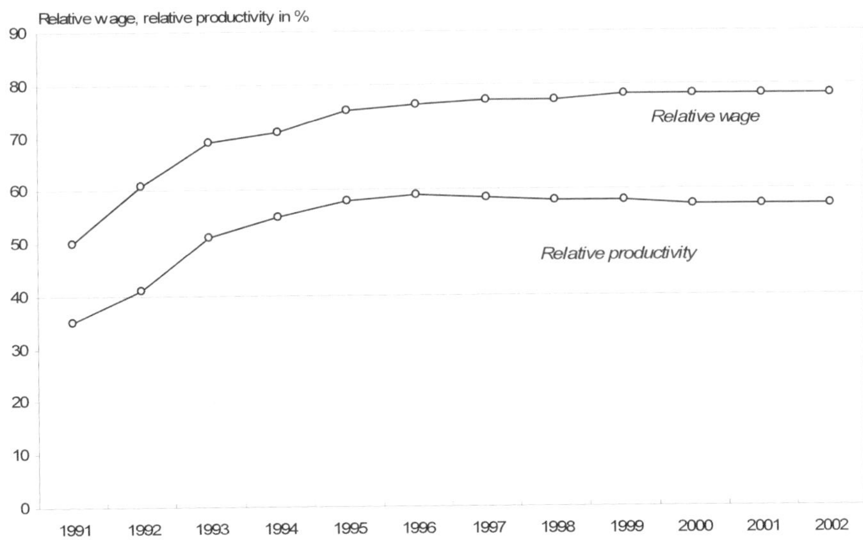

Fig. 7.2b. Relative wage per employee and relative productivity per employee in Eastern versus Western German

Source: Federal Statistical Office, Germany. Reproduced by EEAG, Cesifo 2004

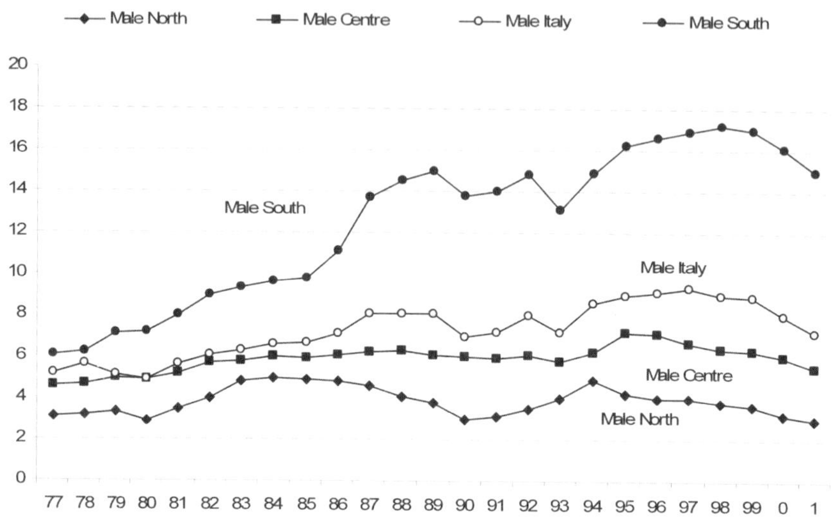

Fig. 7.3. Regional male unemployment in Italy: 1977–2001

Source: Istat and Bank of Italy. Reproduced by Bertola and Garibaldi (2004)

References

Acemoglu, D. and S. Pischke (1998), 'The structure of wages and investment in general training', *Journal of Political Economy*, **107**:539–72.

Agell, J. (1999), 'On the benefits from rigid labour markets: norms, market failures, and social insurance', *Economic Journal*, **109**:F143–F164.

Aidt, T. and Z. Tzannatos (2002), *Unions and Collective Bargaining, Economic Effects in a Global Environment*, Washington DC: The World Bank.

Algan, Y., P. Cahuc and A. Zylberberg, 'Public employment and labour market performance', *Economic Policy*, **34**:7–66.

Belot, M. and J. Van Ours (2003), 'Labour market institutions and unemployment', *CESifo DICE Report,* 2:3–6.

Bertola, G. and P. Garibaldi (2003), 'The structure and the history of Italian unemployment', *CESifo Working Paper 907.*

Blanchard, O. and J. Wolfers (2000), 'Shocks and institutions and the rise of European unemployment: the aggregate evidence', *Economic Journal*, **110**(1):1–3.

Blau, F. and L. Kahn, (1999), 'Institutions and laws in the labor market', in O. Ashenfelter and D. Card (eds), *Handbook of Labor Economics*, vol. 3, Amsterdam: North-Holland, pp. 1399–461.

Blau, F. and L. Kahn, (2002), *At Home and Abroad: U.S. Labor-Market Performance in International Perspective*, New York: Russel Sage.

Boeri, T., A. Brugiavini and L. Calmfors (eds) (2001), *The Role of Unions in the Twenty-First Century*, Oxford: Oxford University Press.

Calmfors, L. and J. Driffill (1988), 'Bargaining structure, corporatism and macroeconomic performance', *Economic Policy*, **6**(3):14–61.

Casadio, P. (2003), 'Wage formation in the italian private sector after the 1992–1993 income policy agreements', in G. Fagan, P. Mongelli, and J. Morgan (eds), *Institutions and Wage Formation in the New Europe*, Cheltenham, UK and Northampton, MA: Edward Elgar.

Crouch, C. (ed.) (2000), *After the Euro, Shaping Institutions for Governance in the Wake of European Monetary Union*, Oxford: Oxford University Press.

Daveri, F. and G. Tabellini (2000), 'Unemployment, growth and taxation in industrialised countries', *Economic Policy*, **15**:48–104.

Dell'Aringa, C. and L. Pagani (2005), 'Collective bargaining and wage dispersion', paper presented at the EALE-SOLE Conference, S. Francisco, 2–5 June.

Dell'Aringa, C., C. Lucifora and F. Origo (2004), 'Public sector and wage decentralisation: a first look at regional public-private wage differentials in Italy', paper presented at the Workshop: 'Public Sector Par Structure and Regional Competitiveness', Ermes-Paris 2, 19th November 2004.

Eironline Netherlands (2002), '2002 Annual review for Netherlands', *European Industrial Relations Observatory on-line*, Dublin: European Foundations for the Improvement of Living and Working Conditions.

Eironline Denmark (2003), '2003 Annual review for Denmark', *European Industrial Relations Observatory on-line*, Dublin: European Foundations for the Improvement of Living and Working Conditions.

European Economic Advisory Group (EEAG), (2004), *Report on the European Economy 2004*, Munich: CESifo.

Flanagan, R.J. (1999), 'Macroeconomic performance and collective bargaining: an international perspective', *Journal of Economic Literature*, **37**:1150–75.

Forni, L. (2004), 'Centralization of wage bargaining and the unemployment rate: revisiting the hump-shaped hypothesis', *Temi di Discussione 492*, Rome: Banca d'Italia.

Iversen, T. (1998), 'Wage bargaining, central bank independence and the real effect of money', *International Organisation*, **52**:469–504.

Nickell, S. (2003), 'Labour market institutions and unemployment in OECD countries', *CESifo DICE Report*, 2:13–26.

Nickell, S. and R. Layard (1999), 'Labour market institutions and economic performance', in O. Ashenfelter and D. Card (eds), *Handbook of Labor Economics*, vol. 3, Amsterdam: North-Holland, pp. 3029–84.

Nicoletti, G., R. Haffner, S. Nickell, S. Scarpetta, and G. Zoega (2001), 'European integration, liberalization and labour market performance', in G. Bertola, T. Boeri and G. Nicoletti (eds), *Welfare and Employment in a United Europe*, Cambridge, MA: MIT Press, pp. 147–235.

Ochel, W. (2005), 'Decentralizing wage bargaining in Germany. A way to increase employment?', *Labour*, **19**(1):91–122.

OECD (1997), *Employment Outlook*, Paris: OECD.

OECD (2004), *Employment Outlook*, Paris: OECD.

Phelps, E. and G. Zoega, (2004), 'The search for routes to better economic performance in continental Europe', *CESifo Forum*, **5**(1):3–11.

Soskice, D. (1990), 'Wage determination: the changing role of institutions in advanced industrialised countries', *Oxford Review of Economic Policy*, **6**(4):36–61.

Tarantelli, E. (1986), 'The regulation of inflation and unemployment', *Industrial Relations*, **25**:1–15.

Traxler, F. (1995), 'Farewell to labour market associations? Organized versus disorganized decentralisation as a map for industrial relations', in C. Crouch and F. Traxler (eds), *Organized Industrial Relations in Europe: what Future?*, Aldershot: Avebury, pp. 3–19.

Traxler, F. (2003), 'The contingency thesis of collective bargaining institutions', *CESifo DICE Report*, 2:34–39.

Visser, J. (2003), 'Unions and unionism around the world', in J. Addison and C. Schnabel (eds), *International Handbook of Trade Unions*, Cheltenham, UK and Northampton, MA: Edward Elgar, pp. 366–413.

Wallerstein, M. (1999), 'Wage-setting institutions and pay inequalities in advanced industrialised societies', *American Journal of Political Science*, **43**(3):649–80.

8 Loops Learning and the Phillips Curve

Piero Ferri

University of Bergamo, Italy

8.1 Introduction*

The objective of the present chapter is to reconsider three topics, one analytical and two of economic policy, that have been at the core of Tarantelli's contribution. The existence of a long-run Phillips curve is the theoretical problem, while the degree of indexation and the role of neo-corporativism on wage and price determination are the policy subjects. In order to deepen these aspects, three analytical aspects will be considered. First of all, a macro model will be examined where endogenous fluctuations can be generated. From a theoretical point of view, these phenomena have been mainly explained by the interplay between exogenous shocks and the mechanism of transmission. However, a medium-run perspective strongly suggests looking for an endogenous explanation of the dynamics. In fact, basing the burden of the explanation exclusively upon the shocks is not a satisfactory approach (as stressed also by Estrella and Fuhrer, 2002). In the second place, the labour market equations are inserted into a broader framework where there are non-neutralities in both labour and capital markets, the latter characterized by a cash flow mechanism that helps generating endogenous cycles (see Fazzari et al., 2006). In this environment, monetary policy is represented by a Taylor rule. Finally, new hypotheses about expectations will be introduced. While the literature refers either to naive or rational expectations, in this chapter 'boundedly rational' agents who learn the parameters of their expectation functions are considered. Bounded rationality approaches have been examined in the literature (see Conlisk, 1996; Evans and Honkapohja, 2001; Sargent, 1993), and their implications depend on the very precise assumptions that are made. In this chapter, agents who do not know the true model are assumed to form their expectations following a Markov switching time series model. According to this scheme, agents expects to have periods of good times and bad times for growth and intervals of low and high inflation, according to some transition probabilities. There are two senses in which they are 'rational'. First, the agents are consistent in the sense that, on average, their expectations match the results of the model. Second, they try to learn the pa-

* This chapter was written while I was honorary Research Professor at the Washington University. I wish to thank S. Fazzari and E. Greenberg for intellectual collaboration and G.M. Rey and C. De Vincenti for stimulating suggestions. A financial support from the University of Bergamo is acknowledged.

rameters of the model, which leads to changing parameters in the Phillips equation, an idea stressed by Sargent (1999) and Akerlof et al. (2000).

The following results, obtained mainly by means of simulations given the relative complexity of the model, are worth mentioning.

i) With calibrated parameters that have empirical underpinnings, the model can generate endogenous cycles in a robust way and, as a consequence, Phillips loops are obtained. The loops are geometrical objects that originate in a dynamical system considered in a medium-run perspective: they are situated between the short-run movements, which are dominated by frictions, and the long-run movements, shaped by the nature of the steady state values, of which the non accelerating-inflation rate of unemployment (NAIRU) is perhaps the most popular example. In this context, the steady state values matters only to center the loops, but they are never reached because of the presence of limit cycles. Referring to a NAIRU, therefore, does not necessarily imply the occurrence of a process of acceleration or deceleration in inflation outside the equilibrium, because there are bounds implied by the structure of the whole model.
ii) The Phillips curve is a system result that does not depend only upon the variables that are inserted in what should be more properly called a supply equation. This claim is not new and has been recently reaffirmed by Haldane and Quah (1999) in a monetary environment based upon rational expectations. The last assumption, however, is not necessary.
iii) In this context, the impact of the so called 'monetary rigidities' and therefore of indexation can be fruitfully analyzed and compared with the results emerging from the coordination between trade unions and monetary authorities.
iv) The assumption of 'boundedly rational' agents who learn the parameters of their expectation functions not only introduces further dynamics (learning as a source of persistence, according to Bullard and Mitra, 2002, and Sargent, 1999) into the system and contributes to a more realistic picture of the Phillips curve but it also shed new lights on the two policy problems. Although these hypotheses have been criticized for being 'ad hoc' (see Buiter and Panigirtzoglou, 2003), the learning process can be justified in terms of the behavioral macroeconomics stressed by Akerlof (2002).

The structure of the chapter is the following. In Section 8.2 a brief description of Tarantelli's framework will be presented. In Section 8.3 the labour market equations are discussed. In Section 8.4, interdependence between monetary and real aspects is introduced through the investment function. Section 8.5 presents the steady state values of the model. The nonlinear nature of the model requires simulations to derive the results; these are presented in Section 8.6. Section 8.7 introduces a learning process based upon Markow-regime switching is considered, while Section 8.8 presents the results of new simulations along with sensitivity analysis. Section 8.9 concludes.

8.2 Tarantelli's framework

In order to understand the nature of the results obtained, it is important to briefly sketch Tarantelli (1986)'s theoretical framework. In this version, the macro aspects will be privileged so that the following system is worth considering:

$$p = m\frac{w}{a} \tag{8.1}$$

$$\dot{w} = \dot{w}(u, \dot{p}) \tag{8.2}$$

$$L = l(Y, \dot{Y}) \tag{8.3}$$

$$LF = j(L) \tag{8.4}$$

$$a = \frac{Y}{L} \tag{8.5}$$

$$u = 1 - \frac{L}{FL} \tag{8.6}$$

where p represents prices, w stands for wages, u, L and LF are respectively unemployment, labour demand and labour supply, a is labour productivity, while m is the exogenous mark-up. (A dot on the variables stand for time derivative). The first equation is referred by Tarantelli to Hall and Hitch, the second to Phillips, the third to Okun, the fourth to Tella, while the two remaining are just definitions.

Tarantelli in order to draw his policy conclusions made two strategic changes in the above model. On the one hand, by considering the Okun relation as a reduced form, he could introduce more structural equations for the labour markets that operate in terms of flows. On the other hand, he chose to close the model in a particular way, by taking the maximum inflation rate as exogenous and this helped him to simplify the analysis.

Three are the main results to be mentioned. First of all, wage determination depends very much on the role of institutional aspects. To this purpose, he underlined two stylized wage equations. The first prevails in a system of decentralized bargain:

$$\dot{w} = \Psi(P_u^a; ..) + \dot{p}_a \tag{8.7}$$

where P_u^a represents the expected probability of finding a job and $\dot{p}_a$ the expected inflation. On the contrary, in a centralized bargaining system, there is a wage-fixer that is represented by the industrial relationships and this can be represented analytically by the following equation:

$$\dot{w}=\phi(P_u^a)+\dot{w}_{pr} \tag{8.8}$$

where $\dot{w}_{pr}$ represents the wage increase predetermined by collective bargaining.

Nesting the two hypotheses and transforming them into an equilibrium price equation, one obtains:

$$\dot{p}=\phi(P_u^a)+\dot{w}_{pr}+\frac{(1-P)}{P}\Psi(P_u^a) \tag{8.9}$$

where P stands for the probability of an income policy. If $P\to 0$, then $\dot{p}\to\infty$ and the monetarist result will be obtained. On the contrary, if $P\to 1$, then $\dot{p}$ will tend to $\phi(P_u^a)+\dot{w}_{pr}$. In this case, a long-run Phillips curve can be obtained and this is the second result worth pointing out. Finally, in a dynamic context where expected unemployment replaces actual unemployment, it is possible to obtain loops in the Phillips curve. In the following, simulations will try to replace the heuristic explanations put forward by Tarantelli.

8.3 The supply equation and the labour market

Let us introduce a very simple wage equation in a discrete dynamic way:

$$g_w=d_3\pi_t^e-d_1u_t+d_2+\tau_t \tag{8.10}$$

where g_w [1] represents the rate of growth of nominal wages, d_3 measures the degree of nominal rigidity on expected inflation (π_t^e), d_1 represents the degree of real rigidity referred to the rate of unemployment (u_t), while d_2 stands for an exogenous factor and τ_t is the rate of growth of labour productivity.

Facing the wage equation, there is price equation based upon a variable mark up that depends on a measure of capital imbalance to be defined later on (h_t):

$$\pi_t=g_w-\tau_t+d_4(h_t-h_0) \tag{8.11}$$

This specification implies that the labour share dynamics can be linearly expressed in the following way:

$$\omega_t=\omega_{t-1}[1-d_4(h_t-h_0)] \tag{8.12}$$

The price dynamics in the case of a fixed mark up becomes[2]

$$\pi_t=d_3\pi_t^e-d_1u_t+d_2$$

[1] The use of g_w and π instead of respectively $\dot{w}$ and $\dot{p}$ reminds there we are operating with difference equations.

[2] For a nonlinear formulation, see Ferri et al. (2001).

If d_3 is equal to 1, then the formula reproduces the NAIRU, which is equal to d_2/d_1 and is the steady state value of unemployment (indicated by a 0 subscript). As stressed by Haldane and Quah (1999), this curve should more properly be called a 'supply curve' and should be distinguished from the Phillips curve that depicts a relationship between inflation and unemployment resulting from the working of the whole model.

As far as expectations are concerned, the so-called 'New Keynesian Phillips curve' (see Roberts, 1995) gets rid of backward expectations by referring to rational expectations. In what follows a different approach is taken because, on one hand, 'bounded rational expectations' will be introduced and, on the other, the Phillips curve will be considered as a system result. For these reasons it is necessary to complete the model, starting from the remaining equations in the supply side.

In this medium-run model, the rate of growth of labour productivity is endogenous. In particular, it depends on both exogenous and endogenous factors, such as capital accumulation:

$$\tau_t = \tau_1\left[(1-\delta)+i_{t-1}\right]+\tau_2 \tag{8.13}$$

where δ is the rate of depreciation, i_t is the accumulation rate given by the ratio of investment to capital, and τ_2 is the exogenous component.[3] It is the dependence on capital accumulation that signals a medium-run analysis. In this perspective, productivity of capital is exogenous, and technical change therefore need not be neutral.

To close the labour market, the definition of the rate of unemployment and its determinants are introduced. Since the labour force (LF) is given and normalized, it follows that the unemployment equation can be written in the following dynamic way:

$$u_t = 1 - L_t \tag{8.14}$$

where L_t is employment which is determined in the following way:

$$L_t = L_{t-1}\left(\frac{1+g_t}{1+\tau_t}\right) \tag{8.15}$$

so that the rate of unemployment today depends negatively on the increase in labour demand, which is the ratio of the growth rate of the product (g_t) and the productivity rate (τ_t).

[3] On the determinants of productivity growth at the world level, see Kumar and Russell (2002), who distinguish between technological change, technological catch-up and capital deepening.

8.4 Closing the model

The model is closed in a different way with respect to Tarantelli. In fact, we explicitly introduce aggregate demand and a monetary policy function. The labour market equations can generate a process of interdependence between real and monetary aspects which are a function of the nature of expectations, as will be examined below. This process of interdependence, however, is strengthened by the presence of a particular specification of the investment equation that becomes very important when the business cycle is not based mainly on the process of stock decumulation but impact on investment and therefore on capital accumulation (on the distinction, see also Zarnowitz, 1999). This specification, which is represented in intensive form and assumes the existence of asymmetric information and uncertainty,[4] is of the form:

$$i_t = \frac{I_t}{K_{t-1}} = \frac{1}{\gamma_1 + \phi_1}\left[(\phi_0 - r_t^*) + \phi_1 \frac{I_t^*}{K_{t-1}} + \gamma_1 \frac{RCF_{t-1}}{K_{t-1}} - \gamma_2 d_{t-1}\right]$$

Given the return on investment (ϕ_0) and an expected medium-run real rate of interest (r_t^*) to be defined below, the other three determinants of the investment ratio, I_t^*/K_{t-1}, RCF_{t-1}/K_{t-1}, and d_t need to be specified.

The desired investment ratio is assumed to be

$$i_t^* = I_t^*/K_{t-1} = i_0 + \lambda\left(K_t^*/K_{t-1} - 1\right)$$

which has a steady state value equal to the steady-state investment ratio i_0. On the assumption that the optimal level of capital K_t^* is proportional to the expected level of output with factor of proportionality v^*, which is the constant optimal capital–output ratio (a reasonable assumption in the medium-run) one finds that

$$g_{K_t^*} = g_t^e \tag{8.16}$$

---

[4] The investment equation is obtained from a pair of equations that represent the (real) external cost of finance and the internal rate of return

$$r_t^s = r_t^* + \gamma_1 (I_t - \frac{RCF_{t-1}}{K_{t-1}}) + \gamma_2 d_{t-1}$$

$$r_t^d = \phi_0 + \phi_1 \frac{I_t^* - I_t}{K_{t-1}}$$

The investment equation (i_t) and the real rate of interest equation (r_t) in the text are obtained by equating these two returns. This is a generalization of the investment equation adopted in Fazzari et al. (2006), which also references the relevant literature. In particular, see Bernanke et al. (1999).

i.e., the rate of growth of optimal capital (i.e. the expression $K_t^*/K_{t-1}^* - 1$) is equal to the expected rate of growth of output. The dynamics of capital accumulation are given by

$$g_{k_t} = (1+\rho)i_{t-1} - \delta \tag{8.17}$$

where ρ is the rate of growth of investment productivity.

Two ratios can be introduced at this point, the actual capital/output ratio v_t,

$$v_t = \frac{K_t}{Y_t} = v_{t-1}\frac{1+g_{k_t}}{1+g_t} \tag{8.18}$$

where Y_t is output, and g_t, its rate of growth. The ratio of optimal to actual capital is given by h_t, a measure of capital imbalance:

$$h_t = K_t^*/K_{t-1} = h_{t-1}\frac{1+g_{\hat{k}_t}}{1+g_{k_{t-1}}} \tag{8.19}$$

From these definitions we obtain the following equation for the real cash flow per unit of capital:

$$\frac{RCF_t}{K_t} = \frac{1}{v_t}(1-\omega_t) - \frac{R_t d_t}{(1+\pi_t)(1+g_{k_t})}$$

Where R_t is the nominal rate of interest. The nominal rate appears in this expression because interest payments are fixed in nominal terms in a monetary economy.

By substituting back into the investment equation, one has

$$\begin{aligned} i_t &= \frac{I_t}{K_{t-1}} = \\ &= \frac{1}{\gamma_1+\phi_1}\left\{(\phi_0 - r^*) + \phi_1 i_t^* + \gamma_1\left[\frac{1}{v_{t-1}}(1-\omega_{t-1}) - \frac{R_{t-1}d_{t-1}}{(1+\pi_{t-1})(1+g_{k,t-1})}\right] - \gamma_2 d_t\right\} \end{aligned} \tag{8.20}$$

where D_t is the nominal debt at the beginning of the period, and $d_t = D_t/(p_{t-1}K_{t-1})$ evolves according to

$$d_t = \frac{1+R_{t-1}}{(1+g_{k_{t-1}})(1+\pi_{t-1})}d_{t-1} + \frac{1}{1+g_{k_{t-1}}}i_{t-1} - \frac{1}{v_{t-1}}(1-\omega_{t-1}) \tag{8.21}$$

In this model, the real rate of interest is given by

$$r_t = \phi_0 + \phi_1(i_t^* - i_t) \tag{8.22}$$

and the nominal rate is determined from a version of the Taylor rule (see Clarida et al, 1999),

$$R_t = R_t^* + \psi_1(\pi_t^e - \pi^*) + \psi_2(g_t^e - g_0) \tag{8.23}$$

There are three (minor) differences from the traditional Taylor rule (see Taylor, 1999) that are more in keeping with the present model. The first is that it is written in terms of the rate of growth of output rather than the level (see Walsh, 2003). Second, the target variables are set equal to an exogenous value in the case of inflation and to the steady state value in the case of growth (g_0). Finally, the optimal interest rate is not fixed but depends on a changing real rate of interest:

$$R_t^* = (1+r_{t-1})(1+\pi^*)-1 \tag{8.24}$$

Given R_t^*, the nominal rate of interest reacts to the gaps of inflation and growth from their respective steady state values. In words, expected returns are function of the 'golden rule' relationship, i.e., they depend on the rate of growth, while the expected cost of capital is some average of the rate of interest fixed by he Central Bank deflated by expected inflation.

To close the model the consumption function and the equilibrium condition relating aggregate demand and supply are specified. Consumption is a function of expected and past disposable income,[5]

$$C_t = c_1 Y_t^e + c_2 Y_{t-1}$$

while the requirement that aggregate demand equals aggregate supply implies

$$g_t = c_1(1+g_t^e) + c_2 + i_t v_{t-1} - 1 \tag{8.25}$$

8.5 The steady state values of the model

Given g^e and π^e, it is possible to specify a temporary equilibrium for a system. Furthermore the steady state values can be computed. In case that $d_3 = 1$, then a NAIRU is obtained that is equal to:

$$u_0 = \frac{d_2}{d_1}$$

Since the rate of unemployment must be constant, we have $g_0 = \tau_0$ and $g_{k_0} = g_0$. In turn, this makes the steady state investment ratio equal

$$i_0 = \frac{g_0 + \delta}{1+\rho}$$

while the steady state rate of growth is

[5] This formulation is compatible with the hypothesis of habit formation in the utility function. See Fuhrer (2000).

$$g_0 = \frac{\{\tau_1(1-\delta_1)\rho + (1+\tau_2)(1+\rho)\}(1+n)}{(1+\rho)-\tau_1(1+n)} - 1$$

The steady state value of the capital output ratio is

$$v_0 = \frac{g_0(1-c_1)+(1-c_1-c_2)}{i_0}$$

The steady state of inflation π_0 is given by the exogenous target fixed by monetary authorities, while R_0 is determined by the Fisher equation:

$$R_0 = (1+\pi_0)(1+r_0) - 1$$

The steady state values of the wage share and the debt ratio are endogenously determined by the following equations:

$$\omega_0 = 1 - \frac{AD + Bi_0}{CD + BE}$$

$$d_0 = \frac{i_0 C - AE}{CD + BE}$$

where

$A = \gamma_1 i_0 - (\phi_0 - r*)$, $B = \frac{\gamma_1 R_0}{(1+g_0)(1+\pi_0)} + \gamma_2$, $C = \frac{\gamma_1}{v_0}$, $D = \frac{g_0 - r_0}{1+g_0}$, and $E = \frac{1+g_0}{v_0}$.

This last equation can be written in a more intelligible way:

$$d_0 = \frac{i_0 - (1-\omega)(1+g_0)/v_0}{g_0 - r_0}$$

Four observations are worth considering. First of all, in accordance with the no Ponzi game assumption, this number must be bounded in order to avoid an infinite amount of debt. In the second place, the steady state value must be greater than zero because an economy with debt is analyzed. Finally, in the dynamic simulations the value of d_t is allowed to become negative, but this can only happen temporarily. In other words, consumers are not allowed to become indebted on a permanent basis. All these assumptions imply that there must be restrictions in the sensitivity analysis when changes in the values of the parameters are examined. Of course, the other restriction is that $R_t \geq 0$.

8.6 Simulating the dynamics

In order to study the dynamics of the model it is necessary to specify how expectations are formed. As a first approximation we assume static expectations,

$$g_t^e = g_{t-1}$$

$$\pi_t^e = \pi_{t-1}.$$

Under this naive assumption the model that has been discussed can be simulated. Initially, d_3 in the wage equation has been taken equal to 1. Under the expectational hypothesis made, this implies that wages are fully indexed to last period inflation. Furthermore, d_4 in the price equation has been set equal to zero so that income distribution is fixed. The details of the simulation are presented in the Appendix. The system is disturbed from its steady state with a productivity shock at the beginning of the second period, and it lasts for one period. The system response is illustrated in Fig. 8.1, where the data are quarterly annualized rates.

There are at least three orders of results that are worth stressing. First, the model, once disturbed at the beginning of the period, can produce very prolonged fluctuations. This means that the system does not return to equilibrium but fluctuates for at least 1000 periods. In other words, an endogenous cycle is generated. Second, in this framework, the Phillips curve presents the loops that are a rather common medium-run stylized fact. They do not depend exclusively on the nature of the labour market, but they rather reflect the relationship between cash flow-investment, on one hand, and the labour market forces. Finally, one has to stress the ambiguity of the NAIRU concept. Even though it helps to center the loop, the NAIRU is never reached. At the same time, the system does not necessarily create

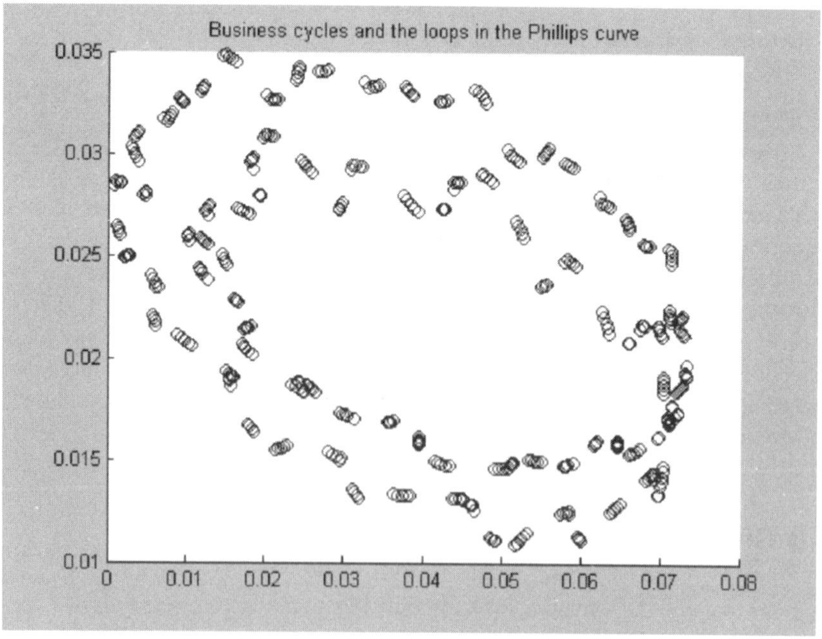

Fig. 8.1. Business cycles and the loops of the Phillips curve (π_t, u_t)

explosive situations, because it wanders around for a long period of time. This stability property, which corresponds to an interval of values for unemployment, is seldom underlined in the literature (for an exception, see Solow, 1998) that stresses the razor's edge property of the NAIRU.

One can try to refer to different specifications in order to test the robustness of the results obtained. For instance, one can introduce the following wage specification:

$$g_w = d_3\pi_t^e - d_1u_t + d_2 + \tau_t - d_5(u_t - u_{t-1})$$

where d_5 measures the so called hysteresis effect (see Layard et al., 1991).

Also in this case the system fluctuates. In particular, Table 8.1 shows the correlations between inflation and unemployment and the degree of persistence of unemployment under the different hypothesis.

Table 8.1. The impact of different specifications of the wage and price equations

Specification	Correlation π, u	persistence of u
$d_4 = 0$	–0.43	0.61
$d_4 \neq 0$	–0.22	0.83
$d_4 \neq 0,\ d_5 \neq 0$	–0.06	0.87

Hysteresis in the wage equation clearly increases the persistence of unemployment, as appears from the last line of Table 8.1. (On this point, see also De Vincenti and Marchetti, 2005). However, one needs not manipulate the wage and the price equations in order to have persistence because this is really a system result that depends on the properties of the system.

Another sensitivity exercise consists in changing the values of d_3, a parameter that governs the nominal rigidities in general and the degree of indexation in particular. [6] As is well known, the literature has tended to examine the problem of indexation within the framework of an exogenous business cycle driven by shocks. In this perspective, the conclusion has been straightforward: 'In the general case, it it easy to show that the optimal degree of indexation is a decreasing function of the variance of supply shocks relative to that of monetary shocks. Thus, to the extent that the 1970s were a period of large supply shocks, full indexation was indeed a bad idea' (Blanchard and Fischer, 1989, p. 525. See also Turnovsky, 2000).

[6] Of course, in this case the steady state value of unemployment is not the NAIRU, but the expression:

$$u_0 = \frac{(d_3 - 1)}{d_1}\pi_0 + \frac{d_2}{d_1}$$

In the present context, the situation is different and the results are less clear as appears from Table 8.2.

The relationship between d_3 and σ is non linear. A higher value of d_3 initially increases the amplitude of the cycle but, after a certain interval, it starts decreasing.

Furthermore, one can investigate what happens when one change the degree of centralisation in the bargaining process. In the present case, mimicking Tarantelli, one can assume that d_3 is equal zero and that d_2, the exogenous component in price determination, is the price-fixer for the monetary authorities, so that in the Taylor rule one has to write

$$\pi^* = d_2$$

In this case, the scenario is different. The business cycles becomes less pronounced and may also disappear. This seems to confirm Tarantelli's intuition about the different macro impact of the various wage bargaining system.

A caveat, however, must be considered. This result are depend very much on the values of other parameters. For instance, limiting out attention to the labour market, a different value of d_1, a parameter that according to Layard et al. (1991) measures real flexibility in the market, can alter the conclusions. In this context, a higher value of d_1 can generate fluctuations and this depends on the interaction between the labour market and other markets in the system. The challenge is to study whether a different set of hypotheses about expectations can make the dynamics more robust.

Table 8.2. The impact of changing d_3 on σ

d_3	σ_u	σ_π	σ_g
1	2.38	0.70	2.27
0.8	3.26	0.99	3.18
0.4	3.11	0.92	3.11

8.7 Bounded rationality and the learning process

So far a very naive process of expectation formation has been used[7] and this is in sharp contrast with the literature, where rational expectations are considered (see, for instance, Woodford, 2005). In the remainder of the chapter, another approach is presented. Agents do not know the precise structure of the model, but depend on empirical regularities to form expectations. In particular, we suppose that, over a medium-run perspective, people expect a dynamic pattern characterized by differ-

[7] According to Ball (2000) this is exactly what happened for the post-1960 period.

ences in performance between 'good times' and 'bad times.' This state of knowledge is specified as a two-state Markovian model with a high growth and a low growth state (see Hamilton, 1989) and 'high' and 'low' periods of inflation. In this perspective agents are supposed to form their expectations according to a particular form of bounded rationality.[8] Hommes and Sorger (1988) argue that expectations must be consistent with data in the sense that agents do not make systematic errors; e.g., the forecasts and the data should have the same means and autocorrelations (see also Grandmont,1998).

At the end of period $t-1$, agents believe that the growth rate in period t will be (see also Clements and Hendry, 1999)

$$g_t^e = \alpha_1 + \beta_1 s_t + (\rho_1 + \mu_1 s_t) g_{t-1} + \varepsilon_t$$

where ε is a random variable with the properties assumed by Hamilton (1988) and s_t is a random variable that assumes the value 0 in the low state and 1 in the high state. It evolves according to the following transition probabilities:

$$\Pr(s_t = 0 \mid s_{t-1} = 0) = a_1$$

$$\Pr(s_t = 1 \mid s_{t-1} = 0) = 1 - a_1$$

$$\Pr(s_t = 0 \mid s_{t-1} = 1) = 1 - b_1$$

$$\Pr(s_t = 1 \mid s_{t-1} = 1) = b_1$$

Since s_t is not known at time t, its expected value, conditioned on s_{t-1}, is taken as a forecast.

If $s_{t-1} = 0$, the conditional forecasting rule is

$$\hat{E}(g_t \mid s_{t-1} = 0) = \alpha_1 + (1 - a_1)\beta_1 + \left[\rho_1 + (1 - a_1)\mu_1\right] \; g_{t-1}$$

where the operator E is written as $\hat{E}$ to indicate its subjective character, which is different from the rational expectations objective conditional expectation,[9] while for $s_{t-1} = 1$,

$$\hat{E}(g_t \mid s_{t-1} = 1) = \alpha_1 + b_1\beta_1 + \left[\rho_1 + b_1\mu_1\right] \; g_{t-1}$$

The general forecasting rule is given by

[8] While 'rationality' implies that people maximize, 'bounded' implies that they have limited information and cannot fully maximize (see Sargent, 1993; Conlisk, 1996; Grandmont, 1998; and Evans and Honkapohja, 2001). The differences between the various approaches to modeling bounded rationality lie in the amount of information assumed.

[9] For such a distinction, see Woodford (2003b).

$$\hat{g}_t = E(g_t \mid s_{t-1}) = \alpha_1 + \beta_1\left[b_1 s_{t-1} + (1-a_1)(1-s_{t-1})\right] +$$
$$\left\{\rho_1 + \mu_1\left[(1-a_1)(1-s_{t-1}) + b_1 s_{t-1}\right]\right\} g_{t-1}$$

A similar forecasting rule can be applied to inflation, where the random state variable is denoted by z_t; the forecast for this variable is

$$\hat{\pi}_t = E(\pi_t \mid z_{t-1}) = \alpha_2 + \beta_2\left[b_2 z_{t-1} + (1-a_2)(1-z_{t-1})\right] +$$
$$\left\{\rho_2 + \mu_2\left[(1-a_2)(1-z_{t-1}) + b_2 z_{t-1}\right]\right\} \pi_{t-1}$$

Although s and z are unobserved (latent) random variables that introduce regime switching, this does not imply that they have no economic meaning,[10] or that correlation with other variables is ruled out. Regime-switching is interpreted as a convenient device to apply time series analysis to the problem of forecasting, and, in view of its popularity among forecasters, it may reflect their practices.

The value of the parameters of the expectations function are learned by the agents as assumed by Sargent (1999) and Akerlof, Dickens, and Perry (2000). Learning takes place by means of rolling regressions.[11] The Hamilton-type forecasts are embodied in the simulation model in the following way. To get the model started, naive expectations for the first 50 periods are assumed. After the first 50 periods, to make a forecast for period t, s_{t-1} is first considered. If, for example, it equals 1, a first order autoregressive regression with a constant is fitted to the previous observations on g_t for which $s_{t-1} = 1$, but no more than 50 observations are included in the regression. The parameters estimated by the regression and the current value g_{t-1} are then used to compute $\hat{g}_t$. An analogous computation is used to forecast $\hat{g}_t$ when $s_{t-1} = 0$ and to forecast π_t.

8.8 A more complex dynamics

To understand the overall dynamics, one cannot refer to the E-stability concept (see Evans and Honkapohja, 2001), since the nonlinearity does not allow us to get to closed form solutions. One rather has to consider simulations. In particular, on one hand, we are interested in studying the impact of the centralisation in the wage determination. Since a generic specification of the wage equation is the following

$$g_w = d_3 \pi_{t-1} + (1-d_3)\pi_t^e - d_1 u_t + d_2 + \tau_t$$

[10] An association with 'animal spirits' is made by Howitt and McAfee (1992). See also Farmer (1999).

[11] For an analysis of the stability of learning process with the latter method, see Bullard and Mitra (2002).

$d_3 = 0$ is in line with the hypothesis of centralisation. On the other hand, since a coordination with monetary authorities is implied, the Taylor rule has been modified as before. The results are presented in Fig. 8.2 (and in the Appendix).

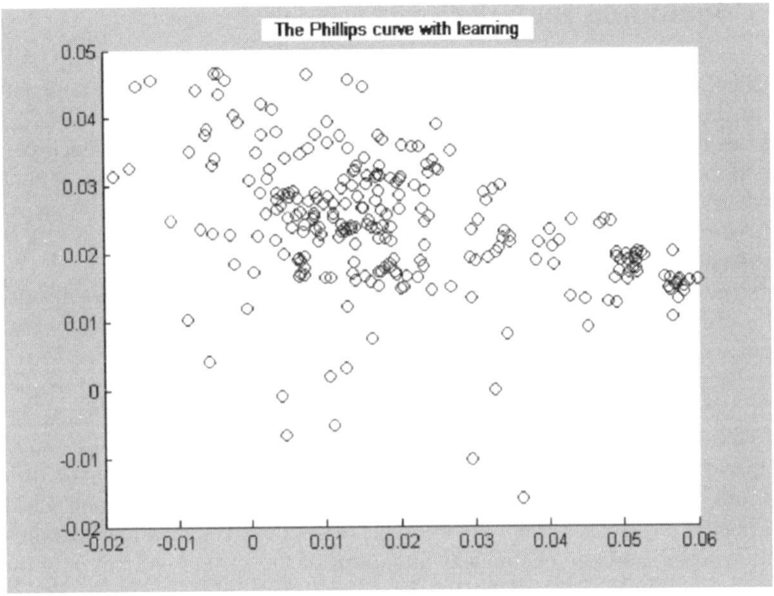

Fig. 8.2. The Phillips curve $(\pi_t,\ u_t)$ in a monetary economy with learning

Some points are worth stressing. First of all, the introduction of learning within a regime switching mechanism maintains the fluctuations in spite of a centralized bargaining. In the second place, there is an increase in the frequency of the cycle and this makes the Phillips loops appear less stylized and therefore more realistic. Finally, it is possible to detect an interval of unemployment that is compatible with inflation stability. The result is that in this case it is even more appropriate to talk about 'a band of unemployment' (see Solow, 1988) than of a unique rate of unemployment as has been noted above.

The robustness of the results can be discussed also in this case. For instance, in order to be closer to Tarantelli's suggestion, the expected rate of unemployment have replaced actual unemployment in the above wage equation. The results do not change.[12] Furthermore, sensitivity analysis can be replicated also for this

[12] We made the assumption that the expected rate of unemployment is obtained by the following rule of thumb:

$$u_t^a = u_{t-1}\frac{(1+\tau_t)}{(1+\hat{g}_t)}$$

specification of the model. For instance, the model is robust to changes in d_1 and this is in contrast with the result of the previous section.

8.9 Concluding remarks

The chapter has tried to evaluate some of Ezio Tarantelli's main contributions both to economic analysis and policy. To reach this target, it has presented a medium-run model of the economy where there is strong interdependence between real and monetary phenomena via the labour market and the investment function, and where agents update expectations functions based upon a Markov process by means of rolling regressions. Within this perspective, the following results should be stressed.

First, the model can produce endogenous business cycles in a robust way. In other words, the presence of strong interdependence between monetary and real aspects results in limit cycles for different constellations of parameters. This result differs both from the real business cycle school, where productivity is exogenous, and from the endogenous school of self-fulfilling expectations (see Farmer, 1999), where the burden of the dynamics is entirely on expectations and learning. Second, the Phillips curve manifests itself in a dynamic setting in the shape of loops. The loops can be more or less regular, but they are present in a great variety of situations. In these cases, there are intervals of unemployment values that are compatible with the absence of runaway situations of the system and not only one value as claimed for the case of the NAIRU. Third, the Phillips curve is a system result and does not reflect only changes that occur in the supply equation. However, this does not mean that changes in the parameters reflecting nominal rigidities are without consequences. On the contrary, their impact depends on their specification and on the nature of the overall model. Finally, expectations and learning, by introducing an extra source of dynamics, can enrich the picture from a realistic point of view and make the results of the simulations more robust.

This analytical apparatus allows to better understand the issues of indexation and the role of 'new corporativism' studied by Tarantelli. In particular, indexation seems to create a greater variability, although in a nonlinear way, while wage centralisation can improve the situation even though its effects are conditioned on a series of factors. In general these results depend very much on the nature of the model in which they are examined, on the technicalities through which they are implemented and on the amount and of the timing in which information is available. In particular, there are three caveats that are worth mentioning. First of all, behind these results and in particular those referring to the so-called wage coordination, there is a game between monetary authorities and trade unions, where the latter is supposed to be the Stackelberg leader. However, the results are compatible with the opposite hypothesis, i.e. with the monetary authorities playing the Stackelberg leader (see Hansen and Sargent, 2000). In the second place, there is too much symmetric information in the system in the sense that both economic agents and monetary authorities have the same expectations. The results could be different with different hypotheses made about the structure of information. Finally, the results pertain to a macro model, where all the institutional complexities made by Tarantelli are set aside and, if this contributes to simplify the analysis, it certainly makes the policy conclusions less reliable.

The analysis can be enriched in different directions. From an analytical point of view, three further tasks should be considered. First of all, the Hamilton model can be generalized in various ways (see Aoki, 1996). For instance, the probabilities of the Markov scheme could be endogenized (see Filardo, 1994). Second, information problem could be made more complex. This, in turn, depends on the structure of the economy, on one hand, and on the degree of institutional depth, on the other, that one is prepared to include into the analysis. Finally, one should try to extend the analysis in order to cover also a deflationary situation, where the employment emerges in a dramatic way. Certainly, something that Tarantelli would not hesitate to study and appreciate.

Appendix

The parameters of the simulations (all carried out with a Matlab program) have been chosen similar to those used in the so called 'monetary policy debate'. For the investment function parameters, we have stayed as close as possible to those used in Fazzari et al. (2006). The econometrics of the investment equation of the type:

$$i_0 = \xi_0 - \xi_1 r_0 + \xi_2 i^* + \xi_3 rcf_0 - \xi_4 d_0$$

gives parameters for the financial aspects of this order of magnitude:

$$\xi_1 = 0.4;\ \xi_2 = 0.1;\ \xi_3 = 0.5;\ \xi_4 = 0.3$$

In the simulations we tried to stay as close as possible to these values.

A.1 Simulations generating Fig. 8.1 and Tables 8.1 and 8.2

Parameter values

$N = 1000$	$\tau_1 = 0.025$	$\tau_2 = 0.005$	$d_1 = 0.25$	$d_2 = 0.01$	$d_3 = 1$
$c_1 = 0.749$	$\phi_3 = 0.82$	$\phi_1 = 1.75$	$\delta = 0.10$	$\rho = 0.03$	$\lambda = 0.01$
$\gamma_1 = 0.2$	$\gamma_2 = 0.75$	$\phi_2 = 0.7$	$\psi_1 = 1.8$	$\psi_2 = 0.4$	$\pi^* = 0.0242$

where N is the number of the periods in the simulations. The shock is equal to 0.001 in the aggregate demand equation and lasts one period.

Finally, we have supposed that $\phi_0 = \phi_3 g_0$ and that $r^* = \phi_2 * r_0$.

In Table 8.1, $d_4 = 0.02$, while $d_5 = 0.1$.

A.2 Simulation of Fig. 8.2

The values of the parameters for Fig. 8.2 are the following:

$N = 500$ $\tau_1 = 0.025$ $\tau_2 = 0.005$ $d_1 = 0.15$ $d_2 = 0.01$ $d_3 = 0$

$c_1 = 0.765$ $\phi_3 = 0.82$ $\phi_1 = 1.75$ $\delta = 0.25$ $\rho = 0.03$ $\lambda = 0.10$

$\gamma_1 = 0.7$ $\gamma_2 = 0.5$ $\phi_2 = 0.7$ $\psi_1 = 1.8$ $\psi_2 = 0.4$ $\pi^* = d_2$

The parameters of the stochastic components are the following:

$$\alpha_1 = g_0\left[1-(\rho_1 + \mu_1 b_1)\right] - \beta_1 b_1$$

$$\alpha_2 = \pi_0\left[1-(\rho_2 + \mu_2 b_2)\right] - \beta_2 b_2;$$

these are obtained by setting $s = z = 1$ (resp., $s = z = 0$) and solving from the steady state expectation formula.

The other parameters are:

$a_1 = 0.4$ $a_2 = 0.45$ $b_1 = 0.6$ $b_2 = 0.8$ $\beta_1 = 0.001$

$\beta_2 = 0.0002$ $\rho_1 = 0.55$ $\rho_2 = 0.5$ $\mu_1 = 0.43$ $\mu_2 = 0.49$

while ϕ_0 and r^* are set as before.

A.3 List of definitions

$d_t = \dfrac{D_t}{p_{t-1}K_{t-1}} =$ real debt per unit of capital at the beginning of period t;

$g_t = \dfrac{y_t}{y_{t-1}} - 1 =$ rate of growth of output;

$g_{k_t} = \dfrac{I_t - \delta K_{t-1}}{K_{t-1}} =$ rate of growth of capital accumulation;

$i_t = \dfrac{I_t}{K_{t-1}} =$ gross investment per unit of capital;

$i_t^* = \dfrac{I_t^*}{K_{t-1}} =$ optimal investment ratio;

$h_t = \dfrac{K_t^*}{K_{t-1}} =$ degree of disequilibrium of the capital stock;

$v_t = \dfrac{K_t}{Y_t} =$ capital–output ratio.

References

Akerlof, G.A. (2002), 'Behavioral macroeconomics and macroeconomic behavior', *American Economic Review*, **92**:411–33.

Akerlof, G.A., W.T. Dickens and G.L. Perry (2000), 'Near-rational wage and price setting and the long-run Phillips curve', *Brookings Papers on Economic Activity*, **1**:1–60.

Aoki, M. (1996), *New Approaches to Macroeconomic Modeling*, Cambridge: Cambridge University Press.

Ball, L. (2000), 'Near-rationality and inflation in two monetary regimes', Cambridge, MA: *NBER Working Papers Series*.

Blanchard, O.J. and S. Fischer (1989), *Lectures on Macroeconomics*, Cambridge, MA: MIT Press.

Bernanke, B.S., M. Gertler and S. Gilchcrist (1999), 'The financial accelerator in a quantitative business cycle framework', in J.B. Taylor and M. Woodford (eds), *Handbook of Macroeconomics*, Volume I, Amsterdam: Elsevier, pp. 1342–93.

Bullard, J. and K. Mitra (2002), 'Learning about monetary policy rules', *Journal of Monetary Economics*, **49**:1105–29.

Buiter, W.H. and N. Panigirtzoglou (2003), 'Overcoming the zero bound on nominal interest rates with negative interest on currency: Gesell's solution', *Economic Journal*, **113**:723–47.

Clements, M.P. and D.F. Hendry (1999), *Forecasting Non-Stationary Economic Time Series*, Cambridge: MIT Press.

Conlisk, J. (1996), 'Why bounded rationality?', *Journal of Economic Literature*, **34**:669–700.

De Vincenti, C. and E. Marchetti (2005), *Temi di macroeconomia contemporanea*, Rome: Carocci.

Estrella, A. and J.C. Fuhrer (2002), 'Dynamic inconsistencies: counterfactual implications of a class of rational-expectations models', *American Economic Review*, **92**:1013–28.

Evans, G. and S. Honkapohja (2001), *Learning and Expectations in Macroeconomics*, Princeton: Princeton University Press.

Farmer, R.E.A. (1999), *Macroeconomics of Self-fulfilling Prophecies*, Boston: MIT Press.

Fazzari, S., P. Ferri and E. Greenberg (2006), 'Cash flow, investment and the Keynes-Minsky cycles', *Journal of Economic Behavior and Organization*, forthcoming.

Ferri, P., E. Greenberg and R. Day (2001), 'The Phillips curve, regime switching and the NAIRU', *Journal of Economic Behavior and Organization*, **46**:23–37.

Filardo, A. (1994), 'Business-cycle phases and their transitional dynamics', *Journal of Business and Economic Statistics*, **12**:299–308.

Fuhrer, J.C. (2000), 'Habit formation in consumption and its implications for monetary-policy models', *American Economic Review*, **90**:367–90.

Grandmont, J.M. (1998), 'Expectations formations and stability of large socioeconomic systems', *Econometrica*, **66**:741–81.

Hamilton, J.D. (1989). 'A new approach to the economic analysis of non-stationary time series and the business cycle', *Econometrica*, **57**:357–84.

Hansen, L.P. and T.J. Sargent (2000), 'Elements of robust control and filtering for macroeconomics', New York University, mimeo.

Hommes, C. and G. Sorger (1998), 'Consistent expectations equilibria', *Macroeconomic Dynamics*, **2**:287–321.

Kumar, S. and R.R. Russell (2002), 'Technological change, technological catch-up and capital deepening: relative contributions to growth and convergence', *American Economic Review*, **92**:527–48.

Layard, R., S. Nickell and R. Jackman (1991), *Unemployment*, Oxford: Oxford University Press.

Phillips, A.W. (1958), 'The relation between unemployment and the rate of change of money wages in the United Kingdom, 1861–1957', *Economica*, **25**:283–99.

Roberts, J.M. (1995), 'New Keynesian economics and the Phillips curve', *Journal of Money, Credit and Banking*, **27**:975–84.

Sargent, T.J. (1993), *Bounded Rationality in Macroeconomics*, Oxford: Clarendon Press.

Sargent, T.J. (1999), *The Conquest of American Inflation*, Princeton: Princeton University Press.

Solow, R. and J.B. Taylor (1998), *Inflation, Unemployment and Monetary Policy*, Cambridge, MA: MIT Press.

Tarantelli, E. (1986), *Economia politica del lavoro*, Turin: UTET.

Taylor, J.B. (ed) (1999), *Monetary Policy Rules*, Chicago: Chicago University Press.

Turnovsky, S.J. (2000), *Methods of Macroeconomic Dynamics*, Cambridge, MA: MIT Press.

Walsh, C.E. (2003), 'Speed limit policies: the output gap and optimal monetary policy', *American Economic Review*, **93**:265–78.

Woodford, M. (2003), *Interest and Prices*, Princeton: Princeton University Press.

Woodford, M. (2005), 'Firm-specific capital and the new Keynesian Phillips curve', *NBER Working Paper 11149*.

Zarnowitz, V. (1999), 'Theory and history behind business cycles: are the 1990s the onset of a golden age?', *Journal of Economic Perspectives*, **13**:69–90.

9 Wage Inequality in Europe: the Role of Labour Market and Redistributive Institutions*

Elisabetta Croci Angelini[1] and Francesco Farina[2]

[1] University of Macerata, Italy
[2] University of Siena, Italy

9.1 Introduction

The debate over income inequality in the era of globalization has been revived by evidence showing that economic growth does not necessarily convey a reduction in income disparities. As for the *between-country* income inequality, in the last decade the rocketing growth rates of the emerging countries seem to have given rise to a slight decrease of the Gini indicator of income inequality with respect to its long-run stable value (Bourguignon and Morisson, 2002). Yet, the population-weighted measurement of world income inequality, which also takes into account the size of countries (e.g., the growth-induced changes in interpersonal income disparities after the polarization between urban and rural incomes in India and China), suggests that the worldwide interpersonal income inequality is widening (Milanovic, 2002). As for the *within-country* income disparities in advanced countries, although a general and stable trend over a long time for the majority of economies is difficult to detect, a clear increase of disparities has been highlighted in the Anglo-Saxon countries (Atkinson and Brandolini, 2005).

This chapter aims at a deeper understanding of the determinants of wage inequality – the most important component of income inequality – in European countries. Wage inequality is influenced by the interaction between labour demand-and-supply and institutional factors. Broadly speaking, after the increase in income inequality determined by market forces within many European economies in the 1980s, income redistribution was intensified and labour market deregulation expanded. Our research effort intends to disentangle the impact on wage inequality of government regulation in the labour market and redistribution operated by the social protection system, also controlling for the impact of the effect of the skill-premium related to technical change.

We investigate on how labour market and welfare institutions affect the earnings distribution and argue that on average the overall degree of governance of the European labour markets was not modified, but a changing balance between de-

* Financial support from Miur is gratefully acknowledged (PRIN 2004–133384. Project title: *Globalisation, Income Distribution and Growth: A Research Agenda*). We thank A. Brandolini, C. De Vincenti and A. Del Boca for useful comments. The usual disclaimers apply.

creasing labour market regulation and increasing redistribution seems to characterise the 1990s. While job and wage protection has been recently eased across Europe, income redistribution was strengthened, though its size differs across four clusters of European countries – depending on the majority voting preference for 'risk insurance', as shown by econometric estimates. To explain the continuously rising wage inequality in Europe, two regression models of wage inequality are employed each one using a different database. The Luxembourg Income Study (LIS) database, which collects and homogenises national statistics, allows to differentiate income distribution between factor income (FI) and disposable income (DPI) and so makes an assessment of the overall income redistribution possible. The European Community Household Panel (ECHP) database, which is based on a specific socio-economic survey, allows the breakdown of wage distribution across sectors and workers' occupations. The assessment of the impact of labour-demand-and-supply for each skill level, as determined by the technological choices of the firms, can be singled out, and so permits to understand the forces behind the increase in earning disparities.[1]

9.2 Employment rates and wage inequality in Europe

During the period of high macroeconomic instability, which started in the 1970s and lasted till the 1990s, the European economies suffered from high (albeit slowly declining) inflation, as well as inadequate employment and sluggish growth rates. The theoretical framework to interpret these decades has centred on the interaction between shocks and labour market institutions.

One interpretation (Blanchard and Wolfers, 2001) argues that the more wage and job adjustments are regulated by labour market institutions, the more a rise in the unemployment rate translates into unemployment hysteresis. After total factor productivity (TFP) fell below the real wage in the 1970s, rigid labour markets produced long lasting unemployment, and skill obsolescence held back workers in finding a new job. Moreover, much higher real interest rates since the 1980s magnified the negative effect of TFP on labour demand, thus determining an upward shift in the equilibrium unemployment rate. An additional explanation for unemployment persistence points to macroeconomic turbulence (Ljungqvist and Sargent, 1998). The higher the frequency of negative shocks, the higher the probability that labour market rigidities would hamper the market adjustment via wages and prices, the larger the ensuing gap between the reservation wage (linked to the

[1] A plurality of economic and institutional factors affect wage inequality across and within countries, first of all international trade. Trade openness depresses the wage and employment levels of low-skilled workers in the advanced countries, due to the rise in the imports of the low-skilled intensive products and the decrease in the relative labour demand for low-skilled workers. Yet, in the European Union in the 1980s and 1990s the shrinking of the traditional sectors was just beginning, and competition from the LDC did not yet exert a differential impact across the economies of the European Union in terms of declining wages of low-skill workers.

unemployment benefits, in turn based on the wage level when employed) and the new lower mean wage, the longer the unemployment spells.

A second interpretation (Nickell et al., 2001) claims that high unemployment rates in Europe are mainly the consequence of an inefficient interaction between labour market institutions and fluctuations in aggregate demand. Empirical evidence about the influence of regulation on the functioning of the labour market is mixed. High union density and long-lasting unemployment benefits exert a negative effect on the employment rates, while coordinated wage bargaining and active labour policies appear to favour a better matching between labour demand and supply. As revealed by the relevant shifts of the Beveridge curves of European countries in the last decades, a high unemployment rate results from the changing capacity of the labour market in making the unemployed match the vacancies, rather than from the distortion caused by institutions to macroeconomic adjustment after shocks.

A third interpretation (Fitoussi et al., 1999) points to the long period of real interest rates higher than growth rates as the origin of higher structural unemployment. Till the first half of 1980s, macroeconomic policies alleviated the consequences on employment of oil price shocks and fast wage dynamics. Since the second half of the 1980s, the monetary and fiscal policy-mix was geared to restriction. The Maastricht criteria and the subsequent introduction of the Stability Pact have imposed on European governments an accelerated reduction of public deficits and debts, despite the priority attributed to monetary stability was procrastinating slow growth. Poor macroeconomic governance of the integration process, and consequently the virtual dismissal of stabilization policies by national governments, is regarded as the main cause of the slow employment and growth rates of European economies.

None of these interpretations establishes a specific link between the depressed labour demand experienced by many European countries after macroeconomic shocks, and the evolution of their indicators of wage inequality. Therefore, the analysis of possible connections between employment and wage disparities in Europe has been sunk in the broad interpretation of globalization as a major cause of increasing inequality either in wages or in unemployment, depending on labour market institutions (Krugman, 1994). While in the literature a comprehensive investigation over the determinants of rising wage inequality in Europe has still to come, some empirical studies have started to cast light on the question. Yet, the opinion is sharply divided.

The OECD, mainly focusing on data referred to the workforce looking for low-pay jobs, finds a positive correlation between employment rates and wage inequality: countries where earnings inequality has risen less than average appear to have experienced a relative increase in unemployment and a relative decrease in employment.[2] This view corroborates the Krugman hypothesis, which points to a

[2] 'Employment and unemployment developments – in particular, the relative employment of youths and older persons of working age – tended to be less favourable in countries in which earnings inequality increased more slowly since 1970 (or fell), than in countries where the earnings inequality rose more rapidly' (OECD, 2004, p. 129). '(C)ountries in

negative causal relationship between wage compression and low-skill employment in Europe, on the assumption that regulation has been preventing the wage reduction required by those sectors more exposed to harsher international competition, thus provoking the shift in structural unemployment. A much lower Gini wage inequality with a much lower employment rate in Europe, as compared to the US, stems from labour market institutions, protecting jobs and wages of the 'insiders' at the cost of a reduction in employment and participation rates of the low-skill and low-wage labour force.

Other studies, mainly focusing on data for jobs in traditional sectors[3] and wage dispersion for the household indicator,[4] have put forward the opposite view of a negative correlation between employment rates and earnings inequality. It is worth noticing that these findings are hardly compatible with the Krugman hypothesis, where limited earnings inequality in Europe determines market pressures fostering a fall in the employment rate, mainly due to a declining relative demand for low-skill workers.

The scattered diagram in Fig. 9.1 collects the data on employment rates, supplied by Eurostat, and the Gini indices, calculated on wages for 13 European countries, under the five waves running from 1979 to 2000, now available from the LIS database[5]. Four clusters of countries are identified (Scandinavian, Continental, Mediterranean and Anglo-Saxon countries), corresponding to the usual aggregation based on the features of their social protection models.

This evidence indicates that the portrayal of Europe as a whole as the land of wage compression – as opposed to high wage flexibility in the US – is misleading. The four Scandinavian countries (Denmark, Finland, Norway and Sweden) present both wage inequality and employment rates much higher than the EU average; the Anglo-Saxon countries (United Kingdom and Ireland) share about the same wage inequality but show lower employment rates, the Mediterranean countries (France, Italy and Spain) display both wage inequality and employment rates lower than EU average and gather in the circle just opposite to Scandinavian countries. Due to higher employment rates, the Continental countries (Belgium, Germany, Luxembourg and the Netherlands) are placed over the Mediterranean countries. Despite their large overlapping in terms of low wage inequality, the

which and a more equal distribution of earnings appears to have worsened consistent with relative labour demand having shifted towards high-skilled workers' (Ibid., p. 140).

[3] 'In sum, our examination of the wage compression hypothesis (like that of the other empirical researchers) finds little support for the belief that lack of jobs in the EU is due to the effect of the compression of wages on employment in low skill industries' (Freeman and Schettkat, 2001, p.25).

[4] 'Unlike for earnings inequality among full-time employed individuals, for pre-tax–pre-transfer income among households we observe sizeable increases over time in most countries. This development appears to have been driven to an important extent by changes in employment. In countries with better employment performance, low-earning households benefited relative to high-earning ones; in nations with poor employment performance, low-earning households fared worse' (Kenworthy and Pontusson, 2005, pp. 21–2).

[5] The FI data for Belgium, France, Italy and Spain are net of taxes.

identities of the former and the latter cluster, will be vindicated in Figs. 9.2 and 9.3 where the much higher redistribution in the Continental countries is shown.

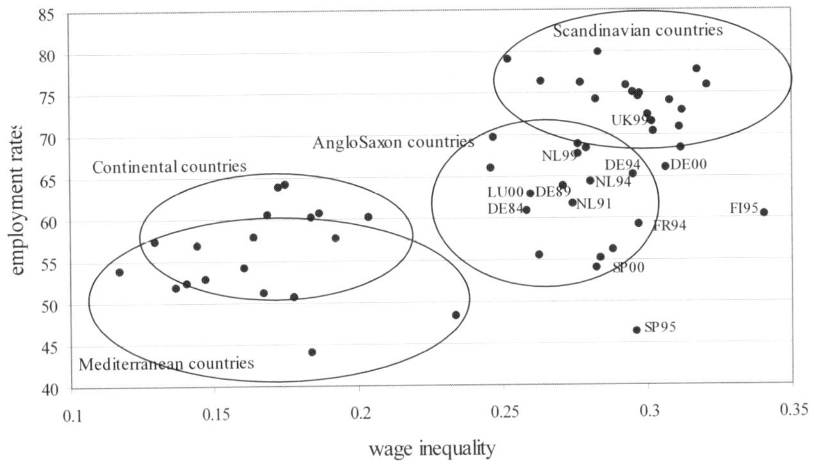

Fig. 9.1. Employment rates and wage inequality in European countries (1979–2000)

The picture in Fig. 9.1 evolves from the mid-1980s to the year 2000. Named spots identify those countries moving outside their original clusters in particular years. For many countries belonging to the Continental and Mediterranean clusters, the Gini coefficient computed on wages moved rightwards while employment rates did not change much.

Overall, the evidence of Fig. 9.1 shows that the poor performance of employment rates in Europe – going downward in the 1980s but upward in the 1990s – is associated to an increase in wage inequality. While the Scandinavian countries keep their corner for the whole period, many Continental and some Mediterranean countries, after their earlier waves, moved rightwards and, to a somewhat lesser extent, upwards. In more recent times, the Anglo-Saxon countries have been joined by non-belonging members and the association between employment rates and wage inequality is less clearly identified by their original clusters, than it used to be. Therefore, our diagram is at odds with what one would expect according to the Krugman hypothesis. The divide within Europe – four clusters each characterized by a different combination of high or low values for employment and wage inequality – seems to be withering during the 1990s.

Were the Krugman hypothesis proven true, one would have found that a disproportionate rise in low-skill and low-pay unemployment ended up in a compression of the wage distribution, due to the lack of jobs for the new entrants and the dismissal of low-wage workers from the bottom half of the wage distribution. Quite on the contrary, during the whole period from 1979 to 2000 Gini wage coefficients have steadily increased in European countries, with no comparable changes in unemployment rates for all sections of the labour force. During the 1980s, the labour market regulation might not have allowed a prompt adjustment via the price of labour. Yet, the alternative adjustment via a lower quantity of the low-skill and low-wage employed, far from causing a compression in wage distribution, has been unable to discontinue the rise in wage inequality. During the 1990s, the high wage inequality at high employment rates in the Scandinavian and the Anglo-Saxon countries, and, more importantly, the trend towards a higher wage inequality at slightly increasing employment rates in the other two clusters is a clue to revealing that more complex dynamics have been at work.

9.3 A view on labour market regulation and redistributive institutions in Europe

The econometric estimates, that will be performed in the Sections 9.4, 9.5 and 9.6, aim at maintaining the hypothesis that the main causality link goes from a depressed labour demand to wage and employment performances, depending on the evolution of strictly interwoven labour market and redistributive institutions. Here is the conceptual framework for the empirical investigation.

In Europe, regulation and redistribution have heavily impinged on labour demand-and-supply, and conversely in each country institutions are moulded by the specific labour market conditions (Katz and Autor, 1999). After the upward shift of the equilibrium unemployment rate at the end of the 1970s, in many European countries employment protection and minimum wage became more effective. High levels of union density and collective bargaining coverage strengthened the unions bargaining power in negotiations and the rigidity of the minimum wage paid to the low-skill workers in excess of their productivity levels. Employment protection legislation (EPL) restrained the capacity of firms to fire workers at low legal costs and raised the reservation wage of the unemployed (Bertola et al., 2002). The sluggish creation of new jobs prevented the low-skill young workers from entering the labour market. The unemployment rate experienced a shift upwards in many European countries. Labour market regulation avoided a downward effect of depressed labour demand on the employment rates of prime-age males. The negative impact of the increasing earnings inequality on the households' income and consumption levels was smoothened by the income redistribution provided by the tax-and-transfers system.

However, job protection has been eased in many European countries in the 1990s. The distortions inflicted to wage determination in the market by EPL (Bertola and Boeri, 2002), by a rigid minimum wage (Card and Di Nardo, 2002), by the centralised wage-setting system (Blau and Kahn, 1996), and by union density and labour contracts coverage (Brugiavini et al., 2001) have been reduced. In the Scandinavian countries, and mainly in the Netherlands among the Continental countries, wage moderation has been traded for the strengthening of unemployment protection, that is a longer duration of unemployment transfers and a higher level of the replacement rates, though under tighter eligibility criteria. While reforms of wage-setting mechanisms, such as lower coordination across wage negotiation and bargaining at the firm level, allowed local market conditions to be taken into account, the diffusion of temporary and part-time contracts helped the increase in employment rates, mostly concentrated in temporary jobs as well as higher women participation and older workers staying in the labour market. Moreover, a more encompassing composition of active labour market policies (ALMP), with more funds devoted to in-work benefits, job matching and re-employment services, have partially substituted for EPL and the fall of net union density has been accompanied by the government replacing the unions as the provider of risk insurance (OECD, 2004).[6]

9.4 Heterogeneity across redistributive systems

In this section, we perform time-series cross-country econometric estimates on the redistributive effort of the European welfare institutions in mid-1980s and mid-1990s.

Under the assumption that income redistribution is the outcome of the political pressure by the median voter's relative factor income position, the redistribution indicator is constructed as the difference between the Gini inequality index for factor income (FI) and the Gini inequality index for disposable income (DPI).[7] The regression model below links the dimension of redistribution to the society's preference for 'risk insurance' expressed by the majority voting political mechanism where the 'median voter' is decisive. The econometric tests conducted show that different countries may have different attitudes towards risk insurance, with idiosyncratic propensities towards redistribution.

Provided that the median voter hypothesis in principle could be ascertained irrespective of time and space (Model 1), at first all available information, which amounts to 44 observations, have been gathered into a single pooling regression model. An OLS regression (eq. 9.1) connects the extent of a country's income redistribution to the distance of the median voter income from mean income in that country, one period lagged.

$$(GiniFI_i - GiniDPI_i)_t = \alpha + \beta \left(\frac{YmdFI_i}{YmnFI_i} \right)_{t-1} + u_{i,t} \tag{9.1}$$

---

[6] The exception is the so called 'Ghent system' operating in some Continental countries, mainly in the Netherlands, whereby the unions keep being involved in the administration of unemployment benefits (Checchi and Lucifora, 2002).

[7] We endorse the view that the median voter 'should … be taken more as a metaphor representing the aggregation of voter's preferences than as a direct explanation of political decisions' (Atkinson, 1999, p. 117). The median voter is to be conceived as a metaphorical agent expressing the sense of precariousness that the majority of the electorate derives from their market earnings, and the consequent demand for 'risk insurance' by redistribution through tax-and-transfers. In fact, the majority voting in favour of redistribution should be regarded as the joint effect of a series of factors – pressure groups, political regimes, government fragmentation, etc. – rather than the decisive preference of the isolated individual occupying the median position in the electorate.

The dependent variable – the reduction in income inequality assessed by the difference between a country's Gini indices on factor income (*GiniFI*) and disposable income (*GiniDPI*) – accounts for the extent of redistribution. The independent variable describing the political pressure – i.e. how much poorer-than-average the median voter is – is the median-to-mean factor income ratio (*YmdFI*/*YmnFI*), ranging between zero and one and signalling less inequality as its value goes up.[8]

The regression is meant to test the reliability of the postulated theoretical relationship between the income level of the median voter (relative to the mean income) and the extent of redistribution. The significant increase appearing in the average FI Gini coefficient mid-1990s *vis-à-vis* that for the mid-1980s, by reinforcing the findings which emerged by looking at the *Ymd*/*Ymn* ratios, extends to the whole income distribution the assessment of an increase in income inequality effected by the operation of market forces from the mid-1980s to the mid-1990s. To prove that the preference of a median voter hit by a decrease in their factor income level determines a wider redistribution through tax-and-transfers, one would expect a negative relationship linking the dependent to the independent variable: a decrease in the median-to-mean factor income ratio is associated to an increase in redistribution. The more distant is the income level of the median voter from the mean income, the wider the expected difference between *ex ante* (FI) and *ex post* (DPI) Gini coefficients, as redistribution should provoke a fall in the DPI Gini coefficient.

Fig. 9.2 shows the scattered diagram where the abatement of the Gini coefficient, from FI to DPI, is on the horizontal axis and the median-to-mean factor income ratio is on the vertical axis. Although no neat relationship emerges from the whole set of observations, and a first glance observation may suggest a very mild positive relationship between the two variables, one can also appreciate four rather blurred groupings, with a somewhat similar and negatively sloping shape, which are placed in parallel to each other along the main diagonal. This finding could be traced back to the influence of different cultural values and psychological attitudes of society at large in different clusters of countries. Since preferences for public goods and social insurance may sharply diverge from preferences on private goods, the range of social protection institutions and the degree of redistribution involved may be large. Market economies at the same technological level and with the same consumption model differ as to the degree of desired risk insurance. To capture this cross-country heterogeneity in the society's choice for redistribution, three dummy variables were included in the model.

The new specification of the regression model is therefore modified as shown in eq. (9.2):

$$(GiniFI_i - GiniDPI_i)_t = \alpha + \beta\left(\frac{YmdFI_i}{YmnFI_i}\right)_{t-1} + d1 + d2 + d3 + u_{i,t} \tag{9.2}$$

[8] The indicator for the median voter's preference for redistribution – the median-to-mean income ratio – is an indicator of income inequality just as the Gini coefficient. A lagged variation in the *Ymd*/*Ymn* ratio is regressed onto the difference between the Gini FI and Gini DPI indicators of income inequality, so preventing spurious correlations.

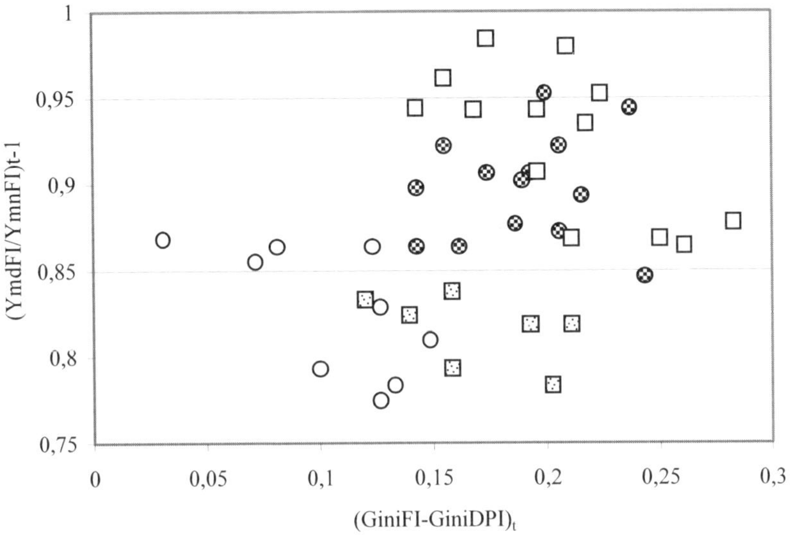

Fig. 9.2. Scatter diagram of the Median Voter equation

where *d*1, *d*2 and *d*3 indicate the dummies added to allow for structural differences in preferences for clusters of countries characterised by different models of Welfare State. The first dummy (*d*1) is meant to single out the peculiarities of the social-democrat model in Scandinavian countries (Denmark, Finland, Norway and Sweden) and is expected to show a positive sign, so to reflect that this is the welfare state which is reputed the most generous in Europe. The other dummies cover respectively (*d*2) catholic Mediterranean countries (France, Italy and Spain) and (*d3*) liberal Anglo-Saxon countries (Ireland and the UK). As they are all characterised by a narrower Welfare State,[9] both dummies *d*2 and *d*3 are expected to show a negative sign. The limited extent of redistribution in Mediterranean and Anglo-

[9] The general reference for different Welfare State models existing in different socio-economic environments and reflecting different institutional characters as well as different preferences about the mix of private and public goods is Esping-Andersen (1999). Many studies considering different clusters of Welfare State systems in Europe, place France in the Continental group of countries. Empirical evidence casts doubts on this affiliation, by showing a surprising homogeneity among the labour market institutions of France, Italy, Spain, Portugal, Greece. These countries, usually gathered under the 'Mediterranean' heading, are characterised by a high employment protection legislation and a low percentage of individuals under social benefits (see Boeri et al., 2001). This striking inverse correlation between the two main forms of labour market regulation, compared to the more mixed evidence of other European countries, suggests that the inclusion of France in the Mediterranean group is the most sensible choice. Moreover, the Eurostat Social Protection Database presents very close low values of social benefits and employment rates for Italy, Spain, Greece and France.

Saxon countries might be traced back, along with other factors, to the segmentation by which in both clusters of countries the labour market is characterised. In other words, the political pressure exerted by the median voter may be weaker due to his relatively higher probability of still being an insider *vis-à-vis* the other two clusters of countries. The remaining countries (Belgium, Germany, Luxembourg and the Netherlands), taken as reference countries, belong to the group of the so-called corporatist Continental Europe countries, characterised by a welfare state with a medium redistributive impact.

Table 9.1 presents the results of the two regression models. While the first model connecting income inequality to redistribution finds a positive relation, but gives unsatisfactory results as to the quality of the estimates, the second model identifies a rather strong negative relation, supported by considerably higher significance levels and explanatory power. The regression results therefore show that the median voter hypothesis is consistent with the empirical evidence: after having controlled for different institutional features characterising the four clusters of countries, all the parameters show the expected sign and are highly significant. The relevant χ^2 critical values state that for both tests – the Jarque-Bera/Salmon-Kiefer test for errors being normally distributed and the Breusch–Pagan test for homoskedasticity – the null hypotheses can be accepted at a very satisfactory significance level.

Table 9.1. Heterogeneity across clusters of countries

		Model 1	Model 2
α		–0.074	0.599
	t	(–0.613)	(4.516)
β		0.283	–0.456
	t	(2.057)	(–3.097)
*d*1 (Nw Sw Fi Dk)		–	0.0299
	t	–	(2.324)
*d*2 (Fr It Es)		–	–0.118
	t	–	(–6.802)
*d*3 (Ie Uk)		–	–0.057
	t	–	(–2.980)
Adj.R^2		0.07	0.606
n. obs.		44	44
Jarque-Bera/Salmon-Kiefer		1.222	0.742
Breusch-Pagan		0.761	1.537

One may observe that regressions linking such variables like income inequality and redistribution are exposed to the problem of reverse causation. The direction of causality may be ambiguous: is it a lower median-to-mean ratio to determine an increase in redistribution (the causality link implied by our estimates), or is it the variation in redistribution to determine the change in the median voter's income position? The negative sign obtained by the correlation between redistribution and the lagged independent variable mitigates the relevance of this issue. In fact, were the direction of causality from redistribution to the median voter's relative income position one would expect a positive relationship – i.e. more redistribution implying a higher median-to-mean factor income ratio – which is not supported by the regression results (see Table 9.1, Model 1). Moreover, in our model specification, the inequality index referred to the political mechanism is measured by the FI data, while redistribution regards the recovery in the DPI inequality with respect to FI. Hence, the possibility of a positive relationship according to a reverse causation is ruled out on theoretical grounds. In fact, it would amount to imagine that the independent variable – indicating income inequality after the tax-and-transfers reshuffling – positively feeds-back on a dependent variable represented by the income inequality before the tax-and-transfers reshuffling, which is clearly implausible.

Therefore, the view is confirmed that the larger the income inequality conditions experienced by the metaphorical agent expressed by the median-to-mean ratio, the larger the need for risk insurance, the larger the extent of redistribution obtained by majority voting, once the link is tested at the cluster level. The regression results for the four clusters of countries support the hypothesis – conveyed by the own specific intercept of each cluster – that the negative relationship between the median voter's relative income position and redistribution is sensitive to the particular inequality aversion, which is peculiar for each group. In all clusters, a change of the median-to-mean FI ratio brings about a redistributive reaction, estimated by the common β coefficient (–0.456) indicating an inverse relationship, which is located at a height in the plan different for each group of countries.

9.5 Redistribution and wage inequality

In Fig. 9.3 the Gini wage values are plotted against the difference between the FI and the DPI Gini coefficients, weighted by the FI indicator for redistribution, used in our time-series cross-country econometric investigation. The four clusters identified by the correlation of wage inequality with employment show up again for the correlation between wage inequality and redistribution.

The upward moving spots inside the circle for Scandinavian countries support the view that the larger is income redistribution, the more unions have allowed for labour market deregulation. In the Anglo-Saxon cluster, wage disparities not only increase in the period 1979–2000 (the two spots for UK in the 1980s are at the left out of the circle), but keep being associated to a much lower degree of redistribution. The Continental cluster shows values for wage dispersion lower than in the Scandinavian one, suggesting that a large social transfers system combines with a limited labour market deregulation. Instead, in the Mediterranean cluster both variables present low values, which is seen as a signal that the lasting paucity of redistributive institutions is compensated by labour market regulation which restraints wage dispersion by putting a hold on market forces.

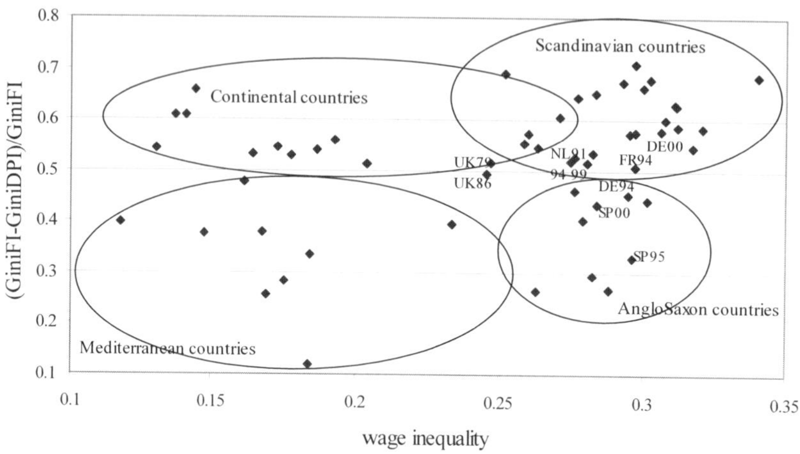

Fig. 9.3. Redistribution and wage inequality in European countries (1979–2000)

Therefore, a substitutability process among institutions seems to have occurred in many European countries, in the form of a shifting combination between labour market and welfare institutions. As Figs. 9.1 and 9.3 show, during the 1990s wage inequality has not reversed its course, but many countries of the Continental or Mediterranean Europe appear to join the high wage inequality league (Scandinavian and Anglo-Saxon clusters). While a lower union density and milder job protection allowed jobs to expand, in particular for women and the new entrants into the labour market, the pay for low-skill workers could have been reduced by an extent even more significant than that describing by how much employment had risen.

A different mix of lower regulation coupled with higher redistribution across European countries has increased heterogeneity in wage and employment performances within European countries. In some countries, a weakening of job protection was accompanied by more generous unemployment benefits and effective ALMP, so that a rising wage inequality came with the increase of temporary labour contracts. In other countries, the polarisation between the stable working position of the high-skill 'insiders' and the long unemployment spells of the low-skill workers has been reinforced. The extensive recourse to flexible labour contracts has created the segregated market for part-time jobs. On the one hand, the bargaining power of the prime-age male workers has further strengthened. On the other hand, the demise of job protection has increased the length of time preceding the passage to permanent labour contracts for low-skill workers, as in many European countries appropriate measures meant to facilitate re-employment of the workers at the end of temporary labour contracts are still lacking.[10] Hence, labour

[10] The varying extent of labour market deregulation across the European economies was also connected to different degrees of deregulation in the market for goods, whereby a weaker price power of firms following harsher competition, by shrinking rents to be shared between producers and workers, hinders the unions' bargaining power (Blanchard

market deregulation has prompted a significant downward wage flexibility, but a strong recovery in employment rates is still to come. A tentative explanation is that the boost to labour supply elasticity could have been insufficient to raise the employment and the participation rates of the low-productivity sections of the labour force.[11] The main impact of deregulation has been on earnings disparities, the effects of which on disposable income inequality has been mitigated by the redistribution operated by welfare institutions.

Given the upward trend for wage inequality at slowly rising employment rates across clusters (Fig. 9.1), and a similar pattern for the correlation between wage dispersion and redistribution (Fig. 9.3), one may suggest that labour market deregulation nourishes wage inequality, while income redistribution compensates for the fall in wage levels at the bottom of the earnings distribution. The labour market deregulation which took place in many European countries, impinging both on the low-skill workers' pay in the labour market and on the number of unemployed workers eligible for social transfers, has probably benefited from the support to the households' disposable income represented by larger redistribution countervailing a rising downward wage flexibility and a variable job involvement inside the household. This interpretation will be tested in the next two sections.

9.6 Wage inequality in Europe: a regression model with the LIS database

Econometric estimates are conducted in this section through a regression model which looks at wage inequality as a function of four variables. First, as we consider that a prolonged period of low labour demand was at the origin of the upward trend in wage inequality in Europe the youth employment rate has been introduced as a proxy for the more or less difficult matching of the labour force with job vacancies. The variable actually used is male employment rates for the age groups 20–24, 25–29, 30–34, as supplied by Eurostat, to reduce the interference both by the upward trend of women participation and by fertility. Second, net union density, that is unions membership excluding pensioners and the self-employed, has been considered to indicate the degree of labour market regulation.

---

and Giavazzi, 2003). Many other factors prompted the recovery of employment rates in many EU countries in the second half of the 1990s, the most important of which is tax cuts, in particular the reduction in social contributions which has shrunk the wedges between the labour costs to employers and employees' effective pay.

[11] A too high effective marginal tax rate in the lower end of the income distribution may discourage the very unskilled to enter the labour market for low-pay jobs, though recent studies report a negligible influence of the tax wedge (the non-wage labour costs due to social contributions paid by the employees as well as by the employers) in the labour market. An econometric analysis of the wage formation mechanism in a dynamic contest indicates that in the EU countries an increase in the tax wedge (or a shift of the tax burden from the employers to the employees) has only a temporary and very small effect on the real wage (Arpaia and Carone, 2004).

Third, redistribution enters as a determinant of wage inequality as unions may trade wage moderation in labour contracts negotiations with a strengthening of unemployment benefits and other social transfers by welfare institutions. The extent of redistribution is quantified by the difference between the FI and the DPI Gini coefficients, weighted by the Gini FI. Fourth, we aim at separating out the role of labour market and welfare institutions in the evolution of wage inequality from the impact exerted on the employment and wage rates by technical change, as reflected in the shift of the sectoral composition towards the ICT industries and services, and by the skill upgrading of human capital, as reflected in the functions performed by the workers. Hence, this regression model regards higher education, whether or not obtained by a university institute, as an indicator of the upgrading of the technological level of the productive system, which is supposed to determine the widening of the skill premium and to discriminate against low-skill workers.

The panel of 13 countries over 5 waves yields 56 actual observations (over a theoretical maximum of 65 observations, were the panel complete) for the dependent variable, which has been extracted from the LIS database, just like all other information on the FI and the DPI distribution. Data on the remaining variables have been collected from published sources: net union density, which gathers percentages of union membership on the labour force net of self-employed and retired workers, is taken from Ebbinghaus and Visser (2000) and integrated with adjusted administrative data surveys as reported by OECD (2004); educational attainment, which refers to the tertiary level (L3), is taken from de la Fuente and Domenech (2002) and has been included with a three periods lag, as this variable is meant to be an indicator of the average human capital level of the existing labour force, relying on the assumption that those who graduated ten-fifteen years earlier are presently employed and represent a substantial part of the skilled workers. A time period corresponds to 5 years, which is the approximate length of time separating the five waves of the LIS database from each other. Table 9.2 summarizes the dependent and independent variables summary statistics.

In addition to the independent variables discussed above, the regression equation includes a drift on union density so to estimate a separate coefficient for the more deregulated labour markets of the Anglo Saxon and Scandinavian countries (as revealed by Fig. 9.1). The regression equation, therefore, reads as follows:

$$
\begin{aligned}
Giniwages = \alpha + \beta netunden + \gamma \frac{GiniFI - GiniDPI}{GiniFI} + \\
+ \delta emplrt_{t-1} + \varphi EduL3_{t-3} + \lambda(netundenAS) + u
\end{aligned}
\tag{9.3}
$$

Given the cross-country time-series nature of the data, one would have hoped for a fixed effect panel regression analysis. A single equation model, pooling all available observations, was instead preferred to a multiple equation model, as the non-negligible number of erraticly missing observations results in a rather unbalanced panel, with a substantial overall loss of information.

Rising wage disparities, determined in European countries by market forces, may have compelled the unions to engage in a stronger quest for 'risk insurance'.

Table 9.2. Summary statistics for the regression model 1

	Giniwages	netunden	$\frac{GiniFI - GiniDPI}{GiniFI}$
min	0.1176	8.9	0.25507
max	0.3406	97.35	0.70848
mean	0.2560	45.498	0.51534
st.dev.	0.0596	23.785	0.12221

$emplrt20–24_{t-1}$	$emplrt25–29_{t-1}$	$emplrt30–34_{t-1}$	$EduL3_{t-3}$
43.9	68.2	76.7	3.51
79.2	94.5	95.8	18.3
63.71	82.666	88.263	10.212
9.399	5.7094	4.6080	4.2038

Thus, the Gini wage coefficient could endogenously feedback on the redistribution operated by welfare institutions, so that reverse causation may occur. Moreover, complementarity or substitutability between the regulatory function of legislation and labour market institutions, and the redistributive function of welfare institutions, may also apply. Therefore, the pooling panel regression does not escape the suspect of endogeneity: income (re)distribution, union density and educational attainment may be seen as a rather interwoven set of variables. Despite this conceptual interrelation, when it comes to their measurement, which is done through the proxy variables employed in the regression, the correlation coefficients between each couple of variables, shown in Table 9.2, are rather low.[12]

Table 9.3. Correlation coefficients model 1

	Giniwages	netunden	$\frac{GiniFI - GiniDPI}{GiniFI}$	$emplrt30–34_{t-1}$
netunden	0.289773			
$\frac{GiniFI - GiniDPI}{GiniFI}$	0.276183	0.65079		
$emplrt30–34_{t-1}$	–0.449696	–0.12753	–0.12524	
$EduL3_{t-3}$	0.188982	0.11257	0.37375	0.171988

[12] The size of the feed-back effect seems to be less than expected in Europe. Despite redistribution from mid-1980s to mid-1990s substantially reduced income inequality for disposable income with respect to factor income, in many European countries the Gini coefficient calculated on disposable income remained higher than that determined by market forces in the previous decade (Croci Angelini and Farina, 2006).

To tackle this possible source of endogeneity a regression equation was estimated making recourse to 2SLS estimators. As the same variables, one-period lagged, have been employed as instrumental variables, more observations were lost to the sample, which is constrained by the availability of the LIS information.

Table 9.4 shows the estimates resulting from the regression equation. The first three columns present the same model where, for the sake of comparisons, the youth employment rate variable is estimated for three different age groups. The negative sign for youth employment rate reflects the expansionary effect on wage inequality due to the low labour demand and a worsening match between the unemployed and job vacancies. None of the three age ranges conveys fully satisfactory estimates, though their significance improves with age. The better performance of the 30-34 range may be interpreted on the one hand as the better position of this age group in overcoming the difficult access to the job market, and on the other hand as a decreasing interference of the education system. Net union density is always highly significant. The negative sign of this variable is a signal that Continental and Mediterranean countries have joined the other two clusters in rising wage inequality following the withering of the unions' bargaining power. The positive sign of the drift on net union density for Scandinavian and Anglo-Saxon countries expresses the lower slope for the more deregulated labour markets of

Table 9.4. Regression results model 1 (LIS database)

Variables	2SLS estimate	2SLS estimate	2SLS estimate	2SLS estimate
netunden	–0.00317 ***	–0.00327 ***	–0.003101 ***	–0.00353 ***
t-value	(–2.961)	(–2.924)	(–3.008)	(–2.581)
$\frac{GiniFI - GiniDPI}{GiniFI}$	0.4444 **	0.45899 **	0.36590 *	0.527153 *
t-value	(2.030)	(2.004)	(1.785)	(1.798)
$emplrt30{-}34_{t-1}$	–0.0043 *			–0.00415
t-value	(–1.716)			(–1.420)
$emplrt25{-}29_{t-1}$		–0.00197		
t-value		(–1.005)		
$emplrt20{-}24_{t-1}$			0.001145	
t-value			(1.096)	
$EduL3_{t-3}$				-0.00096
t-value				(-0.238)
Drift netundenAS	0.00193 ***	0.00215 ***	0.00215 ***	0.00207 ***
t-value	(3.193)	(3.533)	(3.815)	(2.611)
Constant	0.49548 **	0.26800	0.07239	0.45966 *
t-value	(2.208)	(1.571)	(0.677)	(1.703)
R-square	0.27471	0.20254	0.31608	0.15825
Effective sample size	32	32	32	32

Note: Estimates significantly different from zero at the 10 per cent (*), 5 per cent (**) and 1 per cent (***) levels

these two clusters. The positive sign of redistribution confirms that higher wage inequality may depend on more generous redistribution, as higher unemployment spells, due to lower job protection and lower low-skill workers' wages, are compensated by higher duration and coverage of unemployment benefits. Instead, a negative relationship would have been traced back to the persistence of labour market regulation: a lower number of low-pay workers reduces wage dispersion while redistribution in terms of unemployment benefits widens it.

The last column, which adds education, presents the results for the complete model. The inadequate performance of the education variable, with unexpected sign and non-significant estimate, suggests that the indicator of technological level fails to live up to our expectations. The slope of the skill-educational profile, that is the form of the relation between skill level and educational attainment, greatly differs across countries, as university educational programmes for the same graduate or post-graduate degree are idiosyncratic across countries. Pairwisely, the link between skills and productivity levels differs too, depending on the varying production techniques adopted by firms belonging to the same sector but participating into different economic environments.

The two last decades are a sufficiently long period of time for the interaction between the short-term macroeconomic shocks and the long-term technological trajectories to develop. In the recent transition of European economies to a knowledge-based economy, which started in the second half of 1990s, those sectors characterised by high knowledge intensity reflected in the high educational levels of the workforce, such as the ICT sectors, experienced the strongest employment growth. Indeed, technological shifts in the productive processes have set off, either in the form of the sectoral composition moving towards an increasing share of high-tech manufacturing and services, or in the form of a higher proportion of highly educated and high-skilled workers compared to the medium and low-skilled workers. Both these structural changes could have distorted the composition of labour demand towards high-skill workers, thus depressing the low-skill workers' employment and wage rates.

A possible explanation for the scant relevance of the educational variable is that the educational attainment has no direct effect on the probability that the workers occupy the function or mansion which is appropriate to their professional background and thus that their wage level matches with their productivity. Overall, the general educational performance of the whole population is too loose an indicator of the skill structure of the labour force, and cannot be taken as an appropriate measure for the productivity of the employed labour force, not to mention poor data reliability and comparability across countries. The failure of this regression model to get a better understanding of technological choices leaves unanswered the question whether wage inequality, in addition to the impact of labour market regulation on the bottom of the wage distribution, is also influenced at the top by technical factors at the sectoral and firm levels prompting skill premium differentials.

The most severe obstacle in the investigation of links between wage inequality, institutions and technology is by all means the difficulty to find appropriate indicators. Indeed, the youth employment rate is just a proxy for the growth trend of labour demand; and the redistribution indicator, computed by the LIS database, is regressed on wage inequality across employed workers but includes – in addition to the social transfers to in-work individuals – also unemployment benefits and pensions.

The problem to be tackled is that all four independent variables refer to the population at large. In the next section we employ the ECHP database, and accordingly modify our econometric model, so to get more appropriate indicators for the three determinants of wage inequality here considered.

9.7 Wage inequality in Europe: a regression model with the ECHP database

The next regression model relates to the same conceptual framework, but employs data entirely coming from another source, the ECHP. The econometric investigation has been performed on four countries only, one for each cluster: Denmark, Italy, the Netherlands and the UK; and two waves: the first (1994) and the fourth (1997), so that a four-years time lag may be compared to the five-years period introduced in the previous model. For each country and wave the Gini coefficients have been calculated for wages disaggregated according to 18 economic sectors[13] and three occupational levels: managers, white and blue collars.[14] Each wave therefore amounts to a theoretical maximum of 216 observations, which is reduced to 180 observations as not all countries have all sectors, and not all sectors have workers in all occupations in sufficient numbers. The same breakdown has been employed to inquire whether the job contract was intended as permanent, the workers had obtained social transfers under any headings in the preceding year, and what had been their educational attainment, i.e. the maximum grade of schooling successfully attended. In particular, since the Gini coefficient of wage inequality per sector and per skill is expected to capture the between-sectors dispersion, the educational attainment regressed on the Gini measures of wage inequality should convey the effect of the educational gap magnifying divergences at the within-sector and within-skill levels. Information about wages, job tenure, social transfers and educational attainment have been employed to write the second regression model which also includes a few dummy variables and reads as follows:

$$\begin{aligned} Giniwages_i = \alpha + \beta\, jobtenure_i + \gamma\, socialtransfers_i + \\ + \delta\, edu1/3_i + dwhi + dblue + dservices + dDK + u_i \end{aligned} \tag{9.4}$$

[13] Information about the economic activity sectors was obtained by the variable PE007 which identifies the sectors according to the NACE (classification of economic activities in the European Community) code system and covers nine varieties of services (private and public) along with manufactures and other activities.

[14] The three occupational levels were obtained by ri-classifying the occupational variable PE006 into three groups.

The first independent variable, which enters as the percentage of tenured jobs per sector and occupational levels, is regarded as a more appropriate proxy, at disaggregate level, for the impact of labour market deregulation, which to a large extent has consisted in an increasing percentage of temporary contracts. The second independent variable, which enters as the ratio between the amount of social transfers accruing to the workers per sector and occupation and the amount of their earned income (wages and salaries), is an indicator for redistribution which does not refer to the whole tax-and-transfers reshuffling but just to the social transfers declared by the workers. This redistribution accruing to the employed labour force also comprehends unemployment benefits received in the unemployment spells which have been allowed by the relaxation of labour market regulation. Therefore, the redistribution indicator considered in this regression model is a measure of the actual 'mutual risk insurance' taking place among the employed labour force, which is permitted by the 'pooling' of contributions to the national social protection institutions by workers and firms. The variable 'social transfers to workers' is expected to account for institutional complementarity or substitutability between labour market regulation and welfare institutions influencing the wage and employment differentials in the European countries.

A higher level of monetary benefits provided by welfare institutions to the employed labour force is expected to allow for a widening wage inequality. A positive sign of the coefficient linking wage inequality to social transfers accruing to employed workers, can be interpreted as a clue of a 'corporatist' agreement between unions and governmental institutions, that is a larger social insurance traded for a lower pay for thc low-skilled workers at the bottom of the wage distribution.

Finally, the education variable now refers to the actual educational attainment of the labour force as declared by workers, and is regarded as a more insightful indicator than that employed in the former model. The impact of technical change on both wage inequality and the unemployment rate depends on the growth potential of a country, which in turn is a function of its technological trajectories as reflected by the weight of industries intensively using new technologies and human capital. In some countries the impact on the employment rate mainly comes from the aggregate demand fluctuations, while in others supply-side forces are more important, so that different earnings dispersion might result even if similar technological paths are followed by the EU countries. These considerations suggest to look for an indicator conveying information on skill levels, so to check for the direct impact of technical progress on wage differentials across the employed labour force. The education variable enters as the ratio of the number of workers with higher education (ISCED5-7) to the number of workers who have failed to complete secondary education (ISCED0-2) again per sector and occupation.

The summary statistics for the variables employed in the second regression model are reported in Table 9.5.

The regression model again incurs the problem of possible reverse causation for the redistribution indicator. As with the first regression model, we have made recourse to 2SLS estimators by including a one period lagged variable and employing the vector of wave 1 as instrumental variables to estimate the parameters of wave 4. Therefore, in contrast with the previous model, which spanned over two

Table 9.5. Summary statistics for the regression model 2

	giniwages	jobtenure	socialtransfers	edu1/3
min	0.0032943	0.4026846	0	0.001
max	0.5672744	1	0.4083306	49
mean	0.2275286	0.8841157	0.0792788	1.9404229
st.dev.	0.1057347	0.0963618	0.0872835	5.1565745

decades, this model only covers a very limited length of time. This circumstance, together with a more limited sample of countries and a much more detailed information per country, makes a proper comparison between the two sets of results awkward, yet one may notice that they embrace different angles of a same picture.

The correlation coefficients computed for all variables are reported in Table 9.6.

Table 9.7 reports the regression results for three specifications of the regression model: the first excludes the education variable, while the third also includes the services dummy. All variables, except education, show the expected sign and vary little across columns. The significance level is overall satisfactory. Labour market (de)regulation, proxied by the relative frequency of permanent jobs, is found to be an explanation of wage inequality reliable enough. Redistribution to workers is able to explain the most of variability in the Gini coefficient computed on wages when sector and occupation are accounted for. While education does not appear to be a very relevant factor, its unexpected sign may stand to signal that, other things equal, more education is accompanied by less wage inequality, a result that may sound less surprising, than upon a first glance analysis. In fact, other things being equal in addition to the above discussed variables include dummies (dwhite, dblue) to take care of the worker's occupation.

The disaggregation of the four countries by economic sector and occupation, while permitting to focus on the worker's occupation as a relevant condition to explain wage inequality, ends up in hiding those national characters which used to be so important in identifying the relevant cluster in the former analysis. The exception is the dummy dDK which insulates the Scandinavian Denmark where e.g. female employment in the public sector is exceptionally high. A tentative indicator for high technological level is provided by the dummy variable which singles out the service sector (dservices). Had its significance be more adequate, one could have ventured in the suggestion that this is a more telling proxy for technical change than education.

Table 9.6. Correlation coefficients model 2

	Giniwages	jobtenure	socialtransfers
jobtenure	–0.32433		
socialtransfers	0.50804	–0.37962	
edu1/3	–0.15857	0.15805	–0.04167

Table 9.7. Regression results model 2 (ECHP database)

Variables		2SLS estimate		2SLS estimate		2SLS estimate	
jobtenure		–0.19225	**	–0.172653	**	–0.164168	**
	t-value	(–2.358)		(–2.123)		(–2.037)	
socialtransfers		0.912572	***	0.929963	***	0.889359	***
	t-value	(6.736)		(6.907)		(6.390)	
edu1/3				–0.003329	**	–0.003558	**
	t-value			(–2.374)		(–2.544)	
dwhite		–0.047726	***	–0.061375	***	–0.060411	***
	t-value	(–2.808)		(–3.436)		(–3.407)	
dblue		–0.043489	***	–0.05825	***	–0.054672	***
	t-value	(–2.595)		(–3.279)		(–3.063)	
dDK		–0.104169	***	–0.096535	***	–0.096619	***
	t-value	(–5.397)		(–4.999)		(–5.050)	
dservices						0.018633	
	t-value					(1.334)	
constant		0.370179	***	0.365905	***	0.350509	***
	t-value	(4.702)		(4.694)		(4.515)	
R-square		0.3628		0.3799		0.3948	
Adj R-square		0.3440		0.3579		0.3696	
Nobs		176		176		176	

Note: Estimates significantly different from zero at the 10 per cent (*), 5 per cent (**) and 1 per cent (***) levels

The positive sign of the correlation between variations in social transfers accruing to workers and variations in wage inequality sustains the hypothesis that wage decompression has been accompanied by a tighter orientation of social protection to the employed labour force.

9.8 Conclusions

A depressed labour demand in the 1980s started a trend of increasing wage inequality in Europe, accompanied by sluggish employment growth, which eventually prompted a fall in unions' bargaining power and an easing in labour market regulation. During the 1990s, wage inequality kept rising, despite a recovery in the employment rates at the end of the decade. We have investigated whether the interaction between labour market and redistributive institutions has to be taken into account in explaining wage inequality, also with education as a proxy controlling for technical change. To assess why small increases in the employment rates are associated to continuously rising wage inequality in Europe, the hypothesis was put forward of a changing balance between decreasing labour market regulation (job and wage protection) and increasing income redistribution. The widening experienced by wage inequality in Europe during the 1990s might have been caused by labour market deregulation, under the permissive condition of income redistribution compensating for the fall in wage levels mainly at the bottom of the earnings distribution.

Our regression model centred on the median voter's decisiveness on redistribution has indicated that in Europe from mid-1980s to mid-1990s the worsening of income distribution in the market was partially reverted by income redistribution through tax-and-transfers, conditional on the degree of 'risk insurance' desired in each of the four European clusters of countries. The econometric estimate of wage inequality has been conducted on the LIS and ECHP databases. The first regression model (LIS) highlighted the importance of labour market deregulation in the upsurge of wage inequality, but has proven unable to provide reliable answers, mainly due to indicators for the four independent variables referring to the population at large. The second regression model (ECHP) allowed for the breakdown of the sequence from traditional to high-tech sectors and from low to high skill composition of the labour force, as well as more precise indicators for labour demand, regulation, redistribution and education. In fact, each of the three indicators for labour market institutions is linked to each specific occupational level, also warranting a better control for technical change as proxied by each individual's educational attainment.

Though with different characters across the clusters of European countries, the recovery in disposable *vis-à-vis* factor income distribution indicates that redistribution has compensated for the downward wage flexibility, in particular for the wage levels of low-skill workers. After that job and wage protection were eased in many European countries during the 1990s, institutional substitution between labour market regulation and income redistribution seems to back the upward trend in wage inequality. Overall, the degree of labour market governance does not seem to have substantially changed during the 1990s, but more redistribution traded off for regulation, thus allowing for higher wage inequality.

References

Arpaia, A. and G. Carone (2004), 'Do labour taxes (and their composition) affect wages in the short and the long run?', *European Commission,' Economic Papers 216.*

Atkinson, A.B. (1999), *The Economic Consequences of Rolling Back the Welfare State*, Cambridge, MA: MIT Press.

Atkinson, A.B. and A. Brandolini (2005), 'The panel-of-countries approach to explaining income inequality: an interdisciplinary research agenda', in S.L. Morgan, D.B. Grusky and G.S. Fields (eds), *Mobility and Inequality: Frontiers of Research from Sociology and Economics*, Stanford: Stanford University Press.

Bertola, G. and T. Boeri (2002), 'EMU labour markets two years on: microeconomic tensions and institutional evolution', in M. Buti and A. Sapir (eds), *EMU and Economic Policy in Europe. The Challenge of the Early Years,* Cheltenham, UK and Northampton, USA: Edward Elgar.

Bertola, G., F.D. Blau and L.M. Kahn (2002), 'Comparative analysis of labour market outcomes: lessons for the US from international long-run evidence', in A. Kruger and R.

Solow (eds), *The Roaring Nineties: Can Full Employment be Sustained?*, Russell Sage and Century Foundations, pp. 159–218.

Blanchard, O. and F. Giavazzi (2003), 'Macroeconomic effects of regulation and deregulation in goods and labour markets', *Quarterly Journal of Economics*, **118**:879–907.

Blanchard, O. and J. Wolfers (2000), 'The role of shocks and institutions in the rise of European unemployment: the aggregate evidence', *Economic Journal*, **110**(462):C1–33.

Blau, F. D. and L.M. Kahn (1996), 'International differences in male wage inequality: institutions versus market forces', *Journal of Political Economy*, **104**:791–837.

Boeri, T., A. Boersch-Supan, and G. Tabellini (2001), 'Would you like to shrink the welfare state? The opinions of European citizens', *Economic Policy*, **32**:7–50.

Brugiavini, A. et al. (2001), 'What do unions do to the welfare states', in T. Boeri, A. Brugiavini, and L. Calmfors, *The Role of Unions in the Twenty-First Century*, Oxford: Oxford University Press.

Card, D. and J.E. Di Nardo (2002), 'Skill biased technological change and rising wage inequality: some problems and puzzles', *NBER Working Paper 8769.*

Checchi, D. and L. Lucifora (2002), 'Union density. The economic roles of unions and institutions', *Economic Policy*, **35**:363–408.

Croci Angelini, E. and F. Farina (2006), 'The size of redistribution in OECD countries: Does it influence wage inequality?', in F. Farina and E. Savaglio (eds), *Inequality and Economic Integration*, London: Routledge.

De la Fuente, A. and R. Domenech (2002), 'Educational attainment in the OECD (1960–1995)', *CEPR Discussion Paper 3416.*

Ebbinghaus, B. and J. Visser (2000), *The Societies of Europe, Trade Unions in Western Europe since 1945*, London: Macmillan.

Esping-Andersen, G. (1999), *Social Foundations of Post-industrial Economies*, Oxford: Oxford University Press.

Fitoussi, J.P., D. Jestaz, E.S. Phelps, and G. Zoega (2000), 'Roots of the recent recoveris: labor reforms or private sectors forces?', *Brookings Papers on Economic Activity*, **1**:237–91.

Freeman, R. and R. Schettkat (2001), *Differentials in Service Industry Employment Growth: Germany and the US in the comparable German American Structural Database*, Bruxelles: European Commission, DG Employment and Social Affairs.

Katz, L.F. and D.H. Autor (1999), 'Changes in the wage structure and earnings inequality', in O.C. Ashenfelter and D. Card (eds), *Handbook of Labour Economics*, Vol. 3, Amsterdam: Elsevier Science Publisher.

Kenworthy, L. and J. Pontusson (2005), 'Rising inequality and the politics of redistribution in affluent countries', *Perspectives on Politics*, **1**:1–44.

Krugman, P. (1994), 'Past and prospective causes of high unemployment', in *Reducing Unemployment: Current Issues and Policy Options*, Kansas City: Federal Reserve Bank of Kansas City.

Ljungkvist, L. and T.S. Sargent (1998), 'The European unemployment dilemma', *Journal of Political Economy*, **106**:514–50.

Nickell, S., L. Nunziata, W. Ochel, and G. Quintini (2002), 'The Beveridge curve, unemployment and wages in the OECD from the 1960s to the 1990s', in F. Aghion, R. Frydman, J. Stiglitz, and M. Woodford (eds), *Knowledge, Information and Expectations in Modern Macroeconomics*, Princeton: Princeton University Press.

OECD (2004), *Employment Outlook 2004*, Paris: OECD.

PART V

FOR A THEORY OF SOCIAL PACTS

10 Searching for the EU Social Dialogue Model

Richard B. Freeman

Harvard University, Massachusetts, USA

10.1 Introduction

'Collective bargaining and social dialogue were designed into the European project from the very beginning' (John Monks, European Trade Unions Congress Secretary, May 2004).

The European Union and the United States operate different variants of market capitalism. Both systems base economic transactions on private property and rule of law. Both have open economies with sound monetary and macro-economic policies. Where the EU and US differ is in the role of institutions in affecting outcomes, particularly in the labor market.

The EU relies on collective bargaining between employer associations and trade unions to determine wages and employment and on social dialogue between the 'social partners' of labor and capital, often working in concert with government, to choose social and economic policies. The US relies on firms and individual workers to determine employment and wages in competitive markets. The EU has high taxes that provide a strong social safety net for workers. The US has lower taxes and a weak safety net for workers. The differences are sufficiently large to have generated a 'war of the models' about how best to organize a market economy (Freeman, 1998).

From the 1960s through the 1970s oil shock and productivity slowdown, the rapid growth and low unemployment of Western European economies led some analysts to generalize that neo-corporatist centralized bargaining wage systems work better than more market based systems (Bruno and Sachs, 1984). In the 1980s Japan's rapid economic growth and export success directed attention at the virtues of Japanese institutions. During his visit to Harvard in 1986–87, Ezio Tarantelli and I debated whether the Japanese economy was more aligned to the EU institution-affected system than to the more market-driven US.[1] But Japan went into a bad economic decade while US performance improved. From the 1990s

[1] The modest unionization rates, company level unions, use of bonuses related to profits, and limited political role of unions suggested that Japan was closer to the US than to the EU system. But the Shunto offensive, coordination of wage settlements, lifetime employment, lead bank system, industrial concentration, and protection of small firms in the service sector suggested that Japan was closer to the EU than to the US.

through the mid 2000s, the rapid growth and low unemployment in the US shifted sentiment in favor of more market driven variants of capitalist economies.[2]

Regardless of whether more market-driven or institution influenced economies do better in a given period of time, there is generally a wide range of economic outcomes within each group. In the 1990s the US performed well in productivity and employment but Canada, with much the same economic system, had an horrific economic record. From the 1990s through the mid 2000s several smaller EU economies – Ireland, Denmark, Austria, and to some extent the Netherlands – performed better than Germany and France, among others. Supporters of the EU system often cite the smaller successes as evidence that social dialogue economies can deliver economic efficiency as well as economic security and desirable distributions of income.

When market economies run into trouble, the natural response of economists has traditionally been to seek out imperfections in the market and to suggest ways to eliminate those imperfections. This response builds on the powerful framework that economic theory provides for analyzing real market economies. The model of a perfectly functioning competitive system gives economists and policy-makers a benchmark for measuring real world divergences from the ideal and directs attention at reforms designed to bring the real world closer to the competitive ideal.

When EU economies have gotten into trouble, the economists' response is often the same: to identify market imperfections and seek ways to eliminate them. But this seems less appropriate in a social dialogue economy than in a market-dominated economy. Why not seek out imperfections in the social dialogue institutions and search for ways to improve institutional interventions? One reason why economists do not pursue this approach is that we lack a well-specified model of the ideal institution driven economy to benchmark real world divergences from the ideal.

In the world of ideas and in policy discourse the absence of a social dialogue model creates an uneven playing field for assessing the two capitalist models and improving their performances.

EU social dialogue model, where art thou?

This chapter begins the search for such a model. Section 10.2 documents the differences between the EU's social dialogue and collective bargaining system and the US's market driven economy. Section 10.3 presents my principal theme: that efficient bargaining models and the Coase theorem offer the best framework for developing the missing social dialogue model. Section 10.4 assesses evidence on efficient bargaining from laboratory experiments. Section 10.5 considers the implications from game theory analyses of bargaining for developing an efficient social dialogue system. Section 10.6 is a short conclusion.

---

[2] For instance, in 2004, 4.9 per cent of the German labour force had been unemployed for over a year, compared to 0.7 per cent of the US labour force. OECD, *Employment Outlook*, 2005, tables A and G.

10.2 The two economic systems

Fig. 10.1 gives a capsule summary of the differences between the EU and US economic systems. The exhibit shows that the EU relies on collective bargaining to set wages and working conditions to a far greater extent than does the US. In the EU 77 per cent of workers[3] were covered by agreements in 2000, many through mandatory extension of contracts to firms outside the bargaining group. In the US bargaining covers only 13 per cent of workers, and most collective bargaining contracts are at the firm level. Although EU centralized bargaining allows for 'wages drift' (by which firms deviate from the agreement due to their particular circumstances), and although most EU countries have devolved some bargaining to firms or plants, the difference in reliance on institutions in wage-setting with the US remains stark. The 2003 Global Competitiveness Report gave the US the 3rd highest rank in terms of having wages set by the company vs by institutions while the median ranking for EU countries was 68 out of 80 countries in the listing (World Economic Forum, 2003, table 10.19).

The US and EU also differ greatly in the rules that govern 'ownership' of jobs. The US has employment at will, which allows firms to lay off or fire workers at their discretion with no legally mandated severance pay. During a strike, the employer can replace strikers and need not re-employ them after the dispute. By contrast, EU employment protection legislation gives partial ownership of jobs to workers. The OECD's index of employment protection legislation, which gives higher scores to countries with greater protection, gave the US a score of 0.7 compared to a score of 2.3 for EU countries in 2003.[4] Strikers in the EU have a right to return to their job after a labor dispute.

In the product market the US has fewer regulations governing business activity and makes it easier to form and end businesses than the EU. It takes 64 days to form a business in the EU compared to 7 days in the US. The OECD index of regulations, which codes countries from 0 to 2 in three different areas of regulations, gave the US in 2003 a 1 in product market regulations, 1.1 in administrative regulations, and 1.3 in economic regulations compared to 1.4, 1.5, and 2.0 in these three areas for the EU.[5]

Finally, the US has a more limited welfare state than EU countries. In the US the primary source of economic security is working; unemployment benefits are modest and of limited duration; and income support for single parent families is limited. The US offers health care insurance through employers or private purchase; government provision is limited to the elderly and poor. While state and local governments fund primary and secondary education, a large proportion of higher education is paid by students and their families and by private donations.

[3] OECD, *Employment Outlook 2004*, table 3.3, where I have averaged collective bargaining coverage figures for 2000 for 13 EU countries and Norway, excluding the new East European members.

[4] OECD, *Employment Outlook 2004*, table 2.A2.3, where I averaged the EPL scores for the EU countries and Norway, exclusive of the new entrants.

[5] Djankov et al. (2000); Conway et al. (2005, table 24).

Fig. 10.1 The EU and US Economic Systems

	US: Invisible Hand	EU: Social Partners
ECONOMY		
Labor Market:		
Wages	market–employer driven	collective bargaining with extension
Employment	employment at will – employers own job	employment protection legislation – workers own job
Company level formal dialogue	illegal under Section 8a of the Labor Management Relations Act unless union involved; employee involvement committees	European Works Councils (EC 94/45/EC); different country council legislation
Product Market	less regulated, with ease of entry and exit, bankruptcy laws favorable to debtors	greater regulation of business, harder entry and exit
GOVERNMENT		
Safety nets	limited, short duration of unemployment benefits	high replacement for unemployment with long duration, so long spells
Health	health care through employer/private purchase	national health care
Higher education	universities dependent on private support, tuition, business linked	publically funded, free universities

Source: Author's analysis

By contrast, the welfare state is the EU's primary source of economic security. All EU countries offer high replacement rates for unemployed persons for long periods. All have some form of national health insurance. Many provide housing assistance for workers who lose their job and offer other benefits so that loss of a job does not devastate their living standards. In addition to providing free primary and secondary education, the EU provides low tuition higher education through state support of universities.

To fund the wider role of government in 2004 governments in the EU received 48 per cent of GDP compared to the US government receipts of 32 per cent of GDP.[6]

[6] US Bureau of the Census, Statistical Abstract 2006, table 1335.

10.2.1 Social dialogue vs market lobbying

The EU uses social dialogue institutions to bring the voices of business and labor into social and economic policy-making. Most EU countries encourage dialogue at workplaces through mandated works councils. Depending on the country, from 25 per cent to 50 per cent of workers are represented by elected works councils, and almost all workers in middle to large establishments have the option to establish a council at their workplace. The EU social charter requires EU-level councils for larger firms.

By contrast, US labor law discourages firms from setting up systems of dialogue with workers outside of collective bargaining. Section 8a of the US's Labor-Management Relations Act forbids firms from establishing non-union systems of collective representation for fear that companies will create company-dominated organizations to avoid genuine worker organizations. Many firms have employee involvement committees but these committees are legally allowed to deal only with issues that concern the firm such as productivity rather than with worker concerns such as pay, benefits or working conditions.

At the national level, the EU relies on social dialogue committees to ascertain the views of labor and management on diverse issues. The US relies on a very different mechanism for interest groups to contribute to national policy-making – lobbying in which the groups that fund political campaigns meet with legislators to argue for their views.

Fig. 10.2 contrasts the EU social dialogue system with the US lobbying system. The upper panel gives the EU's own description of its system, as reported at the 2005 EU social dialogue summit. While the description focuses on dialogue at the EU level, it notes that 'the European social dialogue complements the national practices of social dialogue, which exist in most Member States'. Indeed, it is at the national level where social partnership arrangements are particularly important and where collective bargaining occurs. When an EU government deviates from the consultative model, as the De Villepin government did in France in 2006 when it enacted a new youth labor law without consultation, it risks enraging the groups that were not consulted – in this case, students and unions, whose protests forced the government to withdraw the law.

The lower panel describes the US lobbying system. It is a market-based system built on the US mode of funding political campaigns through private contributions. Lobbyists buy access to candidates through their contributions and use that access to present their case for/against legislation in private closed-door meetings. The opinion polls summarized in the exhibit show that in the 1990s-2000s most Americans believed that political lobbyists had too much power and bribed members of Congress regularly. As a result most citizens were concerned about the corruption this engendered in Washington.

There is an extensive social science literature on lobbying activities and on the impact of campaign contributions on legislator's decision, but no comparable analysis of the operation of social dialogue committees.

EU social dialogue model, where art thou?

Fig. 10.2 EU social dialogue from workplace to national policy

European social dialogue (Social Dialogue Summit, Brussels, Sept 2005)

European social dialogue is the discussions between employee and employer representative organisations (the social partners). These can take the form of consultations, negotiations and joint actions undertaken by the social partner organizations.

At European level, social dialogue takes two main forms – bipartite dialogue between the European employers and trade union organizations, and tripartite dialogue involving interaction between the social partners and the public authorities.

These are the essential means by which the social partners help define European social standards, and play a vital role in the governance of the Union. European-level social dialogue has received strong institutional recognition in the EC Treaty and in the conclusions to a number of key European Council meetings, notably those of Laeken and Barcelona. Combining the values of responsibility, solidarity and participation, the European social dialogue complements the national practices of social dialogue, which exist in most Member States.

US Lobbying

As of mid 2005, the US had nearly 35,000 registered lobbyists for Congress alone. Lobbyists in the US target the Senate, the House of Representatives, and state legislatures. They may also represent their clients' or organizations' interests in dealings with federal, state, or local executive branch agencies or the courts. Lobbyists sometimes also write legislation. Since 1998, 43 percent of the 198 members of Congress who left government to join private life have registered to lobby. Former lawmakers are hired as lobbyists because of their relationships with their former colleagues as well as other contacts. In 2006, 273 former members of Congress or heads of federal agencies were lobbyists.

Attitudes of Americans toward lobbying:

75% believe political lobbyists have too much power, 1994-2001 (Harris)
81% believe it is common for lobbyists to bribe members of Congress, 2006 (Pew)
91% concerned about corruption in Washington, 2006 (Fox)

Source:
EU, Europa, European Commission, http://europa.eu.int/rapid/pressReleasesAction.do?reference=MEMO/05/344&format=HTML&aged=0&language=EN&guiLanguage=en.
US, Knowlton, B., 'Lobbyists's scandal has a K street home', *International Herald Tribune*, January 11, 2006, www.iht.com; http://en.wikipedia.org/wiki/Lobbyist; under lobbying. Harris Poll #23, May 16, 2001, table 2, www.harrisinteractive.com/harris_poll/printerfriend/index.asp?PID=233, www.citizen.org/print article.fm?ID=14945 for Pew and Fox polls.

10.3 The social dialogue model and efficient bargaining

The main theme of this chapter is that the theory of efficient bargaining and Coase Theorem provide the best framework for answering the 'where art thou?' question.

The notion of efficient bargaining has a distinguished pedigree in economics. In chapter 7 of the *Theory of Wages* (first edition, 1932), John Hicks argued that collective bargaining should produce agreement rather than impasse in most situations. After all, most strikes lower the joint output of capital and labor and thus make no rational sense. He asserted that 'the majority of actual strikes are doubtless the result of faulty negotiation' (Hicks, [1932],1963, p. 146). Efficient bargaining between employers and unions ought to yield the same patterns of outcomes that the efficient market hypothesis predicts for financial markets: randomness. Labor specialists should be no more able to predict strikes from public information than financial specialists can predict financial returns from such information.

In 1946 Wassily Leontief applied the efficient bargaining model to the 'guaranteed annual wage' that the US United Automobile Workers negotiated with General Motors. In this contract the Automobile Workers insisted that GM pay for at least a minimal number of hours of work from the existing work force. Leontief interpreted this as bargaining over employment as well as wages and pointed out that through such a strategy the union could shift distribution to labor while maintaining the presumably efficient pre-union wage employment and output.

In 1986 Mancur Olson argued that 'all-encompassing' unions – those that represent all workers – should internalize the externalities associated with inefficient bargains and produce more efficient outcomes than unions that represent only some workers in a country. In 1988 Lars Calmfors and John Driffill further developed the notion that centralized or coordinated bargaining yields outcomes comparable to competitive markets while industry level bargaining yields less efficient outcomes.

But the most influential analysis of efficient bargaining lies outside of labor economics. This is the Coase theorem on property rights and externalities, which has generated a huge literature in law and economics (Coase, 1960). The theorem holds that, absent transactions costs, the clear allocation property rights/decision-making power suffices to assure efficient outcomes. The reason is that, regardless of who owns what, economic agents should bargain to the most efficient point of production and then divide the maximum output. They ought to leave no money on the table. The prediction that efficiency depends solely on clear property rights suggests that economies with egalitarian rules governing distribution can be as efficient with more unequal income distributions.[7]

10.3.1 But real world bargaining is not efficient

'Using the Coase theorem as the starting point for the analysis of EU economies is more Chicago than Chicago. Bargainers often do not reach efficient solutions' (Ed Lazear, commenting on the theme of this essay).

The criticism is right. There are many cases of real world bargaining that fall short of efficient agreements. In labor economics, the most widely studied failure of efficient bargaining is in strike behavior. In contrast to Hicks' prediction that

[7] Medema and Zerbe (1999, p. 838) note that some versions of the Coase theorem add a stronger claim: that the final allocation of resources will itself be invariant to the assignment of property rights. Since the redistributions associated with social dialogue economies are highly likely to affect the allocation of resources as well as the distribution, I deal solely with the efficiency proposition.

strikes should have no predictable pattern across time or space, strikes are procyclical, occur frequently in some sectors and firms and not in others, are more common in some countries than in others, and occur in narrow time periods. Striking is less common in sectors where the costs to labor and capital are largest but occurs sometimes even when both sides end up as big losers. Game theory, models of asymmetric information, detailed models of negotiations – whatever economists have thrown at the problem – have failed to put a rational efficient market interpretation onto the strike data.

Labor economists have also examined the prediction that efficient union-management negotiations should alter pay but maintain employment and output. Given that most collective contracts have some form of 'management rights' clause that reserves control over hiring to the firm, the claim that the union determines employment seems on the face of it unrealistic. In the few cases where unions have negotiated employment as well as pay, the outcome has often been featherbedding rather than efficient work arrangements (for example, musicians sitting in a studio with recorded music in the early days of radio). Since US unions raise compensation and unionized firms/sectors/workplaces tend to have lower employment growth than their non-union counterparts, most economists reject the notion that collective bargaining produces employment off the demand curve in an efficient way.

In a similar vein, studies of productivity among sectors and firms find that competitive pressures can induce producers to raise productivity so greatly that they almost certainly had previously unexploited opportunities to increase efficiency – what Leibenstein (1966) called X-efficiency. Galdon-Sanchez and Schmitz (2002) have documented a particularly striking example of this in the recovery of US and Canadian iron ore producers from the collapse of steel production in their home markets in the 1980s. The iron ore producers raised their productivity massively compared to otherwise comparable iron ore producers operating in markets that had little or no increase in competitive pressures. The intensified competitive pressure led the firms to reform work and staffing rules that they could readily have done before they faced great competitive pressures.

10.3.2 Empirical studies of the Coase theorem

Law and economics analyses of the Coase theorem in diverse other settings also give a mixed picture of its real world applicability. Steven Medema and Richard Zerbe (1999) reviewed studies of the effect on agricultural production of the property right to control animal trespassing on farmlands. Two studies found efficient outcomes but both attributed the outcomes to social pressures/norms to keep animals off farm lands rather than to efficient bargaining between farmers and ranchers. The third study rejected the efficiency outcome. In 1989 John Donohue examined the 1980s Illinois employment experiment, which paid bonuses to workers or to firms to encourage the unemployed to find employment quickly from the perspective of the theorem. One variant of the experiment paid the bonuses to unemployed workers who found a new job quickly. Another variant paid the bonuses to the firms for hiring unemployed workers quickly. The Coase Theorem predicts that the property right to the bonus ought not affect the employment outcome. But the payments to workers led to greater employment and bonus receipt than did the payments to firms. Whether the Coase theorem failed because transactions costs were higher than the experiment envisaged as some critics of Donohue's work argued (see Medema and Zerba, 1999, pp. 869–71), or because of some other form of non-optimizing behavior, the important conclusion is that in this real world example, the allocation of property rights affected efficiency.

Studies of divorce laws, where the state changes the law from requiring both sides to agree to a divorce (so that the side most eager for the divorce would pay more to the other side to accept it) to allowing one side to insist upon the divorce, have also found the Coase theorem wanting. Peters (1992) reported that changes in divorce laws from mutual to unilateral divorce had effects consistent with the theorem: a change in the division of family assets but no change in the frequency of divorce. But ensuing work, summarized in Allen (2006), has found that rates of divorce rise when the law moves from mutual divorce to unilateral divorce, contrary to efficient bargaining. Wolfers' (2006) analysis offers further evidence and analysis of the problems with the Coase theorem in this setting.

The most widely studied Coase theorem prediction relevant to EU labor problems relates to employment protection laws (EPL). The Coase theorem predicts that EPL will not affect aggregate outcomes but will alter the distribution of income. Many policy analysts dismiss the prediction and argue that weaker EPL laws would reduce unemployment, but empirical analyses find no such consistent effect. The OECD (2004) review of studies of EPL concluded that 'the numerous empirical studies of this issue lead to conflicting results, and (notes further that) moreover their robustness has been questioned.' Baker et al.'s (2005) analysis showing that empirical results vary greatly with modest variation in the models, countries, time period, and measures used to assess the impact of EPL is more consistent with EPL having no effect on the volume of employment or unemployment than with the belief that it has effects.

This does not mean the EPL does not impact labor market outcomes. Stronger EPL regulations are associated with lower flows of labor from employment into unemployment, which benefits older workers, and with lower flows from unemployment to employment, which generally harms younger workers and other new entrants to the job market (OECD, 2004). What is important is that the effects are on the distribution of employment rather or more than on the volume of employment or unemployment, consistent with the Coase theorem.

Still, the EPL studies aside, the bulk of empirical work in labor and in law and economics indicates that the efficient bargaining model does not fit reality well. Does this make Coase theorem style thinking irrelevant for assessing social dialogue economic systems?

I think not. Empirical analyses of market driven economies show that real markets often fall short of 100 per cent efficiency, but the competitive model still provides a valuable framework for analyzing market performance. In finance the efficient market hypothesis is a useful first approximation and benchmark, even though researchers have uncovered numerous empirical regularities that reject the model. By analogy, the efficient bargaining/Coase theorem model can still be a valuable ideal for illuminating social dialogue systems even though the world does not evince efficient bargaining as a general rule.

10.4 Laboratory experiments and behavioral economics

Another way to judge the relevance of efficient bargaining models to real situations is through laboratory experiments. The bulk of experiments in which efficient production requires cooperation among people – the prisoner's dilemma[8]; public goods games[9]– shows that people attain efficient or near efficient solutions in many cases even without formal side agreements. For example, tit for tat behavior tends to dominate prisoner's dilemma games, producing efficient outcomes. And while participants in public goods games rarely contribute 100 per cent to the pot, they almost never contribute the 0 per cent that theory predicts. If people approach efficient solutions without side agreements, perhaps a modicum of bargaining would bring them even closer.

The experiments on the Coase theorem by Elizabeth Hoffman and Matthew Spitzer highlight the strength and weakness of the theorem. Their experiments assigned a number to each of two participants, one of which could be cashed in for real money. A coin toss gave the property right/power to determine which number gets cashed in to one of participants. Without bargaining the person who won the toss would presumably select their number for that is the most that they can get. They should do this even if the second party has a larger number, producing a socially inefficient outcome from the perspective of the pair. But bargaining ought to yield the efficient outcomes. The person with the power to determine which number cashes in ought to pick the highest number subject to a side arrangement in which they obtain more money than they could earn from cashing in their own number (arguably, the entire reward less some minimal payment to the second party, who would otherwise get nothing).

Hoffman and Spitzer found that over 90 per cent of the sets of bargainers brought the higher number to the experimenter for an efficient allocation. But the bargainers distributed the rewards in a manner inconsistent with rational bargaining. They tended to divide the money equally even though that meant that the party with the property right accepted less than he/she would have gained by selecting their own number! When Hoffman and Spitzer altered the allocation of the property right from a coin flip to the winner of a contest and educated the winner about choosing in their own interests, the majority of pairs chose the joint maximum but only 60 per cent bargained for more than they would have gotten by selecting their own number.

[8] The prisoner's dilemma is the most widely studied cooperation game. Efficient production requires that the two participants choose to cooperate even though there is an incentive to defect. See Wikipedia.

[9] In public goods games subjects invest money in a public pot whose value increases, often with higher returns the greater the amount invested, and keep the money they did not invest in the pot plus an even share of the money in the pot. See Wikipedia.

In sum, these experiments yielded efficient outcomes, but they also found that participants got to the efficient outcome through decision processes far from the self-interested economic rationality that underlies the Coase Theorem.

Stewart Schwab's (1988) experiment used a more complicated bargaining design that failed to produce efficient solutions. In Schwab's experiment students were divided into union and management teams that bargained over 3 items: wages, vacation days – which up to 15 days benefited workers more than they cost management but which after 15 days cost management more than their worth to workers – and a contract clause that allowed the firm to move work from the union plant to a non-union plant. In half of the experiments, the work clause produced more value to the management team than to the union team. In the other half, keeping the clause out of the contract meant more to the union. A fully efficient bargain required that the parties agree to 15 days of vacation and adopt the transfer clause in the first variant and reject the clause in the second variant. The wage ($1 benefit to workers = $1 cost of the firm) gave the parties an easily transferable way to redistribute output from the optimal solution. But Schwab found that 'neither item was bargained to a fully efficient result' (Schwab, 1988, p. 251). The contracts produced an average of 11 days of vacation pay and the optimal solution for the transfer clause in 2/3rds of the cases. The bargaining left money on the table.

Surprisingly, even though bargainers did not reach optimal efficiency, the experiment validated the prediction of the Coase theorem that changes in property rights do not affect allocation. In one variant of the experiment the firm had the initial property right to transfer the work. In another variant the union had the initial right to forbid the transfer. The two property rights regimes produced contracts with similar outcomes (approximately 2/3rds efficient) while giving a greater share of the joint output to the party with the property right.

Thus, like the 'real world' assessments, laboratory experiments give a mixed picture of Coase theorem/efficient bargaining. Bargaining pairs sometimes reach efficiency and sometimes not. Distributive outcomes are sometimes consistent with the model and sometimes not. These findings raise what is arguably the critical stumbling block for the theme of this essay: whether actual behavior diverges so much from rational optimizing as to invalidate the use of efficient bargaining/Coase Theorem models as benchmarks for analyzing EU social dialogue economies.

10.4.1 Behavioral economics and efficient bargaining

A large growing body of evidence from psychology and behavioral economics shows that people make decisions in ways that deviate substantially from the rational optimization that economists have historically assumed. Some of these forms of non-rational optimizing behavior make attainment of efficient outcomes more likely – notably the tendencies for cooperation and for fair distribution of outcomes – but others call into question the entire notion of efficient bargaining to a social optimum.

As an example of the latter, consider the evidence that possession of a good raises a person's valuation of it – 'the endowment effect' on preferences. The endowment effects experiments show that random assignment of items to people (such as coffee mugs of a given color) raises their valuation of the item and thus leads them to ask for more money to give up the item than they would be willing to pay for it had it not been in their possession (Kahneman, Knetsch, and Thaler, 1990). When willingness to accept payment diverges from willingness to pay for the same item the volume of trade will be below what the Coase theorem would predict for reasons beyond transactions costs. Two economies with different initial distributions of property rights would have different social optimum.

A second example of behavioral findings that challenge any efficient bargaining analysis is the evidence that individuals choose 'default' options in savings behavior for long periods even when other options dominate the default (Beshears et al., 2006). Since the transaction cost of shifting to a higher return option are nominally modest, the implication is that there are large internal transactions costs that deter rational choice. If a person does not efficiently bargain with themself to make the sensible decision, it seems unrealistic that they can bargain efficiently with others, per any efficient bargaining model.

Without gainsaying the importance of these and related findings from behavioral economics on how people really make decisions, I reject the strong claim that this evidence by itself invalidates the use of efficient bargaining/Coase Theorem models as ideals for social dialogue systems.

One reason why the findings do not invalidate the efficient bargaining ideal is that markets can be efficient even when bargainers make decisions in ways that diverge greatly from economic rationality. Markets based on 'zero intelligence agents' – computer code that chooses randomly among options – give efficient or near efficient outcomes when the agents face budget constraints and/or operate under exit and entry conditions (Gode and Sunder, 1993). The agents that make bad decisions lose their position in the market over time while those who randomly drew good decisions increase their share of the market. In a bargaining situation, the pair of bargainers that reach efficient outcomes, even by chance, will expand their market presence, leading to an evolution toward efficient outcomes.

Another reason is that people may make more rational decisions when they represent others in collective bargaining or social dialogue settings than when they act on their own behalf. For instance, I would expect that pension fund managers who may follow some low return default in their own savings behavior would search carefully for the best returns for the fund as part of their job. Similarly, someone who might take a high risk in a personal investment would choose lower risk options when representing widows and pensioners. Indeed, while society does not care how someone invests their own funds, it places 'fiduciary responsibility' on those investing on behalf of others, which means that they ought to be able to give rational explanations for their decisions. If my expectations are correct, some behavioral anomalies in private decision-making will not generalize to settings where decisions are part of someone's social role.

Finally, collective bargaining and social dialogue usually involve group decision-making, which can also produce decisions that differ from what people make on their own. Studies of group judgment show that under some circumstances groups make better use of information than individuals. This is the 'wisdom of crowds' that improves estimates of parameters and that reduces variation in those estimates (Surowiecki, 2004). But other studies show that group decision-making can lead to erroneous decisions, which members of the group hold with high confidence (Sunstein, 2005).

Sunstein gives a telling example of erroneous group decision-making in an experimental setting. Participants are asked to estimate whether the experimenter is using a Red urn, which has 60 per cent red balls, or a Black urn, which has 60 per cent black balls. The experimenter selects balls from the chosen urn and gives one ball to each person. If each person independently guesses the urn from which the experimenter selected the balls, they would guess the urn whose color they had drawn; and the group would choose the urn with the color of the majority of the balls. Thus, if 3 of 5 persons draw black balls, the group would choose the black urn. But if individuals vote seriatim on the urn (and do not give the color of the ball they drew), the group can go astray. If the first two people drew red and guessed red, and the others drew black, the group might unanimously choose the red urn. The third person might be swayed by the two preceding guesses and guess red as well even though she drew black. The fourth, who also drew black, might also guess red, on the grounds that 3 of 4 draws were red. The fifth would presumably make the same choice. This 'information cascade' leads the group to choose red without dissent.

Reviewing the literature on group judgments, Sunstein concludes that 'group polarization can be heightened, diminished, and possibly even eliminated with seemingly small alterations in institutional arrangements' (p. 45). This suggests that whether groups behave in a more economically rational way than individuals may depend critically on the arrangement and framing of group interactions.

10.5 Game theory and institutional design

The argument that analyses of efficient bargaining/Coase theorem offer the most promising road toward the missing EU social dialogue model directs attention not only at empirical analyses of actual bargaining situations but also at theoretical investigations of bargaining situations by rational (or other) decision-makers and of institutional designs that can produce efficient outcomes. Game theory provides a rich set of models on conditions for efficient bargaining and the Coase theorem. The associated implementation theory (Jackson, 2001) examines ways to design institutions so that the parties reach or approximate efficient equilibrium. Although researchers in these areas have not directed their investigations toward EU social dialogue systems, the work offers potentially useful insight toward the 'holy grail' social dialogue model.

What does the game theory/implementation theory say about bargaining and social dialogue activities?

First, the analyses show that the institutional structure of a bargaining game matters critically as to whether it yields a socially efficient outcome. Using different modelling structures Anderlini and Felli (2001) and Dixit and Olson (2000) find that even modest transactions costs for participating in a bargaining or dialogue system can readily lead to inefficient equilibrium.[10] Since there are always some transactions costs in any negotiation, the implication is that the Coase theorem is non-robust to these costs. In a similar vein Jackson (2001) stresses that particular mechanisms for implementing decision-making can have huge effects on strategic behavior and social outcomes. These analyses also highlight a tension between bargaining systems that allow participants to reach undesirable equilibrium (giving them an incentive to avoid those decisions) and systems in which renegotiation allow participants to escape disaster but which reduce the disincentive to make poor decisions in the first place.

From one perspective, the dependence of results on institutional detail is disappointing, since it suggests that small differences in design can have large effects on the success or failure of social dialogue systems. But this is not a surprising result given the dependence of outcomes on the specifics of game structures broadly (Kreps, 1990). Optimistically, it suggests that experimentation or tinkering with a system has the potential for improving outcomes. It also suggests that EU policies that require bargaining or dialogue may help achieve efficient outcomes.

Second, studies that examine the characteristics of bargainers and bargaining situations show that homogeneous groups, with similar endowments and abilities, operating under stable power relations, are more likely to reach efficient bargains than others (Rajan and Zingales, 2000). Inequality reduces the chance for attaining efficiency because it increases the incentive for the poor or less productive to use their resources for rent-seeking rather than to contribute to social output. Stable relations increase the chance of reaching efficient bargains because parties can be secure that gains from an efficient contract accruing to the other side will not change their relative power in the future. For example, if 80 per cent of an expected gain from an efficiency enhancing economic reform goes to business and business can use this gain to campaign for laws that may restrict union power in the future, unions may refuse to go along with the reform, even though it raises the income of business and workers.[11]

These considerations suggest that EU countries, particularly the smaller ones, are reasonably well-suited to reaching socially efficient outcomes through bargaining. Income inequality is modest compared to the US. Populations are relatively homogenous. And society, including the business community, accepts the legitimacy of labor organizations. The development of EU wide institutions has, moreover, given an additional layer of security to the social partners.

---

[10] Anderlini and Felli use an alternating offer model of negotiation where the bargainers pay a transactions fee at each stage and show that strategic 'hold up' conditions can produce situations where the parties never come to a profitable agreement. Dixit and Olson model a public goods game in which free rider considerations induce many people to opt out of the bargaining process, which leads to failure to produce the good.

[11] Taking a different approach, Hirshleifer (1995) stresses the importance of the technology of conflict in leading parties to allocate different fractions of their resources to fighting over distribution as opposed to producing more output, and shows that under some technologies some resources will always be spent on rent-seeking.

Third, analyses show that the ability of participants to make side payments can affect outcomes substantially. Commitment to make compensating transfers raises the chances of attaining the efficient outcome. In situations where one of the parties loses from an agreement, the ability of the winner to commit to the transfer is necessary for the agreement. But transfers themselves can be inefficient, reducing the value of the bargain, for instance by reducing the incentive of workers and firms in declining industries to shift to more productive activities (Dixit and Londregan, 1995). This appears to be agricultural policy in both the US and EU.

Surprisingly, however, the side contracting or transfers that lie at the heart of efficient bargaining do not always improve efficiency, even in a world of complete information and zero transactions cost. Jackson and Wilkie (2005) show that parties can use side contracts to manipulate the payoff from bargaining so as to redistribute incomes to themselves at the cost of efficiency. They suggest that side payments work better when only one player makes them (for instance where someone pays another party to reduce pollution) than in situations where many participants make side payments (say in encouraging public goods production). They also show that side payments are more likely to support efficient strategies when three or more players are involved in decision-making. The implication is that tripartite bargaining – capital, labor, and government, may be particularly fruitful, at least in some circumstances. The 1987 Irish social pact in which unions accepted small wage increases, so that firms had incentives to expand production, while the government compensated workers with tax reductions may be a case in point. The Pact and succeeding Irish agreements contributed to Ireland's recovery from economic basket-case in the 1980s to Celtic wonder-economy in the 1990s-2000s.

Fourth, information is an important determinant of the likelihood of attaining efficient outcomes. Complete information with each party knowing the other' situation is no guarantee of efficiency, but its absence – private information in which parties know only their own benefits/costs – increases the chance of inefficient results. Bargaining over an indivisible item – say greater authority for the firm to set working hours that will raise output – can result in inefficiencies when each agent privately knows their valuation but is uncertain about the valuation the other party places on it (Myerson and Satterthwaite, 1983). In this case there is an incentive to use private information strategically to gain a larger share of income, which can lead to an agreement that fails to maximize joint surplus or to no agreement at all. Mckelvey and Page (2002) show that the outcome in such circumstances will be tilted toward the party who initially has the property rights rather than being independent of the initial property rights, per the Coase Theorem.

The bottom line of the game theory/implementation theory analyses of bargaining is that the way society – government or social partners – design a social dialogue or bargaining system is likely to affect economic outcomes.

10.6 Conclusion

This chapter has argued that efficient bargaining/Coase Theorem models offer the best starting point for analyzing EU social dialogue economies. Since the evidence shows that these models fit the economic world at best loosely, they are most sensibly viewed as benchmarks comparable to the perfectly functioning competitive model used to benchmark market-driven economies. If the representative agent hypothesis is correct, participants in social dialogue systems may be less prone to anomalous decision-making than laboratory experiments find for individuals acting on their own behalf. On the other hand, if deviations from rational self-interest favor cooperative behavior, as experimental studies indicate, social dialogue systems where decision-makers diverge from economic rationality may reach efficiency more readily than game theoretic models suggest.

Overall, this review of laboratory and theoretic analyses relevant to understanding social dialogue economies suggests the virtue of a research program that examines design factors that lead parties to efficient solutions, not only on the assumption of rational strategic behavior but also on potentially more realistic assumptions about how people make decisions. In any case, whatever the true social dialogue theory turns out to be, it should help level the playing field in the 'war of the models' between the EU and US economies and it should direct attention at ways to improve the efficacy of social dialogue institutions. Given Ezio Tarantelli's commitment to social dialogue as a way for Italy to resolve its economic problems in the 1980s, I would guess that were he with us today, he would look favorably upon these areas of research and be contributing to them.

EU social dialogue model, where art thou?

References

Allen, D. (2006), *Do No-Fault Divorce Laws Matter? A Survey, 1995–2006*, February, http://www.sfu.ca/~allen/divrate95_06.pdf

Anderline, L. and L. Felli (2001), 'Costly bargaining and renegotiation', *Econometrica*, **69**(2):377–411.

Baker, D., A. Glyn, D. Howell and J. Schmitt (2004), 'Labour market institutions and unemployment: a critical assessment of cross-country evidence', in D. Howell (ed.), *Fighting Unemployment: the Limits of Free Market Orthodoxy*, Oxford: Oxford University Press.

Beshears, J., J. Choi, D. Laibson and B. Madrian (2006), 'The importance of default options for retirement savings outcomes: evidence from the United States', *NBER Working Paper 12009.*

Bruno, M. and J. Sachs (1984), *Stagflation in the World Economy*, Cambridge, MA: Harvard University Press.

Calmfors L. and J. Driffill (1988), 'Bargaining structure, corporatism, and. macroeconomic performance', *Economic Policy*, **6**:14–61.

Coase, R.H. (1960), 'The problem of social cost', *Journal of Law and Economics*, **3**:1–44.

Conway, P., V. Janod and G. Nicoletti (2005),'Product market regulations in OECD countries: 1998 to 2003', *OECD Economics Department WP 419.*

Dixit A. and M. Olson (2000), 'Does voluntary participation undermine the coase theorem?', *Journal of Public Economics*, **76**:309–35.

Dixit, A. and J. Londregan (1995), 'Re-distributive politics and economic efficiency', *American Political Science Review*, **89**:856–66.

Donahue, J.J. III (1989), 'Diverting the Coasian River: incentive schemes to reduce unemployment spells', *Yale Law Journal*, **99**:549–609.

Djankov, S., R. La Porta, F. Lopez de Silanes and A. Shleifer (2000), 'The regulation of Entry', *NBER Working Paper 7892.*

Farrell, J. (1987), (1987), 'Information and the Coase theorem', *Journal of Economic Perspectives*, **1**(2):113–29.

Freeman, R.B. (1998), 'War of the models: which labour market. Institutions for the 21st century?, *Labour Economics*, **5**:1–24.

Galdon-Sanchez, J. and J. Schmitz (2002), 'Competitive pressure and labor productivity: world iron ore markets in the 1980s', *American Economic Review*, **92**:1222–35.

Gode, D.K. and S. Sunder (1993), 'Allocative efficiency of markets with zero-intelligence traders: market as a partial substitute for individual rationality', *Journal of Political Economy*, **101**(1):119–137.

Hicks, J. ([1932],1963) *Theory of Wages*, New York: St Martin's Press, 2nd edition.

Hirshleifer, J. (1995), 'Anarchy and its breakdown', *Journal of Political Economy*, **103**(1):26–52.

Hoffman, E. and M.L. Spitzer (1982), 'The Coase theorem: some experimental tests', *Journal of Law and Economics*, **25**:73–98.

Hoffman, E. and M.L. Spitzer (1985), 'Entitlements, rights and fairness: an experimental examination of subjects' concepts of distributive justice', *Journal of Legal Studies*, **14:**259–97.

Jackson, M. (2001), 'A crash course in implementation theory', *Social Choice and Welfare*, **18**(4):655–708.

Jackson, M. and S. Wilkie (2005), 'Endogenous games and mechanisms: side payments among players', Review of Economic Studies, **72**(2):543–66.

Kahneman, K. and R. Thaler (1990), 'Experimental tests of the endowment effect and the Coase theorem', *Journal of Political Economy*, **98**(6):1325–48.

Kreps, D. (1990), *Game Theory and Economic Modelling*, Oxford: Oxford University Press.

Leibenstein, H. (1966), 'Allocative efficiency v. "x-efficiency"', *American Economic Review*, **56**:392–415.

Leontief, W. (1946), 'The pure theory of the guaranteed annual wage contract', *Journal of Political Economy*, **54**(1):76–9.

Maskin, E. (1994), 'The invisible hand and externalities', *American Economic Review*, **84**(2):333–7.

McKelvey, R. and Talbot Page (2002), 'Status quo bias in bargaining', *Journal of Economic Theory*, **107**:336–55.

Monks, J. (2004), 'Is Europe still the workers' best friend?' May Day Celebration, , St Anthony's College, Oxford, 4 June, http://www.sant.ox.ac.uk/esc/esc_lectures/Monks.pdf.

Medema, S. and R. Zerbe (1999), 'The Coase theorem', http://encyclo.findlaw.com/0730book.pdf

Myerson, R. and M. Satterthwaite (1983), 'Efficient mechanisms for bilateral trading', *Journal of Economic Theory,* **29**(2):265–81.

OECD (2004), *Employment Outlook*, Paris: OECD.

Olson, M. (1990), 'How bright are the northern lights? Some questions about Sweden', Institute of Economic Research, Lund University, Sweden, mimeo.

Peters, H.E. (1986) 'Marriage and divorce: informational constraints and private contracting', *American Economic Review*, **76**(3):437–54.

Rajan, R.G. and L. Zingales (2000), 'The tyranny of inequality', *Journal of Public Economics*, **76**(3):521–58.

Schwab, S.J. (1988), 'A Coasean experiment on contract presumptions', *Journal of Legal Studies*, **17**:237–68.

Sunstein, C. (2005), 'Group judgments: deliberation, statistical means, and information markets,' *New York University Law Review*, **80**: 962–1049.

Surowieki, J. (2004) *The Wisdom of Crowds,* Random House 2004,

Wikipedia
http://en.wikipedia.org/wiki/Prisoner's_dilemma
http://en.wikipedia.org/wiki/Public_goods_game

Wolfers, J. (2006), 'Did unilateral divorce laws raise divorce rates? A reconciliation and new results', University of Pennsylvania, Jan 11, 2006 (http://bpp.wharton.upenn.edu/jwolfers/Papers/Divorce(AER).pdf).

World Economic Forum (2003), *The Global Competitiveness Report 2000–2003*, New York: Oxford University Press.

11 From First- to Second-Generation Social Pacts*

Nicola Acocella[1], Giovanni Di Bartolomeo[2] and Patrizio Tirelli[3]

[1] University of Rome 'La Sapienza', Italy
[2] University of Teramo, Italy
[3] University of Milan-Bicocca, Italy

11.1 Introduction

In this chapter we analyze macroeconomic interactions among trade unions, the central bank and the fiscal policymaker. We explicitly model trade unions' concern for public expenditure, paving the way for an analysis of the potential gains from cooperation between the fiscal policymaker and the trade unions, i.e. the so-called corporatist or social pacts that have characterized economic policies in a number of European countries in the last few decades.

Theoretical analyses of macroeconomic outcomes in corporatist economies are relatively scarce. In the 1980s, Cameron (1984) and Tarantelli (1986, 1987), among others, argued that cooperatively determined wages can ensure the same disposable income for wage earners while resulting in a higher level of employment and a lower inflation rate. Summers et al. (1993) pointed out that in corporatist economies interdependence between monopolistic unions and fiscal policymakers limits the distortionary effects of taxes, inducing an exchange between public expenditure increases and wage restraint. More recent contributions suggest that cooperation may improve macroeconomic performance. However the analysis is restricted to the interaction between trade union behaviour and monetary policy.[1] In this chapter we revisit the case for corporatist agreements in a model where labour markets are unionized, the government controls the fiscal stance, and an independent central bank sets monetary policy. We can then analyze the scope for a political exchange between public expenditure and wage setting choices, showing that corporatism may generate quite different macroeconomic outcomes from the traditional exchange between wage moderation and high public expendi-

* Nicola Acocella and Giovanni Di Bartolomeo acknowledge financial support from the University of Rome 'La Sapienza'. Patrizio Tirelli acknowledges financial support from MIUR 60% and MIUR 40% 2004.

[1] See Gylfason and Lindbeck (1994), Burda (1997), Acocella and Ciccarone (1995), Di Bartolomeo (2002), Acocella and Di Bartolomeo (2004), Acocella et al. (2004), and Di Bartolomeo (2006).

ture. In fact our model can give account also of pacts where unions accept a lower level of public expenditure.

Our approach stands in sharp contrast with those in the literature on macroeconomic policy games, where the importance of institutional arrangements in shaping macroeconomic outcomes is a key ingredient, but the focus is restricted to institutional constraints on policymakers. Typically, central bank conservatism and institutional constraints on fiscal discretion are deemed to enhance macroeconomic efficiency, i.e. to produce lower output distortions and inflation. For instance, Beetsma and Bovenberg (1998) obtain these results by implicitly or explicitly assuming a given labour market performance and neglecting interactions between this market and fiscal and monetary policies. Some analyses do in fact endogenize trade union behaviour but focus on monetary policy as the sole tool available for stabilization purposes. Contributions in this vein emphasize that the central banker's idiosyncratic preferences, either conservative or populist, can have a whipping effect on union behaviour, thus inducing a reduction in output distortions.[2] We show that in unionized economies attempts to reduce fiscal distortions either through central bank conservatism or by imposing institutional constraints directly on the fiscal policymaker may be ineffective, as the potential output benefits from fiscal discipline are offset by higher real wages.

The chapter is organized as follows. In Section 11.2 we discuss the different features of the pacts agreed upon in the 1960s and the 1970s, on the one hand, and those of the 1990s, on the other. Section 11.3 presents our model. In Section 11.4 we describe the features of the non-cooperative solutions. In Section 11.5 we compare the outcomes of cooperative and non-cooperative regimes and use our results to suggest an explanation for the observed shift to second-generation pacts. Section 11.6 concludes.

11.2 Types of social pacts

A precise definition of corporatism is hard to give. Following Burda (1997), we define it as a set of rules of the game, i.e. institutional arrangements that involve negotiation, bargaining, collaboration, and accord between major economic groupings in a society. Thus corporatism provides the commitment technology necessary to enforce cooperative agreements between social partners, i.e. social pacts.

Social pacts have different forms, content and outcomes in different countries as they adjust to the political, economic, social, and industrial relations culture (see Ilo).

As to the subjects involved, in addition to workers and firms representatives the government may play a crucial role. The domain of bipartite agreements may simply include terms and conditions of employment. Tripartite agreements usually cover macroeconomic and social policy issues. They usually represent a consensus

[2] See Cukierman (2004) for a review.

between firms, workers and the government on the main directions of economic and social policy.

From a macroeconomic point of view social pacts are the composition of a multiplicity of interests. As we want to analyse macroeconomic performance, we focus on the opposition between wages and employment and limit our analysis to the strategic interaction between the unions and the government. Given the inverse relationship between the wage rate and employment, a social pact between unions and the government is apparently difficult to achieve. However, numerous social pacts have been stipulated after World War II, mainly, but not only, in European countries.

In their golden age (the 1970s and early 1980s) social pacts sought to trade wage moderation for higher public expenditure (namely welfare expenditure) or lower inflation (namely after the oil shocks).[3] Earlier empirical studies pointed out that corporatist economies post better performance in terms of inflation and unemployment (Bruno and Sachs, 1985; Calmfors and Driffill, 1988), but higher levels of taxation. In recent decades there have been rather conspicuous changes in European industrial relations. Since 1987, when the first of five multi-annual pacts was stipulated in Ireland, there have been numerous formal or informal agreements of a corporatist nature in practically all European countries, also in countries without the organizational and institutional preconditions forecast by the neocorporatist literature, with the major exceptions of Belgium and France (Regini, 1997, 2000; Visser, 2006). But the social pacts of the last fifteen years or so appear to differ from earlier ones in at least one important respect, since they establish reductions – rather than increases – in public expenditure and government action to protect employment and labour rights (Regini, 1997; Visser, 2002). This may be thought of as the consequence of some new occurrences taking place, in relation to the increase in competition deriving from globalisation, on the one hand, and from the specific requirements of the European Monetary Union (the Maastricht criteria for taking part to the Union), on the other. A kind of 'competitive corporatism' (Rhodes, 1998) thus emerged to face the challenges of globalisation, economic integration and the monetary unification in Europe.[4] We will refer to the corporatist agreements of the 1970s and early 1980s as 'first generation social pacts', whereas we will call those of the late 1980s and the 1990s as 'second generation social pacts'.

---

[3] Unionized labour markets and a pervasive welfare system have long been the hallmark of European corporatist economies (OECD, 1997; Traxler and Kittel, 2000; and Rhodes, 2001).

[4] In addition, in a number of central and eastern European countries, social pacts were agreed to deal with specific aspects of the transition from a planned to a market economy.

11.3 The model

The standard supply function is defined as follows[5]

$$x = \pi - \pi^e - t - \tilde{x} \tag{11.1}$$

where output deviations from the competitive non-distortionary baseline level, x, are caused by an index of tax distortions, t, real wage distortions due to monopolistic unions, $\tilde{x}$,[6] and inflation surprises, $\pi - \pi^e$ (π^e defines inflation expectations).

In this economy there are three players: the government, the monopoly trade union, and the central bank.

The government's loss function is defined over inflation, output and public expenditure deviations from the target, $g - \tilde{g}$:

$$G = \frac{1}{2}\left\{\alpha_{\pi f}\pi^2 + x^2 + \alpha_{gf}\left(g - \tilde{g}\right)^2\right\} \tag{11.2}$$

As in Debelle and Fischer (1994), $\tilde{g}$ is interpreted as the optimal share of non-distortionary output to be spent on public goods if non-distortionary lump-sum taxes were available. In setting the public expenditures level, the government faces a balanced budget constraint:[7]

$$g = t \tag{11.3}$$

The trade union's loss function is

$$U = -\tilde{x}\beta_{\tilde{x}} + \frac{x^2}{2} + \frac{\beta_{gu}(g - \tilde{g})^2}{2} \tag{11.4}$$

The union's welfare increases with the real wage but falls with output distortions (see Cukierman, 2004, for an extensive survey of the literature).[8] The assumption that the trade union is concerned with expenditure deviations from the target is perhaps less straightforward and requires some discussion. In fact union members may be concerned with specific components of public expenditures, such as pension funds, training schemes, unemployment benefits, health insurance for workers, social policies, labour policy, and any government action in the area of income distribution. More generally, we can say that the union is interested in

---

[5] Eq. (11.1) is akin to Alesina and Tabellini (1987) and Beetsma and Bovenberg (1998).

[6] More precisely, $\tilde{x}$ is defined as the real wage mark-up over the competitive wage rate, which is exogenous.

[7] For the sake of simplicity we do not consider either the seigniorage component of the budget or debt service payments.

[8] In the literature it is sometimes assumed that the union penalises real wage deviations from an exogenous real wage target. This would cause minor changes in our results. See Acocella and Di Bartolomeo (2004) for a discussion on the different specifications of the union loss function.

the level of total government expenditure. In addition, we assume that the monopolistic union sets the labour market distortion, i.e. a real-wage mark-up over the competitive rate. If we accept a social welfare perspective of the government's preferences, the loss functions (11.2) and (11.4) will differ insofar as the government takes the preferences of non-workers into account (as in Beetsma and Bovenberg, 1998).[9]

Monetary policy is delegated to an independent central bank (CB henceforth), which is interested in minimizing both the inflation rate and output deviations from a non-distortionary equilibrium.

$$V = \frac{1}{2}\left\{\alpha_{\pi m}\pi^2 + x^2\right\} \tag{11.5}$$

where $\alpha_{\pi m} > \alpha_{\pi f}$. We assume that the CB directly controls the inflation rate.

11.4 The non-cooperative solution

The timing of the game is as follows. The union and the government simultaneously set labour and tax distortions. After that, the CB chooses monetary policy.

Our analytic results referred to this timing have been presented elsewhere (see Acocella et al., 2006). They can be extended to the case where the government action follows the union wage-setting decision The graphical presentation we will give here includes both the case of the Nash and the Stackelberg equilibrium.

Solving the model by backward induction we find that Nash outcomes are characterized as follows:

1. The output level is policy invariant and depends only on the trade union's preference for the real wage rate.
2. Inflation depends both on the trade union's preference for the real wage rate and the degree of conservatism of the central bank.
3. Labour and tax distortions are perfect substitutes: the output effect of a tax change is fully offset by a real wage adjustment in the opposite direction.
4. The more the union is concerned with the real wage objective, the lower the tax rate.

Our results stand in sharp contrast with those obtained in models where labour market distortions are exogenous. First of all, production subsidies are often seen as a remedy to labour market distortions (Alesina and Tabellini, 1987; Dixit and Lambertini, 2003). In fact, instead of raising production, our model shows that the expectation of a subsidy would trigger a real wage increase. Second, the expenditure bias identified in Beetsma and Bovenberg (1998) has no impact on output distortions, which are independent of fiscal policy.

[9] For the sake of simplicity we assume that the public expenditure targets in eq. (11.2) and (11.4) are identical.

11.5 The cooperative solution

The Nash equilibrium implies three sources of inefficiency related to the timing of the game and the existence of externalities. First, the government cannot internalize the impact of its actions on inflation expectations. Second, the government does not internalize the real wage reaction to its tax policy. Third, the trade union neglects the adverse effects of its actions on the level of public expenditure.

As usual, cooperation is defined as the joint minimization of a convex combination of the difference between the two players' loss functions and their outside options, i.e. the generalized Nash product $(G-G^N)^{\phi}(U-U^N)^{(1-\phi)}$ with $\phi \in [0, 1]$. For our purposes, a graphical analysis is exhaustive.

In order to compare the effects of the cooperative and non-cooperative solutions on players' preferences, it is useful to identify the two players' preferred combinations of expenditure gap and output.

Two different cases are relevant and they refer to the preferences of the union. A first situation is characterized by union's preferences such as its most preferred solution in terms of public expenditures is higher than that given by the Nash one. In other terms, the union's bliss point lies to the South of the Nash solution as in figure 1, where output distortions and the public expenditure gap are represented along the horizontal and the vertical axis, respectively. In this figure the loci RG and RU identify the combinations of output distortions and expenditure gap that obtain along the two players' reaction functions, and points Σ, Ω define the outcomes[10] preferred by the government and by the trade union respectively (their second-best outcomes). Points N and S identify the Nash and Stackelberg equilibria. With regard to the Stackelberg equilibrium, it is worth noting that union now internalizes the trade off between the real wage mark-up and public expenditure. Therefore the union's ability to commit to a real wage distortion leads to a better economic performance relative to the Nash equilibrium. Further benefits accrue from cooperation. In fact cooperative equilibria lie along the contract curve as e.g. point C in Fig. 11.1,[11] entailing a reduction in both output distortions and the public expenditure gap. This, in turn, implies that the trade union is willing to discipline wage claims in order to benefit from an increase in expenditure.

In a second situation the union has a lower preference for public expenditure or, more precisely, the union's most preferred solution in terms of public expenditures is lower than that given by the Nash one. In this case, depicted in Fig. 11.2, both the Stackelberg and the cooperative solutions are substantially modified. With regard to the Stackelberg equilibrium, the union's ability to internalize the trade off between the real wage mark-up and public expenditure causes an increase in out-

[10] Note that point Σ must lie above the locus RG because in Σ the government internalizes the adverse effect of taxes on inflation expectations and chooses a lower level of public expenditure.

[11] We consider the Nash non-cooperative equilibrium as the outside option of the players in the cooperative Nash solution. In the Stackelberg case, of course, the feasibility set has to be computed by considering a different outside option.

put distortions relative to the Nash equilibrium. This happens because the trade union is now less interested in public expenditures. By contrast, cooperation brings output distortions below the Nash equilibrium. In this case the trade union benefits from a real wage increase, but such an increase is sufficiently moderate to leave the government better off despite the fall in expenditures.

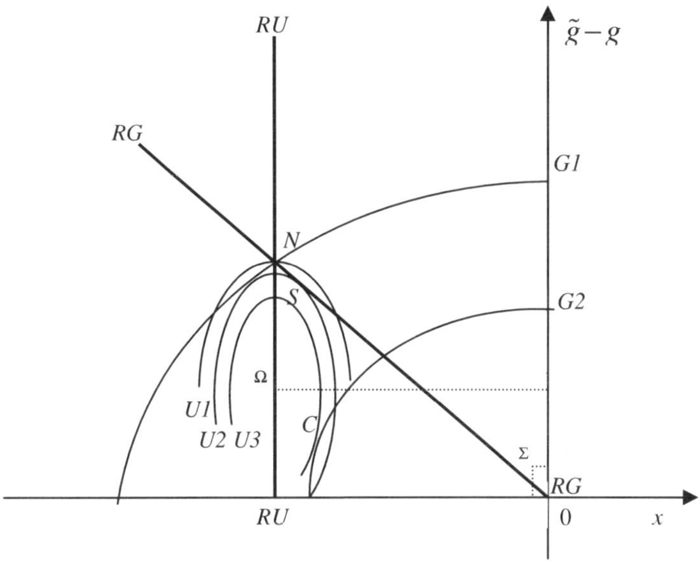

Fig. 11.1

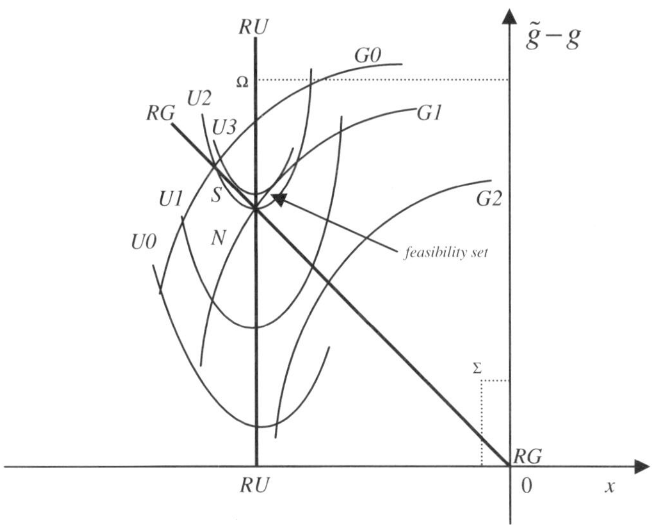

Fig. 11.2

Summarizing, our model is consistent with the acceptance by the union of both an increase and a reduction in public expenditure. Any cooperative agreement entails a reduction in output distortions and an increase in employment. If the union has a high preference for public expenditure, the government will agree to reduce the public expenditure gap (i.e., it will raise public expenditure) in exchange for wage moderation as in the golden age social pacts. By contrast, if the union has a lower preference for public expenditure, the government agrees on a reduction in this variable, i.e. a reduction in taxation, leaving some room for a wage increase.

Can we use the model to rationalize the observed shift to second-generation pacts? Our analysis shows that these are possible only if we are in the second situation depicted above, which implies that:

$$\frac{\beta_{\tilde{x}}}{\beta_{gu}} > \frac{\beta_{\tilde{x}}}{\alpha_{gf}} \frac{\alpha_{\pi f} + \alpha_{\pi m}^2}{\alpha_{\pi m} + \alpha_{\pi m}^2} \tag{11.6}$$

In the light of eq. (11.6) we may discuss the potential role of some facts which happened in the 1980s and 1990s.

- *Fall in union militancy*. There is evidence that union militancy began to fall in the 80s.[12] This could have either disciplined wage claims or induced the unions to accept a reduction in public expenditure. However, from (11.6) it is clear that this would not change the nature of the political exchange between the unions and the policymaker.
- *Political change*. Let us consider the effects of a political change in terms of our model. A fall in α_{gf}, i.e. a political shift to the right, produces an increase in the slope of the government reaction function *RG*. Fig. 11.3 describes a polarized system, where a political shift reverses the nature of the exchange that characterizes the cooperative solution. Points N^{LW} and N^{RW} describe Nash equilibria under left- and right-wing parties, respectively, for given trade union preferences. At point N^{RW} cooperation between the right-wing government and the union involves the traditional exchange between wage restraint and public expenditure laxitysm. By contrast, cooperation between the left-wing government and the union entails a reduction in public expenditure and a real wage increase. The level of public expenditure is, however, still higher under a left-wing government, thus confirming a central tenet of the political economy literature, i.e. public expenditure is systematically higher under left-wing governments.[13]

---

[12] See e.g. Visser (2000, 2006).

[13] Fig. 11.3 describes a situation where, in a cooperative agreement, the left-wing government would accept a decrease in expenditure in exchange for an increase in macroeconomic efficiency. This rationalizes the apparent paradox in the behaviour of left-wing governments, which are sometimes criticized for committing to policy agreements that seem to betray their fundamental (ideological) values.

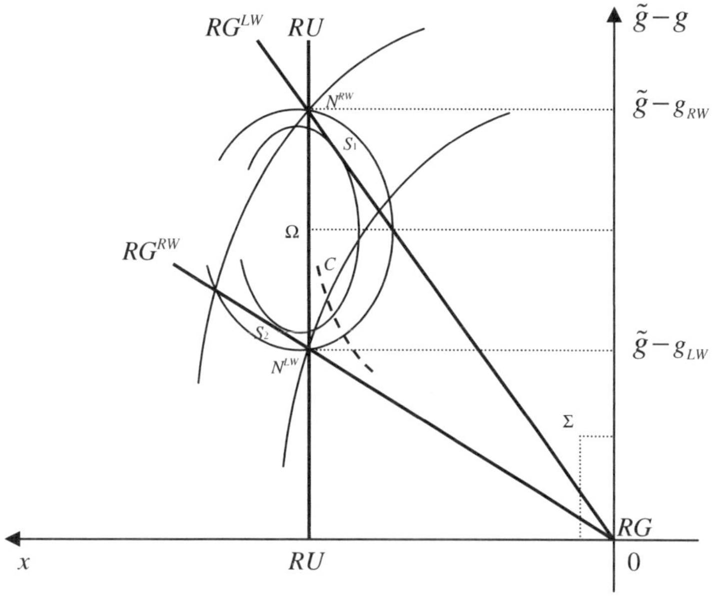

Fig. 11.3

A political shift to the left of European governments could thus help explaining the shift from first to second generation pacts. However, quite the contrary happened in many European countries in the early Nineties as a number of right-wing governments came to power (Swank, 1999).

- *Central Bank commitment to low inflation.* There is a widespread consensus (e.g. Clarida et al., 1998) that in the 80s Central Banks adopted a more conservative stance. In our model, the monetary policy reaction to fiscal and labour market distortions affects the fiscal policymaker decision to levy distortionary taxes. As discussed in Section 11.4, this is the Beetsma and Bovenberg effect, captured by changes in $\alpha_{\pi m}$. From condition (11.6), it is easy to see that an increase in conservatism can reduce cooperative public expenditure only under implausible conditions.
- *The rules adopted for gaining the European Monetary Union membership.* These might have put pressure on both the governments and 'the social parts' in many European countries to adopt social pacts of the second generation. In fact, as we saw in Section 11.2, a number such pacts were agreed upon in the 1990s, after stipulation of the Maastricht treaty, under which admission to EMU was made conditional to fulfilment of certain prerequisites, entailing monetary policy independence and control of inflation and debt accumulation.[14] It is widely

[14] These pacts followed those stipulated since 1982 in the Netherlands and 1986 in Ireland under the pressure of the emergence of a kind of 'competitive corporatism' (see Rhodes, 1998; Fajertag and Pochet, 1997, 2000).

acknowledged that this enhanced the conservativeness of many European central banks and disciplined governments. A similar conclusion should hold for wage-setting behaviour, to the extent that labor unions saw benefits from EMU.[15] In our framework, the role of the Maastricht criteria for debt and inflation can be mimicked by adding linear penalties in inflation and public expenditure to the loss functions (11.2), (11.4).

$$G=\frac{1}{2}\left\{\alpha_{\pi f}\pi^2+x^2+\alpha_{gf}\left(g-\tilde{g}\right)^2\right\}+\alpha_{\pi}^{EU}\pi+\alpha_{gu}^{EU}g \tag{11.7}$$

$$U=-\tilde{x}\beta_{\tilde{x}}+\frac{x^2}{2}+\frac{\beta_{gu}(g-\tilde{g})^2}{2}+\beta_{EU}^{\pi}\pi+\beta_{gu}^{EU}g \tag{11.8}$$

By minimizing (11.7) and (11.8) we can derive the result that the Maastricht effect induces trade unions to choose a smaller level of output distortions for any level of public expenditures. The effect on the cooperative public expenditure gap is ambiguous. On the one hand, the fiscal stance is tighter because the policy-maker sees more costs from increases in inflation and public expenditures. On the other hand, greater wage discipline leaves room for a looser fiscal policy. However, the effect on the trade union's preferred expenditure gap is unambiguously positive, i.e. the gap is higher (the level of public expenditure most preferred by the union is lower). This gives the possibility to explain the emergence of second generation pacts in countries where the Maastricht criteria had a relatively strong impact on trade unions. This conclusions is reinforced for countries where commitment to low inflation had already been established.

11.6 Concluding remarks

In this chapter we have shown that cooperation between the unions and the governments can improve economic performance and the positions of the 'social parts'. Cooperation can take essentially two forms, which differ one from the other as to the different combination of the wage rate and the level of the public budget. The outcomes vary with the preferences of the union and the government, expressed in relation to the various circumstances that can emerge in real life, as well as to incentivating rules and institutions.

The first key to our results lies in the consideration that, in addition to the traditional objectives, i.e. the real wage rate and employment, unions may be interested in the level of public expenditure, as suggested by Ezio Tarantelli when he advocated a 'political exchange' between the unions and the government. The second key lies in our re-examination of corporatism as a feasible set of institutional arrangements designed to internalize certain negative macroeconomic externalities

[15] Consider for instance the welfare gains outlined in the Cecchini report (see Cecchini, 1988). We must in any case stress that the importance of the Maastricht treaty lies in the possibility that it acted as an incentivating rule for the union.

and to provide a positive solution to them as an alternative to the punishment suggested by much of the previous literature. The third key is the characterization of the government budget as a two-faced Janus, i.e. in its double role of providing public expenditure valuable for union members and extracting distortionary taxes. This characterization of the budget makes our model consistent with the observed evolution of social pacts in recent decades, which appear to move in many European countries towards a reduction in public expenditures. This might have been prompted by the occurrence of the Maastricht criteria, which induced greater emphasis on the pursuit of inflation and public expenditure targets.

Our analysis suggests that corporatist institutions should be regarded as valuable tools in enhancing macroeconomic performance, in line with the Lisbon Strategy approach, which emphasizes the role of social partnership. It could help explain the major difference noticed by Visser (2006) between Tarantelli's advocation of a political exchange in order to prevent a monetarist cure (see, e.g., Fitoussi and Tarantelli, 1985) and the second-generation social pacts, which appear to have been signed to make monetarism by means of a conservative European Central Bank possible. In the terms of our model acceptance of a reduction in public expenditure by the unions could have been a way to pursue some limited wage increase in the presence of the constraints (and the opportunities) introduced by the Maastricht Treaty.

References

Acocella, N. and G. Ciccarone (1995), 'Moderazione salariale e "scambio politico": un'analisi microfondata', *Rivista Italiana di Economia*, **0**:111–38.

Acocella, N. and G. Di Bartolomeo (2004), 'Non-neutrality of monetary policy in policy games', *European Journal of Political Economy*, **20**: 695-707.

Acocella, N., G. Di Bartolomeo and W. Pauwels (2004), 'Is there any scope for corporatism in stabilization policies?', *FEEM Working Paper 154*.

Acocella, N., G. Di Bartolomeo and P. Tirelli (2006), 'The macroeconomics of social pacts', mimeo.

Alesina, A. and G. Tabellini (1987), 'Rules and discretion with noncoordinated monetary and fiscal policies, *Economic Inquiry*, **25**:619–30.

Beetsma, R.M.W.J. and A.L. Bovenberg (1998), 'Monetary union without fiscal coordination may discipline policymakers', *Journal of International Economics*, **45**:239–58.

Bruno, M. and J. Sachs (1985), *Economics of Worldwide Stagflation*, Cambridge, MA: Harvard University Press.

Burda, M.C. (1997), 'Corporatism, labor unions and the safety set', *European Economic Review*, **41**(3-5):635–46.

Calmfors, L. and J. Driffill (1988), 'Bargaining structure, corporatism and macroeconomic performance', *Economic Policy*, **6**:14–61.

Cameron, D.R. (1984), 'Social democracy, corporatism, and labour quiescence: The representation of economic interest in advanced capitalist society', in J.H. Goldthorpe (ed.), *Order and Conflict in Contemporary Capitalism*, Oxford: Oxford University Press, pp. 143–78.

Cecchini, P. (1988), *The European Challenge 1992. The Benefits of a Single Market*, Aldershot, UK: Wildwood House.

Clarida, R.H., J. Gali, and M. Gertler (1998), 'Monetary policy rules in practice: some international evidence', *European Economics Review*, **42**(6):1033–68.

Cukierman, A. (2004), 'Monetary institutions, monetary union and unionized labor markets – Some recent developments', in R. Beetsma, C. Favero, A. Missale, V.A. Muscatelli, P. Natale, and P. Tirelli (eds), *Monetary Policy, Fiscal Policies and Labour Markets: Key Aspects of Macroeconomic Policymaking in EMU*, Cambridge: Cambridge University Press.

Debelle, G. and S. Fischer (1994), 'How independent should a central bank be?', in J. Furher (ed.), *Goals, Guidelines, and Constraints Facing a Policymakers*, Federal Reserve Bank of Boston, Conference Series No. 38.

Di Bartolomeo, G. (2002), *Unions, Governments and Central Banks: Macroeconomic Performance in a Simple Game Theoretical Approach*, Ph.D. Dissertation, Rome: Università di Roma 'La Sapienza'.

Di Bartolomeo, G. (2006), 'Interest group and the monetary policy management', in F. Columbus (ed.), *Focus on Monetary Policy*, New York: Nova Science.

Dixit, A. and L. Lambertini (2003), 'Interactions of commitment and discretion in monetary and fiscal policy', *American Economic Review*, **93**(5):1522–42.

Fajertag, G. and P. Pochet (1997), 'A new era for social pacts in Europe', in G. Fajertag and P. Pochet (eds), *Social Pacts in Europe*, Brussels: European Trade Union Institute.

Fajertag, G. and P. Pochet (2000), 'A new era for social pacts in Europe', in G. Fajertag and P. Pochet (eds), *Social Pacts in Europe. New Dynamics*, Brussels: European Trade Union Institute.

Fitoussi, J.P. and E. Tarantelli (1985), 'Una politica dei redditi contro i guasti del monetarismo', *Politica ed Economia*, June and July-August, reproduced in E. Tarantelli, *L'utopia dei deboli è la paura dei forti*, Milan: Angeli, 1988.

Gylfason, G. and A. Lindbeck (1994), 'The interaction of monetary policy and wages', *Public Choice*, **79**:33-46.

Ilo, 'Social pacts in Europe' (http://www.ilo.org/public/english/dialogue/ifpdial/info/pacts/index.htm)

OECD (1997), 'Economic performance and structure of collective bargaining', *Employment Outlook*, 63–92, Paris: OECD.

Piazza, J. (2001), 'De-linking labor. Labor unions and social democratic parties under globalization', *Party Politics*, **7**:413–35.

Regini, M. (1997), 'Still engaging in corporatism? Recent Italian experience in a comparative perspective', *European Journal of Industrial Relations*, **3**:259–78.

Regini, M. (2000), 'Between deregulation and social pacts: The responses of European economies to globalisation', *Politics and Society*, **28**:5–33.

Rhodes, M. (1998), 'Globalization, labor markets and welfare states: A future of "competitive corporatism"?', in M. Rhodes and Y. Mény (eds), *The Future of European Welfare: A New Social Contract?*, London: Macmillan.

Rhodes, M. (2001), 'The political economy of social pacts: "Competitive corporatism" and European welfare reform', in P. Pierson (ed.). *The New Politics of the Welfare State*, Oxford: Oxford University Press, pp. 165–94.

Summers, L.H., J. Gruber and R. Vergara (1993), 'Taxation and structure of labor markets: The case of corporatism', *Quarterly Journal of Economics*, **108**:385–411.

Swank, D. (1999), 'Pooled time series data base on the comparative political economy of advanced capitalist democracies', electronic data base, Marquette University.

Tarantelli, E. (1986), 'The regulation of inflation and unemployment', *Industrial Relations*, **25**:1–15. Reprinted in P. Garonna, P. Mori and P. Tedeschi (eds), *Economic Models of Trade Union*, London: Chapman&Hall, 1996, pp. 305–18.

Tarantelli, E. (1987), 'Monetary policy and the regulation of inflation and unemployment', in M. Gunderson, N.M. Meltz and S. Ostry (eds), *Unemployment: International Perspectives*, Toronto: University of Toronto Press, pp. 94–102.

Traxler, F. and B. Kittel (2000), 'The bargaining system and performance: A comparison of 18 OECD countries', *Comparative Political Studies*, **33**:1154–90.

Visser, J. (2000), 'From Keynesianism to the third way: labour relations and social policy in Western Europe', *Economic and Industrial Democracy*, **21**:421–56.

Visser, J. (2002), 'Unions, wage bargaining and co-ordination in European labour markets', in P. Pochet (ed.), *Wage Policy in the Eurozone*, Brussels: P.I.E. Peter Lang, pp. 39–77.

Visser, J. (2006), 'Wage bargaining institutions in Europe. A Happy marriage or preparing for divorce?, this volume.

PART VI

ALTERNATIVE SOLUTIONS TO CONFLICTS

12 Inflation Inertia, Monetary Policy and Market Competition: Tarantelli Revisited

Fabrizio Coricelli

University of Siena, Italy

12.1 Introduction*

Recent literature shows that different institutional arrangements and preferences of central banks can affect real variables in models with imperfect goods and labour markets (Lippi, 2003). Defining conservatism as the case in which the central bank assigns a large weight to inflation in its objective function, the effects on the economy of the degree of conservatism crucially depend on the monopoly power of economic actors. One result in the literature is that conservatism of the central bank has beneficial effects on the real economy when deviations from perfect competition are large (Soskice and Iversen, 2000). According to this view, a key role of central bank conservatism (CBC from now on) is to counteract inflationary pressure arising from non-atomistic actors. The experience of the Bundesbank has been considered as a typical example of such 'game' between the central bank and unions/firms. Interestingly, the creation of the European Monetary Union has reduced the market power of actors that previously accounted for a significant share of their national markets. These actors became much 'smaller' within the Europe-wide context. Such an increased competition, according to various observers, would reduce the benefits of having a conservative European Central Bank, relative to the Bundesbank (see Franzese, 2000).

So far, the relationship between CBC and degree of competition in markets (both goods and labour), has been analyzed in a static framework, as if the main relevance of such interaction would be in the long run. This is perhaps the main reason why this literature has largely remained separated from the standard macroeconomic modelling widely used for guiding macroeconomic policy. In this chapter we take a different approach and analyze the interaction between degree of conservatism of the central bank and degree of imperfections in goods market in the context of a typical dynamic New Keynesian dynamic macro-model (Woodford, 2003), that emphasizes the short and medium run horizon for assessing effects of policies, rather than steady states. Indeed, it is not easy to justify that a relevant trade-off between output and inflation applies to the long run.

* I thank Nicola Acocella, Renato Filosa and Riccardo Fiorito for very useful comments on an earlier draft of the chapter.

In contrast to the findings of the static models, we show that the need for a conservative central banker increases, rather than declines, with higher competition in goods market. The more competitive the markets are, the more conservative the central bank should be. In the dynamic setting, the role of the characteristics of the central banker has to be assessed in connection with the dynamic properties of equilibria.

First, the speed of adjustment to steady states decreases with the degree of competition in goods markets, while it increases with the degree of conservatism of the central bank. Therefore, when markets are highly competitive deviations from long-run equilibrium tend to be persistent (a point made by Calvo, 2000). The reason for this effect is that higher competition tends to induce 'herding behaviour' by firms. As the economy approaches perfect competition each firm sets the same price. Individual firms tend to 'follow the pack', thus retarding the adjustment to steady states. Such persistence can be reduced or even eliminated by a sufficiently conservative central banker. Second, we show that with high degree of competition in goods markets, determinacy of equilibria requires a conservative central bank. Satisfaction of the so-called 'Taylor principle' for determinacy of equilibria requires a conservative central bank when markets are competitive, while it is compatible with a more liberal central bank when markets are less competitive. Focusing on an optimal feedback interest rate rule for the central bank, we show that the coefficient linking interest rates to inflation depends on the relative size of the degree of conservatism of the central bank and the degree of competition in goods markets.

Summing up, in the context of monopolistic competition and Calvo-type inflation dynamics, liberalization of markets, and increased competition, makes more important, not less, to have a conservative central bank. Rather than counteracting the degree of monopoly power by firms, optimal policy should eliminate the adverse effects of competition on the dynamic properties of equilibria. Superficially, these results appear far apart from the topics debated by Tarantelli. In fact, there is a connection. If one interprets the need for centralisation of bargaining as a mechanism for coordinating individual actions, the model provides ammunitions against the view that decentralized markets left alone will produce the best outcome. Interestingly, many implications of the New Keynesian approach rests on coordination problems (Blanchard and Kiyotaki, 1987; Cooper and John, 1988). The implication is that policy-makers cannot step out of the picture when markets are liberalized, as monetary policy can serve as an antidote to coordination problems. In fact, in line with Tarantelli's work, centralisation of wage setting, whatever the nature of the labour market, would also contribute to solve the coordination problem of firms.

The chapter is organized as follows. Section 12.2 briefly discusses the reasons for our emphasis on goods rather than labour market imperfections. Section 12.3 contains an example of the relationship between degree of accommodation of monetary policy and degree of competition in the goods market, focusing on the speed of adjustment to steady states. Section 12.4 discusses the relationship between market competition and optimal monetary policy. Section 12.5 concludes.

12.2 Product and labour market imperfections

When looking back at the debate in the 1970s and 1980s on the role of institutions in affecting macroeconomic outcomes in European countries, the emphasis was largely on labour markets, especially bargaining structures. In Tarantelli's work, the main message was that centralized bargaining structures would lead to better macroeconomic outcomes (in terms of both inflation and employment). One condition for such positive effect of centralisation was the 'socially responsible' behaviour of unions that would internalize the macroeconomic effects of their behaviour. In more recent jargon, we would summarize these prescriptions in terms of Nash bargaining, in which unions and the other players divide the 'cake', or the surplus, arising in concluding an agreement. The equilibrium would be efficient, and employment and real wages could both increase. Of course, Nash bargaining could characterize bargaining at the firm level, in a totally decentralized market. However, the subtle point was that high decentralisation of bargaining would lead to worse outcomes, as at the firm level unions would not internalize the potentially adverse macroeconomic effects of their behaviour. Later on, it became popular the so-called hump-shaped relationship between bargaining structure and macroeconomic outcomes, due to Calmfors and Driffill (1988). The corner solutions, either high decentralisation or high centralisation, would dominate intermediate solutions. The additional element with respect to previous work was that in a decentralized bargaining unions or workers would have very little power and high wage demands could place out of business firms operating in a competitive, albeit monopolistically, market.

Empirical work has never entirely solved whether the relationship between degree of centralisation of bargaining and macroeconomic outcomes is monotonic or hump-shaped.

Starting from the 1990s the debate shifted. More and more attention has been devoted to product market imperfections. Recent analytical work (e.g. Blanchard and Giavazzi, 2003) highlights the role of imperfections in both labour and goods markets. While, in the long run, both markets are important for determining the equilibrium rate of unemployment and real wages, Blanchard and Giavazzi stress that imperfections in goods markets are a pre-condition for imperfections in labour markets. Under perfect competition in goods markets there is no room for bargaining over a cake that does not exist. This view is supported by empirical work done especially at the OECD (Nicoletti et al., 2000), that, with all caveats, has shown a very high correlation between goods market and labour market imperfections (Fig. 12.1).

Thus, both for theoretical and empirical reasons we frame the analysis focusing on imperfections and market power in goods markets. Of course, we do not believe that imperfections in labour markets do not matter, but we place them on a level of importance below imperfections in goods markets. In our view, macroeconomic outcomes in terms of the level of output and inflation depend crucially on goods market imperfections. From a theoretical point of view, the properties of a NK model that takes into account also non-competitive labour markets are not qualitatively different from those of a NK model with imperfect competition in the goods market and staggered prices (see Woodford, 2003). The focus on goods market shifts the perspective from the internalization of macroeconomic effects of behaviour of non-atomistic actors, such as unions, that is the core of Tarantelli's work, to a coordination problem, typical of New Keynesian macroeconomics. The implications are not far from those of Tarantelli, as the result is that when left alone from policy interference the market is not conducive to the best outcome. Liberalizing markets, while of course beneficial in the long run from an efficiency point of view, does not per se solve issues of macroeconomic management. When pushed away from its long run equilibrium, an economy populated by a large number of firms, operating in a monopolistically competitive market, will remain persistently away from the long run equilibrium the higher is the degree of competition in the market. The reason is that decentralized and un-coordinated behaviour is characterized by a high degree of inertia. The subtle, often neglected, feature of New Keynesian models is that higher degree of price flexibility does not imply faster convergence to the efficient steady state, but slower adjustment.

The second fundamental ingredient of the analysis has to do with the role of monetary policy, in particular of the role of central bank independence and central bank preferences.

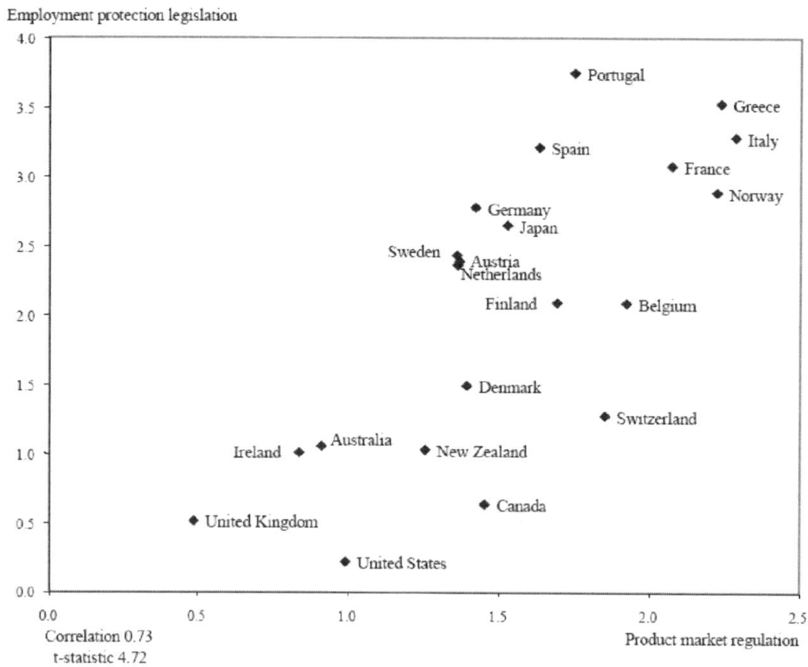

Fig. 12.1. Goods and labour market regulation

12.3 Degree of competition, policy accommodation and dynamics: a simple example

To illustrate the difference between our approach and results of the static literature we focus on a simple example that extends Soskice and Iversen (2000) (SI) by considering inflation dynamics. The rest of the model is directly comparable with SI, as we consider a monopolistically competitive market and their simple policy rule, based on the response of money supply to the price level.

The economy is populated by a large number of firms acting in a monopolistically competitive market. As in Calvo (1983), firms change their prices at random intervals, so that at each point in time there is a fraction α of firms that set new prices and a fraction $1-\alpha$ that keep their prices unchanged. New prices are set optimally by firms facing a downward-sloping demand function with price elasticity $-\theta$. Let us consider for simplicity a Calvo-type model in which aggregate demand is assumed to be a function of real monetary balances and of the real interest rate.[1]

Calvo staggered price model gives rise to the well-known New Keynesian Phillips curve (NKPC). Assuming the absence of an economy-wide labour market determining a unique wage rate across firms, it turns out that the parameter on the output gap in the NKPC depends, among other things, on the degree of competition in the goods market.[2]

Interestingly, with an economy-wide labour market and thus centralized wage determination, the coefficient on the output gap is independent of the degree of competition in goods markets. In such a case we have strategic substitutability among price setters, as the increase in the aggregate price index induces an opposite change in optimal individual prices. In the case of strategic complementarity on which we focus, individual price setters respond in the same direction to changes in the aggregate price. It is apparent that this implies a flatter short-run Phillips curve, given by the effect of the output gap on current inflation, for a given expectation of future inflation. What is more interesting for us is that the speed of adjustment of the system slows down with higher competition. This suggests that the notion of flexibility often seen as a panacea for all problems is in fact a rather complex phenomenon. In our simple example we would conclude that the system is made more flexible through deregulation of goods market that increases competition. At the same time, however, if we look at macroeconomic adjustment we obtain that the system has become less flexible. From the perspective of the ability of the system to quickly eliminate inefficient deviations from the long run equilibrium, we obtain a lower degree of flexibility as a result of higher competition.

[1] This is the discrete time version of the model reported in the textbook by Blanchard and Fischer (1989).

[2] See Woodford (2003) for a more detailed discussion and Section 12.4 below.

$$\pi_t = \beta E_t \pi_{t+1} + \frac{(1-\alpha)(1-\beta\alpha)}{\alpha} \varsigma(\hat{Y}_t - \hat{Y}_t^n) \tag{12.1}$$

where β is the discount factor and ς a coefficient that characterizes the link between marginal costs and output. It is easy to show that the parameter ς is a decreasing function of the parameter θ, that measures the degree of competition in goods markets (see Woodford, 2003 and Calvo, 2000). As markets become more competitive, ς declines. Under perfect competition $(\theta \to \infty)$, ς becomes zero.

$\hat{Y}_t - \hat{Y}_t^n$ denotes excess aggregate demand or the output gap, where n indicates the natural level. Aggregate demand (or aggregate excess demand) is assumed to be a function of real monetary balances and of the real interest rate

$$(\hat{Y}_t - \hat{Y}_t^n) = x_t = (M_t - P_t) - \frac{1}{\sigma}(i_t - E_t \pi_{t+1} - r_t^n) \tag{12.2}$$

where r_t^n is the natural real rate of interest, that characterizes steady-state equilibrium. The nominal interest rate is determined in the money market. Assuming that demand for real monetary balances is a decreasing function of the nominal interest rate, in equilibrium

$$i_t = -(M_t - P_t)/k \tag{12.3}$$

Following Soskice and Iversen (2000) we define the policy rule of the central bank in terms of a feedback rule from the price level to the stock of nominal money. The parameter ρ is an index of the degree of accommodation of monetary policy

$$M_t = \rho P_t \tag{12.4}$$

The nominal interest rate can thus be rewritten as

$$i_t = -(\rho - 1) P_t / k \tag{12.5}$$

When $\rho = 1$, we define monetary policy as fully accommodative.[3]

After substituting the expression for the stock of money and the nominal interest rate in the aggregate demand function, we obtain the full dynamic system in real time,

$$\pi_{t+1} = \pi_t - b\varsigma x_t \tag{12.6}$$

$$x_{t+1} = \left[\frac{1}{B} + (1 + \frac{1}{\sigma k})\frac{(1-\rho)b\varsigma}{B}\right] x_t + \left[(1 + \frac{1}{\sigma k})\frac{(1-\rho)}{B}\right] \pi_t \tag{12.7}$$

[3] Dornbusch (1980) studies an open economy model with the same specification of the policy rule. We could have considered also negative values of ρ, without changing our results.

where $B=1+\frac{(1-\rho)b\varsigma}{\sigma k}$ and $b=\frac{(1-\alpha)(1-\alpha)}{\alpha}$.

As shown in the appendix, the system displays saddle path instability and thus a unique dynamic path to the steady state, related to an initial condition on the state variable of the system, namely real monetary balances.

As policy becomes less accommodative, the speed of adjustment increases. Indeed, the absolute value of the stable root increases with the degree of competition in goods markets and with the degree of accommodation of monetary policy.

As $\rho \to 1$, the adjustment becomes infinitely slow, and at $\rho=1$ the stable root becomes equal to 1. Therefore, the adjustment of the system to shocks that cause a deviation from steady-state values tends to slow down as markets become more competitive. A conservative central banker can counteract such tendency, increasing the speed of adjustment to the steady state, speed of adjustment that is proportional to the degree of toughness of the central bank. If we allow for negative values of ρ, an ultra-conservative central bank could make the response to price increases infinitely negative and this would imply an infinite speed of adjustment.[4]

Such a simple example illustrates that increased market competition and central bank conservatism are complements rather than substitutes. Results are robust to a more general specification in which the demand side of the model is derived from optimizing behaviour of consumers (see Appendix A.2).

A central issue in the analysis of the dynamics of New Keynesian models is the determinacy of equilibria under different policy rules. Determinacy implies uniqueness of the convergent path to the long run equilibrium and is thus associated to equilibria that are not subject to arbitrary path of main macroeconomic variables, induced by behaviour based on sentiment and expectations unrelated to fundamentals. Indeterminacy makes policy makers unable to affect the path of inflation in an economy. Focusing on monetary policy, the conditions for determinancy of a NK model are associated to the well-known Taylor principle (see Appendix A.2), that is related to a sufficiently strong response to inflation of the interest rate set by of the central bank. In an optimizing model of central bank behaviour the coefficients of the feedback rule of the central bank depend on the parameters of the objective function of the central bank. We show next that in the presence of a highly competitive market and an optimizing central bank, this condition is satisfied only when the central bank is sufficiently conservative.

4 Berger and Woitek (2004) discuss the link between degree of conservatism and degree of accommodation and find empirical evidence on the fact that more conservative central banks follow less accommodative, or more activist, monetary policy.

12.4 Optimal interest rate rule and the link between central bank conservatism and market competition

Let us consider a central bank that maximizes welfare (minimizes losses) $\tilde{W}_t$

$$\tilde{W}_t = \frac{1}{2}(\omega x_t^2 + \pi_t^2) + F_t \tag{12.8}$$

subject to

$$\pi_t = \kappa x_t + s_t + f_t$$

with

$$F_t = \tfrac{1}{2} E_t \textstyle\sum_{j=1}^{\infty} \beta^j (\omega x_{t+j}^2 + \pi_{t+j}^2)$$

denoting all future expected components of the loss function, and

$$f_t = \beta E_t \{\pi_{t+1}\}$$

the expected component of the Phillips curve. Focusing on discretionary policy allows us to concentrate on maximization period by period, as the central bank can re-optimize every period and does not take into account the effect of its behaviour on expectations. Thus, the optimization problem reduces to the simple period-by-period optimization. Such optimization gives rise to an interest rule that can be expressed in terms of a feedback of nominal interest rate with respect to inflation (see Appendix A.3)

$$\hat{i}_t = r_t^n + \frac{\sigma\kappa}{\omega}\pi_t \tag{12.9}$$

12.4.1 Competition, price flexibility and policy rule

The Taylor principle for determinacy requires

$$\frac{\sigma\kappa}{\omega} > 1$$

or

$$\omega < \sigma\kappa$$

Substituting the value of κ,

$$\omega < \sigma \frac{(1-\alpha)(1-\beta\alpha)}{\alpha} \varsigma$$

Note that under the assumption of $\sigma = 1$, the above inequality can be rewritten as

$$\omega < \frac{(1-\alpha)(1-\beta\alpha)}{\alpha}\varsigma$$

Therefore, the inequality necessary for the Taylor rule is harder to be satisfied the higher is the degree of competition in the goods markets. As the system tends to perfect competition

$$\theta \to \infty$$

$$\varsigma \to 0$$

Thus, when markets are close to perfect competition, the Taylor principle is satisfied only when the central bank is ultra-conservative ($\omega \to 0$). Thus, from the point of view of determinacy, the importance of having a tough central bank increases with the degree of competition in goods market. Thus, the results of the static model do not survive in the dynamic context of New Keynesian models.

12.5 Concluding remarks

In a static model with non-atomistic actors, Guzzo and Velasco (1999) found that an ultra-liberal central bank would be optimal. Although their result does not appear to be robust (see Lippi, 2002 and Coricelli et al., 2002), their intuition proves relevant in a dynamic context. Guzzo and Velasco derive their result in the case of a monopoly union. In our model with imperfections in goods market their example can be thought as a case of highly monopolistic market structure. Indeed, we showed that the higher is product market competition the more important is to have a conservative central bank. With low product market competition, and thus with large monopoly power by economic actors, determinacy of equilibria and the so-called Taylor principle can be achieved with a rather liberal central bank. By contrast, a conservative central bank is crucial when markets are highly competitive. This chapter stressed the interplay between market competition and central bank preferences, showing that contrary to widespread views central bank conservatism and market competition are complements rather than substitutes. This result could have implications for the debate on central bank policy, especially in the context of the European Monetary Union. Indeed, the presumption that increased competition in goods and labour markets brought about by European integration makes less important the presence of a conservative European Central Bank is not well founded in New Keynesian models that seem to dominate current macroeconomic analysis. In fact, the increased competition at the European level calls for a conservative central bank, possibly even more conservative than the Bundesbank. In sum, even when reinterpreted within recent New Keynesian models the insights of Tarantelli remain valid, showing the depths of his ideas.

Appendix A.1 Simulation of a simple monetary rule

Consider the following parameter values

$$\alpha = 0.5$$

$$\beta = 1$$

$$\frac{(1-\alpha)(1-\beta\alpha)}{\alpha} = b = 0.75$$

$$\varsigma = 0.1$$

$$(\eta + \frac{1}{\sigma}) = a = 1.5$$

$$\eta = 0.5$$

$$\sigma = 1$$

$$k = 0.1$$

$$\rho = 0.1$$

$$B = 1 + \frac{(1-\rho)b\varsigma}{0.1} = 1 + \frac{0.9\times 0.75\times 0.1}{0.1} = 1.\ 675$$

The matrix of coefficients

$$\begin{matrix} 1 & -b\varsigma \\ -\left((1+\frac{1}{\sigma k})\frac{(1-\rho)}{B}\right) & \left(\frac{1}{B}+(1+\frac{1}{\sigma k})\frac{(1-\rho)b\varsigma}{B}\right), \end{matrix}$$

becomes

$$\begin{matrix} 1 & -0.75\times 0.1 \\ -\frac{0.9}{11\times 1.675} & 1/1.675+\frac{11\times 0.75\times 0.9\times 0.1}{1.675} \end{matrix}$$

with eigenvalues: 1.028; 0.956 , and the latter being the stable root.

Consider an increase in the degree of policy accommodation (increase ρ from 0.1 to 0.9).

$$B = 1 + \frac{(1-\rho)b\varsigma}{0.1} = 1 + \frac{0.1\times 0.75\times 0.1}{0.1} = 1.075$$

$$\rho = 0.9$$

$$\begin{matrix} 1 & -0.75 \times 0.1 \\ -\dfrac{0.1}{11 \times 1.075} & 1/1.075 + \dfrac{11 \times 0.75 \times 0.1 \times 0.1}{1.075} \end{matrix}$$

with eigenvalues: 1.028; 0.956.

Thus, the value of the stable eigenvalue increases.

Let us now consider an increase in competition in goods market and thus the reduction in ς.

Assume $\varsigma = 0.001$

$$B = 1 + \frac{(1-\rho)b\varsigma}{0.1} = 1 + \frac{0.1 \times 0.75 \times 0.001}{0.1} = 1.0008$$

The matrix becomes

$$\begin{matrix} 1 & -0.75 \times 0.001 \\ -\dfrac{0.1}{11 \times 1.0008} & 1/1.0008 + \dfrac{11 \times 0.75 \times 0.001 \times 0.1}{1.0008} \end{matrix}$$

with eigenvalues: 1.003; 0.997.

Similarly to an increase in accommodation, an increase in the degree of competition in goods markets reduces the speed of adjustment.

Appendix A.2 An optimizing model of staggered prices

The economy is populated by a large number of household-workers that have the following utility function (C is consumption and h labour)

$$U(C_t,\ h_t(i)) = \frac{1}{1-\theta} C_t^{1-\theta} - \frac{1}{1+\gamma} h_t(i)^{1+\gamma},$$

and by a large number of firms acting in a monopolistically competitive market. There is no unified economy-wide labour market. Wages are set in local markets (associated with each individual product). Production of each firm i comes from a well behaved production function

$$y_t(i) = h_t(i)^{\varepsilon}$$

$$\varepsilon < 1$$

Supply side

Assume that a fraction $0<\alpha<1$ of good prices remain unchanged each period, while a fraction $1-\alpha$ of firms change their price. The aggregate price index is a simple Dixit–Stiglitz price index

$$P_t = \left[(1-\ \alpha)p_t^{*1-\theta} + \ \alpha P_{t-1}^{1-\theta}\right]^{1/(1-\theta)}$$

where p_t^* is the optimal new price set by the fraction (1– α) of firms and θ denotes the constant elasticity of substitution between each pair of goods, and the elasticity of demand for each individual good.

In period t, new prices are set in order to maximize the expected discounted value of profits

$$E_t\left[\sum_{T=t}^{\infty}\delta^{T-t}Q_{t,T}\Pi(p_t(i),\ P_T;\ Y_T)\right]$$

subject to

$$y_{t+k}(i) = \left[\frac{p_t(i)}{P_{t+k}}\right]^{-\theta} Y_{t+k}$$

where δ^{T-t} is the probability that the price set at t will still be in place at $T>t$, and $Q_{t,t+k}=\beta(U_{c,t+k}/U_{c,t})(P_t/P_{t+k})$ is the stochastic discount factor and β is equal to $1/(1+\rho)$, where ρ is the subjective rate of time preference.

Assuming the absence of an economy-wide labour market, the profit function is

$$\Pi(p_t^*,\ P_{t+k};\ Y_{t+k}) = p_t(i)y_{t+k}(i) - MC_{t+k}y_{t+k}(i)$$

The first order condition for this problem is

$$E_t\left[\sum_{k=0}^{\infty}\delta^k Q_{t,t+k}(y_{t+k}(i) + (p_t^{new}(i) - MC_{t+k})\frac{\partial y_{t+k}(i)}{\partial p_t^{new}(i)}\right] = 0$$

Define the rate of inflation as

$$\pi_t = \hat{P}_t - \hat{P}_{t-1}$$

then the optimal solution gives rise to:

$$\pi_t = \beta E_t \pi_{t+1} + \frac{(1-\alpha)(1-\beta\alpha)}{\alpha}\hat{mc}_t$$

We can then substitute the value of the log-linearization of the real marginal costs (see Woodford (2003) for details)

$$\hat{mc}_t = \varsigma(\hat{Y}_t - \hat{Y}_t^n)$$

where $\hat{Y}_t^n$ is the natural level of output

$$\pi_t = \beta E_t \pi_{t+1} + \frac{(1-\alpha)(1-\beta\alpha)}{\alpha} \varsigma(\hat{Y}_t - \hat{Y}_t^n)$$

that is the well-known 'New Keynesian Phillips Curve'.

Demand side

Assume that aggregate demand equals consumption. Thus, the dynamics of output is described by the dynamics of consumption, determined by the intertemporal optimization of consumers, summarized by the familiar Euler equation:

$$U_{c,t} = \beta(1+i_t)E_t\left(U_{c,t+1}\frac{P_t}{P_{t+1}}\right)$$

where we use the no-arbitrage condition

$$\frac{1}{1+i_t} = E_t(Q_{t,t+1})$$

Assuming a zero rate of inflation at steady state, we consider the log-linearization around such equilibrium. Note also that at steady state

$$\frac{1}{1+i} = \beta$$

Therefore,

$$\frac{U_{cc}C}{U_c}\hat{C}_t = \beta\frac{1}{1+i}\hat{i}_t + \frac{U_{cc}C}{U_c}E_t(\hat{C}_{t+1}) + E_t(\log P_t - \log P_{t+1})$$

$$\hat{C}_t = (\hat{C}_{t+1}) - \sigma^{-1}\hat{r}_t$$

with $\hat{r}_t = \hat{i}_t - E_t\hat{\pi}_{t+1}$ and $-\sigma^{-1} = U_c / U_{cc}C$.

Equating aggregate consumption to aggregate output

$$\hat{C}_t = \hat{Y}_t$$

Define the output gap as

$$x_t = \hat{Y}_t - \hat{Y}_t^n$$

and the 'natural' real rate of interest as r_t^n (the real interest rate that occurs when $Y = Y^n$), we obtain

$$x_t = E_t x_{t+1} - \frac{1}{\sigma}(i_t - E_t\pi_{t+1} - r_t^n)$$

Thus, combining demand and supply side, we obtain the overall dynamic system:

$$\pi_t = (\beta + b\varsigma\frac{1}{\sigma})E_t\pi_{t+1} + b\varsigma E_t x_{t+1} - \frac{1}{\sigma}b\varsigma(i_t - r_t^n)$$

$$x_t = E_t x_{t+1} - \frac{1}{\sigma}(i_t - E_t\pi_{t+1} - r_t^n)$$

where $b = \left[(1-\alpha)(1-\beta\alpha)\right]/\alpha$.

To close the model one needs to specify a policy rule determining the path of the interest rate i_t.

Assume that the central bank sets the nominal interest rate as a feedback rule with respect to the deviation of inflation from its target rate

$$i_t = \phi(\pi_t / \pi_t^*)$$

Log-linearizing such policy rule around steady state, we obtain

$$\hat{i}_t = \phi_\pi \pi_t$$

Substituting this value of the nominal interest rate in the above system, after some calculations we obtain that the homogeneous part of the system is

$$\pi_t = \frac{1}{\sigma + k\varsigma\phi_\pi}(\beta\sigma + k\varsigma)E_t\pi_{t+1} + \frac{1}{\sigma + k\varsigma\phi_\pi}\sigma k\varsigma E_t x_{t+1}$$

$$x_t = \frac{1}{\sigma + k\varsigma\phi_\pi}\sigma E_t x_{t+1} + \frac{1}{\sigma + k\varsigma\phi_\pi}(1 - \beta\phi_\pi)\ E_t\pi_{t+1}$$

Determinacy of equilibrium requires

$$\phi_\pi > 1$$

The latter condition is the well-known ‘Taylor principle’, and implies that the forward-looking system is stable and thus that the dynamic equilibrium is determinate.[5]

The matrix of coefficient of the model of Section 12.3 is

$$A = \begin{pmatrix} \dfrac{\beta\sigma + b\varsigma}{\sigma + b\varsigma\phi_\pi} & \dfrac{\sigma b\varsigma}{\sigma + b\varsigma\phi_\pi} \\ \dfrac{1 - \beta\phi_\pi}{\sigma + b\varsigma\phi_\pi} & \dfrac{\sigma}{\sigma + b\varsigma\phi_\pi} \end{pmatrix}$$

---

[5] This means that in ‘real time’ the system is unstable, as both variables, inflation and output gap, are completely forward-looking, not predetermined at each point in time. Thus at any initial point in time there is a unique path to the steady state that is obtained by moving immediately to the steady state. This is the familiar condition for determinacy.

$$DetA = \frac{b\sigma\beta\varsigma\phi_\pi + \sigma^2\beta}{(\sigma + b\varsigma\phi_\pi)^2} = \sigma\beta\frac{b\varsigma\phi_\pi + \sigma}{(b\varsigma\phi_\pi + \sigma)^2} = \frac{1}{b\varsigma\phi_\pi + \sigma}\sigma\beta$$

$$TraceA = \frac{\sigma + b\varsigma + \sigma\beta}{\sigma + b\varsigma\phi_\pi}$$

Conditions for determinacy of equilibrium: the number of 'stable' roots (smaller than one in modulus) should be equal to the number of predetermined variables, while the number of unstable roots should be equal to the number of non-predetermined (entirely forward-looking) variables.

In our model, both variables are non-predetermined. Thus, determinacy requires both roots to be outside the unit circle. They have to be with modulus larger than one. If we study the forward-looking system, this condition is reversed, and thus the roots have to be smaller than one in absolute value. This requires

$$|DetA| < 1$$

and

$$|-TraceA| < 1 + DetA$$

The first condition requires

$$\beta < 1 + \frac{b\varsigma\phi_\pi}{\sigma} \text{ that is always true if } \phi_\pi > 0$$

The second condition for determinacy implies that

$$\frac{\sigma + b\varsigma + \sigma\beta}{\sigma + b\varsigma\phi_\pi} < 1 + \frac{\sigma\beta}{b\varsigma\phi_\pi + \sigma}$$

or

$$\sigma + b\varsigma + \sigma\beta < b\varsigma\phi_\pi + \sigma + \sigma\beta$$

or

$$b\varsigma < b\varsigma\phi_\pi$$

Thus determinacy requires

$$\phi_\pi > 1$$

Appendix A.3 Optimal policy

Let us consider a central bank that maximizes welfare (minimizes losses) $\hat{W}_t$

$$\tilde{W}_t = \frac{1}{2}(\omega x_t^2 + \pi_t^2) + F_t$$

subject to

$$\pi_t = \kappa x_t + s_t + f_t$$

With

$$F_t = \frac{1}{2} E_t \sum_{j=1}^{\infty} \beta^j (\omega x_{t+j}^2 + \pi_{t+j}^2)$$

denoting all future expected components of the loss function, and

$$f_t = \beta E_t \{\pi_{t+1}\}$$

the expected component of the NK Phillips curve. Focusing on the discretionary policy allows us to focus on maximization period by period, as the central bank can re-optimize every period and does take into account the effect of its behaviour on expectations. Thus, the optimization problem reduces to the simple period-by-period optimization. Define L the Lagrangean of the above problem:

$$L = \frac{1}{2}(\omega x_t^2 + \pi_t^2) + F_t + \lambda(\pi_t - \kappa x_t + s_t + f_t)$$

The optimal solution requires

$$\partial L / \partial \pi = 0$$

and

$$\frac{\partial L}{\partial x} = 0$$

The first order conditions imply

$$\pi = -\lambda$$

$$\omega x - \lambda \kappa = 0$$

or

$$\pi_t + \frac{\omega}{\kappa} x_t = 0$$

$$-\frac{\kappa}{\omega} \pi_t = x_t$$

Substituting these expressions in the NK Phillips curve

$$\pi_t = \beta E_t \{\pi_{t+1}\} + \kappa(-\frac{\kappa}{\omega} \pi_t) + s_t$$

or

$$\pi_t (1 + \frac{\kappa^2}{\omega}) = \beta E_t \{\pi_{t+1}\} + s_t$$

Iterating forward

$$\pi_{t+1} = \frac{\beta}{(1+\frac{\kappa^2}{\omega})} E_t\{\pi_{t+2}\} + \frac{s_{t+1}}{(1+\frac{\kappa^2}{\omega})}$$

$$\pi_t = \left(\frac{\beta}{(1+\frac{\kappa^2}{\omega})}\right)^j E_t\{\pi_{t+j}\} + \tfrac{1}{\beta} E_t \sum_{j=1}^{\infty} \frac{\beta s_{t+j}}{(1+\frac{\kappa^2}{\omega})^j} = \left(\frac{\omega}{\omega+\kappa^2}\right) s_t$$

because s_t is observed and the expected value of future shocks is zero.

Thus

$$-\frac{\kappa}{\omega}\left(\frac{\omega}{\omega+\kappa^2}\right) s_t = x_t$$

$$x_t = -\left(\frac{\kappa}{\omega+\kappa^2}\right) s_t$$

Substituting the equilibrium values for inflation and the output gap in the demand equation, noting that

$$x_t = -\left(\frac{\kappa}{\omega+\kappa^2}\right) s_t$$

$$E_t\{x_{t+1}\} = 0 = E_t\{\pi_{t+1}\}$$

$$x_t = E_t\{x_{t+1}\} - \frac{1}{\sigma}\left(\hat{i}_t - E_t\{\pi_{t+1}\} - r_t^n\right)$$

$$-\left(\frac{\kappa}{\omega+\kappa^2}\right) s_t = -\frac{1}{\sigma}\left(\hat{i}_t - r_t^n\right)$$

we can derive the optimal interest rate policy implied by maximization of welfare

$$\hat{i}_t = r_t^n + \frac{\sigma\kappa}{\omega+\kappa^2} s_t$$

with

$$s_t = \left(\frac{\omega}{\omega+\kappa^2}\right)^{-1} \pi_t$$

Note that such rule can be expressed in terms of a feedback of nominal interest rate with respect to inflation

$$\hat{i}_t = r_t^n + \frac{\sigma\kappa}{\omega+\kappa^2} s_t = r_t^n + \frac{\sigma\kappa}{\omega+\kappa^2}\left(\frac{\omega}{\omega+\kappa^2}\right)^{-1} \pi_t = r_t^n + \frac{\sigma\kappa}{\omega}\pi_t$$

that is a Taylor rule, with the coefficient on inflation

$$\frac{\sigma\kappa}{\omega} > 1$$

if ω is sufficiently small.

References

Blanchard, O. and S. Fischer (1989), *Lectures on Macroeconomics*, Cambridge, MA: MIT Press.

Blanchard, O. and F. Giavazzi (2003), 'The macroeconomic effects of regulation and deregulation of goods and labor markets', *Quarterly Journal of Economics*, **118**(3):879–908.

Blanchard, O. and N. Kiyotaki (1987), 'Monopolistic competition and the effects of aggregate demand', *American Economic Review*, **77**:647–66.

Berger, H. and U. Woitek (2004), 'Does conservatism matter? A time series approach to Central Bank behavior', CESifo, mimeo.

Calmfors, L. e J. Driffill (1988), 'Centralization of wage bargaining', *Economic Policy*, **6**:13–61.

Calvo, G. (1983), 'Staggered prices in a utility-maximizing framework', *Journal of Monetary Economics*, **12**(3):983–98.

Calvo, G. (2000), 'A note on price stickiness', University of Maryland, mimeo.

Cooper, R. and A. John (1988), 'Coordinating coordination failures in Keynesian models', *Quarterly Journal of Economics*, **103**:441–64.

Coricelli F., A. Cukierman and A. Dalmazzo (2000), 'Monetary institutions, monopolistic competition, unionized labor markets and economic performance', *CEPR DP 2407.*

Dornbusch, R. (1980), *Open Economy Macroeconomics*, New York: Basic Books.

Franzese, R.J. Jr. (2000), 'Credibly conservative monetary policy and wage/price-bargaining organization: a review with implications for monetary policy in the European common currency area', Center for Political Studies, Institute for Social Research, University of Michigan

Guzzo, V. and A. Velasco (1999), 'The case for a populist central bank', *European Economic Review*, **43**:1317–44.

Lippi, F. (2002), 'Revisiting the case for a populist central banker', *European Economic Review*, **46**:601–12.

Lippi, F. (2003), 'Strategic monetary policy with non-atomistic wage setters', *Review of Economic Studies*, **70**(4):909–19.

Nicoletti, G., S. Scarpetta and O. Boylaud (2000), 'Summary indicators of product market regulation with an extension to employment protection legislation', *OECD Economics Department WP 226.*

Romer, D. (2002), *Advanced Macroeconomics*, New York: McGraw Hill.

Soskice, D. and T. Iversen (2000), 'The non neutrality of monetary policy with large price or wage setters', *Quarterly Journal of Economics*, **115**:265–84.

Woodford, M. (2003), *Interest and Prices*, Princeton: Princeton University Press.

13 Creating the 'Neo-Lisbon' Economy*

Robert M. Lindley

University of Warwick, United Kingdom

13.1 Introduction

Policy reform in the labour market field is not always as innovative as it seems. Very often it involves the re-packaging of old measures in the hope that essentially modest changes in approach will have major impacts on outcomes, usually in spite of evidence to the contrary (witness the use of training schemes for the older long-term unemployed, or recruitment subsidies for school-leavers in periods of high unemployment). Sometimes policy reform is underpinned by a new diagnosis of the imperatives facing the country or region concerned. During the 1990s, perceptions of changes in technology, globalisation and demography combined with speculation about developments in the US economy gave rise to visions of the 'knowledge-based society' (Lindley, 2000). The need for the EU to understand what was happening and find ways of catching up with the US without necessarily copying its approach was a central theme of the Portuguese Presidency in 2000 which gave birth to the Lisbon Strategy (Rodrigues, 2003, 2005), which is being renewed during 2005–06 (CEC, 2005).

This chapter concentrates more on the implications of the knowledge-based society for the general orientation of policy rather than on specific policy measures to create more and better jobs; it is concerned mainly with the balance of attention given to broad parts of the overall policy mix. In order to do this, Section 13.2 looks briefly at the experience of the UK which seems, in a number of key respects, to be one of the EU member states that most exemplifies efforts to modernise labour markets, establish macro-economic stability and proceed to pursue the Lisbon Strategy. This is followed by a review of trends towards higher skilled em-

---

* The author is very grateful to the organisers for inviting him to speak at the conference on 'Social Pacts, Employment and Growth: A Reappraisal of Ezio Tarantelli's Thought', held at University of Rome 'La Sapienza' in Spring 2005 – especially to Luigi Frey and Gabriella Pappadà. This chapter includes substantial material taken directly from the author's previously published work on the knowledge-based economy but, in the present case, introducing the UK as an apparent exemplar of the Lisbon strategy. In particular, it reproduces parts of Lindley's (2000) contribution to the work of the Portuguese Presidency that launched the Lisbon Strategy. Portuguese, English and French versions of this much more extensive analysis of the implications of the knowledge-based economy are published in Lindley (2000a), (2002) and (2004), respectively. The chapter also incorporates parts of the author's contribution (Lindley, 2002a) to the Joint United States and European Union Conference on *Labor Markets in the 21st Century: Skills and Mobility*.

ployment in western developed economies, which is then linked, in Section 13.4, to the notion of the knowledge-based society. In the latter context, two factors that attract much attention from the policy community are then examined: investment in education and training and in mobility. However, the possibility of giving too much emphasis to these processes is considered in Section 13.6 which concentrates on the matter of organisational design and the capacity to use skilled people effectively. Some concluding reflections are given in Section 13.7. Overall, the chapter explores some aspects of what might constitute a strategy for creating a 'Neo-Lisbon' economy.

13.2 Stability and the path to growth – The UK

Overall, the monetary and fiscal policy framework, introduced by the Labour Government in 1997, stabilised the UK economy, generated more common and realistic expectations, and provided a budget surplus which gave considerable room for manoeuvre in making choices between additional public spending and tax reductions and between different areas of spending and taxation within the main aggregates (HM Treasury, 2004; Lindsay, 2004).

Yet there was little room for complacency, as the lesson of the early 1990s should have taught the UK. This is not, however, a reference to the debate about the significance of the large UK budget deficit in the early 2000s. Even against the background of more positive signs at the turn of the decade, there were and still are two particular medium-to-long-run problems which remain to be solved.

First, gains to social well-being derived from the economic recovery and reduction in unemployment of the last decade have been severely limited by rising inequality of income and opportunity, and concentration of disadvantage in particular socio-economic groups. Second, whilst it would be churlish to deny successful elements of structural economic reform, there is a lack of dynamic effectiveness that undermines the momentum of UK economic growth. The failure to tackle this problem may be summarised in the following terms.

- Productivity is low relative to that of the larger EU economies (van Ark and McGuckin, 1999; HM Treasury, 2004).
- Entrepreneurial drive is weaker than it needs to be in the face of international competition.
- The science base has not been harnessed sufficiently for business purposes. Institutional conditions for effective university-business co-operation have still not generally been created.
- Product market competition is not vigorous enough in some areas, allowing less efficient producers of goods and services to survive on the back of the domestic market.
- Investment in education, initial training and continuing professional development are inadequate: as regards employer behaviour, too much reliance is still placed on voluntarism and exhortation, despite continuing skills deficiencies.

- Supply-side orientation of policy is too concerned with individual behaviour and too little with organisational effectiveness.

The present and previous Government's own diagnosis of the problem and policy responses to it are strongly linked to the perceived lack of appropriate education and training. Indeed, *Educational reform* is intended to contribute to the solution of both dynamic deficiency and social exclusion. This, however, is a blunt instrument with largely medium-to-long-term results for the *economy*. There is also a danger that education is being over-sold as a general socio-economic strategy.

Moreover, rate of return analysis suggests that three aspects of UK education and training policy are probably questionable (though, in each case, there are also important caveats) (Dearden et al., 2000, 2001, 2004; Harmon and Walker, 2001; McIntosh, 2004; National Skills Task Force, 2000). First, the proliferation of low-level vocational qualifications as substitutes for initial academic qualifications, usually taken at or soon after minimum school-leaving age, is not in the interests of the least able young people they are intended to help. They offer poor returns *unless* they are used as a stepping-stone to something higher.

Second, expanding the range of full-time provision in school sixth forms and in further education colleges may be no more beneficial for the individual than promoting vocational routes involving the co-operation of employers and part-time study. In particular, the least able students who stay in full-time education would probably be better off in intermediate level vocational provision.

Third, whilst there are a number of reasons advanced to justify expanding higher education, the evidence suggests that it is probably wrong to assume that, for most of those benefiting from the increased opportunity, this route is necessarily more financially beneficial than is the case for more vocational qualifications.

To a degree, the UK is addressing each of these points through raising standards in both general education and vocational education and training. Moreover, in the case of higher education, on the one hand, the expansion is in shorter more vocational Foundation Degrees and, on the other hand, it is intended to be accompanied by major efforts by universities to increase the numbers of able but socially disadvantaged students on the best mainstream courses. However, with the intermediate level vocational systems continuing to remain a weak link in the social and occupational mobility chain, there is a strong danger that this will leave some without a stepping stone out of lower skilled employment and push others into higher education unsuited to their real needs.

At the same time, *labour market policies* that focus on enhancing skill supply via boosting initial training in certain sectors and occupations seem not to alter the fundamentals in the ways which are needed. It is as if the problem is the *lack* of skill shortages rather than their presence, since the former reflects the under-performance of organisations in the economy more than does the latter (Wilson et al., 2003).

Recent research has shed important further light on the natures of skills gaps and shortages (Bosworth et al., 2000; Hogarth and Wilson, 2004). Skills gaps, in the form of employees who are not fully proficient in their work are spread throughout the occupational structure and cling to the most and least skilled occupational contexts alike

Skill shortages, through a lack of potential recruits with the particular skills, qualifications and/or work experience, embody concerns about generic skills as well as the technical skills associated with the occupation (Wilson et al., 2004). There is some evidence that these are becoming more important as they enhance the proficiency with which occupation-specific skills are deployed in changing work environments.

The employment structure is shifting in favour of those occupations that require continual opportunities for learning. In addition, as the employment rate rises and a higher proportion of the labour force is drawn into work, at the same time as the population ages, it will be imperative to make work-based learning a much more effective activity.

Although there are significant areas of actual and potential skill deficiency in the UK economy, the policy debate needs to focus not so much on the tackling of very specific situations in sectoral-occupational labour markets but more with creating the capacity to responds to whatever the changing supply and demand situation presents. The current supply-side orientation of policy is too concerned with the behaviour of individuals in the 'markets for learning and labour' and too little with issues relating to organisational effectiveness which influence so strongly the dynamism of the economy and the quality of working life that results.

The case of the UK is instructive in ways which neither Conservative Governments in the 1979–97 period and subsequent Labour Governments have perhaps cared to admit. First, beyond a certain point, the increasing flexibility of labour markets makes little impact on the employment-population ratio or the unemployment rate. Moreover, at the macroeconomic level, it seems to have no consistent impact on either the responsiveness of wages to unemployment or on the growth of productivity.

Second, whilst high levels of unemployment can be reduced by ceasing to make macro-economic policy mistakes, this does not provide an automatic remedy for low levels of productivity. It seems almost that Britain's recent economic history is more a matter of discovering that certain factors do not, after all, explain its low productivity growth rather than discovering those that do, so that they can be put right. Governments exaggerate the impact of macroeconomic stability on the dynamic efficiency of the economy. In a sense, they set the scene but this does not mean that the actors appear or, if they do so, that they will play their roles in the way intended. The UK has yet to adapt to the idea that the knowledge-based scenario is fundamentally about the behaviour of organisations rather than individuals or the state.

Somehow, despite the rhetoric about labour market flexibility and macroeconomic stability, one of the EU member states apparently most exemplifying both achievements has a major problem with low productivity and with engineering the main strategy it has identified for dealing with it.

13.3 Trends towards higher skill requirements

The strong rise in the demand for people with higher levels of skill is due not only to the faster relative growth of sectors that employ such people, but also to their rising proportions among the labour force even *within* sectors that are not growing so fast or which are declining. This is true for both the US and many EU member states. Indeed, in some EU countries, the relative employment effect is stronger and there is little evidence of the element of modest 'polarisation' found in the US, i.e. growth at both ends of the occupational spectrum. In addition, studies of *generic* skills have identified an increase in the demand for these and in the complexity of skill mixes expected from the workforce.

Several explanations have been advanced for the rising employment and earnings of skilled relative to unskilled workers. Factor price equalisation theory addresses the importance of the pressure arising from the availability of unskilled workers in developing countries upon labour market situations in industrialised economies. Paul Krugman and others have acknowledged the existence of the effect but give it minor importance. Richard Freeman has noticed that EU economists are much more likely to attribute relative changes in the fortunes of skilled to unskilled workers in the industrialised countries to the impact of foreign trade.

One reason for the minor effect is the size of the non-traded sector – redistributive social policy can be used to cope with the consequences. Another reason is that studies examining the impact of trade focus on the wrong aspect of trade, that between developed and third world countries, whereas what matters is trade between developed countries – opening their markets and integrating their economies. As a result, skilled working conditions (especially earnings) become 'detached' from those of the unskilled.

However, the most compelling explanation for rising relative employment and earnings for skilled people is skill-biased technological change. This hinges on the complementarity between capital investment and employment of skilled workers. In contrast, for specific tasks requiring modest cognitive skills, substitution is very strong, particularly in the manufacturing sector though the same applies to retail and financial services.

Other reasons come from the supply side especially the notion of 'filtering down' of qualified people as they find jobs at a higher level elude them but those at a lower level can be colonised for as long as this is necessary in an economic recession.

However, although the returns to skill resulting from education and training are buoyant, other points need to be made.

1. Analysis of educational and occupational perspectives on earnings shows considerable variability within educational groups. Thus, even those convinced of their own ability through their accumulated experience of the education system face uncertainty about the labour market returns they are likely to get from their investment.
2. Moreover, at the aggregate rather than individual level, just because the supply of highly skilled people has not out-stripped demand so far, this does not mean that this could not happen in the next decade.

3. However, in both the EU and the US, demographic scenarios generally suggest otherwise.
4. Visions of the knowledge-based society imply a further intensification of demand for the highly skilled. Periodically over-heated labour markets for IT specialists offer fuel for both predictors of crisis and more sceptical commentators. However, it is the *broadly-based* occupational nature of the underlying trend that is most significant rather than situations in particular high-tech labour markets.
5. The uncertainty that attaches to the returns to investments in human capital (noted above) is compounded by an asymmetry in the basic information accessible to individuals and employers about the other. There has been increasing transparency of both education and vocational training qualifications held by individuals in the EU and certification is being extended to include generic skills and to wider areas of work-based training and development. In contrast, independently validated information available to job-seekers about the qualities of organisations is still hard to come by for the average member of the work force.

13.4 The knowledge-based scenario

Over the last three decades various metaphors have assumed a role as currency in the intellectual debate about the relationship between technology, employment and economic growth. The 'micro-economic revolution', 'information society', and the 'learning society' have given way to the 'knowledge-based society' and, to some extent, this further vies for attention with the 'network society', 'weightless economy', or the 'new economy'.

Leaving aside the debate about how appropriate it is to attach the term 'knowledge society' to the present period and imminent future, its use seems to be associated with the following features (Lindley, 2000).

1. A diversification of the location of knowledge production in the economy such that knowledge is not just created at sites of recognised scientific and development activity but arises and is codified in many other settings. This involves some modification to the notion of 'knowledge' and the nature of what might be called 'knowledge production'.
2. At the same time individuals and organisations are likely to differentiate their performance from that of others by how they handle knowledge. An important aspect of this is the relationship between 'explicit' knowledge and 'tacit' knowledge. Organisations that are able to adopt ways of working that encourage the identification and sharing of key elements of knowledge which have hitherto been only tacit amongst their employees, sub-contractors, etc. are likely to be more effective.
3. The application of knowledge-based procedures to the production and exploitation of knowledge itself. This not only involves much better access to information already available in a manner, which makes its use more extensive and ef-

fective. It also covers the development of mechanisms for identifying tacit knowledge held by individuals and making it explicit and capable of being shared.

4. A much greater willingness to seek out and consider what is known and to bring what is practised at work more into line with what is known.
5. Moreover, whilst these ideas may be seen as being related largely to those in higher level occupations, visions of the knowledge-based society imply that such approaches will also be found among people in broader parts of the occupational hierarchy, reflecting on their 'practice'; on why they do their job a particular way, on its relationship with other jobs and how they might do it differently.
6. Finally, one of the profoundest implications of the knowledge-based society is for the way the policy development system itself behaves in its approach to standards of analysis, to the role of routine monitoring and evaluation, and to the overall relationship between policy design and evidence.

Two more specific perspectives on the knowledge-based society may be mentioned at this point. Box 13.1 considers the wider role that the highly qualified might be expected to play in establishing open occupational structures that share the benefits of their situation with other members of the labour force. This will require a change in the climate of opinion. Box 13.2 refers to the need for greater integration of the learning, labour and innovation systems and the much broader mission that universities should adopt in support of this – an issue now emphasised by the Council of Ministers (CEC, 2005).

Box 13.1

The highly qualified and open occupational structures

In the dynamic context of the knowledge-base economy it seems that a new professional ethic may be required to replace the much-debated notion of 'work sharing' at times of very high unemployment, often in the context of agreements between the social partners. This new ethic is that of 'knowledge sharing' in which an obligation is placed upon professional groups to seek out ways of structuring work so as to generate occupational profiles that reach across the gap between professional employment and skilled industrial or office-based work. At the same time, in constructing these and lower-level occupations, it is essential to avoid creating new types of barrier to entry, which undermine both the scope for achieving equal opportunities and the benefits to business. It is not too far-fetched to think in terms of 'fair employment structures' and a forum or agency responsible for identifying problems of access to and limited development of different parts of the occupational structure.

Thus many of the possible paths on the new and evolving landscape cut across the vested interests of the growing numbers of highly qualified professionals. Yet governments will need to harness much greater commitment from professional groups to think creatively and in socially responsive ways about how to reap the benefits of the knowledge-based society. How we promote occupational enrichment and open employment structures rather than produce polarisation within closed structures will be an especially important issue.

Box 13.2

Learning, labour and innovation

The realisation of the knowledge-based society calls for the learning, labour and innovation systems to be linked much more intimately. The first of these will not simply provide highly skilled labour, basic research and strategic research for the innovation system to incorporate into products and processes. This linear model has long been outdated and many of the leading European universities have been involved with industry for many years. The key characteristics of this relationship at its best has been interaction. Moreover, this needs to be the norm for the future rather than a characteristic displayed by particularly innovative universities. Universities, or their equivalent, will be transformed by far more 'engagement' with:

- other major producers and users of knowledge outside the university and other parts of the publicly-funded research system;
- a variety of intermediaries concerned with more intensive knowledge transfer activities for and with small and medium-sized enterprises (SMEs);
- continuing professional development building on (inter)national reputation, regional and local association as well as alumni relationships in which 'graduation' is merely the start of a process of deepening and broadening the knowledge base and imparting higher-level generic and occupationally specific competencies sought by the individual, with varying degrees of involvement of employers;
- regional economic development strategies in which they will play an active part not merely in helping to implement but in helping to construct;
- and local communities.

The importance of the transformation of universities from exclusive producers of knowledge and educators of the highly qualified to partners in complex networks which go far beyond the pedagogical and scientific boundaries of their traditional roles should not be under-estimated as a major force in the development of the knowledge-based economy and society. Great changes in culture, management and structure of these institutions will be needed if the societies within which they are embedded are to benefit fully from their potential. Essentially, universities have an opportunity to become major animators and participants in networks of *practice* as well as networks of knowledge production and dissemination.

13.5 Investment in human capital and mobility

The EU's concerns about its relatively low employment rate and its need to increase investment in human capital are now being brought together more strongly with the longer-standing commitment to the Single Market objective on 'freedom of movement'. The EU Action Plan on Skills and Mobility has been the result. So whilst the extent of structural unemployment in Europe is seen to be moderating, the policy community is not complacent about the importance of driving it down much further partly through promoting mobility. The prospect of enlargement of the EU reinforces the importance of mobility in the form of migration within the larger region.

In both the EU and US but in different ways, the spotlight has turned on the deployment of older workers and on the role of migration in a period of population ageing (Coomans, 2002). In the case of older workers, the EU, starting from a lower base than in the US, is more acutely concerned to increase labour force participation by lengthening working life through questioning early retirement solutions to redundancy situations and sickness, and through re-assessing the normal retirement ages embedded in state and private pension schemes. In both the EU and US, improvements in educational and training opportunities for people over longer periods of working life are seen to be an important part of the policy strategy. This points to high levels of personal and household investment in education and training accompanied by high levels of potential mobility in which people seek to get the best returns from those investments.

In the case of mobility and (external) migration, the EU's emphasis is on the former as a means of improving the matching of jobs to workers whereas the US focuses more on the latter as a means of raising overall labour supply. In effect the EU has more gains to make in allocative efficiency through geographical and occupational mobility whereas the potential for such gains in the US is seen to be very modest. Migration in the EU context is much more a matter of policy relating to citizenship, security and foreign affairs than a tool of economic management. This is not to deny the importance of economic migrants as a social phenomenon, however, nor that it does have significant labour market effects.

Nonetheless, will countries whose populations have higher propensities for mobility be more successful? Should public policy encourage greater mobility and, if so, what kinds of mobility should be fostered?

In both cases, the starting point is the issue of skills and the knowledge-based society. The latter perspective goes beyond the usual view of mobility as a process by which supply and demand are reconciled in the short-to-medium run to that of mobility as a means of maximising the return on investment in human capital over the long run. Thus it emphasises not only increasing allocative efficiency in the labour market but increasing the potential productivity of the labour force. Some loss of allocative efficiency may well be acceptable if it results in higher labour force potential followed by employment in higher value-added activities.

The obvious example of this is where, in order to invest in education and training, it is necessary to reduce the contribution that the individual makes to current production, often even to zero. Concepts of life-long learning extend this process over more of the working-life and, partly in order to do so, explore the extent to which the opportunity cost of such learning can be reduced by making it 'work-based' and fashioning 'learning organisations' that make the process as effective as possible.

At this point, the knowledge-based society metaphor takes over. The organisation then becomes not just a learning organisation but one engaged in knowledge production and sharing. This is highly demanding, requiring well-qualified people at all levels not just because of what they know already but also because their *experience* of education and training is a *necessary* condition for them to participate effectively in the knowledge-driven organisation. (It is not, however, a *sufficient* condition for there are motivational and other personal qualities needed over and above generic and occupation-specific training and experience.) Moreover, if more of such people are produced, the more they will seek out employment opportunities that offer them scope for continuous learning.

Rising educational levels in the EU mean that companies will find it easier to recruit better educated people and, if they are willing to invest in organisational innovation, they will be able to get much more out of them. Moreover, companies that are content to pursue the low skill – low value-added strategy will find it increasingly difficult to find people who want to join them in doing so.

External mobility will tend to facilitate the above process. Yet what seems to matter most in the visions of the knowledge-based society is the degree of adaptability and mobility taking place within the *internal* labour markets of organisations. The data on internal mobility are very weak, all the more so at the international level, but the low level of *external* mobility observed in the EU relative to the US seems not to be the crucial factor that some would claim it to be. Adaptability and mobility within the internal labour market are particularly tested when there is a high obsolescence of skills which are not continually up-dated. The boundaries between 'occupational mobility' and such processes as 'de-skilling', 're-skilling', 'up-grading' and 'multi-skilling' are not hard and fast in that any of those processes can be associated more or less with a change of occupation within the organisation or involve ultimately the external labour market. However, the faster the obsolescence of skills:

- the more difficult it is to identify and deliver in the external education and training systems up-to-date curricula and the certification systems to accompany them;
- the more important it is to concentrate on giving a good *general* education to all young people and offering opportunities for adults to remedy their lack of this;
- the more the employing organisation will find themselves assuming responsibility for promoting learning and the acquisition of new skills;
- yet employers too will find it more costly to design training programmes when skills needs are evolving quite quickly;
- so the balance of attention between supporting education and training in the external markets for provision of these and supporting work-based learning is a crucial policy parameter, whichever country is being considered;
- and addressing these issues is likely to draw public policy into taking more notice of the quality of employing organisation not just the quality of education and training.

In these circumstances, geographical mobility *per se* seems to be less important than occupational mobility and external occupational mobility seems less important than internal mobility and adaptability.

13.6 Organisational design – The missing policy discourse?

The knowledge-based society is not just about knowledge as produced, disseminated and exploited via the external market; it also embraces ideas about relationships within the internal market of the organisation. Certain inconsistencies then seem to arise between advocating greater flexibility of contracts at the same time as trying to nurture processes that foster active organisational learning, sharing knowledge, co-operative creative behaviour and loyalty to organisational goals. It is in this nexus that modern conceptions of social partnership in continental Europe and progressive ideas about what constitutes a high performance organisation in the US begin to have some common ingredients.

In this scenario, it is not then enough for people and organisations to embrace a 'learning culture'. New forms of management, participation, collaboration and contractual relationship need to be explored in order for them to prosper in a more knowledge-intensive environment. Several authors have argued that this will involve re-casting present approaches to human resources at various levels in the economy and society in order to get the right fit between the market for knowledge per se and the markets for work and learning.

Seeing the rising demand for skilled people, noted in Section 13.3, governments have tended to become pre-occupied with raising the quality of the labour force and worker motivation to train and be mobile, as opposed to the quality of organisational designs within which people are subsequently deployed. One reaction might be to say that the latter is the responsibility of business and the state should just concentrate on ensuring that vigorous product market competition will eventually force persistently poor-performing organisations to the wall. This will enable others to step in and offer better uses for the resources freed up. EU policy clearly does not accept that such a strategy is sufficient either to ensure that many more high-performing organisations ultimately emerge or to speed up the process of learning and experimentation that brings this about. Competition policy and the internal market strategy are important but have limited range partly because of difficulties in coping with transnational enterprises and partly because of large non-traded and non-market sectors. Thus, a critical factor in the process of producing stronger organisations is the potential contribution that employees, trade unions and social partnership can make to such development.

If the individual is to reflect on her or his practice and share those reflections with other workers, this requires high levels of co-operation and trust in order to identify and share what would otherwise remain tacit knowledge. These conditions cannot be assumed to be present automatically. Nor can it be assumed that workers who may be willing to share with each other in very informal ways would wish to share with the organisation. It is here where the attention paid to the nature of knowledge and skills in relation to occupations comes together with that paid to the idea of the high performance organisation and to the conditions likely to give rise to their creation and flourishing in the modern economy.

At the heart of the issue is the tension between encouraging individuals and work groups to reflect on *their* practice and refine the knowledge they have, communicating it to others in the interests of the organisation as a whole and *a reluc-*

tance of the organisation itself to reciprocate. The deal needs to be different in order for the organisation to adapt to changing external conditions and to initiate from within change which will require other organisations to respond.

A *learning organisation* is one in which people are able not only to update continually their knowledge and skills but also to learn from the mistakes they will nonetheless make individually and collectively, however competent they are. The *knowledge-based organisation* is located in or across sectors of the economy that trade intensively in the creation and exploitation of knowledge. A crucial competitive advantage will be how it handles its own knowledge of what it is doing and the intangible assets intimately associated with its main activities, especially its intellectual capital. Its other assets, such as possession of highly valued physical assets, access to cheap energy sources, favourable spatial location with respect to suppliers and customers, and even current market position will be of much less importance. In these circumstances the knowledge-based organisation must be a particularly effective learning organisation but the central human resource management task is to *manage knowledge*. Indeed, the research focus on the learning organisation has been gradually replaced from the mid-1990s by that on knowledge management.

The importance of generic skills seems to lie in the capacity to cope with and contribute to the change process. Job-specific and occupation-specific skills do not adapt easily without broader knowledge, skills and attitudes to change. At this point, the consideration of occupational change and the widespread importance attached to generic skills meets the discussion of organisational styles that will promote a knowledge-based economy. The scenario is one in which, over increasing areas of the occupational map, people are being asked to take more responsibility for their work situations: for getting the knowledge and skills to do the job in the first place and updating them appropriately, ensuring they have the information they need to carry out their jobs, responding creatively to changing requirements, and taking initiatives which will benefit the organisation. The latter must, for its part, facilitate this process, i.e. empower the individual and work group to play this role. We are some way from knowing how best to do this.

Notions of the high performance organisation began to emerge in the employment policy debate partly as an antidote to simplistic ideas of what to expect from labour market de-regulation and the preoccupation with 'unburdening management' by removing constraints on their prerogative to manage. Much less attention has been given to the idea that there are shortages of good managers and good organisational designs and that this might have equal or greater significance for the performance of the labour market and the economy at large. What Europe needs is higher quality organisations in which people can work, as well as a better educated and trained labour force.

13.7 Concluding reflections

The Portuguese Government launched its Presidency of the EU with a document that called for 'a new vision and a long-term strategy'.

> 'A new strategic goal needs to be defined for the next ten years: to make the European Union the world's most dynamic and competitive area, based on innovation and knowledge, able to boost economic growth levels with more and better jobs and greater social cohesion.'

Moreover, it asserted that it was essential that 'we regain the condition of full-employment, geared to the needs of the emerging society ...'.

The strategy, both initially and as it has subsequently evolved, seeks to explore different ways of relating the economy to society, exemplified most of all by the commitment to social partnership as a means of conducting relationships between employees and companies and their deeper involvement in the European Employment Strategy and in the 'EU processes'. It also sought to explore further ways of reconciling personal and professional life, for both women and men. It pointed to the need to examine more extensively the scope for harnessing broader values which blur the boundary between what is 'economic' and what is 'social', in stressing the importance of corporate social responsibility and of finding a more substantial place in the overall strategy for the promotion of sustainable social economy organisations.

One of the most striking things about the outcome of the Portuguese Presidency was the adoption of more explicit goals than hitherto. These relate to increasing educational attainment of young people, continuing adult participation in education and training, overall investment in human capital, and employment-population ratios as well as achieving full-employment by 2010 and reducing child poverty.

The UK *strategy* is clearly quite consistent with the Lisbon Strategy. The importance given to education and lifelong learning and to targets is very familiar. What the UK *experience* offers is an illustration of how difficult it is to bring off the strategy even when the basic conditions of reasonable labour market flexibility and macro-economic stability have been achieved. The logic of the Lisbon Strategy lies in its aims to raise the potential productivity of all sections of the population of working age, to promote higher and longer labour force participation in the long run, in order to provide resources for dealing with child poverty now and have sustainable pension systems in the future. In this scenario, however, there is a danger that education and training will be grossly oversold as the key ingredient in the solution to early disadvantage that continues into working-age experience.

In addition to keeping a clear sense of proportion about what investment in human resources can deliver, there are also questions about how to generate the investment in the first place. The commitments to investment in ICT infrastructure (and much wider access to it), R&D, and human capital are clearly essential. However, their ultimate impact on productivity, output and employment will depend on the effectiveness with which organisations use the resulting resources. There is a tendency for the policy system to give less emphasis to the quality of organisational design, though, in the Lisbon Strategy, the buttressing of the 'four pillars' by the introduction of the two 'horizontal sections' which are deemed to be relevant for all pillars and deal with the *role of the social partners* and with *life-long learning* was a step in the right direction.

So the credibility of the strategy depends crucially on there being a strong link between the major boost to education and training on the one hand and *potential* individual productivity at work on the other hand *and* on there being sufficient jobs available in effective organisations so that the higher potential individual productivity can be realised in practice. It also depends on the substantial switch from 'passive' to 'active' measures (moving from out-of-work to in-work social benefits) yielding a higher supply of suitably skilled labour. Demand and supply then rise together, the former faster than the latter, so as to achieve a higher employment-population rate and lower unemployment rate (as a per cent of both the labour force and the population of working age).

For this mutually reinforcing demand and supply shift to materialise, however, there has to be more than a strong link between investing in human capital and increasing potential productivity. Some have to *act on their belief* in the link and invest. Europe would still seem to lack strong enough mechanisms for leveraging sufficient investment from private sector organisations if we are indeed to realise the best knowledge-based society in the world.

Special effort is needed on that part of the strategy concerned with the situations of firms and organisations in parts of the economy, which generate lower quality jobs than they should do. Thus their problem is not the fact of facing highly competitive product markets for low value-added goods and services; nor is it primarily an inability to find suitable employees, though that can exacerbate the situation. The main problem is that they have out-dated entrepreneurial styles and organisational designs. Part of the vision of the knowledge-based society embraces the idea of strengthening the SME through the professional development of entrepreneurs, increasing the flow of well-qualified people into these sectors. It involves universities taking wider roles to promote such outcomes. This would greatly extend the scope for generating higher levels of skill and greater amounts of purposeful mobility towards high performance organisations over wider parts of the economy.

References

Bosworth, D., R. Davies, T. Hogarth, R.A. Wilson and J. Shury (2000), *Employers' Skill Survey: Statistical Report*, Sheffield: DfEE.

Commission of the European Communities (2005), 'Working together for growth and jobs: next steps in implementing the revised Lisbon strategy', *Commission Staff Working Paper*, Brussels: CEC.

Coomans, G. (2002), 'On external and internal labour mobility in the EU and US', in *Labor Markets in the 21st Century: Skills and Mobility,* Proceedings of a Joint United States and European Union Conference, Washington: Department of Labour, pp. 39–57.

Dearden, L., S. McIntosh, M. Myck and A. Vignoles (2000), *The Returns to Academic and Vocational Qualifications in Britain*, London: Centre for the Economics of Education, LSE.

Dearden, L., S. McIntosh, M. Myck and A. Vignoles (2001), *The Returns to Academic, Vocational and Basic Skills in Britain*, Skills Task Force Research Paper, Sheffield: DfEE.

Dearden, L., L. McGranahan and B. Sianesi (2004), *Returns to Education for the 'Marginal Learner': Evidence from the BCS70*, London: Centre for the Economics of Education, LSE.

Harmon, C. and I. Walker (2001), *The Returns to Education: A Review of Evidence, Issues and Deficiencies in the Literature,* DfEE Research Report No. 254, Sheffield: DfEE.

Hogarth, T. and R.A. Wilson (eds) (2004), *Skills in England 2003: Volume 2*, Research Report, Learning and Skills Council.

HM Treasury (2004), *Opportunity for All: The Strength to Take the Long-term Decisions for Britain*, Pre-Budget Report presented to Parliament by the Chancellor of the Exchequer, Cm 6408.

Lindley, R.M. (2000a), 'Economias baseadas no conhecimento: o debate europeu sobre o emprego', in M.J. Rodrigues (ed.), *Para uma Europa de Inovacäo e do Conhecimento – Emprego, Reformas Económicas e Coesão Social,* Lisbon: Celta, pp. 33–78.

Lindley, R.M. (2000), 'Knowledge-based economies: the European employment debate in a new context', Reports prepared for the Portuguese Presidency of the European Union. Action Line: *Employment, Economic Reforms and Social Cohesion – For a Europe of Innovation and Knowledge*, Lisbon: Gabineto de Primeiro Ministo, pp. 33–83.

Lindley, R.M. (2002), 'Knowledge-based economies: the European employment debate in a new context', in M.J. Rodrigues (ed.), *The New Knowledge Economy in Europe*, Cheltenham: Edward Elgar, pp. 95–145.

Lindley, R.M. (2002a). 'Skills, mobility and policy moods in knowledge-based economies', in *Labor Markets in the 21st Century: Skills and Mobility,* Proceedings of a Joint United States and European Union Conference. Washington: Department of Labour, pp. 67–76.

Lindley, R.M. (2004), 'L'économie de la connaissance: le nouveau contexte du débat sur l'emploi en Europe', in *Vers une Société Européene de La Connaissance: La Stratégie de Lisbonne (2000–2010)*, Bruxelles: Institute d'Etudes Européenes, Université de Bruxelles, pp. 95–141.

Lindsay, C. (2004), *State of the Labour Market*, London: ONS Labour Market Division, Office for National Statistics.

McIntosh, S. (2004), *Further Analysis of the Returns to Academic and Vocational Qualifications*, London: Centre for the Economics of Education, LSE.

National Skills Task Force (2000), *Skills for All: Research Report from the National Skills Task Force*, Sheffield: DfEE.

Rodrigues, M.J. (2003), *European Policies for A Knowledge Economy,* London: Edward Elgar.

Rodrigues, M.J. (2005), 'The debate over Europe and the Lisbon strategy for growth and jobs', Background Paper, Advisory Group to the European Commission – Social Sciences and Humanities in the European Research Area, Brussels, mimeo.

van Ark, B. and R.H. McGuckin (1999), 'International comparisons of labor productivity and per capita income', *Monthly Labor Review*, July, 33–41.

Wilson, R.A. and T. Hogarth with D. Bosworth, A. Dickerson, A. Green, C. Jacobs, E. Keep, K. Mayhew and S. Watson, S. (2003), *Tackling the Low Skills Equilibrium: A Review of Issues and Some New Evidence*, London: DTI.

Wilson R.A., K. Homenidou and A. Dickerson (2004), *Working Futures: New Projections of Employment by Sector and Region: Volume 1 National Report*, Warwick Institute for Employment Research / Cambridge Econometrics/ SSDA (Sector Skills Development Agency).

List of Contributors

Acocella Nicola, Professor
Department of Public Economics, University of Rome 'La Sapienza'
Via Castro Laurenziano 9, 00161 Rome
Italy

Brandolini Andrea, Researcher
Economic Research Department, Bank of Italy
Via Nazionale, 91, 00184 Rome
Italy

Casadio Piero, Researcher
Economic Research Department, Bank of Italy
Via Nazionale, 91, 00184 Rome
Italy

Ciocca Pierluigi, Deputy Director General
Directorate, Bank of Italy
Via Nazionale, 91, 00184 Rome
Italy

Cipollone Piero, Researcher
Economic Research Department, Bank of Italy
Via Nazionale, 91, 00184 Rome
Italy

Coricelli Fabrizio, Professor
Department of Economics, University of Siena
Piazza San Francesco, 7, 53100 Siena
Italy

Cristini Annalisa, Professor
Department of Economics 'H.P. Minsky', University of Bergamo,
Via dei Caniana, 2, 24128 Bergamo
Italy

Croci Angelini Elisabetta, Professor
Department of Studies on Economic Growth, University of Macerata
Piazza Oberdan 3, 62100 Macerata
Italy

Dell'Aringa Carlo, Professor
Department of Economics, Catholic University of Milan
Via Necchi 5, 20123 Milan
Italy

Di Bartolomeo Giovanni, Associate Professor
Department of Media, University of Teramo
Via Coste S. Agostino, 64100 Teramo
Italy

Farina Francesco, Professor
Department of Economic Policy, Finance and Development,
University of Siena
Piazza S. Francesco 7, 53100 Siena
Italy

Ferri Piero, Professor
Department of Economics 'H.P. Minsky', University of Bergamo,
Via dei Caniana, 2, 24128 Bergamo
Italy

Freeman Richard B., Herbert Ascherman Professor
Department of Economics, Harvard University
National Bureauof Economc Research
1050 Mass. Ave, Cambridge, MA 02138
USA

Leoni Riccardo, Professor
Department of Economics 'H.P. Minsky', University of Bergamo,
Via dei Caniana, 2, 24128 Bergamo
Italy

Lindley Robert M., Professor, Pro-Vice-Chancellor and Director
Institute for Employment Research, University of Warwick
Social Studies Building, Coventry, CV4 7AL
United Kingdom

Magnani Marco, Researcher
Economic Research Department, Bank of Italy
Via Nazionale, 91, 00184 Rome
Italy

Rosolia Alfonso, Researcher
Economic Research Department, Bank of Italy
Via Nazionale, 91, 00184 Rome
Italy

Sarcinelli Mario, Professor
Department of Economic Sciences, University of Rome 'La Sapienza'
Via Cesalpino 12, 00161 Rome
Italy

Tirelli Patrizio, Professor
Department of Economics, University of Milan-Bicocca
Piazza dell'Ateneo Nuovo 1, 20126 Milan
Italy

Torrini Roberto, Researcher
Economic Research Department, Bank of Italy
Via Nazionale, 91, 00184 Rome
Italy

Tronti Leonello, Head of Unit
Short-Term Statistics on Industry, Services and Employment, ISTAT
Via Tuscolana, 1788, 00173 Rome
Italy

Visser Jelle, Professor
Amsterdam Institute for Advanced Labour Studies, University of Amsterdam
Plantage Muidergracht 4, 1018 TV Amsterdam
The Netherlands

Printing: Krips bv, Meppel
Binding: Stürtz, Würzburg